D1569818

Human-System Integration in the System Development Process

A NEW LOOK

Committee on Human-System Design Support for Changing Technology

Richard W. Pew and Anne S. Mavor, *Editors*

Committee on Human Factors
Division of Behavioral and Social Sciences and Education
National Research Council

NATIONAL RESEARCH COUNCIL
OF THE NATIONAL ACADEMIES

THE NATIONAL ACADEMIES PRESS
Washington, D.C.
www.nap.edu

THE NATIONAL ACADEMIES PRESS   500 Fifth Street, N.W.   Washington, D.C. 20001

NOTICE: The project that is the subject of this report was approved by the Governing Board of the National Research Council, whose members are drawn from the councils of the National Academy of Sciences, the National Academy of Engineering, and the Institute of Medicine. The members of the committee responsible for the report were chosen for their special competences and with regard for appropriate balance.

The study was supported by Award Nos. W911NF-05-0150 and FA5650-06-1-6610 between the National Academy of Sciences and the U.S. Department of the Army and the U.S. Department of the Air Force. Any opinions, findings, conclusions, or recommendations expressed in this publication are those of the author(s) and do not necessarily reflect the view of the organizations or agencies that provided support for this project.

Library of Congress Cataloging-in-Publication Data

Human-system integration in the system development process : a new look / Committee on Human-System Design Support for Changing Technology ; Richard W. Pew and Anne S. Mavor, editors.
    p. cm.
  Includes bibliographical references and index.
  ISBN-13: 978-0-309-10720-4 (hardback : alk. paper)
  ISBN-10: 0-309-10720-2 (hardback : alk. paper) 1. Human engineering. 2. Systems engineering. 3. User interfaces (Computer systems) I. Pew, Richard W. II. Mavor, Anne S. III. Committee on Human-System Design Support for Changing Technology.
  TA166.H84 2007
  620.8'2—dc22
                          2007012835

Additional copies of this report are available from The National Academies Press, 500 Fifth Street, N.W., Lockbox 285, Washington, D.C. 20055; (800) 624-6242 or (202) 334-3313 (in the Washington metropolitan area); Internet, http://www.nap.edu

Cover images: (1) The Air Force MQ-1 Predator (unmanned aerial system) produced by General Atomics Aeronautical Systems. (2) Controllers in the Combined Air Operations Center at an air base on the Arabian Peninsula monitor the status of ongoing missions supporting Operation Iraqi Freedom. The CAOC was the nerve center for all U.S. Central Command air operations when the first air strike occurred early March 20, 2003. (3) A general-purpose intravenous infusion pump designed primarily for hospital use with secondary, limited feature use by patients at home. (The marketed name is the Symbiq™ IV Pump.) (4) Vehicle screening for port security.

Cover credits: Unmanned aerial system: Photo Courtesy of U.S. Army taken August 10, 2005. Combined Air Operations Center: Photo by Ministry of Defence-Royal Air Force Sgt. Gareth Davies. Courtesy of U.S. Air Force.

Suggested citation: National Research Council. (2007). *Human-System Integration in the System Development Process: A New Look.* Committee on Human-System Design Support for Changing Technology, R.W. Pew and A.S. Mavor, Eds. Committee on Human Factors, Division of Behavioral and Social Sciences and Education. Washington, DC: The National Academies Press.

THE NATIONAL ACADEMIES
Advisers to the Nation on Science, Engineering, and Medicine

The **National Academy of Sciences** is a private, nonprofit, self-perpetuating society of distinguished scholars engaged in scientific and engineering research, dedicated to the furtherance of science and technology and to their use for the general welfare. Upon the authority of the charter granted to it by the Congress in 1863, the Academy has a mandate that requires it to advise the federal government on scientific and technical matters. Dr. Ralph J. Cicerone is president of the National Academy of Sciences.

The **National Academy of Engineering** was established in 1964, under the charter of the National Academy of Sciences, as a parallel organization of outstanding engineers. It is autonomous in its administration and in the selection of its members, sharing with the National Academy of Sciences the responsibility for advising the federal government. The National Academy of Engineering also sponsors engineering programs aimed at meeting national needs, encourages education and research, and recognizes the superior achievements of engineers. Dr. Wm. A. Wulf is president of the National Academy of Engineering.

The **Institute of Medicine** was established in 1970 by the National Academy of Sciences to secure the services of eminent members of appropriate professions in the examination of policy matters pertaining to the health of the public. The Institute acts under the responsibility given to the National Academy of Sciences by its congressional charter to be an adviser to the federal government and, upon its own initiative, to identify issues of medical care, research, and education. Dr. Harvey V. Fineberg is president of the Institute of Medicine.

The **National Research Council** was organized by the National Academy of Sciences in 1916 to associate the broad community of science and technology with the Academy's purposes of furthering knowledge and advising the federal government. Functioning in accordance with general policies determined by the Academy, the Council has become the principal operating agency of both the National Academy of Sciences and the National Academy of Engineering in providing services to the government, the public, and the scientific and engineering communities. The Council is administered jointly by both Academies and the Institute of Medicine. Dr. Ralph J. Cicerone and Dr. Wm. A. Wulf are chairman and vice chairman, respectively, of the National Research Council.

www.national-academies.org

v

COMMITTEE ON HUMAN FACTORS

Acknowledgments

We are grateful to the many individuals who have made a significant contribution to the committee's work by providing information through briefings at our meetings. A complete list of these contributors and their affiliations appears in Appendix A.

In the course of preparing the report, each member of the committee took an active role in drafting sections of chapters, leading discussions, and reading and commenting on successive drafts. We are deeply indebted to them for their hard work, their wiliness in critically weighting a variety of diverse perspectives, and their good spirit in working in concert to produce this volume. It has been a great pleasure and a learning experience to work with all of them. Committee member biographies appear in Appendix B.

Staff at the National Research Council (NRC) made important contributions to our work in many ways. We would like to extend our thanks to Kristen Butler, research assistant, for her support of the committee through her research, her writing, and her extensive work on the report manuscript. Thanks are also due to Matthew McDonough, senior project assistant, who was indispensable in organizing meetings, arranging travel, assembling agenda books, assisting committee members, and preparing the final report for publication. We are also indebted to Christine McShane, who edited the report.

We are most grateful to our sponsors for their insights, encouragement, and support throughout the process. John Lockett, Human Research and Engineering Directorate, Army Research Laboratory, recognized the need for this study and provided early support in getting the committee established. Maris Vikmanis and Edward Martin, Air Force Research Laboratory, added their support once the committee process was under way.

This report has been reviewed in draft form by individuals chosen for their diverse perspectives and technical expertise, in accordance with procedures approved by the NRC's report review committee. The purpose of this independent review is to provide candid and critical comments that will assist the institution in making its published report as sound as possible and to ensure that the report meets institutional standards for objectivity, evidence, and responsiveness to the study charge. The review comments and draft manuscript remain confidential to protect the integrity of the deliberative process. We wish to thank the following individuals for their review of this report: Jonathan Grudin, Adaptive Systems and Interaction Group, Microsoft Research, Redmond, WA; Patricia M. Jones, Human Factors Research and Technology Division, NASA Ames Research Center, Moffett Field, CA; Alex Kirlik, Human Factors Department, University of Illinois at Urbana-Champaign; David C. Nagel, Independent Consultant, Ascona Group, Los Gatos, CA; Christopher Nemeth, Cognitive Technologies Laboratory, The University of Chicago; Mary Beth Rosson, Department of Information Sciences and Technology, Pennsylvania State University; and Andrew Sage, System Engineering and Operations Research Department, George Mason University. Although the reviewers listed above have provided many constructive comments and suggestions, they were not asked to endorse the conclusions or recommendations, nor did they see the final draft of the report before its release. The review of this report was overseen by Thomas B. Sheridan, Engineering and Applied Psychology, Emeritus, Massachusetts Institute of Technology. Appointed by the NRC, he was responsible for making certain that an independent examination of this report was carried out in accordance with institutional procedures and that all review comments were carefully considered. Responsibility for the final content of this report rests entirely with the authoring committee and the institution.

Richard W. Pew, *Chair*
Anne S. Mavor, *Study Director*
Committee on Human-System Design
Support for Changing Technology

Contents

Executive Summary   1
     Principles for Successful System Development, 2
     Policy Recommendations, 4
     Research Agenda, 5
     The Future, 7

1   Introduction   9
     The Problem, 11
     Charge and Scope, 16
     The Context, 18
     Themes, 23
     Report Organization, 27

PART I: HUMAN-SYSTEM INTEGRATION
IN THE CONTEXT OF SYSTEM DEVELOPMENT

2   The System Development Process   31
     Principles for Successful System Development, 32
     The Evolving Nature of System Requirements, 33
     Principles-Based Comparison of Alternative Process Models, 34
     The Incremental Commitment Model, 36
     Views of the Incremental Commitment Model, 39
     Project Experience with ICM Principles, 51
     Conclusion, 53

3   Human-System Integration and the System Development
    Process   55
    Human-System Integration in the Incremental Commitment
        Model, 57
    Communicating HSI Issues and Opportunities through Shared
        Representations, 61
    Conclusion, 66
    Appendix 3-A, 67

4   Managing Risks   75
    Identifying and Analyzing Risk, 78
    Handling Options Assessment, 85
    Executing Risk Mitigation, 88

5   Case Studies   91
    Unmanned Aerial Systems, 92
    Port Security, 97
    "Next-Generation" Intravenous Infusion Pump, 105

        PART II: HUMAN-SYSTEM INTEGRATION METHODS
                 IN SYSTEM DEVELOPMENT

6   Defining Opportunities and Context of Use   135
    Organizational and Environmental Context, 139
    Field Observations and Ethnography, 150
    Task Analysis, 157
    Cognitive Task Analysis, 161
    Participatory Analysis, 169
    Contextual Inquiry, 175
    Event Data Analysis, 177

7   Defining Requirements and Design   189
    Usability Requirements, 191
    Work Domain Analysis, 197
    Workload Assessment, 207
    Participatory Design, 210
    Contextual Design, 216
    Physical Ergonomics, 217
    Situation Awareness, 223
    Methods for Mitigating Fatigue, 226
    Scenarios, 230
    Personas, 233

Prototyping, 235
Models and Simulations, 240

8 Methods for Evaluation 253
Risk Analysis, 253
Analysis of Human Error, 256
Usability Evaluation Methods, 265

PART III: THE FUTURE: SCENARIOS, CONCLUSIONS, AND RECOMMENDATIONS

9 Scenarios for the Future 277
An Integrated Methodology, 278
Knowledge-Based Planning for Human-System Integration, 286
User Participation, 288

10 Conclusions and Recommendations 296
Research and Policy Recommendations, 301

References 331

Appendixes
A Sponsors and Contributors 357
B Biographical Sketches of Committee Members and Staff 358

Index 365

Executive Summary

In April 1991 *Business Week* ran a cover story entitled, "I Can't Work This ?#!!@ Thing," about the difficulties many people have with consumer products, such as cell phones and VCRs. Today, more than 15 years later, the situation is much the same. At quite a different level of scale and consequence of the disconnect between people and technology are the major large-scale systems accidents for which human error was paramount, such as those at Three Mile Island and Chernobyl. Similarly, a major, expensive console update to the nation's air traffic control operations was cancelled because the operational personnel concluded that it would be too complicated and difficult to operate. These examples illustrate the pressures on industry and government as the complexity of the systems they seek to develop increase at the same time they are challenged to shorten the development cycle for those systems. These problems are magnified by the increasing prevalence of systems of systems. Systems of systems arise when a collection of different systems, originally designed for their own purposes, are combined and coordinated to produce a very large system with new issues and challenges.

These problems can be traced to a significant challenge—that human capabilities and needs must be considered early and throughout system design and development. One aspect of the challenge has been providing the background and data needed for the seamless integration of humans into the design process from various perspectives (human factors engineering, manpower, personnel, training, safety and health, and, in the military, habitability and survivability). This collection of development activities has come to be called human-system integration (HSI). A second aspect has been a lack of commitment by funders and program managers to assign priority to these activities. A third aspect has been a lack of effective communication between the system engineers and human-system domain experts.

To address these challenges, the Army Research Laboratory and the Air Force Research Laboratory of the U.S. Department of Defense asked the National Academies, through its Committee on Human Factors, to undertake a study of the current state of methods, tools, and approaches for analyzing human capabilities and needs and to develop a vision for creating an integrated, multidisciplinary, generalizable, human-system design methodology. The Committee on Human-System Design Support for Changing Technology was specifically charged with four tasks:

1.   Provide a comprehensive review of issues involved in design throughout the system life cycle that need to be addressed by a consideration of human cognitive and physical performance characteristics. This review will be used as a framework for further analysis of methodologies.
2.   Evaluate the state of the art in human-system engineering and (a) product development processes, (b) product design methodologies, and (c) product design tools.
3.   Develop a vision for an integrated, multidisciplinary, generalizable, human-system design support methodology and tool set. Identify a set of core methods and tools needed to support design activities associated with a variety of systems.
4.   Recommend a research plan suggesting how to achieve this ideal.

In carrying out its work, the committee's goal was to make recommendations that are relevant not only to the project's military sponsors, but also to other government departments and the private sector, including the process control, manufacturing, and service industries.

PRINCIPLES FOR SUCCESSFUL SYSTEM DEVELOPMENT

The committee identified five principles that are critical to the success of human-intensive system development and evolution: (1) satisficing[1] the requirements of the system stakeholders—the buyers, developers (including engineers and human factors experts), and users; (2) incremental growth of system definition and stakeholder commitment; (3) iterative system defini-

---

[1]Satisficing occurs in consensus building when the group looks toward a solution that everyone can agree on, even if it may not be the best.

tion and development; (4) concurrent system definition and development; and (5) management of project risk.

After analysis of several candidate system development models in terms of the five principles, the committee proposes the incremental commitment model as a useful systems engineering approach and as a framework for examining categories of methodologies and tools that provide information about the environment, the organization, the work, and the human operator at each stage of the design process. Although it is not the only model that could be used on future human-intensive systems and systems of systems, it provides a reasonably robust framework for explaining the study's HSI concepts. A central focus of the model is the progressive reduction of risk through the full life-cycle of system development, to produce a cost-effective system that meets the needs of all the stakeholders. Cost-effectiveness is achieved by focusing resources on high-risk aspects of the development and deemphasizing aspects that are judged to pose a limited risk. All kinds of potential risk, including hardware, software, and HSI risks, must be assessed to identify risk-reduction strategies at each stage in the system development process. The model recognizes that, in very large and complex systems, requirements change and evolve throughout the design process. The approach to acquisition is incremental and evolutionary: acquiring the most important and well-understood capabilities first; working concurrently on engineering requirements and solutions; using prototypes, models, and simulations as ways of exploring design implications to reduce the risk of specifying inappropriate requirements; and basing requirements on stakeholder involvement and assessments. When trade-offs among cost, schedule, performance, and capabilities are not well understood, the model provides a framework to specify priorities for the capabilities and ranges of satisfactory performance, rather than to require precise and unambiguous requirements.

The incremental commitment model has five life-cycle development phases: exploration, valuation, architecting, development, and operation. In each phase, every activity must be considered, from system scoping through goals and objectives requirements and evaluation through operations and retirement. The specific level of the effort on each activity is risk-driven and thus varies across life-cycle phases and from project to project.

The committee concludes that a model such as the incremental commitment model that incorporates the five principles can provide a significant improvement in the design of major systems, particularly with regard to human-system integration. Our policy recommendations follow from this conclusion. These recommendations are followed by an overview of the committee's recommended research agenda.

POLICY RECOMMENDATIONS

Recommendation: The U.S. Department of Defense and other government and private organizations should refine and coordinate the definition and adoption of a system development process that incorporates the principles embodied in the incremental commitment model. It should be adopted as the recommended approach for realizing the full integration of human-related design considerations with systems engineering in organizational policies and process standards, such as the DoD 5000 series and the ISO systems engineering standards.

Recommendation: The U.S. Department of Defense and other government and private organizations should revise current system acquisition policies and standards to enable incremental, evolutionary, capabilities-based system acquisition that includes HSI requirements and uses risk-driven levels of requirements detail, particularly for complex systems of systems and for collaboration-intensive systems.

Recommendation: The U.S. Department of Defense and other government and private organizations should put the operational requirements of human-system integration on a par with traditional engineering requirements at the beginning of the initial *requirements analyses* to determine which requirements have priority and provide an opportunity for negotiation.

Recommendation: When developing system acquisition programs, the U.S. Department of Defense and other government and private organizations should define potential means for verifying and validating HSI requirements to enable supplier program managers to establish clearly specifiable HSI technical performance measures for contracts.

Recommendation: The U.S. Department of Defense and other government and private organizations should account for HSI considerations in developing the technical, cost, and schedule parameters in the business offer. In particular, contracts need to reflect an understanding of how human-system integration affects the ability to reuse existing technical solutions or the feasibility of inserting new technologies, as well as an appreciation of how anticipated HSI risks may affect meeting program award fee criteria. It is also important that the contractor understand how HSI elements in their product offering contribute to achieving market capture goals and subsequently the viability of their business case.

RESEARCH AGENDA

The committee makes research recommendations that the U.S. Department of Defense and other research funders support (1) the development of shared representations for facilitating effective communication among funders, developers, and users, (2) the extension and expansion of current human-system methods and tools, and (3) the full integration of human systems and engineering systems. Chapter 10 provides details.

Shared Representations

Effective and efficient design requires meaningful communication among hardware, software, and HSI designers; among professionals in the domains of human-system design (e.g., personnel, manpower, training, human factors); and among the stakeholders. With a great deal of diversity among the groups tasked with the design of complex systems, the potential for communication and collaboration failures increases if assumptions (and their associated mind sets) are not made explicit. One approach to dealing with such diversity is through shared representations. The production of an explicit representation at various stages in the design process can provide a focus for people from different disciplines to document what they have accomplished and provide a plan for what they will do next. Just as architects provide blueprints, perspective drawings, and physical models to communicate a design, when people from different perspectives collaborate in a design process, they bring the results of various methods and tools to the activity as a shareable representation to communicate design opportunities and constraints. Shared representations can be stories, sketches, models, simulations, prototypes, spreadsheets, or reports in various levels of detail.

The committee recommends research to identify the characteristics of shared representations that communicate effectively across HSI domains and engineering disciplines.

Methods and Tools

There are many human-system methods that inform the system design and development process and many produce shared representations. In this report we review more than 20 categories of methods, many with several variations. Examples include environmental and organizational analysis, task analysis, field observation, participatory analysis and design, event data analysis, physical ergonomics, modeling and simulation, risk analysis, and usability evaluation. Each method is described broadly in terms of general characteristics, types of use, shared representations, contributions to the system design process, and strengths, weaknesses, and gaps. Our review is not exhaustive but presents state-of-the-art examples in the categories of methods that the committee agreed are core contributors and central to the provision of needed information about humans and human-system integration. Besides the strength in terms of sheer number of methods, the methods as a whole can also be characterized as highly flexible, fluid, tailorable, scalable, or modifiable—all characteristics that are critical given the current complexity of systems and their associated design uncertainty.

The committee recommends a detailed agenda to extend existing methods and the development of new methods of human-system integration. The recommendations cover seven major areas:

1.   The development of software tools to capture and disseminate the results of context of use analyses so that they can more easily by applied in various phases of system life-cycle development.

2.   The active participation of users in engineering design, the future of unobtrusive, passive data collection, and the ethical considerations of both.

3.   The further development and validation of human-system models to increase usability and expand their application.

4.   The further development of prototypes for training and organizational design.

5.   The identification and communication of human-system development risk.

6.   The further development of cost-effective usability evaluation methods and the more frequent and effective use of usability objectives at the beginning of a system development effort.

7.   The identification and assessment of human-system integration to system adaptability and resilience.

Full Integration of Human Systems and Systems Engineering

The committee recommends research in seven areas to support the full meshing of human-system integration and systems engineering into the system design and development process. These include

1.   Managing integrated system development.

2.   Providing traceability of HSI design objectives, decision points, and the rationale for decisions across life-cycle design phases.

3.   Developing approaches to human-system integration in the context of systems of systems.

4.   Estimating the size of the HSI development effort.

5. Creating knowledge-based planning tools for including human-system integration in complex system development efforts.

6. Developing human-system integration as a discipline and preparing HSI specialists to be system development managers.

7. Fostering more synergy between research and practice.

THE FUTURE

With the policy and research we recommend, we envision methodology for human-system integration that will be based on anticipated advances in technology in which the products of each design and development activity are manifest in representations that may be shared across the development community. In this approach, each product builds on the reusable components of previous ones. Common threads are provided by storyboards, use cases, scenarios, time lines, models, and system simulations. The stakeholders in a system will cooperate as an integrated team. The resulting design will accomplish much of system integration before implementation begins, and the result will represent a system that is truly responsive to the needs of its users, the ultimate goal of human-system integration.

In addition to the development and application of an integrated methodology, the future would hold the opportunity for the development of a discipline of human-system integration and the opportunity for HSI-led system development, the more active participation by users in system design through the use of new web-based approaches and other technologies, and the development of a set of knowledge-based planning aids to support the sharing of information across domains.

1

Introduction

Although interest in understanding the role of humans in systems and accommodating that role in design has a history of more than 60 years, there has been a continuing concern that, in each phase of development, the human element is not sufficiently considered along with hardware and software elements. When information about the performance characteristics and preferences of operators and users is not introduced early enough in the process, there are higher risks for both simple and catastrophic failures in the systems that are produced. This leads to additional costs required to revise the design late in the development cycle and even sometimes to revisions after it has been fielded. Human-system integration (HSI) is concerned with ensuring that the characteristics of people are considered throughout the system development process with regard to their selection and training, their participation in system operation, and their health and safety. It is also concerned with providing tools and methods meeting these same requirements to support the system development process itself.

This volume provides a vision for integrating an understanding of human capabilities and needs into system design using an incremental model of systems engineering development that continually assesses risks, including risks associated with the human element, at each phase of the system development effort. The chapters present a large variety of methods (1) for describing human capacities, limitations, and needs, their tasks, and the environments in which they work and (2) for characterizing and evaluating alternative designs that require some form of human-system interaction. In the context of developing a single system, these methods are extremely effective for providing needed information in a timely manner when applied by trained human-system design professionals. Ineffective and inappropriate application can be attributed, in part, to lack of communication within the organization and the development team and a dearth of fully trained professionals as team members. Additional methods and approaches are needed to complement the existing methodology as systems become more complex and the focus shifts from the design and operation of individual systems to systems of systems.

A brief history of key events in the development of human factors appears in Box 1-1. Some of these events were driven by the interest of the behavioral science community; others came about as a result of accidents

---

BOX 1-1
Events in the Growth of Human Factors

1. Bell Laboratories established a human factors group in the late 1930s.
2. In Great Britain, a new Medical Research Council Laboratory, the Applied Psychology Research Unit, was created in 1944.
3. In the U.S. military, efforts began during World War II. Immediately after the war, each military service established one or more laboratories for the study and application of human performance principles to the design of military systems. Terms like "Qualitative and Quantitative Personnel Requirements Inventory" and the "Personnel Subsystem" were coined. The military procurement community began requiring the analysis of human factors issues in responding to requests for system development proposals.
4. The Human Factors Society of America (now the Human Factors and Ergonomics Society) was founded in 1957, and the first issue of the *Human Factors* journal was published in 1958.
5. The first conference in the United States that focused on human-computer interaction was held in 1982.
6. The MANPRINT program (Manpower Personnel Integration) was introduced by the Army in 1984.
7. Over the years, interest in human factors issues was stimulated in new domains by safety crises and, sometimes, by the establishment of new government agencies to respond to these crises. Some notable examples include
   • The National Transportation Safety Administration was established in 1970 in response to the public outcry generated by Ralph Nader's book, *Unsafe at Any Speed*.
   • The Occupational Safety and Health Administration (OSHA) was established in 1970 in response to safety concerns of hazardous chemical exposure in industry.
   • The Consumer Product Safety Commission was established in 1972 in response to concerns about child safety in the home.

and safety concerns. In recent years, efforts to effectively incorporate humans into the system have been referred to as human-system integration. Two important features of the HSI approach are (1) a user focus on all aspects of the systems definition, development, and deployment stages and (2) the combined application of human-related technologies to the HSI domains (Booher, 2003a, p. 7). A key element of the HSI approach is the coordination and integration of the HSI domains at each system life-cycle phase (U.S. Department of Defense, 1999). The HSI domains cover issues of manpower, personnel, training, human factors engineering, safety, health, and survivability. While the committee pays particular attention to the integration of human factors engineering in the system life cycle, we also explore approaches to integration across the HSI domains. It is important to note that we are concerned with the application of human-system integration in the commercial context as well as in the military context.

In this report we use the term "human-system integration" to refer to the design activities associated with ensuring that the human-system domains described above are considered in concert with all the other design activities associated with the systems engineering process, so that the resulting designs are truly responsive to the needs, capacities, and limitations of the ultimate users of the systems. Although human factors engineering is but one of the HSI domains, the one concerned with providing the methods and expertise to take account of human performance capacities and limitations in formulating effective system designs, it receives particular emphasis in this report because the methods appropriate to it are often the same methods needed for the other domains. Human-system integration is also concerned with the design process itself. The design process requires humans—stakeholders and design team members—with their own performance capacities and limitations, and with diverse interests, to work together. It is important to ensure that the tools and methods supporting that process meet the requirements of human-system integration as well.

THE PROBLEM

One motivation for undertaking this study now is that industry and government are finding profound changes in the nature and complexity of the systems they seek to develop and at the same time are challenged to shorten the development cycle for new systems. There is pressure to reduce the staff required to support system operation, and this leads to increases in automation. However, not all automation actually reduces required staffing. Sometimes automation changes the job requirements and takes away the hands-on knowledge that has proved to be so useful for maintaining "situation awareness." Sometimes it actually creates more work because now the automation, as well as the system itself, must be monitored and controlled. Sometimes it reduces the reliability and trustworthiness of the overall system and increases the requirements for back-up personnel. System designers, like people in general, can be subject to an "over-confidence" bias, focusing on the potential benefits of new technology while failing to anticipate the complex interactions and new problems that may emerge (Feltovich et al., 2004). This has been referred to as the "envisioned world" problem (Woods and Dekker, 2000). There is an urgent need for improved HSI methods and tools that will enable system designers to anticipate and head off potential problems earlier in the design process (Woods, 2002).

Considering the design of individual interface workstations in isolation is no longer enough. Today's complex systems are operated by teams of individuals whose interactions must be taken into account. Even considering single systems is not enough. Currently there are requirements to operate multiple systems—systems of systems—in interaction with each other. The military is particularly concerned with systems of systems, although they are of equal concern in civilian industry (e.g., hospital systems, complex interlinked communications systems). Furthermore, many of these systems of systems are adding an organizational component and respective complexities to the technological and personnel complexities already inherent in complex systems. Finally, the emergence of service-oriented architectures and the approaches called "Web 2.0" to combinations of functionalities add to the immediate complexity and potential interdependencies of systems and their services.

The field of design is also undergoing rapid change at this time. There is continued pressure to reduce the design cycle time. Software and hardware development methodologies supporting the design process are proliferating, but there is little understanding of which tools and methods are best for which purposes. Similar methods and tools are created by different communities of practice with little awareness of the tools and best practices in the related fields. There has been no comprehensive framework to organize competing methods, and, as a result, comparisons tend to be situational with correspondingly limited generalizability.

In spite of this long history, and in part because design continually faces new challenges, there are many examples of systems that have either failed entirely or have been adopted despite their inadequacies because of the need for their capabilities. Often the reasons these adopted systems were considered unsuccessful are because they failed to meet the requirements of the human users—they required unreasonable workload, induced psychological and physical stress, or resulted in costly human error. They failed because their developers had inadequate understanding of, or overlooked consideration of, the unique capacities and limitations of people. Examples include (1) military command and control vehicles for which the requirement for operation on the move had to be dropped late in the program, because vibration and motion-induced sickness in the operational crew was found to be unacceptable; (2) the costly abandonment of a new air traffic control console before it was introduced into the workplace because it was unreasonably complex and difficult to operate; and (3) the confusion that arises from controlling a home media system with five different remote controls, or even with one "universal" remote with five different modes.

By the same token, there are examples of effective systems that have succeeded specifically because of the attention that was paid to human-system integration during system development. A primary example is the current generation of Navy Tactical Decision Support systems that was designed as part of the TADMUS (Tactical Decision Making Under Stress) program. This successful program was initiated in response to the tragic downing of an Iranian Air Bus in 1986 by the USS *Vincennes*, caused in part by poor human-system integration. TADMUS was a success because it took a human-centered design approach; the research and development (R&D) supporting it was assigned high priority by senior officer staff, and it brought researchers together with operational personnel. The confluence of these considerations gave the project a high profile and has influenced much subsequent design in the Navy.

Another outstanding example of success is the Army Comanche Helicopter program. By modifying the acquisition program specifically to recognize human-system interaction as an integral part and by introducing HSI requirements early and throughout the acquisition program, the government-industry team substantially improved overall human-system performance while realizing a cost saving of 40 times the cost of the HSI investment. This program was abruptly cancelled in 2004, the cause being attributed to "challenges of software integration" not human-system issues. The reader interested in more detail about the human-system features of this program or further examples in Army programs is referred to the excellent review by Booher and Minninger (2003).

An example of the commercial importance of human-system interaction in risk analysis and risk avoidance is the precise human-performance modeling done by the NYNEX Science and Technology organization in the evaluation of a proposed new operator services workstation (Gray et al., 1993). Using keystroke-level analysis and parameter estimation, the NYNEX team was able to show that the proposed new design would paradoxically reduce human productivity. This early analysis, as well as subsequent decisions regarding the product, was credited with saving $2 million annually. In a similar R&D project, HSI observations and analyses of over 500 directory assistance calls at US WEST helped to correct the first voice recognition application for directory assistance (Muller et al., 1995). Initial outcomes showed that the technology-assisted calls took significantly longer than conventional calls and resulted in extremely negative customer response. The information gained through qualitative and quantitative analyses showed how to reverse the negative work outcomes through a simple redesign of the dialogue between customers and the voice recognition technology. In addition to obtaining the labor savings that were promised by the technology, the redesign also improved the customer responses, leading to the voice recognition technology that is part of nearly all U.S. directory assistance calls today.

The reasons some system designs fail are multidimensional and complex. Here are a few that the committee has identified:

• Failure to introduce human factors considerations early enough—in some cases needs and requirements are forecast even before the formal system acquisition process begins.
• Lack of effective methods and tools to predict direct impacts and ripple effects of envisioned future systems early in the design process, particularly in the case of large-scale systems and systems of systems with diverse elements that can interact in complex, difficult to anticipate ways.
• A tendency to focus on people as the error-prone weak links in a system that needs to be "automated away," rather than as important contributors to overall system resilience that enable systems to adapt to unanticipated situations in need of support in that role (Hollnagel, Woods, and Leveson, 2006).
• Failure to apply known good methods routinely in practice, such as those specified in Department of Defense (DoD) and international quality standards (ISO) and recommended practices.
• Lack of ability to abstract generalizable concepts and principles, as well as transportable models, across application contexts, limiting the ability to grow a solid body of human factors design knowledge.
• Lack of synergy between research and practice, with the result that practitioners are not sufficiently aware of relevant research and research is not sufficiently informed by the body of knowledge gained from practice (Norman, 1995; Woods and Christoffersen, 2002).
• Lack of adequate HSI metrics to support progress monitoring, pass/fail reviews, and system-level evaluation.
• Inadequate or poorly documented data on relevant human task performance.
• Lack of effective use of methods and tools to support the HSI process.
• Difficulty of cost-justifying resource allocation to study and resolve human-system integration issues.
• Inadequate education and training of system developers to sensitize them to the HSI issues.
• Limited opportunities for the education of HSI specialists.

- Failure to assign resources as a result of lack of awareness that specific resources are needed to address HSI concerns.
- Conflicting requirements of various stakeholders in the system development process.
- Insufficient advocacy for consideration of human-system integration at the top level of relevant organizations.

This list, developed independently, is quite consistent with the list cited in Booher and Minninger (2003). As previously mentioned, an underlying issue regarding system failures and the inadequacies associated with current system development and human-system integration may be that many systems should actually be regarded as systems of systems.

A consensus view held by the fellows of the International Council on Systems Engineering (INCOSE) is that a system is a collection of different elements that together produce results not obtainable by the elements alone. The elements, or parts, can include people, hardware, software, facilities, policies, and documents; that is, all things required to produce system-level results. The results include system-level qualities, properties, characteristics, functions, behavior, and performance. Furthermore, INCOSE thinks the value-added of the system as a whole, beyond that contributed independently by the parts, is primarily created by the relationship among the parts; that is, how they are interconnected. What has changed in recent years is that, increasingly, these parts are systems themselves.

Over a dozen different definitions of a system of systems have emerged, emphasizing different aspects of product, process, and personnel (Jamshidi, 2005; Lane and Valerdi, 2005). Two fairly definitive treatments, Maier (1998) and Sage and Cuppan (2001), identify their distinguishing features as having component systems that (1) achieve well-substantiated purposes in their own right even if detached from the overall system; (2) manage, in large part, for their own purposes rather than the purposes of the whole, plus (3) exhibit behavior, including emergent behavior, not achievable by the component systems acting independently; and (4) involve the role of a lead systems integrator (LSI) with sufficient capability, authority, and responsibility to architect, acquire, and integrate the component systems into a satisfactorily performing system. Levis (2006) adds a condition that component systems may be added or removed while other parts of the overall system are operating.

Systems of systems may differ in several aspects, such as the number of separately managed component system owners, the number of separate missions (emergency medical, search and rescue, crisis response, insurgency suppression, limited or full-scale warfare), and the degree to which the component systems are newly developed or already developed. Particular challenges for human-system integration are multiowner, multimission systems of systems with numerous already-developed systems, which are likely to have incompatible human-system interfaces, operating modes, assumptions about operator capabilities and underlying infrastructure, and degrees of mission criticality or safety criticality.

As systems become increasingly complex, there is a corresponding increase in complexity in the systems (i.e., enterprises) that develop, operate, and sustain these systems in a global context (Nightingale and Rhodes, 2004). Traditional methods related to systems engineering, enterprise engineering, or enterprise architecting are inadequate for designing and managing systems within systems and systems within enterprises. Broader and more holistic methods within an engineering systems perspective are needed (Nightingale and Rhodes, 2004). While HSI methods offer considerable contributions to analyzing and designing complex systems, methods related to systems of systems and enterprises are still inadequate.

An example of a system of systems under development is the Air Force Falconer Air Operations Center in Arizona; in Central Command, Air Operations Center is described in *The Integrator* (Mayer, 2005) as follows:

> The Electronic Systems Center developed Falconer AOC "system of systems" is the Combined Forces Air Component Commander's weapon system for commanding air and space forces. A Falconer operating with a Theater Response Package—meaning fully equipped and manned for a theater war—can manage and control up to 3,000 air sorties a day.

CHARGE AND SCOPE

Many methods, tools, and techniques are available in the literature for addressing various aspects of human-system integration, and there are several methods textbooks and standards:

*   *Handbook of Human Factors and Ergonomics Methods* (Stanton et al., 2005);
*   *Handbook of Human Factors and Ergonomics* (Salvendy, 2006);
*   *Handbook of Human Systems Integration* (Booher, 2003b);
*   *A Guide to Task Analysis* (Kirwan and Ainsworth, 1992);
*   *Handbook of Human Factors Testing and Evaluation* (Charlton and O'Brien, 2002);
*   *Systems Engineering: System Life Cycle Processes* (International Organization for Standardization, 2002);
*   *Software Engineering: Software Product Quality Requirements and Evaluation* (International Organization for Standardization, 2006); and
*   *Handbook of Systems Engineering and Management, revised edition* (Sage and Rouse, in press).

These claim to offer a systematic approach, but each has serious deficiencies. The methods tend to exist in isolation. Nemeth (2004) has assembled existing methods into a coherent book, but still there are gaps in the existing methods and tools, and more work is needed to improve their integration into a coherent methodology with a suite of tools that would support such an integrated methodology. These are the issues we address in this report. Specifically, the charge to the committee is to

- provide a comprehensive review of issues involved in design throughout the system life cycle that need to be addressed by a consideration of human cognitive and physical performance characteristics. This review will be used as a framework for further analysis of methodologies.
- evaluate the state of the art in human-system engineering and (1) product development processes, (2) product design methodologies, and (3) product design tools.
- develop a vision for an integrated, multidisciplinary, generalizable, human-system design support methodology and tool set. Identify a set of core methods and tools needed to support design activities associated with a variety of systems.
- recommend a research plan suggesting how to achieve this ideal.

Although the U.S. military requested this report, our goal is to provide recommendations that are also relevant to other government departments as well as industry, including the process control, manufacturing, and service industries. Furthermore, the committee defined the scope of its review and analysis to include environmental factors, organizational and work context, and matching the system to users' needs as well as taking account of human cognitive and physical capacities and limitations. Many audiences have a vested interest in, or will benefit from, better methodologies for making systems useful and relevant, such as the following:

- acquisition and program managers,
- developers/engineers/first-level managers,
- contractor management,
- human factors/usability professionals and those representing other MANPRINT domains,
- policy makers and regulators, and
- research funders.

In preparing this report, we tried to remain sensitive to these different constituencies and are hopeful that various chapters and recommendations are relevant to different subsets of them.

THE CONTEXT

The Military Sector

Both the Army and the Navy have active HSI programs that were created to inform system development efforts about the human side of system performance and the decisions that are required throughout the development cycle to adequately consider human roles and contributions. The Air Force is in the process of implementing a similar system. The Army's program, known as MANPRINT, has been operating since the early 1980s; the Navy's system, SEAPRINT (Systems Engineering, Acquisition, and Personnel Integration) was formalized in 2003 to establish a MANPRINT-like approach to Navy system design and acquisition. The military services have control over all decisions related to development, fielding, staffing, and operation of their new systems.

MANPRINT is "a comprehensive management and technical program designed to improve total system (leader, unit/soldier, and equipment) performance by focusing on the human requirements for optimal system performance" (U.S. Army, 2000). It consists of seven domains: manpower, personnel, training, human factors engineering, system safety, health hazards, and soldier survivability. SEAPRINT "provides the Navy with a single, integrated performance-based process that addresses all aspects of Human-System Integration—from capability definition through personnel delivery" (U.S. Navy, 2005). It also includes seven domains, differing from MANPRINT by combining safety and health and adding a domain labeled habitability. Both programs are compatible with the seven HSI domains listed in the defining DoD Instruction 5000.2 Operation of the Defense Acquisition System (U.S. Department of Defense, 2003a).

Representatives of the Army and the Navy have specified two major problems in effectively applying these programs. The first is getting inputs from the required specialists to be considered early enough and at all stages of the system development life cycle. The second is the inability to effectively integrate HSI efforts across domains. In addition, many HSI analyses are applicable to more than one domain, and decisions made in one can significantly constrain or influence decisions in another. Despite these opportunities for integration, those working in each domain tend to function separately, applying their own methods and tools.

The domains of manpower, personnel, and training (MPT) encompass both supply and demand issues. Supply involves the sources of personnel, their background, and how they will be trained. Demand involves the determination of the number and skill levels of personnel required for each job specialty. The committee's focus is on the demand side, where manpower, personnel, and training impact design through their implications for human factors requirements. Managing workload is a critical design issue in human-system integration. The number and type of personnel are intimately tied to workload requirements. Similarly, there are important trade-offs between the usability of a system and the requirements for training. How does one consider the trade-offs among staffing levels, personnel quality, personnel turnover, training requirements, and system design? Complex systems represent a usability challenge that can be solved by better design or by more extensive training. Both of these kinds of issues influence the manpower, personnel, and training investment required in new system development. Although we do not address the supply side directly, it is important to understand the approaches and decisions in supplying manpower, personnel, and training as a context for the committee's work.

Manpower refers to the number and type of personnel who operate, maintain, support, and provide training for systems. Input concerning the number of personnel needed comes from policy makers in the Pentagon at the top and from manpower analysts at the unit and the system levels at the bottom. Although manpower assessment techniques are available to determine the appropriate number of operators/people for each piece of equipment/task, these techniques are often not used because they are labor-, skill-, and knowledge-intensive. A good example is IMPRINT (Improved Performance Research and Integration Tool), a modeling tool developed by the Army Human Engineering Directorate and used by the Army and the Navy for manpower planning and to inform human-system design decisions (Allender et al., 2005). This tool requires substantial training to be used effectively, and personnel with this training are not always readily available.

Another issue concerning the adequacy of input from the bottom up is that results of the analyses are often politically inconvenient or are overshadowed by budget constraints or logistics requirements. Furthermore, expertise in unit-level manpower analysis is rare. Decisions made regarding the number of personnel can have an important influence on the requirements for personnel basic abilities, system features, and training.

Personnel refers to the human aptitudes, skills, and experiences required to perform the jobs of operators, maintainers, and support personnel. The Services apply a standardized set of entry requirements that have changed little over the past decades. The supply of enlisted personnel to the military primarily comes from 18- to 24-year-olds in the general population who have received a high school diploma and can achieve an acceptable score on the Armed Forces Qualification Test (AFQT). The Services are almost completely staffed by applicants with scores in the higher range on the AFQT. The AFQT score and scores on combinations of subtests in the full Armed Forces Aptitude Test Battery (ASVAB) are used to determine qualifications for various jobs. The actual assignment to a job is also driven by the availability of a position opening. It is important to note that the philosophy of the military services is to recruit motivated individuals with an appropriate ability level—the skill and the knowledge needed for each military job is then developed through military training.

Studies examining how well the ASVAB subset scores predict job performance have shown only a weak relationship (National Research Council, 1991). More recently, the level of prediction from the ASVAB to job performance has been further reduced by the fact that, although jobs are changing with the introduction of technology, the old job descriptions remain in place.

Training prepares personnel to perform the tasks necessary to meet the mission or goals and objectives of the system. Development of training requirements, methods, curricula, and training system design are important parts of the overall system design process. The length and intensity of training depends on the background, ability levels, and learning styles of the personnel in the training class; the complexity of the system; and the level of skill and knowledge needed to ensure the desired level of performance speed and accuracy. Some training is designed for individual task performance; some for team or unit-level performance. An important input to effective training is a task analysis that identifies the skills and knowledge needed for acceptable performance—this analysis requires updating as the system configuration changes or as new automation is introduced. Although there may be some task analysis requirements that are unique to the training domain, the methods for creating this task analysis are substantially the same as those used for other system development purposes discussed in this report. Inadequate training can result when work and task descriptions are outdated. Training deficiencies may also result from failure to allocate the necessary training time and budget, lack of flexible training schedules needed to meet learning requirements, and lack of useful proficiency criteria.

Manpower, personnel, and system design decisions should take into account the level of training needed and the feasibility of delivering that training in the allowable time frame.

The Private Sector

The private or commercial sector is more difficult to characterize because of the wide variety of systems and products, of the differences in approaches to human-system design, the central role of marketing, and because in the commercial product environment projects are more likely to be cancelled if milestones are not met in the early stages of the development process. Companies generally develop products for use by other companies, groups, or individuals. Some products require extensive training, and some are subject to safety regulations. Development efforts are driven by market forces; competition; time constraints; safety and liability exposure; and by customer characteristics, requirements, and budgets. HSI activities in the private sector focus on a number of activities, including, but not limited to, market research, risk analysis, product planning, development of product lines and platforms, usability testing, and product evaluation (Rouse, 2003).

Private-sector products cover a wide range of sizes, complexity, and level of human involvement. On one hand, for example, there are complex systems in manufacturing, process control plants, nuclear power plants, network management, and air traffic control systems. These systems include large numbers of personnel performing a highly structured set of jobs requiring technical skills and knowledge. In this context, considerations of manpower, personnel, and training are relevant. On the other hand, there are many smaller scale single-user systems (e.g., commercial products) for which training is critical but manpower and personnel issues are less relevant. Many commercial products are released for which user training is impractical, so they need to have self-evident, intuitive user interfaces to be successful; indeed, for web-based commercial services, user training is impossible, and ease of use becomes a significant, make-or-break attribute.

Many private-sector companies perform a user analysis, or a similar assessment of the intended user, in the early stages of design, using such methods as contextual inquiry, scenarios, task analysis, cognitive task analysis, ethnography, or participatory analysis (these are discussed in Chapter 6). This analysis of users' capabilities is similar to the military's personnel assessment. For some products, such as hospital medical devices, the user can be expected to have advanced skills and knowledge. When designing products intended for use by the general population, companies must account for a wide range of skill levels. With increasing regulatory pressure, companies are also designing for people with a range of disabilities, including visual, auditory, motor, and cognitive/developmental disabilities. A product that is poorly matched to a user's capabilities may create frustration for the user, lower sales, increased need for training and customer support, and an overall increased cost. A product that is created to serve multiple types of users often has additional and unanticipated reach into new markets or applications.

Training takes many forms in the private sector. Most products include such training aids as user manuals, help menus, and product support help lines. For complex or difficult to operate systems, a formal training program may be required. Alternatively, online training may be needed. Training requirements may be established as part of the design process or may be put into place after a product is on the market.

New developments challenge these simple, old ways of thinking about development and deployment—especially the concepts often referred to as Web 2.0 (e.g., O'Reilly, 2005), in which each application provides a standardized interface (typically XML) to other applications, and new services can be created as through simple interfaces among these existing applications (making a "call" between applications, similar to a subroutine call in a conventional program architecture). The standardization of data formats and protocols among these services allows very rapid prototyping and testing of new service concepts, and these integrations can lead to user experiences that appear to be entirely new concepts and functionalities. Each such web site or module uses these standardized formats to offer "services" that can be called from other web sites or modules—hence the more formal description as service-oriented architectures (Erl, 2005; SOA, 2006). We list five classes of these new "social software" services here (Allen, 2004; IBM, n.d.; Teton and Allen, 2007; see also Chi et al., 2007):

1.   Combinations of data from multiple services, creating new services and new user experiences.
2.   Easily consumed updates or "feeds" from user-created dynamic pages called "weblogs or "blogs."
3.   Sharing of annotations of websites, pictures, music, and other web-addressable objects through "social tagging" of web resources in a shared database, as well as the evolution of user-created "folksonomies" as low-maintenance alternatives to high-cost enterprise taxonomies.
4.   Sharing of dynamically updated personal information through person-centric shared databases.
5.   Negotiation and co-creation of shared knowledge, accessible to millions of users, at user-constructed online encyclopedias.

These new service-oriented architectures present new challenges in several areas. First is the speed with which new services can be created: development time in this very open environment decreases from years to days. Second is the rate of change of the data in these new services, which can amount to many thousands of updates daily. Third is the decentralization of the "sourcing" and control of the information, which is typically contributed by thousands of people who do not necessarily have other ties or relationships to one another. Fourth is the current very loose security model for these services, which is likely to be tightened as the commercial and governmental uses of these technologies increase. All of these challenges highlight the need for input from users and analysis of the implications of these design alternatives for their human users, either before or while they are implemented. Without specific human-system requirements, the ease and speed of creation makes it even easier for designers to pursue their own clever but often inappropriate designs.

THEMES

In addressing the charge, the committee identified several major themes that are woven through the chapters of this report. These include adopting a risk-driven approach to determining the need for HSI activity; tailoring the selection of methods to meeting time and budget constraints; developing and using shared representations for communication of issues and results among domains and disciplines; designing systems that can accommodate changing conditions and requirements in the workplace; and integrating HSI inputs across human-system domains as well as across life-cycle phases.

The committee proposes an incremental commitment model as a useful approach to system development. Although it is not the only model that could be used on future human-intensive systems and systems of systems, it serves as a reasonably robust framework for explaining HSI concepts and for evaluating these via a set of case studies presented in Chapter 5.

This model is based on five principles that are critical to success:

1. satisficing of system stakeholders (e.g., users, acquirers, developers);
2. incremental growth of system definition and stakeholder commitment;
3. concurrent system definition and development;
4. iterative system definition and development; and
5. risk management.

The details of this model appear in Chapter 2.

Adopting a Risk-Driven Approach

A central focus of the incremental commitment model is the progressive reduction of risk throughout the system development life cycle with the goal of producing a cost-effective system in which all stakeholders are considered winners. Risk reduction is accomplished through the application of all relevant disciplines. In the past, the risks associated with human-system integration have often been neglected in the system risk analysis process. In this report we emphasize the importance of including human factors and HSI risk as an integral part of this process. Cost-effectiveness is achieved by focusing resources on high-risk aspects of the development while deemphasizing development phases for aspects of the system that are judged to pose a limited risk. Key elements of the model are the anchor points at the end of each cycle that call for stakeholder evaluation and commitment. These anchor points correspond to DoD system development milestone reviews.

Engineering development risks are realized when development is impeded by unforeseen difficulties in implementation or costly overruns. In contrast, HSI risks may be realized only at the conclusion of a system development life cycle when the system is fielded. They may lead to (1) under-utilization or disuse of a product or system because it is difficult, inefficient, or dangerous to use; (2) human error in the use of the product or system, resulting in delays, serious compromises in system performance, or higher operational costs; or (3) both. For safety-critical or defense systems, either of these risks can lead to catastrophic events, including serious injury or death. For the manufacturer of commercial products, loss of sales, product liability lawsuits, and product recalls are major potential results of failure to adequately consider HSI risks.

These operational stage risks are traceable to failures to fully integrate user needs and capabilities at earlier phases of the development cycle. To be effective, all risk-reduction approaches, including human-system integration, must be applied to identify and address risk reduction during early and middle stages of development. The use of such risk-reduction approaches allows developers (or stakeholders) to select one design approach over another, gain an understanding of unanticipated effects through simulation studies, and generally have a higher level of confidence that system development efforts are on track to meet requirements and avoid the operational stage risks of disuse, error, high costs, and lack of sales.

In this report we take the view that the analysis of HSI risks should be considered at the same level of importance as the risks that specific hardware or software functions will not be able to meet the required technical specifications. This consideration places HSI issues at the level of priority required to produce systems that will not fail due to poor attention to the MANPRINT variables of importance.

Tailoring Methods to Time and Budget Constraints

The committee recognizes that human-system integration is in competition with other system development activities for the resources controlled by the project manager. Sometimes the resource demands of the HSI team seem incommensurate with the project manager's perceived benefits. This perception arises partly because much of the resource investment needs to occur very early in the process, yet the benefits are not harvested until late in the development process. Use of risk analysis to focus resources on critical development issues can help to ameliorate this concern. Nevertheless, the committee thinks that it is incumbent on the HSI specialists to tailor the application of their methodologies to the specific needs of a project. Most of the methods and tools described in this report are designed to be adjustable and scalable to meet the needs of specific projects.

Creating Shared Representations for Communication

Effective and efficient design requires meaningful communication among hardware, software, and human-system integration designers; among professionals in the domains of human-system design (e.g., personnel, manpower, training, human factors); and among designers, users, and other stakeholders. Just as an architect provides blueprints, perspective drawings, or physical models to communicate a design, when people from different perspectives collaborate in a design process, they bring various methods and tools to communicate effectively with other experts in the activity. In addition, each group often has its own mind set, language, and work practices. With so much diversity among the groups tasked with complex systems design, the potential for communication and collaboration failures increases if assumptions (and their associated mind sets) are not made explicit. Effective use of multiple shared representations to mediate the activities of these multidisciplinary teams can foster innovation and a more effective design process.

Shared representations "stand in" and mediate communication between and among people engaged in a collaborative process. From the HSI perspective, they can be stories, reports, spreadsheets, models/diagrams, prototypes, or simulations. Physical or electronic models of aspects of the human-machine system are shared representations that provide a bridge between research and design in complex systems. The act of modeling can help teams detect unintended relations and features and lead to new connections and ideas. Prototypes are one form of model that make explicit an aspect of form, fit, or functionality—they can range from simple sketches to full physical mock-ups. By predicting and highlighting potential performance limitations, computer simulations of the human-machine system are another form of model that can support shared understanding by the development stakeholders.

The committee thinks that a current impediment to effective identification of HSI issues and risks and utilization of the resultant recommendations is the often vague nature of the products of HSI analysis. We are therefore emphasizing the importance of shared representations that truly communicate effectively with the other engineering disciplines and project stakeholders.

Shared representations are useful at all phases of the system design life cycle and play an important role at the anchor points at which stakeholders are asked to make commitments and reach agreements. The chapters in Part II of the report describes a variety of shared representations, including stories and scenarios, prototypes, user models, and simulations. The use of these representations is further explored in later chapters.

Designing to Accommodate Changing Conditions and Requirements in the Workplace

New technologies provide new capabilities, and these often generate new expectations, roles, and ways of doing things that are not always anticipated ahead of time (Woods and Dekker, 2000). Unanticipated complexities can arise through increased system interconnectedness and interdependency, which create new sources of workload, problem-solving challenges, and coordination requirements. In turn, individuals in the system will adapt. They will exploit the new power provided by the technology in unanticipated ways, and they will create clever work-arounds to cope with technology limitations, so as to meet the needs of the work and human purposes. To accommodate changes and unintended effects, the system development process should be viewed as incremental and ongoing. It is important to continue observations and analysis, even after a system has been implemented, both to evaluate the validity of designers' assumptions and to drive further discovery and innovation. For a system to remain work-centered over time, it must not only support the elements of work identified at the design stage, but it must also be able to accommodate elements that the initial design did not appropriately capture and be adaptable to meet the changing nature of the work. Systems need to be designed in ways to enable users to adapt the system to evolving requirements.

Researchers have argued for the importance of creating systems that afford the potential for productive adaptation to enable users to "finish the design" locally in response to the situated context of work. This idea can be extended to include not only local responses, but also adaptation of systems to keep pace with a constantly evolving world. The technologies of Web 2.0 represent an extreme version of this approach, emphasizing the importance of users as co-creators of information, co-editors of collections of information, and co-implementers of new features through the increasingly easy technologies that enable the aggregation of features and services into new functionalities, experiences, and utilities (referred to as "mash-up" technologies). In the latter sense, the design is never really finished. A significant challenge currently facing organizations is their ability to adapt to rapid and unpredictable change in more appropriate ways than their competitors, including the adoption of new technologies and business practices (Crisp, 2006). Changes in hardware and software must be accompanied by changes in the use of humans in the rapidly evolving systems.

The notion of designing for evolvability is discussed in more detail in Part II.

Integrating HSI Contributions Across
Life-Cycle Phases and Human-System Domains

The primary features of the HSI concept are consideration of humans in the decisions made in each system life-cycle phase and the integration of inputs across domains dealing with the various human-related development issues at each life-cycle phase. These features have been stated by our military sponsors as critical considerations in effectively applying their programs.

Throughout the report we examine the role of HSI methods at each development phase and discuss how many of these methods provide inputs at several phases. Chapter 6 focuses on methods that are applied early in the life cycle to help identify opportunities, structure the scope, and characterize various aspects of the context of use from the perspective of human attitudes, capabilities, limitations, and needs. Chapter 7 carries some of these methods over into the design phases as well as introducing an additional set of methods. Chapter 8 focuses on evaluation methods and their role throughout each life-cycle phase. When possible, we provide examples of shared representations that can be used for communication among human-related domains as well as among those working with the human elements, the software elements, and the hardware elements.

REPORT ORGANIZATION

Following this introduction, the report is divided into three parts. Part I: Human-System Integration in the Context of System Development consists of four chapters. Chapter 2 describes the system development process, Chapter 3 focuses on human-system integration in the system development process and the use of shared representations for communication, and Chapter 4 addresses HSI program risk. Chapter 5 introduces three case studies: uninhabited aerial systems, port security, and a commercial medical device. These cases were selected because they provide examples of an existing system, a developing system, and a vision for a future system. They are used throughout the report to highlight different approaches, methods, and tools.

Part II: Human-System Integration Methods in System Development contains three chapters characterizing HSI methods and tools. Each of these chapters provides an overview of the relevant methods, how they are used, the shared representations they generate, and their strengths and limitations. It is important to note that these chapters do not provide an exhaustive review but rather focus on the classes of methods that the committee identified as central contributors of information to the system development process about topics relating to people.

Part III: Scenarios, Conclusions, and Recommendations provides the committee's vision for the future and our conclusions and recommendations.

PART I

Human-System Integration in the Context of System Development

2

The System Development Process

The ultimate goal of system development is to deliver a system that satisfies the needs of its operational stakeholders—users, operators, administrators, maintainers, interoperators, and the public—within satisfactory levels of the resources of its development stakeholders—funders, acquirers, developers, suppliers, and others. From the perspective of human-system integration (HSI), satisfying operational stakeholders' needs can be broadly construed to mean that a system is usable and dependable, permits few or no human errors, and leads to high productivity and adaptability. Developing and delivering systems that simultaneously satisfy all these stakeholders usually requires managing a complex set of risks, such as usage uncertainties, schedule uncertainties, supply issues, requirements changes, and uncertainties associated with technology maturity and technical design. Each of these areas poses a risk to the delivery of an acceptable operational system within the available budget and schedule. End-state operational system risks can be categorized as uncertainties in achieving a system mission, carrying out the work processes, operating within such constraints as cost or personnel, satisfying operational stakeholders, and achieving an acceptable operational return on investment.

This chapter summarizes the committee's analysis of candidate models of system design, development, and evolution processes with respect to a set of study-derived principles critical to the success of human-intensive system development. It presents the results of synthesizing the contributions of these models along with key human factors processes into an incremental commitment model (ICM) that is used as a process framework for application of the study's recommended processes, methods, and tools, as well as for illustrating their successful application in three human-system design case studies (see Chapter 5).

PRINCIPLES FOR SUCCESSFUL SYSTEM DEVELOPMENT

The five principles critical to the success of human-intensive system development and evolution were evolved during the study and validated by analysis of the critical success factors of award-winning projects and application to the case studies in Chapter 5:

1. *Stakeholder satisficing.* If a system development process presents an operational or development stakeholder with the prospect of an unsatisfactory outcome, the stakeholder will generally refuse to cooperate, resulting in an unsuccessful system. Stakeholder satisficing involves identifying the stakeholders critical to success and their value propositions; negotiating a mutually satisfactory set of system requirements, solutions, and plans; and managing proposed changes to preserve a mutually satisfactory outcome.

2. *Incremental growth of system definition and stakeholder commitment.* This characteristic encompasses the necessity of incremental discovery of emergent human-system requirements and solutions via such discovery methods as prototyping, operational exercises, and the use of early system capabilities. Requirements and commitment cannot be monolithic or fully prespecifiable for complex, human-intensive systems; understanding, trust, definition, and commitment are achieved through a cyclic process.

3. *Iterative system definition and development.* Incremental and evolutionary approaches lead to cyclic refinements of requirements, solutions, and development plans. Such iteration helps projects to learn early and efficiently about operational and performance requirements.

4. *Concurrent system definition and development.* Initially, this includes concurrent engineering of requirements and solutions, as well as integrated product and process definition. In later increments, change-driven rework and rebaselining of next-increment requirements, solutions, and plans occur simultaneously with development of the current-system increment. This allows early fielding of core capabilities, continual adaptation to change, and timely growth of complex systems without waiting for every requirement and subsystem to be defined.

5. *Risk management—risk-driven activity levels and anchor point milestones.* The level of detail of specific products and processes will depend on the level of risk associated with them. If the user interface is considered a high-risk area, for example, then more design activity will be devoted to this component to achieve stakeholder commitments at particular design anchor points. If, however, interactive graphic user interface (GUI) builder

capabilities make it low risk not to document evolving GUI requirements, much time-consuming effort can be saved by not creating and continually updating GUI requirements documents while evolving the GUI to meet user needs.

THE EVOLVING NATURE OF SYSTEM REQUIREMENTS

Traditionally, requirements have served as the basis for competitive selection of system suppliers and subsequent contracts between the acquirer and the selected supplier. As such, they are expected to be prespecifically complete, consistent, unambiguous, and testable. Frequently, progress payments and award fees are based on the degree to which these properties are satisfied.

However, particularly as systems depend more and more on being parts of a network-centric, collaboration-intensive system of systems, the traditional approach to system requirements has encountered increasing difficulties that these key ICM principles have been evolved to avoid. These difficulties include

- *Emergent requirements.* The most appropriate user interfaces and collaboration modes for a human-intensive system are not specifiable in advance but emerge with system prototyping and usage. Forcing them to be prematurely and precisely specified generally leads to poor business or mission performance and expensive late rework and delays (Highsmith, 2000).
- *Rapid change.* Specifying current-point-in-time snapshot requirements on a cost-competitive contract generally leads to a big design up front and a point-solution architecture that is hard to adapt to new developments. Each of the many subsequent changes then leads to considerable nonproductive work in redeveloping documents and software, as well as in renegotiating contracts (Beck, 1999).
- *Reusable components.* Prematurely specifying requirements (e.g., hasty specification of a 1-second response time requirement when later prototyping shows that 4 seconds would be acceptable) that disqualify otherwise cost-effective reusable components often leads to overly expensive, late, and unsatisfactory systems (Boehm, 2000).

These key principles focus on (1) incremental and evolutionary acquisition of the most important and best-understood capabilities; (2) on concurrently engineering requirements and solutions; (3) on using prototypes, models, and simulations as ways of obtaining information to reduce the risk of specifying inappropriate requirements; and (4) on basing requirements on stakeholder negotiations once their implications are better understood.

These principles work best when stakeholders adopt a different vocabulary for dealing with requirements. The primary dictionary definition of a requirement is "something required, i.e., claimed or asked for by right and authority." It is much easier to make progress toward a mutually satisfactory negotiated solution if stakeholders use more negotiation-oriented terms such as "goals," "objectives," or "value propositions" rather than assuming that they are dealing with nonnegotiable "requirements." And when trade-offs among cost, schedule, performance, and capabilities are not well understood, it is better to specify prioritized capabilities and ranges of mutually satisfactory performance, rather than to insist on precise and unambiguous requirements. However, following Principle 5 above on the risk-driven level of product detail, it is important to converge on precise requirements when the risk of having them be imprecise is high. Some good examples are human-computer interaction protocols for safety-critical systems and interfaces among separately developed mission-critical subsystems.

PRINCIPLES-BASED COMPARISON OF ALTERNATIVE PROCESS MODELS

Our study included an analysis of candidate systems development process models with respect to the five critical principles for success. The candidate models include the waterfall, V, spiral, and concurrent engineering process models discussed in the first two chapters of the *Handbook of Systems Engineering and Management* (Sage and Rouse, 1999a, 1999b; Patterson, 1999), plus emerging candidates, such as agile methods (Beck, 1999; Highsmith, 2000), V-model updates (Federal Republic of Germany, 2004), and 2001 extensions of the spiral model (Boehm and Hansen, 2001).

Our analysis, summarized in Table 2-1, indicates that all of the models make useful contributions but exhibit shortfalls with respect to human factors considerations, particularly in explicit guidance for stakeholder satisficing. Pure-sequential implementations of the waterfall and V-models are not good matches for human-intensive systems. Although they are becoming less frequent, they are still often encountered due to the imposition of existing contracting clauses and standards. More recently, the V-Model XT has adopted more risk-driven and incremental approaches that encourage concurrent engineering (Federal Republic of Germany, 2004), but it takes some skill to build in stakeholder satisficing and to avoid overly heavyweight implementations and difficulties in coping with rapid change. Risk-driven evolutionary development is better at coping with rapid change, but it can have difficulties in optimizing around early increments with architectures that encounter later scalability problems. Concurrent engineering explicitly addresses incremental growth, concurrency, and iteration. Although com-

TABLE 2-1 Principles-Based Comparison of Alternative Process Models

Process Models	Principles				
	Stakeholder Satisficing	Incremental Growth	Concurrency	Iteration	Risk Management
Sequential waterfall, V	Assumed via initial requirements; no specifics	Sequential	No	No	Once at the beginning
Iterative, risk-driven waterfall, V	Assumed via initial requirements; no specifics	Risk-driven; missing specifics	Risky parts	Yes	Yes
Risk-driven evolutionary development	Revisited for each iteration	Risk-driven; missing specifics	Risky parts	Yes	Yes
Concurrent engineering	Implicit; no specifics	Yes; missing specifics	Yes	Yes	Implicit; no specifics
Agile	Fix shortfalls in next phase	Iterations	Yes	Yes	Some
Spiral process 2001	Driven by stakeholder commitment milestones	Risk-driven; missing specifics	Yes	Risk-driven	Yes
Incremental commitment	Stakeholder-driven; stronger human factors support	Risk-driven; more specifics	Yes	Yes	Yes

patible with stakeholder satisficing and risk management, it lacks much explicit guidance in addressing them.

Agile methods are even better at coping with rapid change, but they can have even more difficulties with scalability and with mission-critical or safety-critical systems, in which fixing shortfalls in the next increment is not acceptable. There is a wide variety of agile methods; some, such as lean and feature-driven development, are better at scalability and criticality than others. The version of spiral development in Boehm and Hansen (2001), with stakeholder satisficing and anchor point milestones, covers all of the principles, but it is unspecific about how risk considerations guide iteration and incremental growth. Our analysis of these models indicates primary shortfalls in support of human factors integration and unproven ability to scale up to the future process challenges involving emergent, network-centric, massively collaborative systems of systems (Maier, 1998; Sage and Cuppan, 2001).

The committee undertook to integrate human factors considerations into the spiral 2005 process model (Boehm and Lane, 2006), a generalization of the win-win spiral model being used in the future combat systems system of systems (Boehm et al., 2004). The result is the incremental commitment model, discussed in the next section. Although, it is not the only model that could be used on future human-intensive systems of systems, it has served as a reasonably robust framework for explaining the study's HSI concepts, and for evaluating these via the case studies presented in Chapter 5.

THE INCREMENTAL COMMITMENT MODEL

An overview of the ICM life-cycle process is shown in Figure 2-1. It identifies the concurrently engineered life-cycle phases; the stakeholder commitment review points and their use of feasibility rationales to assess the compatibility, feasibility, and risk associated with the concurrently engineering artifacts; and the major focus of each life-cycle phase. There are a number of alternatives at each commitment point: (1) the risks are

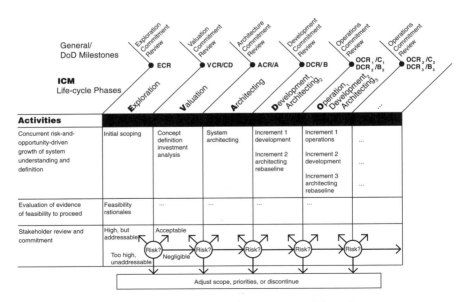

FIGURE 2-1 Overview of the incremental commitment life-cycle process.

negligible and no further analysis and evaluation activities are needed to complete the next phase; (2) the risk is acceptable and work can proceed to the next phase; (3) the risk is addressable but requires backtracking; and (4) the risk is too great and the development process should be rescoped or halted. These risks are assessed by the system's stakeholders, whose commitment will be based on whether the current level of system definition gives sufficient evidence that the system will satisfy their value propositions (see Box 2-1).

The incremental commitment model builds on the early verification and validation concepts of the V-model, the concurrency concepts of the concurrent engineering model, the lighter-weight concepts in the agile and lean models, the risk-driven concepts of the spiral model, the phases and anchor points in the rational unified process (RUP) (Royce, 1998; Kruchten, 1999; Boehm, 1996), and recent extensions of the spiral model to address systems of systems acquisition (Boehm and Lane, 2006). In comparison to the software-intensive RUP, the incremental commitment model also addresses hardware and human factors integration. It extends the RUP phases to cover the full system life cycle: an exploration phase precedes the RUP inception phase, which is refocused on valuation and investment analysis. The RUP elaboration phase is refocused on architecting; the RUP construction and transition phases are combined into development; and an additional operations phase combines operations, production, maintenance, and phase-out. An integration of the RUP and the incremental commitment model is being prepared for use in the open-source eclipse process frameworks.

In comparison to the sequential waterfall (Royce, 1970) and V-models (Federal Republic of Germany, 2004), the incremental commitment model explicitly emphasizes concurrent engineering of requirements and solutions, establishes explicit feasibility rationales as pass/fail milestone criteria; explicitly enables risk-driven avoidance of unnecessary documents, phases, and reviews; and provides explicit support for a stabilized current-increment development concurrently with a separate change processing and rebaselining activity to prepare for appropriate and stabilized development of the next increment. These aspects can be integrated into a waterfall or V-model, enabling projects required to use such models to cope more effectively with systems of the future.

The ICM commitment milestones correspond fairly closely with the Department of Defense (DoD) acquisition milestones as defined in DoD Instruction 5000.2 (U.S. Department of Defense, 2003a). For example, the ICM milestone commitment to proceed into development based on the validated life-cycle architecture package (an operations concept description, requirements description, architecture description, life-cycle plan, working prototypes or high-risk elements, and a feasibility rationale providing

BOX 2-1
Value-Based Systems and Software Engineering

In order for a system's stakeholders to commit their personal material and financial resources to the next level of system elaboration, they must be convinced that the current level of system elaboration provides evidence that their value propositions will be satisfied by the system. This success condition is consistent with the theory W (win-win) approach to value-based systems and software engineering, which states that a project will be successful if and only if it makes winners of its success-critical stakeholders. If the project does not create a satisfactory value proposition for some success-critical stakeholders (a win-lose situation), they will refuse to participate or will counterattack, generally creating a lose-lose situation for all stakeholders.

The associated key value-based principles for creating a success-critical stakeholder win-win outcome are (1) to identify the success-critical stakeholders and their value propositions; (2) to identify, confront, and resolve conflicts among these value propositions; (3) to enable the stakeholders to negotiate a mutually satisfactory or win-win solution region or opportunity space; and (4) to monitor the evolution of the opportunity space and apply corrective or adaptive actions to keep the opportunity space viable or increase its value (Boehm and Jain, 2005).

The associated key value-based practices address these principles and also involve using alternative terminology to traditional project or system acquisition terminology: early-stage "goals, objectives, value propositions, or win conditions" rather than "requirements"; "solution space" rather than "solution"; "desired and acceptable levels of service" rather than "the required level of service"; "satisficing" rather than "optimizing"; and "success-critical stakeholder or partner" rather than "vendor, supplier, or worker."

Key value-based practices for identifying the success-critical stakeholders and their value propositions include ethnographic techniques, plus a technique called results chains (Thorp, 1998) for identifying success-critical stakeholders. Other useful techniques include scenarios, prototypes, brainstorming, quality function deployment, business case analysis, and participatory design, plus asking "why?" for each "what" or "how" identified by a stakeholder.

Key value-based practices for identifying, confronting, and resolving conflicts among stakeholder value propositions include inventing options for mutual gain (Fisher and Ury, 1981), expectations management, business case analysis, and group-based techniques for prioritizing desired capabilities and for identifying desired and acceptable levels of service.

Key value-based practices for enabling stakeholders to negotiate a mutually satisfactory or win-win solution region or opportunity space include the conflict resolution techniques just described, plus negotiation techniques (Raiffa, 1982); risk-based techniques for determining how much of an activity, artifact, or level of service is enough, such as real options theory (Black and Scholes, 1973; Amram and Kulatilaka, 1999); and groupware support systems for negotiating stakeholder win-win requirements.

Key value-based practices for monitoring and keeping the opportunity space viable or increasing its value include market-watch and technology-watch techniques, incremental and evolutionary development, architecting to accommodate future change, adaptive control techniques, and business-value-oriented earned value management systems.

evidence of their compatibility and feasibility) corresponds fairly closely with DoD's Milestone B commitment to proceed into the development and demonstration phase.

VIEWS OF THE INCREMENTAL COMMITMENT MODEL

The following section provides multiple views of the incremental commitment model, including a process model generator view, a concurrent level of activity view, an anchor point milestone view, a spiral process view, and an incremental development view for incorporating rapid change and high assurance using agile and plan-driven teams. It concludes with a comparison of the incremental commitment model with other often-used process models.

Process Model Generator View

As shown by the four example paths through the incremental commitment model in Figure 2-2, the incremental commitment model is not a single monolithic one-size-fits-all process model. As with the spiral model, it is a risk-driven process model generator, but the incremental commitment model makes it easier to visualize how different risks create different processes.

In Example A in the figure, a simple business application based on an appropriately selected enterprise resource planning (ERP) package, there is no need for a valuation or architecting activity if there is no risk that the ERP package and its architecture will not cost-effectively support the application. Thus, one could go directly into the development phase, using an agile method, such as a scrum/extreme programming combination. There is no need for big design up front (BDUF) activities or artifacts because an appropriate architecture is already present in the ERP package. Nor is there a need for heavyweight waterfall or V-model specifications and document reviews. The fact that the risk at the end of the exploration phase is negligible implies that sufficient risk resolution of the ERP package's human interface has been done.

Example B involves the upgrade of several incompatible legacy applications into a service-oriented web-based system. Here, one could use a sequential waterfall or V-model if the upgrade requirements are stable, and its risks are low. However, if for example the legacy applications' user interfaces were incompatible with each other and with web-based operations, a concurrent risk-driven spiral, waterfall, or V-model that develops and exercises extensive user interface prototypes and generates a feasibility rationale (described below) would be preferable.

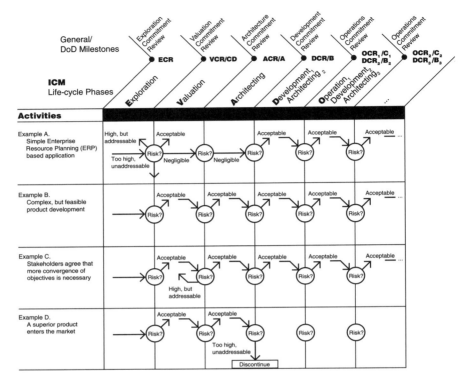

FIGURE 2-2 Different risks create different ICM processes.

In Example C, the stakeholders may have found during the valuation phase that their original assumptions were optimistic about the stakeholders having a clear, shared vision and compatible goals with respect the proposed new system's concept of operation and its operational roles and responsibilities. In such a case, it is better to go back and ensure stakeholder value proposition compatibility and feasibility before proceeding, as indicated by the arrow back into the valuation phase.

In Example D, it is discovered before entering the development phase that a superior product has already entered the marketplace, leaving the current product with a nonviable business case. Here, unless a viable business case can be made by adjusting the project's scope, it is best to discontinue it. It is worth pointing out that it is not necessary to proceed to the next major milestone before terminating a clearly nonviable project, although stakeholder concurrence in termination is essential.

Concurrent Levels of Activity View

The concurrent levels of activity view shown in Figure 2-3 is an extension of a similar view of concurrently engineered software projects developed as part of the rational unified process (Kruchten, 1999). As with the RUP version, it should be emphasized that the magnitude and shape of the levels of effort will be risk-driven and likely to vary from project to project. In particular, they are likely to have mini-risk/opportunity-driven peaks and valleys, rather than the smooth curves shown for simplicity in the figure. The main intent of this view is to emphasize the necessary concurrency of the primary success-critical activity classes, shown as rows in Figure 2-3. Thus, in interpreting the exploration column, although system scoping is the primary objective of this phase, doing it well involves a consider-

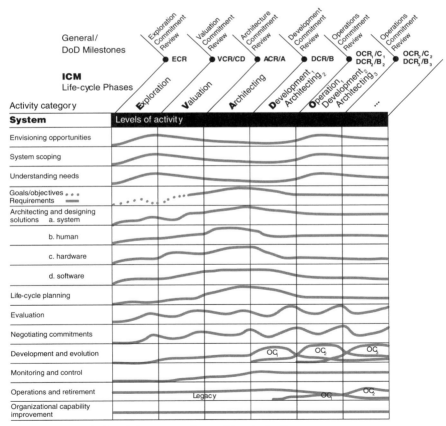

FIGURE 2-3 ICM activity categories and level of effort.

TABLE 2-2 Primary Focus of HSI Activity Classes and Methods

Activity Class	Examples of HSI Methods Described in This Volume	Systems Engineering
1. Envisioning opportunities	–Field observations and ethnography –Participatory analysis	–Modeling –Change monitoring (technology, competition, marketplace, environment)
2. System scoping	–Organizational and environmental context analysis –Field observations and ethnography –Participatory analysis	–Investment analysis –System boundary definition –Resource allocation –External environment characterization –Success-critical stakeholder identification
3. Understanding needs	–Organizational and environmental context analysis –Field observations and ethnography –Task analysis –Cognitive task analysis –Participatory analysis –Contextual inquiry –Event data analysis –Prototyping –Models and simulations –Usability evaluation methods	–Success-critical stakeholder requirements –Competitive analysis –Market research –Future needs analysis
4. Goals/ objectives and requirements	–Usability requirements methods –Scenarios –Personas	
5. Architecting solutions	–Task analysis –Usability requirements methods –Work domain analysis –Workload assessment –Participatory design –Contextual design –Physical ergonomics –Situation awareness –Methods for mitigating fatigue –Prototyping –Models and simulations –Usability evaluation methods	–Architecture frameworks –Commercial off the shelf/reuse evaluation –Legacy transformation analysis –Human-hardware-software allocation –Quality attribute analysis –Synthesis –Facility/vehicle architecting –Equipment design –Component evaluation and selection –Supplies/logistics planning –Construction/maintenance planning –Architectural style determinants –Component evaluation and selection –Physical/logical design –Evolvability design

TABLE 2-2 Continued

Activity Class	Examples of HSI Methods Described in This Volume	Systems Engineering
6. Life-cycle planning	–Usability requirements methods (common industry format) –Risk analysis	–Phased objectives (increments, legacy transformations) –Milestones and schedule –Roles and responsibility –Approach –Resources –Assumptions
7. Evaluation	–Usability requirements methods (common industry format) –Prototyping –Models and simulation –Risk analysis –Usability evaluation methods	–Evidence of fitness to proceed –Feasibility (usability, functionality, safety) –Other quality attributes –Cost/schedule risk –Business case mission analysis –Stakeholder commitment –Simulations, models, benchmarks, analysis
8. Negotiating commitments	–Usability requirements methods (common industry format) –Risk analysis	–Dependency/compatibility trade-off analysis –Expectation management, prioritization –Option preservation –Incrementing sequencing
9. Development and evolution	–Usability requirements methods (common industry format) –Models and simulation –Risk analysis –Usability evaluation methods	Material/operational solution analysis; make or buy analysis; acquisition planning; source selection; contracting/ incentivization; human/hardware/ software element development and integration; legacy transformation preparation; incremental installation
10. Monitoring and control	–Organizational and environmental context analysis –Risk analysis	Progress monitoring vs. plans; corrective action; adaptation of plans to change monitoring
11. Operations and retirement	–Organizational and environmental context analysis	Planned operations and retirement; OODA (observe, orient, decide, act) operations and retirement; adaptation of operations to change monitoring
12. Organizational capability improvement	–Organizational and environmental context analysis	Organizational goals and strategy definition; resource allocation; capability improvement activities

NOTE: HSI methods often span multiple activity classes.

able amount of activity in understanding needs, envisioning opportunities, identifying and reconciling stakeholder goals and objectives, architecting solutions, life-cycle planning, evaluation of alternatives, and negotiation of stakeholder commitments. Many HSI best-practice tables confine each recommended practice to a single phase-activity cell. Experts treat these confinements as suggestions that need not be followed, but nonexpert decision makers often follow such confinements literally, seriously reducing their effectiveness.

Table 2-2 shows the primary methods and work products involved in each activity class. The second column of the table shows the primary HSI methods that are discussed in Part II. The third column shows the primary corresponding systems engineering methods. Appendix Table 3-1 in Chapter 3 is a more detailed presentation of activities, methods, and best practices contained in ISO/PAS 18152 (International Organization for Standardization, 2003).

The Development Commitment Anchor Point Milestone Review

Figure 2-3 suggests that a great deal of concurrent activity is planned to occur within and across the various ICM phases. This gives rise to two main questions. First, more specifically than in Figures 2-2 and 2-3, what are the main concurrent activities that are going on in each phase? Second, how are the many concurrent activities synchronized, stabilized, and assessed for risk at the end of each phase? Figure 2-4, an elaboration of Figure 2-2, provides the next-level answer for the first question.

The elaboration of the concurrent engineering and feasibility evaluation activities makes it clearer just what is being concurrently engineered and evaluated in each phase. For example, at the development commitment review (DCR), the stakeholders and specialty experts review the life-cycle architecture (LCA) package for the overall system and for each increment to assure themselves that it is worthwhile to commit their human, financial, and other resources to the next phase of system development.

During the architecting phase, the project prepares for the DCR by concurrently engineering the system's operational aspects into a detailed operational concept and set of system requirements; the various commercial off the shelf, custom, and outsourced capabilities into a compatible build-to architecture; and the business case and resource constraints into a set of compatible plans, budgets, and schedules for each phase and for the overall system.

The next-level answer for the second question on synchronization, stabilization, and risk assessment is provided by the contents of the ICM architecture commitment review (ACR) and DCR anchor point milestone feasibility rationales referred to in Figure 2-4 and shown in Box 2-2. The

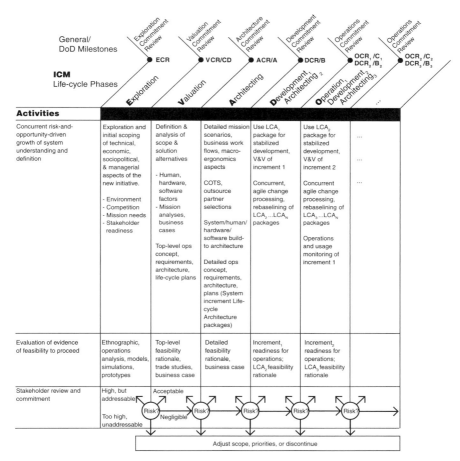

FIGURE 2-4 Elaboration of the ICM life-cycle process.

contents indicate that the project is responsible not only for producing a set of artifacts, but also for producing the *evidence* of their compatibility and feasibility. This evidence—from models, simulations, prototypes, benchmarks, analyses, etc.—is provided to experts and stakeholders in advance of the milestone review. Shortfalls in this evidence for compatibility and feasibility of the concurrently engineered artifacts should be identified by the system developer as potential project risks and addressed by risk-management plans. Any further shortfalls in the evidence or the risk management plans found by the reviewers should be communicated to

---

BOX 2-2
ICM Architecture Commitment Review and Development Commitment Review for the Anchor Point Milestone Feasibility Rationale Content

- Evidence provided by the developer and validated by independent experts that if the system is built to the specified architecture, it will
    - Satisfy the requirements: capability, interfaces, level of service, and evolution
    - Support the operational concept
    - Be buildable within the budgets and schedules in the plan
    - Generate a viable return on investment
    - Generate satisfactory outcomes for all of the success-critical stakeholders
- All major risks resolved or covered by risk-management plans
- Serves as basis for stakeholders' commitment to proceed

---

the developers in time for them to prepare responses to be presented at the DCR review meeting.

At the DCR milestone review meeting for the LCA package, the project then either provides adequate additional evidence of feasibility or additional risk-management plans to address the risks. The stakeholders then decide whether the risks are negligible, acceptable, high but addressable, or too high and unaddressable, and the project proceeds in the direction of the appropriate DCR risk arrow in Figure 2-4.

The Other ICM Milestone Reviews

The architecture commitment review criteria and procedures are similar but less elaborate than those in the DCR, as the degree of stakeholder resource commitment to support the architecting phase is considerably lower than for supporting the development phase. The ACR and DCR review procedures are adapted from the highly successful AT&T Architecture Review Board procedures described in Marenzano et al. (2005). For the ACR, only high-risk aspects of the operational concept, requirements, architecture, and plans are elaborated in detail. And it is sufficient to provide evidence that at least one combination of those artifacts satisfies the feasibility rationale criteria, in comparison to demonstrating this at the DCR for a particular choice of artifacts to be used for development.

The review criteria and procedures for the exploration commitment review (ECR) and the valuation commitment review (VCR) are even less elaborate than those for the ACR milestone, as the commitment levels for proceeding are considerably lower. But they will similarly have a risk-driven level of detail and risk-driven stakeholder choice of review outcome. For the ECR, the focus is on a review of an exploration phase plan with the proposed scope, schedule, deliverables, and required resource commitment by a key subset of stakeholders. The plan content is risk-driven and could be put on a single page for a small and noncontroversial exploration phase. For the VCR, the risk-driven focus is similar; the content includes the exploration phase results and a valuation phase plan and a review by all of the stakeholders involved in the valuation phase.

The operations commitment review (OCR) is different, in that it addresses the often much higher operational risks of fielding an inadequate system. In general, stakeholders will experience an increase in commitment level by a factor of 2 to 10 in going through the sequence of ECR to DCR milestones, but the increase in going from DCR to OCR can be much higher. The OCR focuses on evidence of the adequacy of plans and preparations with respect to doctrine, organization, training, material, leadership, personnel, and facilities, along with plans, budgets, and schedules for production, fielding, and operations.

A nonscientific analogy may be useful. The series of ICM milestones has the advantage of reflecting other human life-cycle incremental commitment sequences, such as those of getting married and raising a family. The ECR might be considered similar to a nonexclusive commitment to go out on dates with a girlfriend or boyfriend. The VCR is similar to a more exclusive but informal commitment to "go steady," and the ACR is similar to a more formal commitment to get engaged. The DCR is similar to an "until death do us part" commitment to get married: if one marries one's life-cycle architecture package in haste, one may repent in leisure. The OCR is similar to having one's first child: once the baby arrives, one's lifestyle is changed by the need to maintain its health and well-being.

Another possibly relevant metaphor for the incremental commitment model is a poker game, such as Texas Hold'em. At each round of betting, each stakeholder looks at his or her own hole cards and the jointly visible community cards and decides whether it is worth adding further resources to the pot of resources on the table, in order to see further community cards and to win the pot based on having the best poker hand constructible from one's own hole cards and the community cards. With the incremental commitment model, however, there will be negotiations designed to make win conditions for each success-critical stakeholder.

The Spiral View

A simplified spiral model view of the incremental commitment model appears in Figure 2-5. It avoids sources of misinterpretation in previous versions of the spiral model and concentrates on the five key spiral develop-

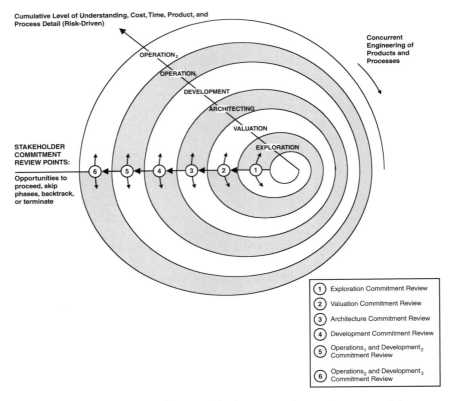

FIGURE 2-5 Simplified spiral view of the incremental commitment model.

ment principles. Stakeholder satisficing is necessary to pass the stakeholder commitment review points or anchor point milestones. Incremental growth in system understanding, cost, time, product, and process detail is shown by the spiral growth along the radial dimension. Concurrent engineering is shown by progress along the angular dimension. Iteration is shown by taking several spiral cycles both to define and develop the system. Risk management is captured by indicating that the activities' and products' levels of detail in the angular dimension are risk-driven, and by the risk-driven arrows pointing out from each of the anchor point commitment milestones.

These arrows show that the spiral model is not a sequential, unrollable process, but that it incorporates many paths through the diagram, including skipping a phase or backtracking to an early phase based on assessed risk. The fourth arrow pointing toward rescoping or halting in Figure 2-4 is omitted from Figure 2-5 for simplicity; it would be pointing down underneath the plane of the figure. Other aspects of the spiral model, such as the specific artifacts being concurrently engineered and the use of the feasibility rationale, are consistent with their use in Figure 2-4 and the other figures, in which they are easier to understand and harder to misinterpret than in a spiral diagram. Also for simplicity, the concurrent operation of increment N, development of increment N + 1, and architecting of increment N + 2 are not shown explicitly, although they are going on. This concurrency is explained in more detail in the next section.

Incremental Development for Accommodating Rapid Change and High Assurance

Many future systems and systems of systems will need to simultaneously achieve high assurance and adaptation to both foreseeable and unforeseeable rapid change, while meeting shorter market windows or new defense threats. Figure 2-6 shows an incremental view of the incremental commitment model for addressing such situations. It assumes that the organization has developed artifacts that have passed a development commitment review, including

- a best-effort definition of the system's envisioned overall capability;

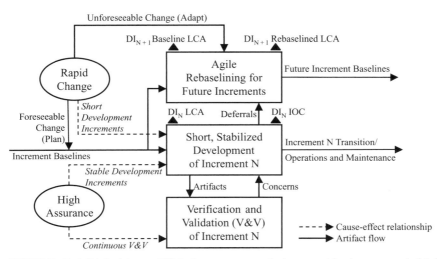

FIGURE 2-6 Risk-driven ICM for accommodating rapid change and high assurance.

• an incremental sequence of prioritized capabilities culminating in the overall system capability; and

• a feasibility rationale providing sufficient evidence for each increment and the overall system that the system architecture will support the increment's specified capabilities; that each increment can be developed within its available budget and schedule; and that the series of increments create a satisfactory return on investment for the organization and mutually satisfactory outcomes for the success-critical stakeholders.

The solid lines in the figure represent artifact flows. For example, the baselined operational concept, requirements, architecture, and development plans for increment N enter the center box and guide the plan-driven development of increment N to be transitioned into operations and maintenance. This development is stabilized by accepting only changes that have been architecturally anticipated (or occasional exceptional showstoppers). The corresponding baselines for future increments enter the top box, in which an agile team addresses unforeseeable changes and unavoidable content deferrals from increment N into future increments. The agile team's output is a rebaselined set of specifications and plans to be used in developing increment N + 1 and counterpart rebaselined specifications and plans for future increments to be updated during increment N + 1.

The dotted lines in Figure 2-6 represent cause-effect relationships. For example, the need to deliver high-assurance incremental capabilities on relatively short fixed schedules (to avoid delivery of obsolete capabilities in an era of increasingly rapid change) means that each increment needs to be kept as stable as possible. This is particularly the case for very large systems of systems with deep supplier hierarchies (often 6 to 12 levels), in which a high level of in-process change adaptation traffic can easily lead to the developers spending more time processing changes than doing development. In keeping with the use of the incremental commitment model as a risk-driven process model generator, the risks of destabilizing the development process make this portion of the project into a build-to-specification subset of the concurrent activities, in which the only changes accommodated are potential showstoppers or foreseeable changes that have been accommodated in the increment's architecture. The need for high assurance of each increment also makes it cost-effective to invest in a team of appropriately skilled personnel to continuously verify and validate the increment as it is being developed, as shown in the lower box in Figure 2-6.

In order to avoid delays and shortfalls in getting increment N + 1 specifications and plans ready for development, the agile team is concurrently assessing the unforeseen change traffic and rebaselining the next increment's LCA package and feasibility rationale, so that the stabilized build-to-specifications team will have all it needs to hit the ground running

TABLE 2-3 Number of Top-5 Projects Explicitly Using ICM Principles

Year	Concurrent Engineering	Risk-Driven	Evolutionary Growth
2002	4	3	3
2003	4	3	2
2004	2	2	4
2005	4	4	5
Total (of 20)	14	12	14

in rapidly developing the next increment. More detail on this process and its staffing and contracting implications is provided by Boehm (2006).

PROJECT EXPERIENCE WITH ICM PRINCIPLES

The incremental commitment model uses the critical success factor principles to extend several current spiral-related processes, such as the rational unified process, the win-win spiral process, and the lean development process, in ways that more explicitly integrate human-system integration into the system life-cycle process. A good source of successful projects that have applied the critical success factor principles is the annual series of top-5 software-intensive systems projects published in *CrossTalk*[1] (2002-2005).

The top-5 quality software projects are chosen annually by panels of leading experts as role models of best practices and successful outcomes. Table 2-3 summarizes each year's record with respect to usage of four of the five principles: concurrent engineering, risk-driven activities, and evolutionary and iterative system growth (most of the projects were not specific about stakeholder satisficing). Of the 20 top-5 projects in 2002 through 2005, 14 explicitly used concurrent engineering, 12 explicitly used risk-driven development, and 14 explicitly used evolutionary and iterative system growth, while additional projects gave indications of their partial use. Table 2-4 provides more specifics on the 20 projects.

Evidence of successful results of stakeholder satisficing can be found in the annual series of University of Southern California e-services projects using the win-win spiral model as described in (Boehm et al., 1998). Since 1998 over 50 user-intensive e-services applications have used the win-win

---

[1]For examples of annually chosen top-5 quality software projects, see http://www.stsc.hill. af.mil/crosstalk/2002/01/index.html; http://www.stsc.hill.af.mil/crosstalk/2003/07/index.html; http://www.stsc.hill.af.mil/crosstalk/2004/07/index.html; and http://www.stsc.hill.af.mil/cross-talk/2 005/09/index.html [accessed April 2007].

TABLE 2-4 Critical Success Factor (CSF) Aspects of Top Five Software Projects

Software Project	CSF Degree	Concurrent Requirements/ Solution Development	Risk-Driven Activities	Evolutionary, Incremental Delivery
STARS Air Traffic Control	*	Yes	HCI, safety	For multiple sites
Minuteman III Messaging (HAC/RMPE)	*	Yes	Safety	Yes; block upgrades
FA-18 Upgrades	*	Not described	Yes	Yes; block upgrades
Census Digital Imaging (DCS2000)	**	Yes	Yes	No; fixed delivery date
FBCB2 Army Tactical C3I	**	Yes	Yes	Yes
Defense Civilian Pay (DCPS)		No; waterfall	Yes	For multiple organizations
Tactical Data Radio (EPLRS)	**	Yes	Yes	Yes
Joint Helmet-Mounted Cueing (JHMCS)	*	Yes; IPT-based	Not described	For multiple aircraft
Kwajalein Radar (KMAR)	*	Yes; IPT-based	Not described	For multiple radars
One SAF Simulation Test Bed (OTB)	**	Yes	Yes	Yes
Advanced Field Artillery (AFATDS)		Initially waterfall	Not described	Yes; block upgrades
Defense Medical Logistics (DMLSS)		Initially waterfall	Not described	Yes; block upgrades
F-18 HOL (H1E SCS)		Legacy requirements-driven	Yes; COTS, display	No
One SAF Objectives System (OOS)	**	Yes	Yes	Yes
Patriot Excalibur (PEX)	**	Yes; agile	Not described	Yes
Lightweight Handheld Fire Control	**	Yes	Yes	Yes
Marines Integrated Pay (MCTFS)		Initially waterfall	Not described	Yes; block upgrades
Near Imaging Field Towers (NIFTI)	**	Yes; RUP-based	Yes	Yes
Smart Cam Virtual Cockpit (SC3DF)	**	Yes	Yes	Yes
WARSIM Army Training	**	Yes	Yes	Yes

NOTE: COTS = commercial off the shelf; HCI = human-computer interaction; IPT = integrated project team; RUP = rational unified process. For CSF Degree: blank = "generally not used," * = "generally used," and ** = "strongly used."

spiral model to achieve a 92-percent success rate of on-time delivery of stakeholder-satisfactory systems.

CONCLUSION

Future transformational, network-centric systems will have many usage uncertainties and emergent characteristics. Their hardware, software, and human factors will need to be concurrently engineered, risk-managed, and evolutionarily developed to converge on cost-effective system operations. They will need to be both highly dependable and rapidly adaptable to frequent changes.

This chapter has described the incremental commitment model, which builds on experience-based critical success factor principles (stakeholder satisficing, incremental definition, iterative evolutionary growth, concurrent engineering, risk management) as well as the strengths of existing V, concurrent engineering, spiral, agile, and lean process models, to provide a framework for concurrently engineering human factors into the systems engineering and systems development processes. The chapter provides capabilities for evaluating the feasibility of proposed HSI solutions and for integrating HSI feasibility evaluations into decisions on whether and how to proceed further into systems development and operations. The chapter also presents several complementary views showing how the principles are applied to perform risk-driven process tailoring and evolutionary growth of a systems definition and realization; to synchronize and stabilize concurrent engineering; and to enable simultaneous high-assurance development and rapid adaptation to change. The chapter analyzes the use of the critical success factor principles on the best-documented government software-intensive system acquisition success stories, the 2002-2005 *CrossTalk* top-5 projects, and shows that well over half of them explicitly applied these principles. The next three chapters will elaborate on how HSI practices fit into the ICM process and provide case studies of successful projects that have used the principles and practices.

The current path of least resistance for a government program manager is to follow a set of (existing) regulations, specifications, and standards that select, contract with, and reward developers for doing almost the exact opposite. Most of these legacy instruments emphasize sequential versus concurrent engineering; risk-insensitive versus risk-driven processes; early definition of poorly understood requirements versus better understanding of needs and opportunities; and slow, unscalable, contractual mechanisms for adapting to rapid change.

This chapter has provided a mapping of the ICM milestones to the current DoD 5000.2 acquisition milestones, showing that they can be quite compatible. It also shows how projects could be organized into stabilized build-to-specification increments that fit current legacy acquisition instruments, along with concurrent agile change-adaptation and verification and validation functions that need to use alternative contracting methods. Addressing changes of this nature will be important if organizations are to realize the large potential value offered by investments in HSI processes, methods, and tools.

3

Human-System Integration and the System Development Process

An important theme of this report is the integration of human-system methods within the system development process, so that multiple human-system integration (HSI) concerns can be addressed effectively with the least resource expenditure. This reflects the position of Miller (1953) in his initial description of the task analysis method as a procedure that can serve design and training needs analysis equally well. The committee findings indicate that a core set of human factors method classes can serve as integrating links across the diverse HSI concerns of human factors, manpower, personnel, training and system safety, health hazards, and survivability. Furthermore, shared representations of the outputs of these methods can be developed that effectively will communicate findings and conclusions among HSI domains as well with hardware and software developers and other stakeholders.

Three general classes of human factors methods provide a robust representation of the multiple HSI concerns, and are applicable at varying levels of effort throughout the development life cycle. These broad classes include methods to:

- *Define opportunities and context of use:* Methods for analyses that contribute to early definitions of opportunities and requirements and that attempt to characterize the context of use, including characteristics of users, their tasks, and the broader physical and organizational environment in which they operate so as to build systems that will effectively meet the needs of users and their work and will function smoothly within the broader physical and organizational context.

- *Define requirements and design solutions:* Methods to identify requirements and design alternatives to meet the requirements revealed by prior front-end analyses.
- *Evaluate:* Methods to evaluate the adequacy of proposed design solutions and propel further design innovation.

These methods generate objective data concerning critical human-system issues, leading to incremental growth of system definition and stakeholder commitment.

In Chapter 2 we showed how system development activities of the incremental commitment model (ICM) were distributed across system life-cycle phases (see Figure 2-3). Here, Figure 3-1 illustrates broadly how the four major classes of HSI activity relate to these phases. For example, activities related to understanding the context of use are likely be concentrated early in system development, when characteristics of the users, their work, and the environmental context are first being understood. However, because the context of use is constantly evolving and introduction of new technology is likely to produce operational and organizational changes, not all of which will have been anticipated ahead of time, it is important to continue to devote some (albeit lower) level of effort to examination of the context of use and how it evolves throughout the system development and deployment process, both to guide midcourse design corrections and to lay the groundwork for next-generation system development.

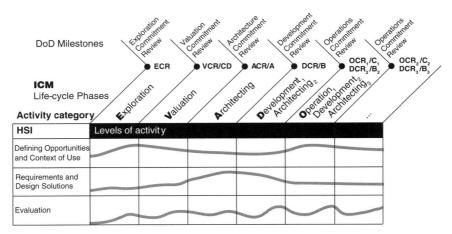

FIGURE 3-1 Activity level of HSI methods across system life-cycle phases.

HUMAN-SYSTEM INTEGRATION IN THE
INCREMENTAL COMMITMENT MODEL

In order to place human-system integration and its associated methods in the risk management context that is central to the incremental commitment model, it is important to distinguish several types of risk. *End-state operational system risks* include low usability, high rates of human error, low productivity, and safety problems. These types of risks tend to become manifest during the development process as a failure to properly manage *HSI risks*. They include such problems as specifying the user interface too early in design (or alternatively not considering it all), poorly understood work domain constraints, insufficient stakeholder engagement, and lack of personnel–organizational system interoperability in systems of systems. Often these types of risks are simply accepted or minimized because they pose a threat to maintaining program cost and schedule (*program management risks*).

Properly balancing these various categories of risk can be accommodated in the incremental commitment model, as it is a risk-driven process that aims to identify and properly manage these various risk categories. By engaging appropriate HSI methods during the incremental development process, risks can be reduced throughout the engineering life cycle, increasing the likelihood of a system's meeting user requirements and satisficing stakeholders. Appendix Table 3-A1 lists best practices for human-system integration taken from ISO/PAS 18152 (International Organization for Standardization, 2003) and categorized by activity category. Each of these practices is valuable for successful human-centered design. Examples of methods to use in implementing these practices are also shown in the table. A risk assessment can be used to decide how much effort is needed to implement each practice in the context of a particular project.

- Are the objectives that the user or user organization wants to achieve through use of the system already known, or is some field investigation necessary?
- How important is it to establish measurable usability criteria for the system in its intended context of use?
- What are the risks if end-users are not involved in each evaluation?

Figure 3-2 illustrates the links between desired system end-state (stakeholder satisficing), system phases, and HSI activities. This figure conveys the multiple determinants of the ultimate system design goal, stakeholder satisficing. The system development principles identified in Chapter 2 are shown as inputs to the system engineering processes or phases. Each of the phases is conducted iteratively, as described in the incremental com-

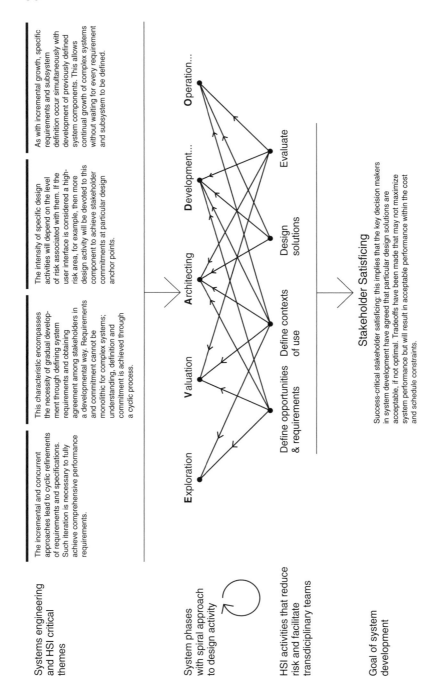

FIGURE 3-2 Linkage of system engineering principles to HSI activities that reduce risks.

Systems engineering and HSI critical themes

The incremental and concurrent approaches lead to cyclic refinements of requirements and specifications. Such iteration is necessary to fully achieve comprehensive performance requirements.

This characteristic encompasses the necessity of gradual development through defining system requirements and obtaining agreement among stakeholders in a developmental way. Requirements and commitment cannot be monolithic for complex systems; understanding, definition and commitment is achieved through a cyclic process.

The intensity of specific design activities will depend on the level of risk associated with them. If the user interface is considered a high-risk area, for example, then more design activity will be devoted to this component to achieve stakeholder commitments at particular design anchor points.

As with incremental growth, specific requirements and subsystem definition occur simultaneously with development of previously defined system components. This allows continual growth of complex systems without waiting for every requirement and subsystem to be defined.

System phases with spiral approach to design activity

Exploration   Valuation   Architecting   Development...   Operation...

HSI activities that reduce risk and facilitate transdisciplinary teams

Define opportunities & requirements   Define contexts of use   Design solutions   Evaluate

Goal of system development

Stakeholder Satisficing

Success-critical stakeholder satisficing: this implies that the key decision makers in system development have agreed that particular design solutions are acceptable, if not optimal. Tradeoffs have been made that may not maximize system performance but will result in acceptable performance within the cost and schedule constraints.

mitment model, and requires inputs from multiple HSI methods. This is illustrated by the network of links between HSI activities and the systems engineering phases. As with the level of activity diagram in Figure 3-1, our main point is that HSI activities are concurrent, iterative processes carried out as needed to reduce development risks at various incremental stages of system design.

The role of human-system integration in the management of engineering development risk is a relatively new concept. Human factors engineering methods are traditionally conceived as design-aiding techniques, to be used when it is time to design or test very specific elements of the human-system interface. However, this conception is too narrow for complex systems that increasingly involve multiple teams of distributed operational personnel. Instead, human factors methods can be more broadly conceived both as design-aiding techniques *and* as methods for progressive risk reduction during the life cycle. In this sense, human factors methods contribute to the development process in much the same way as, for example, prototyping or simulation is employed by systems engineers and can be used during the early to middle stages of development to evaluate alternatives and to narrow design choices based on various constraints. The use of such risk-reduction approaches allows developers to select one design approach over another, gain an understanding of unanticipated effects based on simulation, and generally to have a higher level of confidence that system development efforts are on track to meet requirements and avoid the operational stage risks of disuse, error, and high life-cycle costs.

Extensive experience with major system development efforts by committee members and colleagues in the profession suggests that human factors issues have often been underutilized during system development because of a perception by program managers that the risks of cost and schedule delay associated with human-system integration exceed the benefit to be delivered. Part of this perception is associated with a standard waterfall model of design, in which specific milestones are set in time, and HSI analytic methods tend to be time-intensive if performed in a linear fashion. Program managers often perceive human factors professionals as overly focused on comprehensive application of methods, while the art of engineering is to accommodate the realities of schedule and cost, conducting studies and analyses only as necessary to manage risks. It is thus important for HSI practitioners to adopt an incremental and iterative approach to analysis and design, recognizing that if there are no HSI risks associated with a particular aspect of a project, then it is unnecessary to apply various methods. The HSI profession has seen a trend in this direction with the development of such approaches as quick look reports[1] in which the precision of laboratory experiment or exhaustive observation is traded off with the expedience of providing the most critical design inputs through rapid prototyping, contextual inquiry, and various forms of participatory design.

By incorporating human-system integration as an integral thread within the incremental commitment model, the balance of program risks with HSI risks can be accommodated. This is especially true if HSI professionals are incorporated as members of an integrated product team structure that is involved continuously throughout the design cycle. Early iterations of work domain analysis, for example, may be conducted at a fairly high level to ensure that all appropriate stakeholders are identified and represented. As designs become more elaborated, participatory techniques can be applied to the point of reaching stakeholder consensus for purposes of a specific increment. This linkage of HSI activities to incremental development permits the design and risk management process to serve as a way to select the most appropriate HSI methods (and their extent of application) for a particular phase of the engineering cycle. It is not necessary to apply HSI techniques in a monolithic fashion, and in some cases it may not be necessary at all because there is no risk associated with a particular HSI issue; alternatively, program managers may accept certain identified risks (e.g., commercial off-the-shelf user interfaces) in order to preclude rejecting the use of certain technologies.

An important aspect of the incremental commitment model and the spiral representation for HSI professionals is the notion that methods are not only progressive, but also iterative, and that risk analysis determines the frequency and extent of their application. This has important implications for sizing the HSI effort, since the resources devoted to HSI activities should reflect the requirements for their application. This is a difficult task to accomplish currently, since there are no well-established methods for estimating the resource requirements for human-system integration. Various systems engineering approaches to level of effort sizing include activity-based costing, comparison with previous projects of similar scope, applying a unit-cost basis (as when a request for proposal specifies how many human factors engineers should work on a system), parametric models that link effort to project complexity, expert consensus, and risk trade-off analysis. None of these approaches has been systematically examined for sizing HSI efforts, and this area represents a knowledge gap that could be addressed through research.

---

[1]Quick look report is a term used primarily by the National Aeronautics and Space Administration and the Department of Transportation to describe the results of a rapid field observation or appraisal of a prototype system in a test situation. These appraisals are less detailed than formal operational test and evaluation procedures.

COMMUNICATING HSI ISSUES AND OPPORTUNITIES THROUGH SHARED REPRESENTATIONS

A critical concern of HSI professionals and a major theme of the committee's work is the need not only to communicate effectively within the specific HSI domain but to share findings across all systems engineering domains. This can be a daunting challenge for groups tasked with complex systems design. In addition, there is a clear need to share design and process artifacts at all phases in the systems development process, especially with the software and hardware developers who are actually implementing the system, and who are not only relying on clear specifications for development, but who are also expected to contribute to the generation of those specifications at critical decision points in the process. As a consequence, the committee has pursued the concept of *shared representations* as a means of addressing this concern. Shared representations—particularly diagrammatic models and other more visual, holistic representations—can serve as the fundamental medium for interactions among individuals, teams, and the organization.

Imagine a scenario from the commercial software development world. A team meets to kick off a new project. Groups of people from business, technology, and human systems discuss the goals of the project, the timeline, and other variables. Notes from the meeting are distributed within a few hours. Each group works on its tasks for several weeks. At the next meeting, team members discover that each discipline has taken its interpretation of the goals in directions different from those of the other groups, and now weeks have gone by with little truly collaborative progress to show for their efforts. Everyone attended the meeting and everyone read the notes, so what happened? The verbal description of goals and the written documentation of the events were not enough to provide *common ground* for the team. They lacked a shared representation of the event, their views, and what needed to be done by each of the groups.

A shared representation is an artifact or experience that mediates the interaction between and among people coming from multiple perspectives (different organizational roles, distinct technical or business backgrounds, etc.). It can be useful for an individual, a team, or an organization (Curtis, Krasner, and Iscoe, 1988). A representation can provide support or scaffolding for effective collaboration among people in transdisciplinary design teams, and at the same time be used at the organizational level to "communicate up" to forge understandings between and among the various project stakeholders. A shared representation is most powerful when used not only to facilitate activities, but also to make people's assumptions and individual mind sets explicit.

Shared representations act as a means for synchronization, clarification, and grounding in the socially constructed process of design (D'Astous et al., 2004; Olson et al., 1992). In the process, solutions are negotiated, the representation acts as mediator, and subsequent modifications made to the representation make explicit the result of those negotiations.

Why Shared Representations Are Useful

Models, diagrams, and other, more visual shared representations are effective for people as they participate in design activities. Don Norman writes: "Without external aids, memory, thought, and reasoning are all constrained. But human intelligence is highly flexible and adaptive, superb at inventing procedures and objects that overcome its own limits." He goes on to suggest that one can enhance cognitive ability by producing representations or artifacts to help one think (Norman, 1993; see also Hutchins, 1995; Nardi, 1996; Pasztory, 2005). When people externalize their thinking via representations (e.g., get their ideas out on paper or on screen), they produce a representation of their thinking that not only can be examined critically, but also can be used to reduce their working memory load (Nardi, 1996; Suwa and Tversky, 2002).

In addition, by producing the representation and taking the information beyond words into a new form or medium, relationships among meaningful elements of the design must either be made *explicit* or must *emerge*, by the simple act of creating an explicit shared representation of the component elements in a well-framed *space* (e.g., a two-D sketch, a three-D volumetric representation, or some higher dimensional parametric space characterizing the design elements). Seeing these placements can not only lead the reader or the originators to recognize previously unacknowledged connections or relations, but also produce new connections and ideas. Suwa and Tversky (2002) call the activity *detection of unintended relations and features*. For example, in the applied cognitive work analysis (ACWA) method, the functional abstraction hierarchy is designed to highlight critical domain relationships that define the problem-space confronting domain practitioners. Each subsequent artifact in the process builds on the original model and, through negotiation, points to a model of what the system should be in such a way that it can finally be prototyped.

Shared representations act as mediators in the collaborative and iterative construction of knowledge in the design process. When multiple people build, share, comment, and change a shared information base, they are collaboratively constructing new knowledge (Bucciarelli, 1988; Suthers, 2005). If participants produce different types of artifacts, representations, or models as they engage in the design and development process—these should, as Norman suggests, "help them think" and make their assumptions explicit. In a sense, shared representations work in the same way that blueprints work for architects in moving from what might be to what is built. Many different views are produced. Everyone involved in the process—from stakeholders to the various disciplines involved—is able to use the abstraction reflected in the blueprints to make meaningful decisions. For all these reasons, producing shared representations in transdisciplinary teams can be critical to creating innovative solutions because they help teams collectively see and communicate about novel connections, spawn new ideas, and facilitate a more effective design process (Détienne, 2006; Evenson, 2005).

There is a dynamic between the representation's role in facilitating externalization (making explicit the group's assumptions and beliefs) and its role in acting as an environment for conversation, to facilitate subsequent negotiations and elaboration. The task of creating the representation initiates the process of making explicit the underlying goals, assumptions, and viewpoints of the different design team members; the process of updating the representation following design team negotiations captures the results of negotiating *design meaning* out of nonverbal, semiverbal, and verbal conversations engaged in by the various team members while discussing the *current* model or representation (Suthers, 2005).

Attributes of Good Shared Representations

Nearly every activity in the system development life cycle results in some form of tangible design artifact, but it may not necessarily be a good shared representation. To be useful, a shared representation should

1. establish a shared language that is appropriately aligned with the development or communication problem to be solved.
2. provide a strategically chosen extent of ambiguity versus definition.
3. facilitate the desired social process (e.g., critique and redesign versus accept/reject decisions).
4. make differences and relationships apparent.
5. facilitate group "thinking with" (Norman, 1993) to transform knowledge and create new understandings (Carlile, 2002).
6. provide a meaningful structure, content, and appearance to both the creators of the shared representation and the consumers of that shared representation.

Of the six attributes listed above, the two most important are the shared language and facilitation of a social process.

To establish the language, a shared representation should be easily read by all of its users (creators and recipients)—that is, the structure and content should be easily perceived and comprehended, reflect the structure and content of the ideas or mental representation, and create a sort of resonance. The participants in the construction process should agree that the thing produced adequately represents what they want it to (Tversky, Morrison, and Betrancourt, 2002).

To facilitate the social process, the representation must stand in and mediate communication between and among people engaged in the collaborative process (Boland and Collopy, 2004). In other words, the representation must be suitable for facilitating negotiation among the participants.

Shared Representations in the Design Process

What is useful as a shared representation can change over time in the systems development process. In practice, the process of constructing the shared representation may be more important for team building than the artifact itself. Early on, mapping out the territory the system is expected to address can draw out existing preconceptions and knowledge held by the various team members, helping to bound research activities. A territory map is an example of a shared representation that captures more a gestalt or overview of the system. It is suggestive of everything the system is and—by virtue of what is left out—everything it is not. A good territory map accounts for all the stakeholder interests in the system; a great territory map provides a picture of the system that is comprehensive, cohesive, and visionary. Completed early enough in the process, a territory map can even serve to mediate the communication of the participants in the acquisition process. Teams that agree on what is in the territory have established common ground that can be carried forward throughout the design and development process.

Documentation that focuses on activities identified from a territory map often becomes successful shared representations. They are produced in the midst of extensive task, process, or environmental research and provide a way to discuss what currently happens and what should or could happen. A standard recording language (UML, activity diagrams, business process modeling notation, etc.) facilitates discussion and contributes to the production of the shared representation. A less common but often effective shared representation early in the process can be developed with a focus on the target users of the system. For example, the findings from user-generated field journals (incorporating a standardized and embedded framework for users to record their observations) helps to extend the language of the team and build a model of system attributes important to the target user group.

Sometimes shared representations can function as a vehicle for the clarification of ideas (e.g., Suthers, 2005) or as an opportunity for groups to combine their different perspectives and knowledge into new insights (Muller, 2003; Muller et al., 1994). This is often the case when a low-fidelity prototype (such as a blank shape that is used symbolically "in place of" a real device or prototype) is used as a candidate for eliciting different stakeholders' ideas about what would be done with the product, system, or service, as well as for eliciting and exploring different stakeholder concepts and assumptions. This was successfully demonstrated in the UTOPIA project, in which the implications for working relationships from a new print shop technology were explored by placing low-fidelity mock-ups of the new technology in the existing print shop and by acting out the new work practices around those prototypes (Ehn and Kyng, 1991).

Erickson reviewed the importance of "roughness" in a shared representation, noting that less formal and less finished representations were more likely to elicit useful comment, critique, and improvement, whereas more formalized or polished representations were more likely to lead to simple accept/reject decisions (Erickson, 1996). People feel more open to participating in and refining ideas in sketches and than they do in finished prototypes.

Personas are also often an excellent shared representation category because they are composite user archetypes based on behavioral data gathered from many actual people during discovery research (see Chapter 7). Personas are useful because they build on people's expectations about other people's behavior from what is known about that person. Developing solid profiles or personas contributes to serving individual user needs, aids in integration with customer processes, and leads to a design that the various constituents can participate in co-evolving. As a shared representation, personas and profiles are a tool for making user needs explicit, differentiating between and among different stakeholders, and prioritizing different and sometimes competing goals (Cooper, 2004).

Even physical spaces can become successful shared representation of the system or systems to be designed. For example, in a design project intended to reconceptualize 35mm point-and-shoot cameras, a physical design space was built initially to contain the results of qualitative research conducted to understand the existing paradigm (Rheinfrank and Welker, 1994). The space contained images and relevant artifacts that characterized different aspects of use and users of cameras. Initially, each wall of the space individually represented a particular aspect of the experience and was used more as a repository for the information about each dimension. Over time, however, the space was seen as a whole and became a shared representation in the collaborative process to solve a multidimensional camera design problem (Star, 1989). Specifically, the physical space evolved into a shared representation offering the internal and external design teams multiple views of possible 35mm camera futures, in which the view depended on its position on the floor in juxtaposition to the walls of the room (Rheinfrank and Welker, 1994). In later cycles of development, scoping maps (1) illustrate the features, functionality, and content of the designed system, (2) illustrate anticipated user experiences, and (3) enable team members to prioritize a plan for staged release. These types of shared representations allow the stakeholders to make decisions about what can and should be produced from the potential things that could be built. Eventually, a high-fidelity representation, such as a functional prototype, is a good candidate for validating what the team collectively knows about the system and for communicating a clear idea of the system from one design group to another, as well as "up" the organization.

As the design and development process unfolds, and when groups shift from one type of shared representation to another or change the way they are using a shared representation, the shift signals a qualitative change in the know-how needed for continuing to make progress in the design/development process (Cook and Brown, 1999; Gasson, 2005).

CONCLUSION

Effective use of shared representations depends on understanding the team or organization's current issues and needs in communication, and in strategically choosing the right kind of shared representation to mediate at the right time.

When used appropriately, shared representations enable the design team to coalesce around a shared view, while providing a capacity for increasing the conceptual complexity that can be attended to—activities that are crucial in the design of complex systems.

Shared representations can provide a bridge among analysis, design, implementation, and training in complex systems design, development, and fielding. The act of producing the representation can help teams detect unanticipated relations and features that can be exploited to lead to new connections and ideas.

Shared representations can be anything from a simple sketch, to a "wizard of Oz" prototype, to a fully active simulation of system design and behavior. Although conventional project planning schedules or spreadsheets can support the design and development process, they can never take the place of consciously planning, producing, and seeding discussion around shared representations to improve the quality of collaboration and productive outcomes of transdisciplinary design teams (Carroll, 2002). Shared representations provide a means for teams to transcend conventional project management paradigms and to coalesce around their ideas to produce work that is a reflection of their shared understanding of the mission to be supported, the user needs, and the best that technology can deliver.

APPENDIX 3-A

TABLE 3-A1 Best Practices for Risk Mitigation

Activity Category	Best Practices for Risk Mitigation from ISO/PAS 18152	Example HSI Methods and Techniques
1. Envisioning opportunities	–Identify expected context of use of systems [forthcoming needs, trends and expectations]. –Analyze the system concept [to clarify objectives, their viability and risks].	–Field observations and ethnography –Participatory analysis
2. System scoping	–Describe the objectives which the user or user organization wants to achieve through use of the system. –Define the scope of the context of use for the system.	–Organizational and environmental context analysis –Field observations and ethnography –Participatory analysis *Work context analysis*
3. Understanding needs (a) Context of use (b) Tasks (c) Usability needs (d) Design options	–Identify and analyze the roles of each group of stakeholders likely to be affected by the system. –Describe the characteristics of the users. –Describe the cultural environment/ organizational/management regime. –Describe the characteristics of any equipment external to the system and the working environment. –Describe the location, workplace equipment, and ambient conditions. –Decide the goals, behaviors, and tasks of the organization that influence human resources. –Present context and human resources options and constraints to the project stakeholders. –Analyze the tasks and worksystem. –Perform research into required system usability. –Generate design options for each aspect of the system related to its use and its effect on stakeholders. –Produce user-centered solutions for each design option.	–Organizational and environmental context analysis –Field observations and ethnography –Task analysis –Cognitive task analysis –Participatory analysis –Contextual inquiry –Event data analysis –Prototyping –Models and simulations –Usability evaluation methods *Success-critical stakeholder identification* *Context of use analysis* *Work context analysis* *Investigate required system usability* *Usability benchmarking*

continued

TABLE 3-A1 Continued

Activity Category	Best Practices for Risk Mitigation from ISO/PAS 18152	Example HSI Methods and Techniques
4. Goals/objectives and requirements (a) Context requirements (b) Infrastructure requirements (c) User requirements	–Analyze the implications of the context of use. –Present context of use issues to project stakeholders for use in the development or operation of the system. –Identify, specify, and produce the infrastructure for the system. –Build required competencies into training and awareness programs. –Define the global numbers, skills, and supporting equipment needed to achieve those tasks. –Set and agree on the expected behavior and performance of the system with respect to the user. –Develop an explicit statement of the user requirements for the system. –Analyze the user requirements. –Generate and agree on measurable criteria for the system in its intended context of use.	–Usability requirements methods –Scenarios –Personas *Define the intended context of use including boundaries* *Identify staffing requirements and any training or support needed to ensure that users achieve acceptable performance* *Storyboards* *Establish performance and satisfaction goals for specific scenarios of use* *Define detailed user interface requirements* *Prioritize requirements (e.g., QFD)*
5. Architecting solutions (a) System architecting	–Generate design options for each aspect of the system related to its use and its effect on stakeholders. –Produce user-centered solutions for each design option. –Design for customization. –Develop simulation or trial implementation of key aspects of the system for the purposes of testing with users. –Distribute functions between the human, machine, and organizational elements of the system best able to fulfill each function. –Develop a practical model of the user's work from the requirements, context of use, allocation of function, and design constraints for the system. –Produce designs for the user-related elements of the system that take account of the user requirements, context of use, and HF data. –Produce a description of how the system will be used.	–Task analysis –Work domain analysis –Participatory design –Prototyping –Models and simulations *Function allocation* *Generate design options*

TABLE 3-A1 Continued

Activity Category	Best Practices for Risk Mitigation from ISO/PAS 18152	Example HSI Methods and Techniques
(b) Human elements	–Decide the goals, behaviors, and tasks of the organization [that influence human resources]. –Define the global numbers, skills, and supporting equipment needed to achieve those tasks. –Identify current tasking/duty. –Analyze gap between existing and future provision. –Identify skill requirements for each role. –Predict staff wastage between present and future. –Calculate the available staffing, taking account of working hours, attainable effort and nonavailability factor. –Identify and allocate the functions to be performed. –Functional decomposition and allocation of function. –Specify and produce job designs and competence/skills required to be delivered. –Calculate the required number of personnel. –Generate costed options for delivery of training and/or redeployment. –Evolve options and constraints into an optimal [training] implementation plan (4.3.5). –Define how users will be re-allocated, dismissed, or transferred to other duties. –Compare to define gap and communicate requirement to design of staffing solutions.	–Task analysis –Usability requirements methods –Work domain analysis –Workload assessment –Participatory design –Contextual design –Situation awareness –Methods for mitigating fatigue *Human performance model* *Design for alertness* *Plan staffing*
(c) Hardware elements	See (a) System architecting.	–Participatory design –Physical ergonomics –Prototyping –Usability evaluation methods
(d) Software elements	See (a) System architecting.	–Participatory design –Prototyping –Usability evaluation methods *User interface guidelines and standards*

continued

TABLE 3-A1 Continued

Activity Category	Best Practices for Risk Mitigation from ISO/PAS 18152	Example HSI Methods and Techniques
6. Life-cycle planning (a) Planning (b) Risks (c) User involvement (d) Acquisition (e) Human resources	–Develop a plan to achieve and maintain usability throughout the life of the system. –Identify the specialist skills required and plan how to provide them. –Plan and manage use of HF data to mitigate risks related to HS issues. –Evaluate the current severity of emerging threats to system usability and other HS risks and the effectiveness of mitigation measures. –Take effective mitigation to address risks to system usability. –Identify the HS issues and aspects of the system that require user input. –Define a strategy and plan for user involvement. –Select and use the most effective method to elicit user input. –Customize tools and methods as necessary for particular projects/stages. –Seek and exploit expert guidance and advice on HS issues. –Take account of stakeholder and user issues in acquisition activities. –Implement the HR strategy that gives the organization a mechanism for implementing and recording lessons learned. –Enable and encourage people and teams to work together to deliver the organization's objectives. –Create capability to meet system requirements in the future (conduct succession planning). –Develop and trial training solution to representative users. –Deliver final training solutions to designated staff according to agreed timetable. –Provide means for user feedback [on human issues].	*–Usability requirements methods (common industry format)* *–Risk analysis* *Plan to achieve and maintain usability* *Plan use of HSI data to mitigate risks* *Identify HSI issues and aspects of the system requiring user input* *Develop a plan for user involvement* *Select and use the most effective methods* *Customize tools and methods as necessary*

continued

TABLE 3-A1 Continued

Activity Category	Best Practices for Risk Mitigation from ISO/PAS 18152	Example HSI Methods and Techniques

7. Evaluation
  (a) Risks
  (b) Plan and execute
  (c) Validation
  (d) HSI knowledge
  (e) Staffing
	−Assess the health and well-being risks to the users of the system.
	−Assess the risks to the community and environment arising from human error in the use of the system.
	−Evaluate the current severity of emerging threats to system usability and other HS risks and the effectiveness of mitigation measures.
	−Assess the risks of not involving end-users in each evaluation.
	−Collect user input on the usability of the developing system.
	−Revise design and safety features using feedback from evaluations.
	−Plan the evaluation.
	−Identify and analyze the conditions under which a system is to be tested or otherwise evaluated.
	−Check that the system is fit for evaluation.
	−Carry out and analyze the evaluation according to the evaluation plan.
	−Understand and act on the results of the evaluation.
	−Test that the system meets the requirements of the users, the tasks and the environment, as defined in its specification.
	−Assess the extent to which usability criteria and other HS requirements are likely to be met by the proposed design.
	−Review the system for adherence to applicable human science knowledge, style guides, standards, guidelines, regulations, and legislation.
	−Decide how many people are needed to fulfill the strategy and what ranges of competence they need.
	−Develop and trial training solution to representative users.
	−Conduct assessments of usability [relating to HR].
	−Interpret the findings.
	−Validate the data.
	−Check that the data are being used.
		−Usability requirements methods (common industry format)
		−Prototyping
		−Models and simulation
		−Risk analysis
		−Usability evaluation methods
		Obtain user feedback on usability
		Compare with requirements
		Performance measurement
		HR

continued

TABLE 3-A1 Continued

Activity Category	Best Practices for Risk Mitigation from ISO/PAS 18152	Example HSI Methods and Techniques
8. Negotiating commitments (a) Business case (b) Requirements	−Contribute to the business case for the system. −Include HS review and sign-off in all reviews and decisions. −Analyze the user requirements. −Present these requirements to project stakeholders for use in the development and operation of the system. −Identify any staffing gap and communicate requirement to design of staffing solutions.	−Usability requirements methods (common industry format) −Risk analysis *Value-based practices and principles (identify success-critical stakeholder requirements) Environment/ organization assessment*
9. Development and evolution	−Maintain contact with users and the client organization throughout the definition, development, and introduction of a system. −Evolve options and constraints into an implementation strategy covering technical, integration, and planning and manning issues.	−Usability requirements methods (common industry format) −Models and simulation −Risk analysis −Usability evaluation methods *User feedback on usability Performance measurement*
10. Monitoring and control	−Analyze feedback on the system during delivery and inform the organization of emerging issues. −Manage the life-cycle plan to address HS issues. −Take effective mitigation to address risks to system usability. −Take account of user input and inform users. −Identify emerging HS issues. −Understand and act on the results of the evaluation. −Produce and promulgate a validated statement of staffing shortfall by number and range of competence.	−Organizational and environmental context analysis analysis −Risk analysis *User feedback Work context analysis*

continued

TABLE 3-A1 Continued

Activity Category	Best Practices for Risk Mitigation from ISO/PAS 18152	Example HSI Methods and Techniques
11. Operations and retirement (a) Operations (b) Retirement	–Analyze feedback on the system during delivery and inform the organization of emerging issues. –Produce personnel strategy. –Review the system for adherence to applicable human science knowledge, style guides, standards, guidelines, regulations, and legislation. –Deliver training and other forms of awareness-raising to users and support staff. –Assess the effect of change on the usability of the system. –Review the health and well-being risks to the users of the system. –Review the risks to the community and environment arising from human error in the use of the system. –Take action on issues arising from in-service assessment. –Perform research to refine and consolidate operation and support strategy for the system. –Collect and analyze in-service reports to generate updates or lessons learned for the next version of the system. –Identify risks and health and safety issues associated with removal from service and destruction of the system. –Define how users will be re-allocated, dismissed, or transferred to other duties. –Plan break-up of social structures. –Debriefing and retrospective analysis for replacement system.	–Organizational and environmental context analysis *Work context analysis*

continued

TABLE 3-A1 Continued

Activity Category	Best Practices for Risk Mitigation from ISO/PAS 18152	Example HSI Methods and Techniques
12. Organizational capability improvement (a) HSI capability data collection, analysis, and improvement (b) Organizational skill/career and infrastructure development planning and execution	–Identify and use the most suitable data formats for exchanging HF data. –Have a policy for HF data management. –Perform research to develop HF data as required. –Produce coherent data standards and formats. –Define rules for the management of data. –Develop and maintain adequate data search methods. –Feedback into future HR procurement, training, and delivery strategies. –Define usability as a competitive asset. –Set usability, health, and safety objectives for systems. –Follow competitive situation in the market place. –Develop user-centered infrastructure. –Relate HS issues to business benefits. –Establish and communicate a policy for human-centeredness. –Include HR and user-centered elements in support and control procedures. –Define and maintain HCD and HR infrastructure and resources. –Increase and maintain awareness of usability. –Develop or provide staff with suitable HS skills. –Take account of HS issues in financial management. –Assess and improve HS capability in processes that affect usability, health, and safety. –Develop a common terminology for HS issues with the organization. –Facilitate personal and technical interactions related to HS issues. –Feedback into future HR procurement, training, and delivery strategies. –Create capability to meet system requirements in the future (conduct succession planning). –Identify any opportunities for redeployment. –Develop a strategy for [HR] data gathering.	–Organizational and environmental context analysis *Assess and improve HSI capability* *Develop and maintain HSI infrastructure and resources* *Identify required HSI skills* *Provide staff with HSI skills* *Establish and communicate a policy on HSI* *Maintain an awareness of usability*

NOTES: Italicized items are methods not covered in Chapters 6-8. HF = human factors. HS = human-system. HR = human resources. QFD = quality function deployment. HCD = human-centered design.

4

Managing Risks

R isk management is one of the five key principles underpinning the
incremental commitment model of system development because
understanding risks and managing them effectively are paramount
to effective program execution. At a high level, the concept of risk encompasses subjective or objective determination of an event's likelihood of occurrence and the detrimental impact of that event's occurrence. Typically,
program execution risk is grouped into three primary categories: (1) technical (i.e., a product's ability to meet technical requirements), (2) cost (i.e.,
executing the program within the contracted budget), and (3) schedule (i.e.,
executing the program within the contracted duration). Risk can be defined
as the product of estimated probability of each occurrence and the level
of undesirable contingent consequences added across the set of events and
consequences under consideration. Essential to the concept of risk is that
the probability of occurrence must fall between 0 (i.e., total success—risk
will never be realized) and 1 (i.e., total failure). In opposition to the concept of risk, but maintaining the same underlying principles and practices
as risk management, is opportunity and opportunity management, wherein
an opportunity's consequence has a positive impact on technical, cost, or
schedule program variables.

Human-system integration (HSI) analyses to identify risks are typically
conducted at two levels: the finer grain relating to aspects of system design
(e.g., safety, product usability), and the coarser grain contributing to overarching program risk management, which is the focus of this chapter. To
explain how human-system integration fits into program risk-management
efforts, an example methodology is presented; however, it should be noted

that other approaches may also be utilized. In addition, although a Department of Defense (DoD) program is the context for discussion, we note that the risk-management concepts and HSI interwoven thread have direct applicability to commercial development as well. Finally, although the chapter focuses on program risk management, the concepts can also be applied to managing opportunities that arise during program execution.

Before delving into HSI contributions to risk management, it is important to understand the DoD acquisition program context in which these activities are carried out and must be integrated to be effective in achieving system performance goals. Risk, issue, and opportunity management is a concept grounded in a continuous, forward-looking, structured, informative approach that is planned early in the life cycle and aggressively executed. This affords an organized, comprehensive, and iterative means for identifying and assessing the risks and handling options required to ensure technical, schedule, and cost aspects are appropriately balanced and accounted for.

An important aspect of the DoD risk-management approach is the concept of cost as an independent variable (CAIV) (U.S. Department of Defense, 2003b). In this concept, the highest priority in executing an acquisition program is reduction of procurement and in-service costs balanced by maintaining a high level of system performance for the user. In essence, CAIV entails establishing aggressive cost objectives, bound by maximum acceptable risk, so that if costs are too great and viable opportunities exist to reduce them, then the user and developer may compromise system performance requirements to meet cost objections. The important aspect to glean is that, as HSI risks are identified, their subsequent prioritization must be presented in a manner that shows a pragmatic and balanced understanding of the risk/opportunity's likelihood and consequence traded against acquisition and in-service cost impacts. In essence, the HSI field must be able to concretely demonstrate the cost-benefit trade-offs for the technical, cost, and schedule modifications being proposed (Sager and Grier, 2005). Figure 4-1 depicts an overview of a representative program risk-management process. In each step, the HSI practitioner contributes valuable information enabling development and sustainment of a system that meets CAIV objectives and user needs. These steps should be undertaken with a holistic system view covering hardware, software, the human element, and related systems.

We have chosen to describe program risk management as applied to DoD acquisition programs because of its applicability to development of highly complex systems and systems of systems. The methods can also be tailored and scaled for less complex military or commercial projects.

In addition to the CAIV concept, there are additional program management practices that should be considered to effectively manage HSI

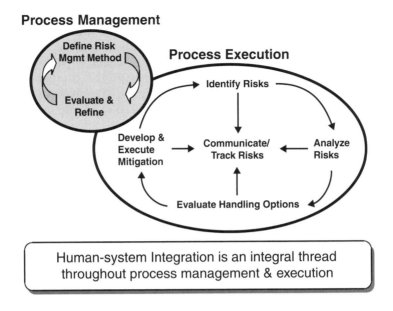

FIGURE 4-1 The risk-management process.

risks and opportunities during program execution. These aspects are not covered in detail in this report, but their importance and relationship to risk management and human-system integration are summarized here. The first practice relates to the business proposal on which the program's execution is based. The business offer is critical because in this process estimates and assumptions are formulated and agreed on by all stakeholders: they cover the customer's requirements and value proposition, measures of compliance with technical requirements (technical performance measures), schedule milestones, and requisite baseline program resources. If HSI specialists are not involved in the business offer process, their perspective and knowledge are not accounted for in formulating the program baselines, often making it necessary to use management reserve or negotiated requirements relief to resolve technical risks and issues that may have been otherwise accounted for during proposal activities.

The second important program management practice is creating a program organization—in particular, a product-based organization with clear team charters and integration teams at appropriate organizational levels. From a risk management perspective, understanding the organizational breakdown is important because it is a source of program execution risk and may hinder proactive risk management if not done properly. From the point of view of human-system integration, understanding where the team resides in the organization is critical because it influences their ability to be effective. In addition, understanding the organizational composition affords the HSI team an opportunity to determine whether they should be represented in integration teams or in other organizational components to create the multidisciplinary skill set that is required to meet that component's charter.

The final program management practice of interest is a culture of openness in which "help needed" (that flows up the organizational structure) and independent reviews are viewed as positive elements. From a risk-management perspective, help needed and independent reviews are important because they encourage early identification and timely mitigation of risks and issues.

The remainder of this chapter focuses on managing risks; however, it should be noted that considering opportunities is just as important and can be managed similarly to risks. In many cases, the HSI practitioner is well suited to identify and exploit opportunities that yield program execution benefits.

IDENTIFYING AND ANALYZING RISK

Risk Identification

Risk identification is the problem definition stage at which risks are identified and quantified in terms of the likelihood of occurrence and detrimental consequences, forming the basis for most risk management actions (Hall, 1998; Boehm, 1991; U.S. Department of Defense, 2003b). Assessments provide insight into the likelihood of achieving desired outcomes in terms of program cost, schedule, and technical objectives and in-service system performance requirements. The risk identification component entails screening candidate risks to ensure validity, deletion of duplicates, clear statement of the risk, and creation of records used to summarize and track risks throughout the program life cycle. Due to the heterogeneity and nuances of program objectives, program life-cycle stages, and skill areas contributing to risk identification, detailed standard approaches are generally not promoted; however, some high-level steps are universal. The steps presented in Figure 4-2 are intended to provide insight into risk identification focus areas.

To effectively identify risks, several qualities of the effort must be in place before focusing on external and internal sources of risk. In the committee's collective experience, the qualities listed below have been found to be indicators of a healthy and dedicated risk-management commitment:

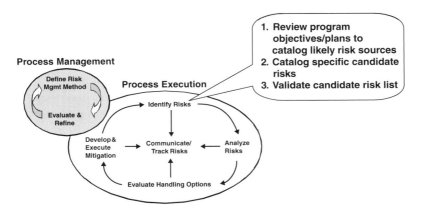

FIGURE 4-2 Steps in risk identification.

- Involvement of all stakeholders and clear communication of program objectives.
- Continual iteration of risk identification until program objectives are met.
- Utilizing nonadvocate technical experts to assist with risk identification.
- Program management culture encouraging risk identification and recording.
- Risk-management processes that afford consistent documentation.

As the HSI practitioner begins risk identification efforts, he or she should be aware that acquisition programs tend to have numerous, often interrelated, risks at all program levels and life-cycle stages that are not always obvious or understood by all skill areas. This can at times mask HSI risks or make it difficult to tease out the HSI component in a larger multi-attribute risk. However, lessons learned from DoD acquisition programs have revealed program aspects containing HSI risk sources that tend to be more critical and should receive heightened attention (U.S. Department of Defense, 2003b). These aspects include

- system performance (technical) requirements and characteristics that do not satisfy user requirements.
- mismatch of user manpower or skill profiles with system design solutions.

- user interface problems (software and hardware).
- proper mix (experience, skills) of HSI personnel assigned to the program management office or contractor team (or both); frequent rotation of HSI personnel.

Listed below are additional program risk sources that HSI practitioners should be concerned about that may reside at the procuring agency's program management office, contractor, and/or suppliers.

- Missing, incomplete, insular, out of scope, or uncertain HSI activity plans, schedules, cost estimates, resources, and processes; HSI team budget/staff size.
- Program management perspective on the HSI discipline and HSI technical risks.
- Inclusion in risk review boards.
- Working relationships with stakeholders; access to users.
- Clarity and validation of HSI requirements and ability to verify compliance; appropriateness of cited standards.
- Supplier HSI processes and requirements.

When reviewing these HSI risk sources, one or more of the identification methods enumerated below can be used to populate a candidate risk list. These methods may be undertaken individually by the HSI practitioner, but they are most effective when multiple methods are executed in the setting of an integrated product team (IPT).

- Risk-identification checklists and likelihood/consequence tables built on collective knowledge and lessons learned regarding processes, specific technologies, and design phases.
- Earned value management metrics analyzed for plan deviations.
- Product operations and program processes analyzed for potential failures/anomalies.
- Program statement of work or work breakdown structure analyzed for risk sources in managed items (resources, deliverables, or events).

Once a candidate's HSI risk has been identified, it is assigned to an HSI team member who becomes the "risk owner" and is responsible for managing it. In some instances, the interrelated nature of HSI risks may require that it is co-owned by more than the HSI team. Candidate risks are subsequently recorded in a risk-management database.

The next step entails establishing a risk review board or risk-management IPT for screening and validating the candidate risk list to avoid duplication, gaps, and inaccuracies. It is essential that HSI practitioners are actively involved in the risk review board or IPT that serves this purpose—at the very least, a representative voice that understands the HSI perspective. Without HSI involvement in this screening and validation step, it is possible that critical HSI risks may be marginalized or ignored. The completeness of the risk identification activity, as well as the candidate risk itself, should be validated using the following criteria:

- Each organization of the program has contributed to risk identification; no gaps.
- Candidate risks are deemed significant by the owner and those affected by it.
- Risks, their source, and consequence are well defined and consistent with known data. (This can be challenging for human-system integration given the skill's subjective nuances).
- Risk consequences describe the unfavorable effects on the program objectives.

Upon completing the candidate risk validation process, HSI risks are included in a program risk watch list that serves as the deliverable for risk identification activities.

Risk Analysis

Risk analysis determines the levels of likelihood, consequence, and overall risk for each candidate risk, then categorizes (technical, schedule, or cost) and prioritizes the risks (low, moderate, or high) to select risk-handling actions (Garvey and Lansdowne, 1998; Hall, 1998). The overarching intent is to zero-in on areas of high and moderate HSI risk for which risk-handling actions can have the greatest impact.

Figure 4-3 provides a synopsis of the risk analysis steps in which human-system integration plays an important role championing an end-user's perspective on risk likelihood and consequence. When progressing through these steps, risk analysis is first conducted on individual risks followed by analysis of their effect on managed items (deliverables or scheduled events) and the entire program to prioritize risk-handling strategies. It is important that HSI engineers are part of the risk review board performing the analysis to describe the risks and lobby for appropriate resources to manage HSI risks effectively, as well as to coordinate with others where a HSI thread is woven into other risks.

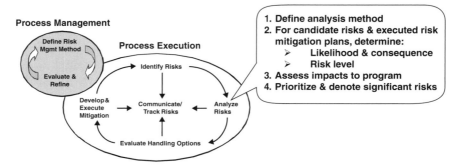

FIGURE 4-3 Steps in risk analysis.

Determine the Risk Analysis Method

As noted in Figure 4-3, the first step in risk analysis is to determine the method of analysis for "measuring" the risk. Methods of risk analyses range from simple, qualitative approaches to quantitative methods to hybrids combining qualitative and quantitative techniques. Typically, qualitative and hybrid methods are utilized, whereas complex quantitative methods are applied to specialized, in-depth risk analyses. This is particularly true for HSI risks in which subjective data predominates, thereby necessitating a qualitative approach, as explained below. When deciding which method to employ, it is important to consider the type of likelihood and consequence values that will be generated—ordinal (qualitative, relative values, not an actual numerical difference) or ratio (quantitative, calibrated to a known scale with a fixed zero point). This is critical because mathematical operations performed on results from uncalibrated ordinal scales are meaningless and yield erroneous risk ratings (Conrow, 1995). Quantitative analyses should use only values from ratio scales having calibrated, measurable values.

Assess Likelihood and Consequence Levels

The second step in risk analysis is to determine the likelihood and consequence levels for each identified risk. For HSI risks, assessing their likelihood and consequence is particularly challenging for a number of reasons (subjective nature of the risk, lack of previous examples or analogies to reference, individual differences of end-users, etc.) and is an area in which HSI specialists may lack experience. Aside from the risk that the HSI team may not adequately accomplish the risk analysis on time and within budget, most HSI risks involve the potential failure of the system's design specifications or user interface specifications to meet the performance requirements of the end users. Quantifying these risks is difficult and requires the participation of the design team as well as the HSI specialist. In addition, it is paramount that method, tools, and criteria are consistently applied to create an equitable basis for comparison. Chapter 8 discusses in more detail aspects of assessing the likelihood and consequence of a risk using failure modes and effects analysis and fault tree analysis.

Determine the Risk Level

Next, the risk level (i.e., a holistic "measurement" of risk) is determined based on combining the assessed likelihood and consequence levels. Risk levels are described as high, moderate, or low and are often portrayed in risk grids (likelihood and consequence are the axes) with stoplight colors (red represents high risks, yellow for moderate risks, and green for low risks).

Assess Program Impacts

Thus far, risk owners have assessed individual risk levels, but individual risk impacts on the program need to be assessed. The program impact of the individual risks is determined by a risk review board that examines the relationships of individual risks to one another or a higher level program item (managed items, deliverables, or scheduled events) to perform a collective risk assessment. The risk review board also takes into account the dependencies of higher level program items to ensure a holistic program-level risk assessment. HSI risks are often marginalized in this process due to the specialty engineering nature of human-system integration, unless an HSI representative is present to elucidate the issue. If an HSI representative is not a part of the risk review board, the result may be inadequate resources being allocated to HSI risks or disregard of their potential impact when examining higher order dependencies because it is masked by other risks.

The holistic, integrated perspective is important because individual risk analysis treats risks as mutually exclusive and independent of each other; typically this is not the case for HSI risks in complex system development. Individual risks frequently have common elements that make them interdependent despite their independent occurrence; this is especially true for HSI risks. As a result, the potential relations of individual risks to higher level program items may have a collective effect of increasing the risk level of that higher level program item—hence the importance of collective risk analysis in which the first step in assessing program impacts is to determine the relationship of individual risks to higher level program items and then assessing their collective effect on the risk level of a higher level program item.

The next step in assessing program impacts is an integrated risk analysis to determine risk interdependencies that may amplify one or more of the interrelated risks. In this analysis it is important for HSI practitioners to explain how disregarding HSI risks, particularly those masked by other risks or marginalized due to underappreciation of the HSI risk, may have implications later requiring rework to resolve or additional risk management activities. This need for clearly explaining how HSI risks may significantly contribute to the program's risk "critical path" is particularly crucial for software development, in which a "we can fix that later, it's software" mind set, or the fallacy of reusing software to improve program cost and schedule metrics, at times prevails.

Once the risk review board has completed the collective and integrated risk analyses, the program risk critical paths may be determined. The risk-critical path of a program can be identified only by determining the predecessor and successor relationships and success dependencies of managed items and conducting the integrated risk analysis. All individual risks in the risk-critical path should be given the highest priorities in the program for risk handling.

Prioritize Risks

Individual risks should be prioritized for their handling options by individual risk levels, effect on higher level program items, relationship to the program's risk-critical path, and urgency based on time to when the risk may occur and/or customer priorities and preferences. Prioritization is done by adjusting the risk priorities up or down from the risk level based on the risk prioritization factors. If the risk levels and prioritization factors all have ratio scales with absolute values, the risk level may be a calculated function of these quantities. Otherwise, prioritization must be done by manually assessing the effect of the prioritization factors on risk level.

Successful completion of the risk analysis step culminates in the generation of individual risk likelihood and consequence assessments, risk levels (low, moderate, high) for individual risks and higher level program items, an identified program risk-critical path, and prioritized individual risks to steer subsequent risk-handling activities. Given the extent of influence that risk analysis has on resource allocation, it is important that HSI practitioners are actively involved in this component of risk management. The HSI team is typically working with suboptimal resources, and it is imperative they are not further diminished because the issues associated with HSI risks are not fully understood or appreciated by decision makers.

HANDLING OPTIONS ASSESSMENT

Assessing risk-handling options includes evaluating each significant risk to determine the appropriate handling strategy (Hall, 1998; Boehm, 1991). Typically, only moderately or highly prioritized risks require a risk-handling strategy, whereas low-priority risks are monitored and periodically reassessed. The most appropriate handling strategy for each risk is selected based on its urgency, level of the risk, resources and schedule constraints, and customer satisfaction expectations. The risk-handling options to choose from include avoiding the risk, transferring the risk, assuming the risk, and mitigating the risk; these options are depicted in Figure 4-4. The HSI practitioner is well suited to offer a range of risk-handling options given the flexibility in HSI techniques and bringing a mind set of the impact of those options on user and system performance when the system is operational.

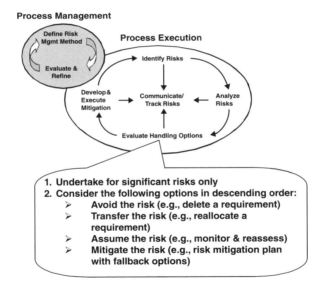

FIGURE 4-4 Decision flow of risk-handling options.

Avoiding the Risk

Avoiding the risk is an option that is usually viable only in the earliest phases of a program, when concept development permits redefining plans and approaches with minimum impact. A decision to avoid the risk and the method of avoidance typically involves not only the team responsible for the risk, but also program management and the customer. The limited window of opportunity for avoiding the risk and the need for extensive coordination is illustrated by its associated options, which include (1) choosing an alternative approach with a lower risk, (2) deleting specific requirements, (3) changing specific requirements, (4) changing the overall technical solution, (5) modifying the program schedule, and (6) modifying the funding level or funding profile.

An additional, yet untraditional, perspective is that HSI risks can often be avoided by further defining requirements to remove the nebulous ("soft") attributes (in Chapter 7 see the section on usability requirements methods). Traditionally, HSI requirements are vaguely defined and hard for the contractor to prove compliance; jointly refining them creates clarity in the development process. Before deciding on a risk avoidance handling strategy, options of risk transfer, risk acceptance, and risk mitigation should be evaluated.

Transferring the Risk

Transfer is a strategy to shift the risk elsewhere (e.g., another team, supplier, customer, or requirement) so that overall program risk is optimized and risk ownership is assigned to the party most capable of reducing or accepting the risk. Options for transferring the risk include

- reallocating requirements to reduce overall program risk.
- developing a research and development (R&D) project that takes the risk with it and substitutes a lower risk contractual alternative with an option to evaluate the R&D results for later product improvement.
- pushing the risk to the next program phase and addressing it later if the current program is successful.

Deferring the risk can have dire consequences from an HSI perspective. Delaying the handling of an HSI risk is often the option chosen because decision makers do not fully appreciate the importance of managing HSI risks proactively and early in the program life cycle. This is particularly true in software development and hardware design, in which ergonomic (anthropometry and biomechanics) and human factors (usability) aspects of the system design may necessitate costly fixes because the HSI risks were not given appropriate attention at the proper program life-cycle phase, or it was deemed that transferring the risk by pushing it to a later program phase would be more effective. Having assessed risk avoidance and transfer, the options of risk acceptance and risk mitigation should be evaluated.

Assuming the Risk

Risk assumption is a deliberate decision to accept a known risk, and it should be based on cost-benefit analysis, showing that it is more beneficial to assume the risk than it is to choose any of the other risk-handling options. This decision is made only when all relevant facts have been presented to the decision makers. If assuming the risk is the option chosen, then the risk owner needs to monitor the risk continuously for change, reassess it as appropriate, and take action as needed. As long as the risk's parameters are within predetermined acceptable ranges, no action is needed. If they fall outside these predetermined acceptable ranges, action is triggered, and a decision must be made for how to bring the risk level back into the acceptable range. At this point, a reassessment of the possibilities of avoiding, transferring, or assuming the risk also is recommended.

Risk assumption is another often-used approach for handling HSI risks, primarily because the decision makers do not fully grasp the implications, or the seriousness of the risk does not surface in demonstrable manner until the system is operational. Human-in-the-loop evaluations of system prototypes and system build releases within the spiral life cycle are the most effective means for demonstrating when an HSI risk should not be assumed, but these activities require competing for highly utilized program resources. It is also crucial that the tolerable bounds for assuming an HSI risk are succinctly documented along with the impact of crossing them. After examining the alternative of assuming the risk, risk mitigation should still be evaluated, especially for risk items that exceed acceptable risk assumption parameters.

Mitigating the Risks

For items judged to be significant risks and avoiding, transferring, and assuming risks are not acceptable options, risk mitigation is chosen. Risk mitigation is a strategy for developing options and alternatives that lower or eliminate the risk by reducing its likelihood or consequences. This usually applies to technical risks (e.g., subsystem design), but it may also apply to schedule risks (e.g., a supplier who has a significant on-time delivery risk). For high-risk items, a fallback plan needs to be identified to cover the possibility of mitigation plans failing. The purpose of the fallback plan is to allow the program to continue while still meeting most of the program objectives.

Human-system integration has an amalgam of tools and techniques for mitigating risk that are integrated into everyday practices—for example, software prototyping, anthropometric modeling, usability evaluations, and cognitive workload modeling. By effectively performing the role of an HSI engineer, the practitioner is continuously mitigating risk in the design and development of the system, with a focus on the risks that impact the operational effectiveness of both the system and the user.

EXECUTING RISK MITIGATION

The risk mitigation option, when chosen, establishes detailed plans for the risks that require them, covering required resources, schedules, tasks, success criteria, expected resulting risk level for each successfully completed task, and plan approval. In addition, this step creates fallback plans for all high risks, along with decision gates and criteria for their implementation (U.S. Department of Defense, 2003b). Human-system integration will execute mitigation strategies for its own risks; however, it is also important that human-system integration is involved in defining the collateral impacts of its efforts and understanding the impacts on other skill areas' risk mitigation activities, as well as theirs on human-system integration. Figure 4-5 is a representation of the risk mitigation activity.

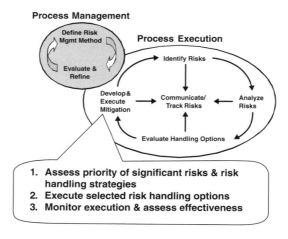

FIGURE 4-5 Steps in risk mitigation.

Develop a Plan

Effective risk mitigation entails reduction of the risk occurrence likelihood, its consequences if it occurs, or both to complete the effort. Subsequently, clearly defining task success criteria is imperative to measure the effectiveness of the risk mitigation plan and determining when to invoke a fallback plan. For human-system integration, defining the success criteria can be tricky due to the subjectivity inherent in a majority of the issues with which the discipline works. In essence, the HSI practitioner is trying to define criteria akin to usability goals with gradations indicating degrees of success and when a fallback plan should be implemented.

When creating a risk mitigation plan, an array of options exists, depending on the nature of the risk; HSI options may include

- trade studies; parallel prototyping; early development HSI evaluation; early and extensive simulation.
- system and/or task analysis; refining, modifying, or eliminating HSI requirements.
- working with suppliers to implement solid HSI processes.
- using an alternate design that already meets HSI requirements.
- extending the schedule; increasing the budget.

When generating the risk mitigation plan, the items below should be explicitly and succinctly stated.

- Task definitions with entry and exit criteria that denote starting and completion points (success criteria defining expected risk-level outcomes and subsequently removing the risk from the significant risk list). Planned start and stop dates with associated cost and required inputs.
- Relationships between tasks in the risk mitigation plan and overarching program plan, as well as collateral impacts on required resources.
- Means for tracking plan variance.

Identify Fallback Plans

Risks that are categorized as high should have fallback plans as part of the risk mitigation strategy. Fallback plans are requisite to ensure that an alternative approach is available to mitigate risks that have a significant likelihood of occurrence, severe consequences, or both.

Incorporate into Program Schedules

Approved risk mitigation plans need to be a formal part of the program schedule and be reflected in the program's metrics to garner the requisite attention needed to accomplish planned mitigation tasks. Generally, "off the books" mitigation efforts suffer from lack of visibility, suboptimal coordination, and improper configuration management. It is extremely important that HSI risk mitigation plans are integrated into the program scheduled because the discipline is often hampered by the perspective of some decision makers that human-system integration is a specialty engineering resource utilized for consultancy purposes. By operating off the books, the HSI team is further isolating itself from the decision makers who control resources.

Evaluate Success Accomplishments and Assess Reductions Achieved

Each mitigation activity has predefined success criteria associated with it. As mitigation tasks are accomplished, they must be evaluated to determine if the expected success criteria were met. In addition, the degree to which the predicted risk reduction was accomplished needs to be assessed. If not fully successful, the plan may need to be adjusted or fallback plan implemented to achieve the planned risk reduction.

Evaluate Remaining Plan Activities

Upon completion of each risk mitigation task, the remaining tasks in the plan should be evaluated to ensure the overall required reduction is still attainable via the defined plan. Decisions are made at this point whether to proceed with the plan as defined, modify it, or implement the fallback plan. As noted previously, any decisions to change the plan need to mandate proper coordination, approval, and incorporation into the program schedule.

Successful completion of the risk mitigation step culminates in detailed mitigation plans documented in team and program schedules, fallback plans, approved resources to execute the risk mitigation plan, and completion of the risk mitigation strategy resulting in the expected reduced level of risk.

5

Case Studies

This chapter provides three examples of specific system development that illustrate application of human-system integration (HSI) methods in the context of the incremental commitment model (ICM). The examples are drawn from the committee's collective experience and specific application of the concepts developed during our work to these particular projects. They represent projects at three stages of development: the early stages of planning, in mid-development, and fully realized.

The first example involves the development of unmanned aerial systems and identifies numerous HSI issues in these systems that will require solution. This example provides a "notional" application of human factors methods and potential implementation of the incremental commitment model. The case study illustrates the theme of designing to accommodate changing conditions and requirements in the workplace. Specifically, it addresses the issue of adapting current unmanned aerial systems to accommodate fewer operators, with individual operators controlling multiple vehicles. The hypothetical solutions to this problem reveal the potential costs of reliance on automation, particularly prior to a full understanding of the domain, task, and operator strengths and limitations. This case study also reveals the tight interconnection between the various facets of human-system integration, such as manpower, personnel, training, and design. In other words, answering the "how many operators to vehicles" question necessarily impacts design, training, and personnel decisions.

The second example focuses on a large-scale government implementation of port security systems for protection against nuclear smuggling. The example discusses the HSI themes and incremental application of methods during the iterative development of the system. This case is useful for illustrating application of human factors methods on a risk-driven basis, as they tend to be applied as needed over time in response to the iterative aspects of defining requirements and opportunities, developing design solutions, and evaluation of operational experience.

The third example describes development of an intravenous infusion pump by a medical device manufacturer. This example is the most detailed and "linear" of the three cases, in that it follows a sequential developmental process; the various systems engineering phases are discussed in terms of the human factors methods applied during each phase. This case study illustrates the successful implementation of well-known HSI methods, including contextual inquiry, prototyping and simulations, cognitive walkthroughs for estimating use-error-induced operational risks, iterative design, and usability evaluations that include testing and expert reviews. The importance of the incremental commitment model in phased decision making and the value of shared representations is also highlighted.

Each of these examples is presented in a somewhat different format, as appropriate to the type of development. This presentation emphasizes one broad finding from our study, which is that a "one size" system development model does not fit all. The examples illustrate tailored application of HSI methods, the various trade-offs that are made to incorporate them in the larger context of engineering development, and the overall theme of reducing the risk that operational systems will fail to meet user needs.

UNMANNED AERIAL SYSTEMS

Unmanned aerial systems (UASs) or remotely piloted vehicles (RPVs) are airplanes or helicopters operated remotely by humans on the ground or in some cases from a moving air, ground, or water vehicle. Until recently the term "unmanned aerial vehicle" (UAV) was used in the military services in reference to such vehicles as Predators, Global Hawks, Pioneers, Hunters, and Shadows. The term "unmanned aerial system" acknowledges the fact that the focus is on much more than a vehicle. The vehicle is only part of a large interconnected system that connects other humans and machines on the ground and in the air to carry out tasks ranging from UAS maintenance and operation to data interpretation and sensor operation. The recognition of the system in its full complexity is consistent with the evolution from human-machine design to human-system design, the topic of this report. It highlights an important theme of this book: the need for methods that are scalable to complex systems of systems.

Unmanned aerial systems are intended to keep humans out of harm's way. However, humans are still on the ground performing maintenance, control, monitoring, and data collection functions, among others. Reports from the Army indicate that 22 people are required on the ground to operate, maintain, and oversee a Shadow UAS (Bruce Hunn, personal communication). In addition, there is a dearth of UAS operators relative to the current need in Iraq and Afghanistan, not to mention the U.S. borders. The growing need for UAS personnel, combined with the current shortage, points to another theme of this report: the need for human-system integration to accommodate changing conditions and requirements in the workplace.

In addition, this issue has strong ties to questions of manning. The manning questions are "How many operators does it take to operate each unmanned aerial system? Can one modify the 2:1 human to machine ratio (e.g., two humans operating one UAS) to allow for a single operator and multiple aircraft (e.g., 1:4)?" Automation is often proposed as a solution to this problem, but the problem can be much more complex. Automation is not always a solution and may, in fact, present a new set of challenges, such as loss of operator situation awareness or mode confusion. Furthermore, the manning question is a good example of how HSI design touches other aspects of human-system integration, such as manpower, personnel, and training. That is, the question of how many vehicles per operator is not merely one of automation, but also involves the number and nature of the operators in question.

A Hypothetical Case

This example is based on an ongoing debate about the manning question, which has not been fully resolved. Therefore some aspects of the case are hypothetical, yet not improbable. In this example we assume that the objective of the design is to change the operator to UAS ratio from 2:1 to 1:4. That is, instead of two operators for one UAS there will be one operator for four UASs. This operator to UAS ratio is a requirement of the type that may be promulgated by the Department of Defense with minimal HSI input. It could be too late for human-system integration, which needs to be fully integrated into the engineering life cycle *before* system requirements have been determined. It could be too late in the sense that up-front analysis might have revealed that an effective 1:4 ratio is beyond the capabilities of current humans and technology under the best of circumstances. If this is the case, then there is a huge risk of designing a system that is doomed to fail. Even worse, this failure may not reveal itself until the right operational events line up to produce workload that breaks the system.

In our example, we present another scenario. The design of a UAS with a 1:4 ratio of operator to system is carried through the ICM development process to illustrate the potential role of human-system integration and one of the themes of this book. The Department of Defense is one of many critical stakeholders in this scenario, all of whom are to be considered in the satisficing process that ensues.

Human-System Integration in the Context of the Incremental Commitment Model

In the earliest exploration phases of ICM development, the problem space and concept of operations are defined, and concept discovery and synthesis take place. Table 5-1 provides highlights of the entire example. It is often the case that human-system integration is not brought into the development cycle at this point, although at great risk. Up-front analyses, such as interviews of UAS operators, observations of operations of 2:1 systems, examination of mishap reports, understanding of the literature and data, an analysis of the 2:1 workload, event data analysis targeted at communications in the 2:1 UAS system, application of models of operator workload, and work flow analysis are all methods that could be used to explore the HSI issues in the current UAS system.

There is much that could come from this kind of up-front analysis. One hypothetical possibility is that the up-front HSI analyses could determine that UAS workload is not constant but peaks in target areas where photos need to be taken or in situations in which the route plan needs to change.

One of the key principles of ICM development is *risk management*, including risk-driven activity levels and anchor point commitment milestones. What are the risks if human-system integration is not considered early in the development life cycle? In this case, the formal requirements that are established may target workload reduction incorrectly. For example, autopilot automation might be developed to help to get multiple UASs from point A to point B and so on. This might have the effect of reducing workload when a reduction was not needed, while providing no relief from the high-workload tasks. Ultimately the neglect of up-front human-system integration could result in a system that is ineffective or prone to error. Consideration of risks like these should guide system development.

What if there is not enough time to interview UAS operators and to do a thorough job in the exploration phase? There is also risk associated with application of costly up-front techniques. The up-front methods used often during the exploration phase of the life cycle can be tailored to meet time and budget constraints—another theme of this book. For example, in this case in which the manning question is the issue and automation appears to be a promising solution, it would make sense to focus on aspects of the task that may be automated and the workload associated with each. One caveat is that decisions on how to scope and tailor the methods require some HSI expertise in order to target the aspects of human-system integration that promise the most risk reduction.

As system development progresses, other principles of ICM development come into play, including incremental growth of system development and stakeholder commitment. This part of the development life-cycle synthesis leads to construction, invention, or design that is iteratively refined as it is evaluated. HSI activities that would be useful at this point include function allocation and the development of shared representations, such as storyboards and prototypes.

Based on the previous finding of fluctuating workload, it may be decided that human intervention is needed at target areas and during route changes, but that the single operator can handle only one of these peak-workload tasks at a time. It may also be determined that, although automation could handle the routine flight task, an even more important place for automation is in the hand-off between the flight tasks and the human planning/replanning operation. The automation would therefore serve a scheduling and hand-off function, allocating complex tasks to the human operator as they arise and in order of priority (e.g., priority targets first). There could also be automation that serves as a decision aid for the targeting task.

Because only one nonroutine task can be handled at a time under the 1:4 scenario, it may also be decided that operators should be relieved of the flight functions completely but be on call for hand-offs from automation. For example, four controllers could handle the prioritized hand-offs from the automation, much as air traffic controllers handle multiple planes in a sector. Note that this new design and staffing plan are completely different in terms of operator roles and tasks from the former 2:1 operation. It is human-system integration that guided the allocation of tasks to human and machine; without it there would have been many other possibilities for automation that may not have produced the same end-state.

As the ICM development continues, the system engineers will go from working prototypes to product development, beta testing, product deployment, product maintenance, and product retirement. But there is continual iteration along the way. The incremental growth in the automation for scheduling, hand-offs, and targeting would occur in parallel with the next iteration's requirements and subsystem definitions (i.e., concurrent engineering). Incremental growth will be influenced by stakeholder commitment. The HSI methods in the later stages include interviews and observations in conjunction with the newly designed system and usability testing. Some of the same methods used in up-front analysis (e.g., event data analysis, participatory analysis) can be again used and results contrasted with those of the earlier data collection.

The goal of human-system integration at this stage is to verify that the situation for the user has improved and that no new issues have cropped up in the interim. For instance, it may be determined from testing that the targeting decision aid is not trusted by the human operator (a stakeholder)

TABLE 5-1 Example of Human-System Integration for UASs in the Context of the Risk-Driven Spiral

Life-Cycle Phase	HSI Activity	SE Activities
Exploration	Observe 2:1 system, interview UAS operators, examine literature/data, examine mishap reports, workload analysis and models, event data analysis, communication, work flow analysis	Define problem space, concept discovery, concept of operations, synthesis
Valuation and architecting	Function allocation, storyboards, prototypes	Synthesis, construct, invent, design, refine, hard requirements, working prototypes
Development and operation	Interviews, observations, usability testing, comparisons with previous system	Working prototypes, product development, beta testing, product deployment, maintenance, retirement

NOTE: HSI = human-system integration; SE = systems engineering; UAS = unmanned aerial system.

and as a result is not used (a risk). Through iterations, a new design will be tested or the decision aid will be completely eliminated (i.e., stakeholder satisficing).

Conclusion and Lessons Learned

In this example, human-system integration plays a major role throughout the design process and is critical in the early stages before requirements are established. It can be integrated throughout the design life cycle with other engineering methods. It is also clear that the HSI activities serve to reduce human factors risks along the way and make evident the human factors issues that are at stake, so that these issues can be considered as they trade off with other design issues.

This example illustrates several lessons regarding human-system integration and system design:

- The importance and complexity of the "system" in human-system integration compared with "machine" or "vehicle."
- Design concerns are often linked to manpower, personnel, and training concerns.

Hypothetical Outcome	Risks If No HSI	HSI Value-Added
Workload not constant; heavy at target areas and for route change	Ineffective or error-prone system	Requirements targeted at known system strengths and weaknesses
Automation takes over flight and hand-offs complex tasks to operator-based on priority	Operator who is overwhelmed during high workload and bored during low workload	Design takes into account known machine and human strengths and weaknesses
Targeting decision aid not trusted by human operator	Validation and verification would not consider the human limitations in relation to the new system	Testing takes into account usability and comparison to prior system

• Up-front analysis and HSI input in early exploration activities is critical.

• Methods can be tailored to time and money constraints, but HSI expertise is required to do so.

• Risks are incurred if human-system integration is not considered or if it is considered late. In this case the risk would be a system that is not usable and that ultimately leads to catastrophic failure.

PORT SECURITY

The U.S. Department of Homeland Security (DHS) is in the process of implementing a large-scale radiation screening program to protect the country from nuclear weapons or dirty bombs that might be smuggled across the border through various ports of entry. This program encompasses all land, air, and maritime ports of entry. Our example focuses on radiation screening at seaports, which have a particularly complex operational nature. Seaports are structured to facilitate the rapid offloading of cargo containers from ocean-going vessels, provide temporary storage of the containers, and provide facilities for trucks and trains to load containers for transport to their final destination. The operation involves numerous personnel, includ-

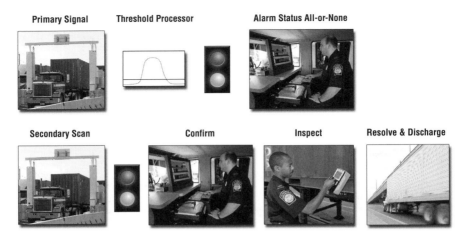

FIGURE 5-1 RPM security screening at seaports involves multiple tasks, displays, and people.

ing customs and border protection (CBP) officers for customs and security inspection, terminal personnel, such as longshoremen for equipment operation, and transport personnel, such as truck drivers and railroad operators. Figure 5-1 illustrates the steps involved in the radiation screening process.

Design and deployment of radiation portal monitoring (RPM) systems for seaport operations engages the incremental commitment model for ensuring commitments from the stakeholders and to meet the fundamental technical requirement of screening 100 percent of arriving international cargo containers for illicit radioactive material.

This example illustrates aspects of the ICM process with specific instances of human-system integration linked to concurrent technical activities in the RPM program. The development of RPM systems for application in the seaport environment entails an iterative process that reflects the overall set of themes developed in this book. We discuss how these themes are reflected in the engineering process.

Human-System Integration in the Context of Risk-Driven Incremental Commitments

The human factors design issues encountered in this program are very diverse, ranging from fundamental questions of alarm system effectiveness at a basic research level, to very practical and time-sensitive issues, such as the most appropriate methods of signage or traffic signaling for controlling the flow of trucks through an RPM system. HSI methods have been applied on a needs-driven basis, with risk as a driver for the nature of the application. With the issue of alarm system effectiveness, for example, it was recognized early in the program that reducing system nuisance alarms is an important issue, but one that requires a considerable amount of physics research and human factors display system modeling and design. The ICM process allowed early implementation of systems with a higher nuisance alarm rate than desirable while pursuing longer term solutions to problems involving filtering, new sensors, and threat-based displays. The nuisance alarm risk was accepted for the early implementations, while concurrent engineering was performed to reduce the alarm rate and improve the threat displays for implementation in later versions.

A contrasting example involves traffic signage and signaling. Since the flow of cargo trucks through port exits is a critical element of maintaining commercial flow, yet proper speed is necessary for RPM measurement, methods for proper staging of individual vehicles needed to be developed. Most ports involve some type of vehicle checkout procedure, but this could not be relied on to produce consistent vehicle speed through the RPM systems. Instead, the program engaged the HSI specialty to assist in developing appropriate signage and signaling that would ensure truck driver attention to RPM speed requirements.

HSI Methods Tailored to Time and Budget Constraints

Since the RPM program focus is homeland security, there has been schedule urgency from the beginning. The need for rapid deployment of RPM systems to maximize threat detection and minimize commercial impact has been the key program driver, and this has also influenced how the HSI discipline has been applied. The primary effect of program urgency and budgetary limitations has been to focus HSI efforts in work domain analysis, the modeling of human-system interactions, and theory-based analysis rather than experiment.

The work domain analysis has typically focused on gaining a rapid understanding of relatively complicated seaport operations in order to evaluate technology insertion opportunities and to better understand design requirements. In contrast to work domain analysis oriented toward cognitive decision aids, which requires time-intensive collaboration with subject matter experts, the RPM analysis worked at a coarser level to characterize staff functions and interactions, material flow, and operational tempo. Similarly, modeling of human-system interactions (such as responding to a traffic light or an intercom system) was performed at the level of detail necessary to facilitate design, rather than a comprehensive representation of operator cognitive processes—this was not required to support engineering.

Theory-based analysis of alarm system effectiveness has been conducted on a somewhat longer time scale, since the problem of human response to alarms is more complex. This work consisted of adapting traditional observer-based signal detection theory, in which the human is an *active* component of the detection system, to RPM systems in which the human operator *evaluates* the output of a sensor system that detects a threat precondition. Various threat probability analyses have been conducted in this effort, and they can be used to guide subsequent advanced RPM designs. This work has been guided by empirical studies, but it has not required an independent data collection effort.

Shared Representations Used to Communicate

The rapid-paced nature of the RPM program places a premium on effective communication between human-system integration and the engineering disciplines. In this program, fairly simple communication mechanisms that use graphics or presentation methods adapted from engineering have the best chance of successful communication. For example, it is important to evaluate the human error risks associated with new security screening systems so that mitigation approaches can be designed. One approach to describing this to the engineering community might be to simply borrow existing taxonomies from researchers in the field, such as Reason (1990). Alternatively, a more graphic and less verbose approach is to represent the approach as a fault tree, shown in Figure 5-2. This type of representation is immediately recognizable to the engineering community and is less subject to interpretation than abstract descriptions of error typologies.

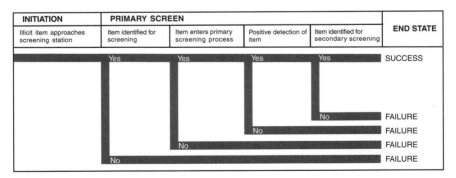

INITIATION	PRIMARY SCREEN				END STATE
Illicit item approaches screening station	Item identified for screening	Item enters primary screening process	Positive detection of item	Item identified for secondary screening	
	Yes	Yes	Yes	Yes	SUCCESS
				No	FAILURE
			No		FAILURE
		No			FAILURE
No					FAILURE

FIGURE 5-2 General model of human error analysis for security screening used as a shared representation to communicate the concept to engineering staff.

Primary Signal

Statistical Processor:
templates/spectra

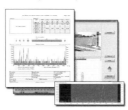

Alarm
Radioactive Threat
Material

Alert
Naturally Occurring
Radioactive Material

Pass
No Material of Concern

Alarm Status Calibrated to
Potential Threat

Resolve & Discharge

FIGURE 5-3 Graphical representation of work flow with a threat-based RPM display.

Human-system integration has used graphics to convey fairly abstract design ideas to the engineering staff, as shown in Figure 5-3. This display conveys the concept of a threat likelihood display, which informs the RPM operator about the contents of a vehicle based on processing algorithms. The graphic contrasts the eight-step process shown in Figure 5-1, with a four-step screening process, illustrating the functional utility of the display in a direct way.

Accommodation to Changing Conditions and Workplace Requirements

The RPM program started with a set of baseline designs for seaports that involved a cargo container passing through an exit gate. As the program expanded to a wider range of port operations, numerous variations in the container-processing operations became apparent. In some instances, the traffic volume is so low that the costs of installing a fixed installation are too high; alternatively, trenching limits or other physical constraints may preclude a fixed portal. Operational differences, such as moving containers direct to rail cars, also present challenges for design.

FIGURE 5-4 Standard truck exit RPM system (left), mobile RPM system (middle), and straddle carrier operation (right).

Figure 5-4 illustrates several variants of RPM operational configurations that have HSI implications. The truck exit shown in the figure is a standard design that accommodates the majority of seaport operations as they are currently configured. In order to accommodate reconfiguration and low volume, a mobile RPM system has been developed, as shown above. For ports at which straddle carriers are used to move containers directly to rail, solutions are currently being evaluated. Human-system integration has been directly responsible for operations studies of straddle carrier operation to discern technology insertion opportunities. The critical issue for seaports is that current operations do not predict future operations; the rapid expansion of imports will fundamentally alter how high-volume ports process their cargo, and HSI studies will be an important element of adapting the security screening technologies to evolving operational models.

Scalable Methods

The RPM program is large in scale—involving geographically distributed installations on a nationwide basis, multiple personnel, government agencies and private-sector stakeholders—and seaports are an element of the nation's critical infrastructure. To make an effective contribution in this context, human-system integration has focused on problems of an aggregate nature that affect multiple installations. The methods generally employed, such as work domain analysis, probabilistic risk modeling, and timeline analysis, are applicable at an individual operator, work group, or port-wide level. Scalability is inherent in the overall goals of method application (i.e., discerning general operational constraints and potential design solutions); in the process there are requirements for "one-off" tailored solutions, but the fundamental goal is to provide generic solutions.

Principles of System Development

The development of RPM systems for application in the seaport environment has entailed an iterative process that reflects the system development principles described in this book. This section discusses how these principles are reflected in the engineering process.

Success-Critical Stakeholder Satisficing

As mentioned above, this program involves the private sector (seaport terminal management and labor), local public agencies such as port authorities, local and national transportation companies such as railroads, federal government agencies (DHS), federal contractors, and, from time to time, other federal law enforcement agencies, such as the Federal Bureau of Investigation. The issues and requirements of all need to be addressed in RPM deployments. The dual program goals of maximizing threat detection and minimizing impact on commerce define the parameters for stakeholder satisficing.

Incremental Growth of System Definition and Stakeholder Commitment

The objective of minimal disruption to ongoing seaport operations and the need to identify traffic choke points and screening opportunities require considerable up-front analysis, as well as continuing evaluation of impact as individualized deployments are designed. The general activities in this category include

- initial site surveys to identify choke points.
- operational process analysis to identify traffic flow and screening procedures for individual seaport sites.
- adaptation of baseline screening systems to specific seaport site constraints.

- continued monitoring and evaluation of impact, including nuisance alarm rates and traffic flow, from design through deployment.
- modification of RPM system elements as required to meet security and operational missions.

This process generally involves initial stakeholder meetings to establish the relationships necessary to adapt the technologies to individual operations. Based on information gathered in operational studies, conceptual designs (50-percent level) are proposed, reviewed, and revised as a more detailed understanding of requirements and impacts is obtained. This leads to more refined definitions of implementation requirements and operational impacts, which in turn lead to commitment at the 90-percent design review.

Risk Management

The multiple operational personnel involved in port security and seaport operations necessarily entails a variety of human factors risks when new technology is introduced. One of the major initial risks involved consideration of staffing, as customs and border protection authorities have not typically placed officers on site at seaports. A number of options for operating security equipment were evaluated, and the decision was made that CBP would staff the seaport sites with additional schedule rotations. This reduced the risk of relying on nonlaw enforcement personnel but increased the cost to the government (a trade-off). Other risks include generally low workload associated with processing alarms (a trade-off of boredom and cost, but physical presence is guaranteed), the gradual erosion of alarm credibility based on the exclusive occurrence of nuisance alarms (a trade-off of high sensitivity of detection system with potential for reduced effectiveness), risks of labor disputes as more complex technology is introduced that may be seen as infringing on private-sector territory (a trade-off of the risk of a complex labor situation with the need for security screening), and transfer of training procedure incompatibilities from one location to another (i.e., procedures vary considerably from one site to another, and staff rotate among these locations—a trade-off of procedural variability with the human ability to adapt).

HSI activities tend to be deployed in this program based on continuing assessment of risks associated with individual seaport deployments. For example, HSI operational studies of straddle carrier cargo operations were undertaken midway through seaport deployments, when it was recognized that existing technology solutions could not be adapted to that type of operation. The risk of using existing technology was that seaport operations would need to fundamentally change—this would lead to an unacceptable impact on commerce. Thus operational studies were undertaken to identify potential technology insertion opportunities that would minimize the risk of commercial impact.

Concurrent System Definition and Development

The RPM program involves substantial concurrent engineering activity. The initial deployments have utilized relatively low-cost, high-sensitivity but low-resolution sensors made of polyvinyl toluene. These sensors are highly sensitive to radioactive material but tend to generate nuisance alarms because of low resolution of the *type* of radioactive material (naturally occurring versus threat material). While this yields high threat sensitivity, it is also nonspecific and creates a larger impact on commerce due to nuisance alarms and the need for secondary inspections.

However, development of advanced spectroscopic portals (ASPs) that utilize high-resolution sensors is taking place concurrently with the installation of lower resolution portals and will be deployed subsequently. These portals will be able to identify specific radioactive isotopes and will help to reduce nuisance alarms that create an adverse impact on commerce. Concurrent human factors research concerning threat-based displays will be used for developing appropriate end-user displays for the new systems.

"NEXT-GENERATION" INTRAVENOUS INFUSION PUMP

The next-generation infusion pump is a general-purpose intravenous infusion pump (IV pump) designed primarily for hospital use with secondary, limited-feature use by patients at home. The device is intended to deliver liquid medications, nutrients, blood, and other solutions at programmed flow rates, volumes, and time intervals via intravenous and other routes to a patient. The marketed name is the Symbiq™ IV Pump. The device will offer medication management features, including medication management safety software through a programmable drug library. The infuser will also have sufficient memory to support extensive tracking logs and the ability to communicate and integrate with hospital information systems. The infuser will be available as either a single-channel pump or a dual-channel pump. The two configurations can be linked together to form a 3- or 4-channel pump. The infuser includes a large touchscreen color display and can be powered by either A/C power or rechargeable batteries.

To ensure that the infuser has an easy-to-use user interface, the development of the product was based on a user-centered design approach. As part of the user-centered design approach, the team involved potential users at each phase in the design cycle. During the first phase, the team conducted interviews with potential users and stakeholders, including nurses, anesthesiologists, doctors, managers, hospital administrators, and biomedical technicians to gather user requirements. The team also conducted early research in the form of contextual observations and interviews in different clinical settings in hospitals as a means to understand user work flow involving infusion pumps. The information from these initial activities was used in the conceptual development phase of the next-generation infusion pump. Iterative design and evaluation took place in the development of each feature. Evaluations included interviews, usability testing in a laboratory setting, usability testing in a simulated patient environment, testing with low-fidelity paper prototypes, and testing with high-fidelity computer simulation prototypes. Computer simulations of the final user interface of each feature were used in focus groups to verify features and to obtain additional user feedback on ease of use before the final software coding began. In the final phases of development, extensive usability testing in simulated patient environments was conducted to ensure design intent has been implemented and that ease of use and usability objectives were met. Throughout the development process, iterative risk analysis, evaluation, and control were conducted in compliance with the federally regulated design control process (see Figures 5-5 and 5-6).

Motivation Behind the Design

The primary motivation was to design a state-of-the-art infusion pump that would be a breakthrough in terms of ease of use and improved patient safety. Over recent decades, the quality of the user interface in many IV pump designs has fallen under scrutiny due to many human factors–related issues, such as difficulty in setting up and managing a pump's interface through careful control and display interplay. In the past 20 years, the type, shape, and use of pumps have been, from outward appearances, very similar and not highly differentiated among the different medical device manufacturers. In fall 2002, Hospira undertook a large-scale effort to redesign the IV pump. Their mission was to create a pump that was easier to set up, easier to manage, easier to oversee patient care, and easier to use safely to help the caregiver prevent medication delivery errors. There was a clear market need for a new-generation IV pump. The Institute of Medicine in 2000 estimated 98,000 deaths a year in the United States due to medical errors (Institute of Medicine, 2000).

The User-Centered Design Process in the Context of the Incremental Commitment Model

The Symbiq™ IV Pump followed a classic user-centered design process, with multiple iterations and decision gates that are typically part of the in-

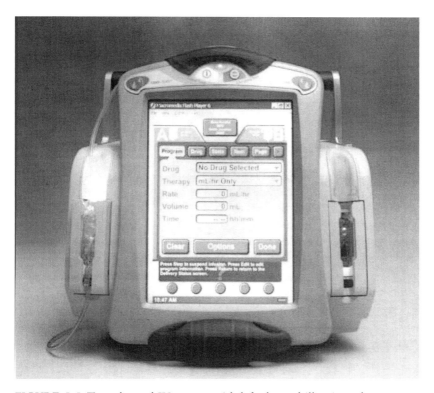

FIGURE 5-5 Two channel IV pumps with left channel illuminated.

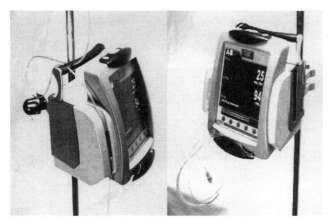

FIGURE 5-6 IV tube management features.

cremental commitment model of product development. Risk management was a central theme in the development, both in terms of reducing project completion and cost risks and managing the risk of adverse events to patients connected to the device. Many of the interim project deliverables, such as fully interactive simulations of graphical user interfaces (GUI), were in the form of shared representations of the design, so that all development team members had the same understanding of the product requirements during the development cycle.

Following a classic human factors approach to device design, the nurse user was the primary influence on the design of the interface and the design of the hardware. Physicians and home patient users were also included in the user profiles. Hospira embarked on a multiphase, user-centered design program that included more than 10 user studies, in-depth interviews, field observations, and numerous design reviews, each aimed at meeting the user's expectations and improving the intelligence of the pump software aimed at preventing medication errors.

Preliminary Research

Much preliminary work needed to be done in order to kick off this development. A well-known management and marketing planning firm was hired to lead concept analysis in which the following areas were researched:

- Comparison of the next-generation pump and major competitors, using traditional strengths/weaknesses/opportunities methodology, included the following features:
  - Physical specifications
  - Pump capabilities, e.g., number of channels
  - Therapies
  - Programming options
  - Set features
  - Pressure capabilities
  - Management of air in line
  - Battery
  - Biomedical indicators
  - Alarms
- Competitive advantages of the next-generation pump were identified in the following areas:
  - Bar code reading capability with ergonomic reading wand
  - Small size and light weight

-Standalone functional channels (easier work flow, flexible regarding number of pumping channels)
-Extensive drug library (able to set hard and soft limits for the same drug for different profiles of use)
-High-level reliability
-Clear mapping of screen and pumping channels
-Vertical tubing orientation that is clear and simple

An extensive competitive analysis was undertaken, against the five largest market leaders. Task flows and feature lists and capabilities were created. A prioritization of the possible competitive advantage features and their development cost estimates was generated and analyzed.

Business risks were examined using different business case scenarios and different assumptions about design with input from the outside management consultants. Engineering consultants assisted Hospira with input on technical development issues and costs, including pump mechanisms, software platforms, and display alternatives.

Extensive market research was conducted as well to identify market windows, market segment analyses, pricing alternatives, hospital purchasing decision processes, and the influence of outside clinical practice safety groups. Key leaders in critical care were assembled in focus groups and individually to assess these marketing parameters. This process was repeated. Key outcomes were put into the product concept plan and its marketing product description document. This document also captured current and future user work needs and the related environments.

The concept team reached a decision gate with the concurrence of the management steering committee. The project plan and budget were approved and development began. Again, business risks were assessed. This step is typical in an ICM development approach.

Design Decisions

A fundamental architecture decision was reached to have an integrated design with either one or two delivery channels in a single integrated unit. Two or more integrated units could themselves be connected side by side in order to obtain up to four IV channel lines. This alternate was chosen over the competing concept of having modular pumping units that would interconnect and could be stacked onto one master unit to create multiple channels. The integrated master unit approach won out based on problems uncovered from the market research, such as a higher likelihood of lost modular units, inventory problems, and reduced battery life.

Feature Needs and Their Rationale

Based on the preliminary market research and on an analysis of medical device reports from the Food and Drug Administration (FDA) as well as complaints data from the Hospira customer service organization, the Marketing Requirements Document was completed and preliminary decisions were made to include the features described in this section. Field studies and contextual inquiry were planned as follow-on research to verify the need for these features and to collect more detail on how they would be designed.

Types of programmable therapies. Decisions were made to offer a set of complex therapies in addition to the traditional simple therapies usually offered by volumetric IV pumps. The traditional simple therapies were

  • continuous delivery for a specified period of time (often called mL/Hr delivery).
  • weight-based dosing, which requires entering the patient's weight and the ordered drug delivery rate.
  • bolus delivery (delivery of a dose of medication over a relatively short period of time).
  • piggyback delivery (the delivery type that requires Channel A delivery suspension while Channel B delivers and then its resumption when Channel B completes).

The more complex therapies included

  • tapered therapy (ramping up and down of a medicine with a programmed timeline. It is sometimes used for delivery of nutritional and hydration fluids, called total parenteral nutrition).
  • intermittent therapy (delivery of varying rates of medication at programmed time intervals).
  • variable time delivery.
  • multistep delivery.

Business risks were examined to understand the sales consequences of including these features of therapy types to address the issue of stakeholder satisficing.

Medication libraries with hard and soft dosage limits. Research uncovered that several outside patient safety advocate agencies, including the Emergency Care Research Institute and the Institute for Safe Medical Practices were recommending only IV pumps with safety software consisting of upper and lower dosage limits for different drugs as a function of the programmed clinical care area in a hospital. (Clinical care areas include emergency room, intensive care unit, oncology, pediatrics, transplants, etc.) It became clear that it would have been imperative to have safety software in the form of medication libraries that were programmed by each hospital to have soft limits (which could be overridden by nurses with permission codes) and hard limits (that could under no circumstances be overridden). It was decided at this time that separate software applications would need to written that would be used by hospital pharmacy and safety committees to enter drugs in a library table with these soft and hard limits, which would vary by clinical care area in the hospital. This is an example of incremental growth and stakeholder commitment in the design process.

Large color touch screen. A human factors literature review was conducted to create a list of advantages and disadvantages of various input and display technologies. This research was supplemented with engineering data on the costs and reliabilities of these technologies. Again, business risks were examined, including reliability of supply of various display vendors. After much research and debate, the list of choices was narrowed to three vendors of touch-sensitive color LCD displays.

This was a breakthrough, in the sense that no current on-market IV pumps were using color touchscreen technology. A large 8.4-inch diagonal color LCD display with resistive touchscreen input was selected for further testing. A resistive touchscreen was believed to reduce errors due to poor screen response to light finger touch forces.

Another issue that required some data from use environment analysis was the required angle of view and display brightness under various use scenarios. Subsequent contextual inquiry data did verify the need for viewing angles of at least +/- 60 degrees horizontal viewing and +/- 30 degrees vertical viewing angles. The minimum brightness or luminance levels were verified at 35 candelas per square meter. A business risk analysis examined the trade-offs between a large touchscreen display and the conflicting customer desire for small footprint IV pumps. The larger display size of 8.4-inch diagonal would allow larger on-screen buttons to minimize use errors due to inadvertent selection of adjacent on-screen buttons as well as allowing larger more readable on-screen text. Again, human factors research literature and standards on display usability were included in these decisions.

Special alarms with melodies. FDA medical device reports and customer complaint data reinforced the need for more effective visual and auditory alarms to alert IV pump users to pump fault conditions, such as air in line, occlusion in IV tubing, pending battery failure, IV bag nearly empty or unsafe dosage rates for a particular drug in a specific critical care area.

The team also decided to adopt the recommendations of the International Electrotechnical Commission (IEC) for an international standard for medical device auditory alarms to use unique melody patterns for IV pumps to distinguish these devices from other critical care devices, such as ventilators and vital sign patient monitors. These auditory alarms were later subjected to extensive lab and field studies for effectiveness and acceptability.

An early beta test in actual hospital settings with extended use subsequently showed user dissatisfaction with the harshness of some of the alarm melodies. The IEC standard had purposely recommended a discordant set of tone melodies for the highest alarm level, but clinicians, patients, and their families complained that they were too harsh and irritating. Some clinicians complained that they would not use these IV pumps at all, unless the alarms were modified. Or worse, they would permanently disable the alarms, which would create a very risky use environment.

This outcome highlights a well-known dilemma for human factors: lab studies are imperfect predictors of user behavior and attitudes in a real-world, extended-use setting. The previous lab usability studies were by their very nature short-duration exposures to these tones and showed that they were effective and alerting, but they did not capture long-term subjective preference ratings. A tone design specialist was engaged who redesigned the tones to be more acceptable, while still being alerting, attention grabbing, and still in compliance with the IEC alarm standard for melodies. Subsequent comparative usability evaluations (group demonstrations and interviews) demonstrated the acceptability of the redesigned melodies. This is a prime example of design iteration and concurrent system definition and development.

Semiautomatic cassette loading. Another early decision involved choosing between a traditional manual loading of the cassette into the IV pump or a semiautomated system, in which a motor draws a compartment into the pumping mechanism, after the clinician initially places the cassette into the loading compartment. The cassette is in line with the IV tubing and IV bag containing the medication. The volumetric pumping action is done through mechanical fingers, which activate diaphragms in the plastic cassette mechanism. Customer complaint history suggested the need for the semiautomated system to avoid use error in loading the cassette and to provide a fail-safe mechanism to close off flow in the IV line except when it was inserted properly into the IV pump.

A major problem with earlier cassette-based volumetric IV pump systems was the problem of "free flow," in which medication could flow uncontrolled into a patient due to gravitational forces, with the possibility of severe adverse events. Early risk analysis and evaluation were done from both a business and use-error safety perspective to examine the benefit of the semiautomated loading mechanism. Later usability testing and mechanical bench testing validated the decision to select the semiautomated loading feature.

A related decision was to embed a unique LED-based lighting indication system into the cassette loading compartment that would signal with colored red, yellow, and green lights and steady versus flashing conditions the state of the IV pump in general and specifically of the cassette loading mechanism. The lights needed to be visible from at least 9 feet to indicate that the IV pump is running normally, pump is stopped, cassette is improperly loaded, cassette compartment drawer is in the process of activation, etc.

Special pole mounting hardware. Again, data from the FDA medical device reports and customer complaints indicated the need for innovative mechanisms for the mounting of the IV pump on poles. Later contextual inquiry and field shadowing exercises validated the need for special features allowing for the rapid connection and dismounting of the IV pump to the pole via quick release/activation mechanisms that employed ratchet-like slip clutches. Subsequent ergonomics-focused usability tests of hardware mechanisms validated the need and usability of these design innovations for mounting on both IV poles and special bed-mounted poles, to accommodate IV pumps while a patient's bed is being moved from one hospital department to another.

Risk analyses for business and safety risks were updated to include these design decisions. Industrial design models were built to prototype these concepts, and these working prototypes were subjected to subsequent lab-based usability testing. Again, these actions are examples of stakeholder satisficing, incremental growth of system definition, and iterative system design.

Stacking requirements. Given the earlier conceptual design decision to have an integrated IV pump rather than using add-on pumping channel modules, decisions were needed on how integrated IV pumps could be stacked together to create additional channels. A concomitant decision was that the integrated IV pump would be offered with either one or two integrated channels. Based on risk assessment, it was decided to allow side-by-side stacking to allow the creation of a 4-channel system when desired. The 4-channel system would be electronically integrated and allow the user interface to operate as one system. Again, trade-off analyses of risks were made against the competing customer need for a smaller device size footprint. A related design decision was to have an industrial design that allowed handles for easy transportation, but would also allow stable vertical stacking, while the units are stored between uses in the biomedical engineering department. Market research clearly indicated the need for vertical stacking in crowded storage areas. To facilitate safe storage of the pumps, the special pole clamps were made removable.

Tubing management. A well-known use-error problem of tangled and confusing IV tubing lines was addressed in the housing design by including several holders for storing excess tubing. Notches were also included to keep tubes organized and straight to reduce line-crossing confusion. These same holders were built as slight protrusions that protected the touchscreen from damage and inadvertent touch activation, if the pump were to be laid on its side or brushed against other medical devices.

Many other preliminary design decisions were made in these early stages that were based on both business and use-error risk analysis. In all cases, these decisions were verified and validated with subsequent data from usability tests and from field trials.

Design Process Details

The development of the Symbiq™ IV Pump followed the acknowledged best practices iterative user-centered design process as described in medical device standards (ANSI/AAMI HE 74:2001, IEC 60601-1-6:2004, and FDA human factors guidance for medical device design controls). The following sections are brief descriptions of what was done. Table 5-2 outlines the use of these human factors techniques and some areas for methodology improvements.

Contextual Inquiry

Contextual inquiry was done by multiple nurse shadowing visits to the most important clinical care areas in several representative hospitals. Several team members spent approximately a half-day shadowing nurses using IV pumps and other medical devices and observing their behaviors and problems. A checklist was used to record behaviors and, as time permitted, ask about problem areas with IV pumps and features that needed attention during the design process. Subsequent to the field visits, one-on-one interviews with nurses were conducted to explore in depth the contextual inquiry observations. These observations and interviews were used to generate the following elements:

- task analyses
- use environment analyses
- user profiles analyses

Figure 5-7 shows an example of one of many task flow diagrams generated during the task analyses phases of the contextual inquiry.

Setting Usability Objectives

Quantitative usability objectives were set based on data from the contextual inquiry, user interviews, and the previous market research. Early use-error risk analysis highlighted tasks that were likely to have high risk, with particular attention to setting usability objectives to ensure that these user interface design mitigations were effective. Experience with earlier IV pump designs and user performance in usability tests also influenced the setting of these usability objectives. The objectives were primarily based on successful task performance measures and secondarily on user satisfaction measures. Examples of usability objectives were

- 90 percent of experienced nurses would be able to insert the cassette the first time while receiving minimal training; 99 percent would be able to correct any insertion errors.
- 90 percent of first-time users with no training would be able to power the pump off when directed.
- 90 percent of experienced nurses would be able to clear an alarm within 1 minute as first-time users with minimal training.
- 80 percent of patient users would rate the overall ease of use of the IV pump 3 or higher on a 5-point scale of satisfaction with 5 being the highest value.

Early Risk Management

Many rounds of iterative risk analysis, risk evaluation, and risk control were initiated at the earliest stages of design. The risk-management process followed recognized standards in the area of medical device design (e.g., ISO 14971:2000, see International Organization for Standardization, 2000a). The risk analysis process was documented in the form of a failure modes and effects analysis (FMEA), which is described in more detail in Chapter 8. Table 5-3 presents excerpts from the early Symbiq™ FMEA. Business and project completion risks were frequently addressed at phase review and management review meetings.

The concept of risk priority number (RPN) was used in the operation risk assessment for the Symbiq™ infusion system. RPN is the resulting product of multiplying fault probability times risk hazard severity times probability of detecting the fault. A maximum RPN value is typically 125, and decision rules require careful examination of mitigation when the RPN

TABLE 5-2 Methodology Issues and Research Needs

Human Factors Engineering Process Step	Explanation
User profiles	All major user categories were analyzed.
Task analysis	All significant task flows were analyzed.
User environment	All significant use environments were analyzed.
Use-error risk analysis	All tasks were analyzed and use-error probabilities were estimated, as were hazard severities and risk priority values. Design mitigations were described.
Set and meet usability objectives	Objectives were set for all critical tasks using both task completion rate and satisfaction ratings.
Prototyping and iterative design	Design was iterated many times over through a series of at least 12 usability test cycles.
Usability testing	A series of formative usability tests were conducted in both usability-testing labs and in the patient simulator. A final summative usability test was completed.
Field studies	Field studies are planned for the postmarketing period. A clinical device study was conducted in two hospitals to obtain real-world usability and product effectiveness data.

NOTE: EEG = electroencephalogram; fMRI = functional magnetic resonance imaging.

Methodology Issues

Disadvantages	Methodological Research Needs
Are personas as descriptive of users as regular user profiles? Can we be sure that we have captured the majority of user profiles?	Studies of design impacts of different ways to capture users and their profiles.
Can we be sure that all significant task flows have been captured and have they been captured at the correct level of detail?	Studies of advantages and disadvantages of different approaches to task analysis, including cognitive task analysis and task modeling techniques.
Can we be sure that all significant use environments have been captured and have they been captured at the correct level of detail?	Studies to develop methods to understand limitations of current ethnographic methods for capturing information about use environments and ways to improve these methods.
When data are not available, then subjective estimates must be made for use-error rate probabilities. Group dynamics can bias the consensus ratings of hazard severity, fault likelihood, and mitigation effectiveness.	Validate estimation methods to reduce bias in consensus ratings, e.g., Delphi techniques. Research methods to improve error rate modeling.
Human performance usability objectives are usually limited to task completion rates and task times, supplemented by subjective measures of satisfaction.	Research better, more reliable, and valid outcome measurements and methods to make these measurements, e.g., fMRI, EEG, or other neuro/physiological measures.
Iteration takes time, even with rapid prototyping tools.	Develop better, quicker, more efficient methods and tools for rapid prototyping.
Usability tests also take a lot of time and resources.	Research more efficient usability evaluation methods.
It is difficult to select the optimal tasks to include in a usability study.	Create tools that allow easier selection of the most important and critical tasks to include in a test.
Can summative usability tests be done with fewer subjects and still be valid?	Investigate the use of alternative statistical analysis methods such as Bayesian statistics to conduct summative usability tests.
Field studies have the advantage of giving real-world validation to lab-based usability evaluations, but are time and resource intensive.	Research techniques that are more efficient in providing the kind of postmarket surveillance data that can be obtained from field studies.

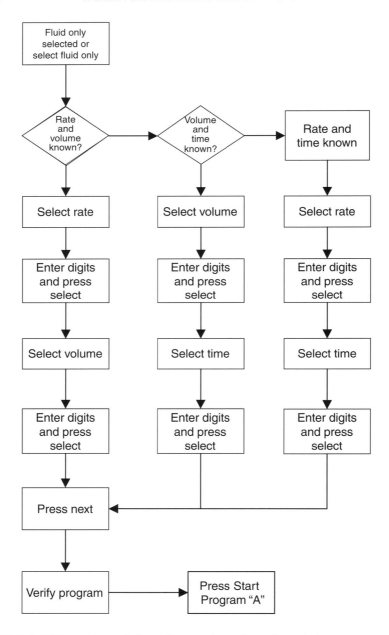

FIGURE 5-7 Illustrative task flow diagram from the task analysis.

values exceed a value of 45. RPN values between 8 and 45 require an explanation or justification of how the risk is controlled.

The product requirements document (PDR) was formally created at this point to describe the details of the product design. It was considered a draft for revision as testing and other data became available. It was based on the customer needs expressed in the marketing requirements document. This document recorded the incremental growth of system definitions and stakeholder commitment and served as a shared representation of the design requirements for the development team.

Prototypes

Many prototypes and simulations were created for evaluation:

- Hardware models and alternatives considered
  –hardware industrial design mock-ups
  –early usability tests of hardware mock-ups.
- Paper prototypes for graphical user interfaces with wireframes consisting of basic shapes, such as boxes and buttons without finished detail graphic elements.
  - GUI simulations using Flash™ animations.[1]
- Early usability tests with hardware mock-ups and embedded software that delivered the Flash™ animations to a touchscreen interface that was integrated into the hardware case.
- Flash animations are excellent examples of shared representations because they were directly used in the product requirements document to specify to software engineering exactly how the GUI was to be developed. All team discussions regarding GUI design were focused exclusively on the Flash animation shared representations of the Symbiq™ user interface.

Integrated Hardware and Software Models with Integrated Usability Tests

As noted earlier, the usability tests performed later in the development cycle were done with integrated hardware mock-ups and software simulations. Usability test tasks were driven by tasks with high-risk index values in the risk analysis, specifically the FMEA. Tasks were also included that had formal usability objectives associated with them. Although the majority of usability test tasks were focused on the interaction with the touchscreen-

---

[1]Flash refers to both a multimedia authoring program and the Macromedia Flash Player, written and distributed by Macromedia, which utilizes vector and bitmap graphics, sound and program code, and directional streaming video and audio.

TABLE 5-3 Excerpts from Symbiq™ Failure Modes and Effects Analysis (FMEA)

Task	Hazard	Use Error (Fault)	Fault Probability	Risk Hazard Severity
Enter concentration for those drugs in library with ___/___ concentration.	Patient receives over-delivery of ordered drug.	Incorrect concentration entered for drug and confirmed.	2	5
Soft limit override.	Patient receives under-delivery of ordered drug.	Soft limit unintentionally overridden and confirmed.	2	4

based graphical user interface, critical pump-handling tasks were included as well, such as IV pump mounting and dismounting on typical IV poles.

Tests of Alarm Criticality and Alerting

The initial alarm formative usability studies, described earlier, had the goal of selecting alarms that would be alerting, attention getting, and properly convey alarm priority, as well as communicating appropriate actions. These formative studies evaluated the subject's abilities to identify and dis-

Method of Control	Detect/ Mitigate Risk	Outcome (Residual Risk)	Reference
The completed program screen shows the drug selected. When START is pressed on a program screen, a second screen (confirmation screen) appears with the programmed values on the screen view looking slightly different. A query is displayed and user must select YES or NO. If YES selected infusion begins. If NO selected, user is returned to PROGRAM screen and has opportunity to correct the concentration before beginning delivery. After delivery is initiated, the user can view the entered concentration and correct if necessary by returning to the programming screen (by selecting the appropriate line A or B). The user manual provides instructions. Trailing zeros have been eliminated for whole numbers, e.g., 50.0 will be 50.	1	10	Study report for User Study Protocol #03-03 Version 3 revealed the experienced users read the confirmation screen and discovered and corrected any mistakes.
When a value entered is not within specified rule sets, a warning appears and the override soft limits icon appears. The warning indicates the value that is outside the rule sets and the clinician must confirm override, YES or NO? If YES is chosen, the confirmation screen appears with the override icon. Query is displayed and user must select YES or NO. If YES selected, infusion begins and override icon remains on screen during infusion. If NO selected, user remains on the PROGRAM screen and has opportunity to correct. The warning icon remains visible.	1	8	Study report for User Study Protocol #03-03 Version 3 revealed the experienced users questioned the messages before overriding.

criminate among different visual alarm dimensions, including colors, flash rates, and text size and contrast. For auditory alarms, subjects were tested on their ability to discriminate among various tones with and without melodies and among various cadences and tone sequences for priority levels and detectability. Subjects were asked to rate the candidate tones relative to a standard tone, which was given a value of 100. The standard was the alternating high-low European-style police siren. Subjective measures were also gathered on the tones using the PAD rating system, standing for perceived tone pleasure, arousal, and dominance, as well as perceived criticality. Data from these studies enabled the team to make further incremental decisions on system definitions for both visual and auditory alarms and alerts.

Tests of Display Readability

Another set of early formative usability tests was conducted to validate the selection of the particular LCD touchscreen for readability and legibility. During the evaluation it was determined that the screen angle (75 degrees) and overall curvature were acceptable. The screen could be read in all tested light conditions at a 15-foot viewing distance.

Iterative Usability Tests

As noted, a series of 10 usability studies were conducted iteratively as the design progressed from early wireframes to the completed user interface with all the major features implemented in a working IV pump. In one of the intermediate formative usability tests, a patient simulator facility was used at a major teaching hospital. Users performed a variety of critical tasks in a simulated room in an intensive care unit, in which other medical devices interacted and produced noises and other distractions. The prototype IV pump delivered fluid to a mannequin connected to a patient monitor that included all vital signs. As the pump was programmed and subsequently changed (e.g., doses titrated), the software-controlled patient mannequin would respond accordingly. The patient simulator also introduced ringing telephones and other realistic conditions during the usability test. This test environment helped in proving the usability of visual alarms and tones, as well as the understandability and readability of the visual displays. Final summative usability tests demonstrated that the usability objectives for the pump were achieved.

Focus Groups

Focus groups of nurses were also used as part of the usability evaluation process. These were used to complement the task-based usability tests. Many of the focus groups had a task performance component. Typically the participants would perform some tasks with new and old versions of design changes, such as time entry widgets on the touchscreen, and then convene to discuss and rate their experiences. This allowed a behavioral component and addressed one of the major shortcomings of typical focus groups, that they focus only on opinions and attitudes and not behaviors.

Field Studies

Field studies in the form of medical device studies have also been incorporated in the design process. Thoroughly bench-tested and working beta versions of the IV pump were deployed in two hospital settings. The hospitals programmed drug libraries for at least two clinical care areas. The devices were used for about 4 weeks. Surveys and interviews were conducted with the users to capture their real-world experiences with the pump. Data from the pump usage and interaction memory were also analyzed and compared with original doctor's orders. This study revealed a number of opportunities to make improvements, including the problem with the perceived annoyance of the alarm melodies and the data entry methods for entering units of medication delivery time (e.g., hours or minutes).

Instructions for Use Development and Testing

Usability testing was also conducted on one of the sets of abbreviated instructions called TIPS cards. These cards serve as reminders for how to complete the most critical tasks. These usability studies involved 15 experienced nurses with minimal instructions performing 9 tasks with the requirement that they read and use the TIPS cards. Numerous suggestions for improvement in the TIPS cards themselves as well as the user interface came from this work, including how to reset the air-in-line alarm and how to address the alarm and check all on-screen help text for accuracy.

Validation Usability Tests

Two rounds of summative usability testing were conducted, again with experienced nurses performing critical tasks identified during the task analysis, including those with higher risk values in the risk analysis. The tasks were selected to simulate situations that the nurses may encounter while using the IV pump in a hospital setting. The tasks included selecting a clinical care area, programming simple deliveries, adding more volume at the end of an infusion, setting a "near end of infusion" alarm, titration, dose calculations, piggyback deliveries, intermittent deliveries, using standby, programming a lock, adjusting the alarm volume, and responding to messages regarding alarms.

Usability objectives were used as acceptance criteria for the summative validation usability tests. The study objectives were met. The calculated task completion accuracy was 99.66 percent for all tasks for first-time nurse users with minimal training. The null hypothesis that 80 percent of the participants would rate the usability 3 or higher on a 5-point scale in the overall categories was met. There were a few minor usability problems uncovered that were subsequently fixed without major changes to the user interface or that affected critical safety-related tasks.

Federal regulations on product design controls require that a product's user interface be validated with the final working product in a simulated work environment. In this instance, the working product was used in a laboratory test, but without having the device connected to an actual patient. Bench testing is also a part of validation to ensure that all mechanical and electrical specifications and requirements have been met.

Revised Risk Analysis

As part of the incremental commitment model, the risk analysis was iterated and revised as the product development matured. FMEAs were updated for three product areas, which were safety-critical risks associated with the user interface, the mechanical and electrical subsystems, and the product manufacturing process. Explicit analysis of the business risks and the costs of continued financial commitment to the funding of development were also incremented and reviewed at various management and phase reviews.

Product Introduction

Product introduction planning included data collection from initial users to better understand remaining usage issues that can be uncovered only during prolonged usage in realistic clinical conditions. The many cycles of laboratory-based usability testing typically are never detailed enough or long enough to uncover all usability problems. The plan is to use the company complaint handling and resolution process (e.g., corrective action and preventive action) to address use issues if they arise after product introduction.

Life-Cycle Planning

The product was developed as a platform for the next generation of infusion pump products. As such, there will be continued business risk assessment during the life cycle of this first product on the new platform as well as on subsequent products and feature extensions.

Summary of Design Issues and Methods Used

This infusion pump incorporated the best practices of user-centered design in order to address the serious user interface deficiencies of previous infusion pumps. The development process took excellent advantage of the detailed amount of data that is derived from an integrated HSI approach and used it to improve and optimize the safety and usability of the design. Because of these efforts, the Symbiq™ IV Pump won the 2006 Human Factors and Ergonomics Society award for best new product design from the product design technical group.

This case study also illustrates and incorporates the central themes of this report:

1. Human-system integration must be an integral part of systems engineering.

2. Begin HSI contributions to development early and continue them throughout the development life cycle.

3. Adopt a risk-driven approach to determining needs for HSI activity (multiple applications of risk management to both business and safety risks).

4. Tailor methods to time and budget constraints (scalability).

5. Ensure communication among stakeholders of HSI outputs (shared representations).

6. Design to accommodate changing conditions and requirements in the workplace (the use of iterative design and the incremental commitment model).

This case study also demonstrates the five key principles that are integral parts of the incremental commitment model of development: (1) stakeholder satisficing, (2) incremental growth of system definition and stakeholder commitment, (3) iterative system development, (4) concurrent system definition and development, and (5) risk management—risk-driven activity levels.

Part II

Human-System Integration Methods in System Development

The chapters in Part II provide overviews of state-of-the-art methods of human-system integration (HSI) that can be used to inform and guide the design of person-machine systems using the incremental commitment model approach to system development. We have defined three general classes of methods that provide robust representation of multiple HSI concerns and are applicable at varying levels of effort throughout the development life cycle. These broad classes include methods to

- *Define context of use.* Methods for analyses that attempt to characterize early opportunities, early requirement and the context of use, including characteristics of users, their tasks, and the broader physical and organizational environment in which they operate, so as to build systems that will effectively meet users' needs and will function smoothly in the broader physical and organizational context.
- *Define requirements and design solutions.* Methods to identify requirements and design alternatives to meet the requirements revealed by prior up-front analysis.
- *Evaluate.* Methods to evaluate the adequacy of proposed design solutions and propel further design innovation.

Figure II-1 presents a representative sampling of methods that fall into each activity category and the shared representations that are generated by these methods. A number of points are highlighted in the figure:

- The importance of involving domain practitioners—the individuals who will be using the system to achieve their goals in the target domain—as active partners throughout the design process.
- The importance of involving multidisciplinary design experts and other stakeholders to ensure that multiple perspectives are considered throughout the system design and evaluation process and that stakeholder commitment is achieved at each step.
- The availability of a broad range of methods in each class of activity. Appropriate methods can be selected and tailored to meet the specific needs and scope of the system development project.
- The range of shared representations that can be generated as output of each of four HSI activities. These representations provide shared views that can be inspected and evaluated by the system stakeholders, including domain practitioners, who will be the target users of the system. The shared representations serve as evidence that can be used to inform risk-driven decision points in the incremental commitment development process.

We realize that the classification of methods for discussion in the three chapters that follow is to some extent arbitrary, as many of the methods

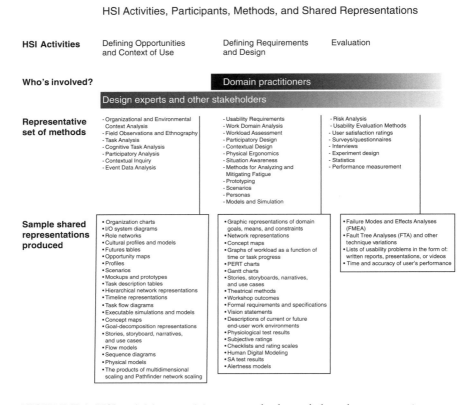

FIGURE II-1 HSI activities, participants, methods, and shared representations.

are applied at several points in the system design process and thus logically could be presented in more than one chapter. The assignment of methods to classes and chapters is based on how the methods are most frequently used and where in the design process they make the greatest contribution. As already noted, the presentation of methods is not exhaustive. We have selected representative methods in each class, as well as some less well-known methods that have been used primarily in the private sector and that we think have applicability to military systems as well. Chapter 1 provides other sources of methods.

The committee further recognizes that many of the methods described (e.g., event data analysis methods, user evaluation studies) build on foundational methods derived from the behavioral sciences (e.g., experimental design methodology, survey design methods, psychological scaling techniques, statistics, qualitative research methods). These foundational methods are not explicitly covered in this report because they are well understood in the field, and textbooks that cover the topics are widely available (e.g., Charlton and O'Brien, 2002; Cook and Campbell, 1979; Coolican, 2004; Fowler, 2002; Yin, 2003). However, two categories of foundational methods that are not explicitly covered but deserve some discussion are briefly described below. Both of these method categories—function allocation and performance measurement—are integral to the application of other methods throughout the design process.

Function allocation is the assignment of functions to specific software or hardware modules or to human operators or users. In the case of hardware and software, it is a decision about which functions are sufficiently similar in software requirements or interfunction communication to collect together for implementation. In the case of assignment to human users versus software/hardware, it is a matter of evaluating the performance capacities and limitations of the users, the constraints imposed by the software and hardware, and the system requirements that imply users because of safety or policy implications. Everyone agrees that function allocation is, at the base level, a creative aspect of the overall design process. Everyone agrees that it requires hypothesis generation, evaluation and iteration. In our view, it spans the range of activities that are represented by the methodologies we are describing and does not, by itself, have particular methodologies associated with it. There have been attempts to systematize the process of achieving function allocation (Price, 1985), but in our view they encompass the several parts of the design process that we are discussing in this section and do not add new substantive information. Readers interested in the topic itself are referred to Price (1985) and a special issue on collaboration, cooperation, and conflict in dialogue systems of the *International Journal of Human-Computer Studies* (2000).

Performance measurement supports just about every methodology that is applied to human-system integration. Stakeholders are interested in the quality of performance of the systems under development, and they would like to have predictions of performance before the system is built. While they may be most interested in overall system performance—output per unit time, mean time to failure, probability of successful operation or mission, etc.—during the development itself, there is a need for intermediate measures of the performance of individual elements of the system as well, because diagnosis of the cause of faulty system performance requires more analytic measures at lower functional levels. From a systems engineering point of view, one may consider system-subsystem-module as the analysis breakdown; however, when one is concerned with human-system integration, the focus is on goal-task-subtask as the relevant decomposition of performance, because it is in terms of task performance that measures specifically of human performance are most meaningful and relevant.

TABLE II-1 Types of Performance Measures

Types of Performance Measures		Potential Uses
a. Integrated system performance measures	• Output per unit time • Mean time to failure • Probability of successful operation or mission	• Is the overall design and implementation successful?
b. System state variables	The values of parameters reflecting the various states of the system as a function of time	• Is the system being controlled appropriately, either by automation or by human controllers? • Are safety boundaries being exceeded?
c. Human performance	• Response time • Percent correct/probability of error • Time to learn/relearn • Measures of remembering –Recognition –Free recall	• Is the system design producing the desired human performance? • Is training effective/efficient? • Is the system requiring unnecessary workload or memory load?
d. Industrial engineering measures	• Activity analysis—measures reflecting the allocation of time to different tasks • Time and motion study—measures describing in detail the literal time taken for each sequential step in a process	• What are the equipment duty cycles? • How are the users distributing their time? • What are the most challenging tasks?
e. Measures derived from human physiology	• Electroencephalographic records –Continuous wave analysis –Evoked potentials • Electro-ocular response –Eye movement tracking –Eye blink response –Pupil size • Cardiovascular measures –Heart rate/heart rate variability • Metabolic levels	• How is attention being allocated? • What information is being sought? • How attention absorbing is the task? • How stressful is the task? • What is the workload?
f. Subjective measures	• Judges/expert ratings • Questionnaire data • Interview/protocol analysis	• What are experts' opinions of user/system performance? • Do the users like the design? • How hard are the users working? • Do the users have situation awareness? • Are the users stressed?

TABLE II-1 Continued

Types of Performance Measures		Potential Uses
g. Team measures	• Time to complete team task • Accuracy/quality of team performance • Judges/expert ratings of team effectiveness • Team process measures of specific behaviors • Cognitive measures of knowledge sharing and team situation awareness	• Are levels of team performance acceptable? • How do different design decisions affect team performance? • What aspects of team performance are most critical?

Table II-1 contains some examples of the kinds of measures that are likely to be of interest.

Since each situation is different, the analyst must consider the context of use under which measurement or prediction is to be undertaken, the goals of the measurement, the characteristics of the users who will be tested or about whom performance will be inferred, and the level of detail of analysis required in order to select specific measures to be used.

6

Defining Opportunities
and Context of Use

In the past when new technologies were introduced, the focus was on what new capabilities the technology might bring to the situation. People then had to find ways to cope with integrating their actions across often disparate systems. Over time, as computational capability has increased and become more flexible, one has seen a shift in focus toward understanding what people need in given situations and then finding ways for technology to support their activities. In other words, people no longer need to adapt to the technology—the technology can be designed to do what people and the situation demand. The challenge is to understand human needs in dynamic contexts and respond with solutions that leverage the best of what technology has to offer and at the same time resonate with people's natural abilities. The emphasis and risks have switched from the technology to the users.

This chapter introduces a range of methods that can be used to gain an understanding of users, their needs and goals, and the broader context in which they operate. The methods provide a rich tool box to support two of the major classes of human-system integration (HSI) activities that feed into the incremental commitment model (ICM): defining opportunities and requirements and defining context of use. They include methods that focus on the capabilities, tasks, and activities of users (e.g., task analysis methods that characterize the tasks to be performed and their sequential flow, cognitive task analysis methods that define the knowledge and mental strategies that underlie task performance), as well as methods that examine the broader physical, social, and organizational context in which individuals operate (e.g., field observations and ethnography, contextual inquiry, analysis of organizational and environmental context).

The chapter covers a variety of complementary approaches, ranging from participatory analysis methods, which include domain practitioners as active partners, to event data analysis methods, which promise the potential of more automated and less obtrusive ways of uncovering user activities and needs. The chapter also covers methods for capturing and communicating knowledge about users and the context of use in the form of compelling shared representations, including storyboards, scenarios, role networks, and input/output system diagrams. Figure 6-1 provides an overview. Each method is discussed in terms of use, shared representations, contribution to the system development process, and strengths and limitations.

The extent to which system requirements can be defined at the beginning of a project varies. When requirements are poorly defined, there may be unanticipated opportunities for new features or new applications of the system. Typically, there are more opportunities than resources to respond to them. It is therefore prudent to define the space of opportunities and then to evaluate those opportunities and choose the most promising ones.

In order to build systems that can support users and their tasks effectively, it is important to understand the broader context of use. This strategy can be particularly important if the system needs are poorly understood, or if a new system is to be designed and deployed into a domain in which there is no predecessor system. In these cases, it is easy to engage in a rush to judgment—that is, to design and deploy a system based on assumptions, rather than on the actual opportunities that old assumptions may not reveal. However, even for systems that will occupy a known niche, it is important to understand the context of use, because field conditions and work practices change, and old solutions may no longer fit the current realities.

As illustrated in Figure 6-2, the context of use includes understanding the characteristics of the users, their motivations, goals, and strategies; the activities and tasks they perform and the range and complexity of situations that arise and need to be supported; the patterns of formal and informal communication and collaboration that occur and contribute to effective performance; and the broader physical, technical, organizational, and political environment in which the system will be integrated. Understanding the context of use is especially important as one moves toward more complex systems and systems of systems.

Context of use analysis methods are particularly important during the exploration phase of the incremental commitment model, when the focus is on understanding needs and envisioning opportunities. Among the promised benefits of leveraging context of use analyses to inform design are systems that are more likely to be successful when deployed because they

HSI Activities, Participants, Methods, and Shared Representations

HSI Activities	Defining Opportunities and Context of Use	Defining Requirements and Design	Evaluation
Who's involved?		Domain practitioners	
	Design experts and other stakeholders		

| Representative set of methods | - Organizational and Environmental Context Analysis
- Field Observations and Ethnography
- Task Analysis
- Cognitive Task Analysis
- Participatory Analysis
- Contextual Inquiry
- Event Data Analysis | | |

| Sample shared representations produced | • Organization charts
• I/O system diagrams
• Role networks
• Cultural profiles and models
• Futures tables
• Opportunity maps
• Profiles
• Scenarios
• Mockups and prototypes
• Task description tables
• Hierarchical network representations
• Timeline representations
• Task flow diagrams
• Executable simulations and models
• Concept maps
• Goal-decomposition representations
• Stories, storyboard, narratives, and use cases
• Flow models
• Sequence diagrams
• Physical models
• The products of multidimensional scaling and Pathfinder network scaling | | |

FIGURE 6-1 Representative set of methods and sample shared representations for defining opportunities and context of use.

address the specific problems facing users and are sensitive to the larger system context. Experience has shown that introduction of new technology does not necessarily guarantee improved human-machine system performance (Woods and Dekker, 2000; Kleiner, Drury, and Palepu, 1998) or the fulfillment of human needs (Muller et al., 1997b; Nardi, 1996; National Research Council, 1997; Rosson and Carroll, 2002; Shneiderman, 2002). Poor use of technology can result in systems that are difficult to learn or use, can create additional workload for system users, or, in the extreme,

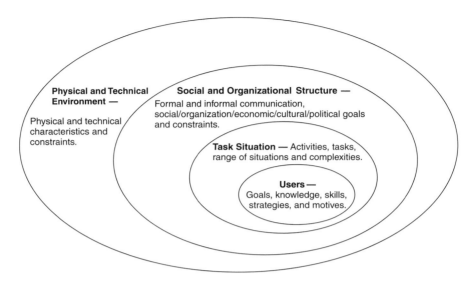

FIGURE 6-2 Context of use encompasses consideration of the user, the task situation, the social and organizational structure within which activities take place, as well as the physical and technical environment that collectively provide opportunities and impose constraints on performance.

can result in systems that are more likely to lead to catastrophic errors (e.g., confusion that leads to pilot error and fatal aircraft accidents).

Context of use analysis methods can play an important role in mitigating the risks of these types of design failures by promoting a more complete understanding of needs and design challenges as part of the incremental commitment model. This more complete understanding can help avoid common design pitfalls, such as local optimizations, in which a focus on improving a single aspect of a system in isolation inadvertently results in degradation of the overall system because of unanticipated side effects. It can also help manage "feature creep" (the proliferation of too many disjointed features in a single release) by integrating new ideas into a few, powerful innovations. Thus, an important benefit of investing in context of use analysis is a reduction in risk exposure by reducing the risk that the design will fail to meet the user's needs and thus not be adopted, as well as by reducing the risk that a design will be put in place that contributes to performance problems with costly economic or safety implications.

While we have focused on the value of context of use analyses during the early exploratory phases of the incremental commitment model, these methods continue to be relevant throughout the system development process, up to and including when systems are fielded. The context of use is constantly evolving, and introduction of new technology can produce operational and organizational changes, not all of which will have been anticipated ahead of time (Woods and Dekker, 2002; Patterson, Cook, and Render, 2002; Roth et al., in press). For example, as part of a recent power plant control room upgrade, computerized procedures were developed that integrated plant parameter information with the procedures so that the lead operator could work through the procedures without having to ask others for plant state information. This had the (anticipated) consequence of improving the lead operator's situation awareness of plant state and the speed with which the procedures could be executed. However, it decreased the situation awareness of the other crew members (an unanticipated negative consequence) because the lead operator no longer needed to keep them as tightly in the loop. This was discovered during observational studies (O'Hara and Roth, 2005) conducted as part of the initial system introduction. As a consequence, crew operating philosophy and training were completely redefined so as to capitalize on the crew members' freed-up mental resources (they could now provide an independent and diverse check on plant state), resulting in improved shared situation awareness of the entire team.

This example highlights the importance of continuing to monitor the context of use up to and beyond system introduction to establish that the intended benefits of new technologies are realized and that unintended side effects (e.g., new forms of error, new vulnerabilities to risk) are identified and mitigated. Analyses of context of use can be used to guide midcourse design corrections, as well as to lay the groundwork for next-generation system development.

ORGANIZATIONAL AND ENVIRONMENTAL CONTEXT

Overview

A guiding tenet of work-centered design approaches in human-system integration is that an understanding of the characteristics of the users, including their motivations, goals, and strategies and the context of work, should be central drivers for the specification of the entire system design and not just the user interface. The advantage of a whole-systems approach is the recognition that an organization is, in itself, a system and some organizational designs can better support the organization's mission and vision (Lytle, 1998) than others. Some context-oriented questions that drive design in a human-centered systems engineering approach include

- Who are the stakeholders, or interested parties, in the system?
- How can the voices of all of the stakeholders be heard?
- How can conflicts among stakeholders' needs be resolved?
- What are the goals and constraints in the application domain?
- What social and interactive patterns occur in the domain of practice?
- What is the broader organizational/sociopolitical context in which the work is placed?

The success of human-system design and integration is to a large extent dependent on the appropriate consideration of organizational, macroergonomic, and sociotechnical factors in a system-of-systems perspective. Macroergonomics, a subdiscipline of ergonomics, promotes an analysis of work systems at the level of subsystems or contributing factors (i.e., personnel, technological, organizational, environmental, and cultural and their interactions) before pursuing traditional microergonomics intervention. At the same time, success also depends on a continual focus on the needs of each stakeholder, as well as an openness to balance and rebalance the design and implementation trade-offs between or among stakeholder needs. In complex designs with many stakeholders, there may in fact be no global optimization, but rather a series of trade-offs that result in a system that delivers some value to each stakeholder group. It is also important to remember that, whereas requirements may become fixed, application domains seldom remain stable. As a result, any optimization scheme may turn out to be short-lived, because the conditions that were considered in crafting the optimization may themselves change.

Here, we focus on a brief introduction to analyzing the enterprise and the environment as relevant contexts for system development, using the sociotechnical systems perspective and focusing on four general methods with associated sources of data and shared representations (Table 6-1). As adapted from sociotechnical systems theory, a guiding assumption is that to evaluate factors in the environment or organization, variances between what is observed and what is desired can be identified by the analyst and should be minimized (Emery and Trist, 1978) by those responsible for operational or process improvement. A variance then is an unexpected or unwanted deviation from a standard operating condition, specification, or norm (Emery and Trist, 1978).

Key variances potentially significantly impact system performance criteria, or interact with several other variances, or both. Performance is broadly defined to include technical performance (e.g., efficiency, productivity) as well as social performance (e.g., safety, satisfaction). Typically, 10-20 percent of variances are considered key variances. The notion is not dissimilar from the notion of special and common causes of variance in quality as-

TABLE 6-1 Organizational and Environmental Methods and Respective Sources of Data and Shared Representations

General Method	Source of Data (input)	Shared Representation (output)
Organizational system scan	Authority and communication analysis Mission, vision, principle analysis Input/output analysis	Organization charts Table of gaps (variances) Input/output system model
Role analysis	Gap-focused survey, focus groups, and/or interviews	Role network
Cultural analysis	Culture survey	Cultural profile
Stakeholder analysis	Gap-focused survey, focus groups, and/or interviews	Futures table

surance. Special causes are the outliers (in a statistical sense) that should be managed first, in order to place the system in control. Once outliers are managed, common or system causes of variance can be reduced to improve overall system performance.

Shared Representations

The main purpose of this section is to make and illustrate the point that understanding and to some extent evaluating organizational context are useful endeavors. The shared representations presented have been selected for their potential appreciation by a wide and diverse audience and are the shared representations that map to a sociotechnical systems approach to organizational context.

Organization Charts: A widely known but often incorrectly or underused representation is the organizational chart, which depicts lines of authority and communication in an organization. In theory, formal, informal, and normative depictions of an organization's lines of authority and communication can be developed. The formal structure is the published chart. The informal chart is a representation of the actual lines of authority and communication in the organization and relates to the informal organization. The normative structure is the theoretical best structure, given a number of considerations.

Regarding communication processes, various theories have been proposed to explain the emergence, maintenance, and dissolution of communication networks in organizational research (Monge and Contractor, 1999). Although a detailed presentation is beyond the scope of this report, these theories consist of self-interest (social capital theory and transaction cost economics); mutual self-interest and collective action; exchange and dependency theories (social exchange, resource dependency, and network organizational forms); contagion theories, (social information processing, social cognitive theory, institutional theory, structural theory of action); cognitive theories (semantic networks, knowledge structures, cognitive social structures, cognitive consistency); theories of homophily (social comparison theory, social identity theory); theories of proximity (physical and electronic propinquity); uncertainty reduction and contingency theories; social support theories; and evolutionary theories. Regarding a theoretical "best" structure, practically, the state of the art is to choose among a set of alternative types, each with its own strengths and weaknesses. These general types and their associated strengths and weaknesses are discussed below.

Table of Organizational Variances: Mission, vision, and principles represent the identity of an organization. Mission is the purpose of the organization, vision is the envisioned future, and principles are the values or underlying virtues that guide organizational behavior. As the contextual environment for a system, the organization portrays the identity it professes through its published mission, vision, and principles statements, and it also has the actual identity represented by the perceptions of organizational members and other stakeholders or observers. Thus, there is sometimes a difference between the organizations preferred and actual profile. A table can be constructed that highlights the gaps between the preferred and the actual mission, vision, and principles and can include action items or interventions that are designed to decrease the gaps.

Input/Output System Diagram: An alternative to the organization chart is the system diagram or map. A system diagram or map is a representation of the organization as an input output model. Such depictions were popularized by Deming (2000), starting with the restoration period following World War II. Rather than depicting who reports to whom, this representation illustrates what the organization does from a process perspective. In a focus group or through a survey, opportunities for improvement are identified. Also, since systems operate as input-output transformers, depicting the organization in such terms provides an opportunity to illustrate where the technical system fits in the organizational context. Finally, as described in Kleiner (1997), performance criteria and metrics can be mapped to these systems.

Role Network: A role network, based on a role analysis, is also a useful shared representation. A job within an organization is defined by the formal job description that is a contract or agreement between the individual and the organization. This is not the same as a work role within the system, which is comprised of the actual behaviors of a person occupying a position or job in relation to other people. These role behaviors result from actions and expectations of a number of people in a role set. A role set is comprised of people who are sending expectations and reinforcement to

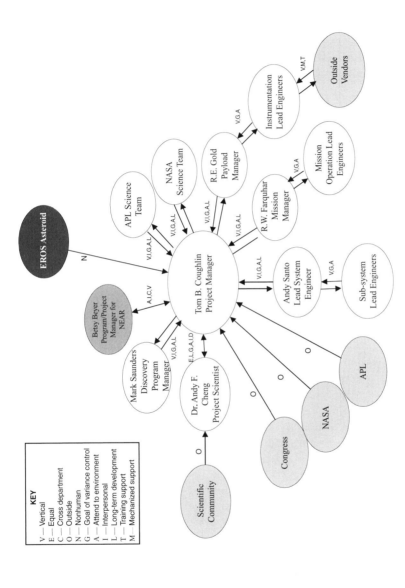

FIGURE 6-3 Role network for National Aeronautics and Space Administration (NASA's) Near Earth Asteroid Rendezvous project.

the role occupant. Figure 6-3 is an example of a role network for the Near Earth Asteroid Rendezvous (NEAR), a project managed by the Applied Physics Lab for NASA.

Cultural Profile: Shared representations related to culture include organizational culture and climate assessment tools. These typically take the form of the results produced by survey instruments. Schein (1993) describes culture at three levels: the artifacts (what is visible), espoused values (attributes that guide behavior), and basic underlying assumptions (deeply held beliefs).

Futures Table: An environmental scan is the major representation shared during environmental analysis. During a scan or analysis of the subenvironments, the key stakeholders are identified. Their expectations for the system are identified and evaluated and gaps are noted in a futures table. Conflicts and ambiguities are seen as opportunities for system or interface improvement. As with other variance or gap analyses, minimizing the variances is the objective.

Uses of Methods

Consistent with the sociotechnical systems approach, we summarize the general methods associated with the presented shared representations. Detailed coverage of nested techniques, such as survey design and analysis or focus group management, is beyond the scope of this report.

Organizational System Scan

The purpose of designing an organizational structure is to create lines of authority and communication in an enterprise in support of a strategy. In the context of system development, these lines of authority and communication establish and define ownership and management of the system in question. This will ultimately serve as a major determinant of the level of system success. The organizational design is also the manner by which an organization distributes its purpose or mission throughout the enterprise. Ideally, a given system supports the mission or purpose of the organization, and the structure facilitates accomplishment of the mission. Also, all employees and users ought to understand the overall purpose of the enterprise, the contributing role of the system, and their personal role in achieving the purposes of the system and enterprise. If the organizational design is appropriate and effective, this is more likely to occur.

Three core dimensions of organizational design underlying all organizational structures can be analyzed: these are referred to as complexity, formalization, and centralization (Hendrick and Kleiner, 2001). Complexity has two components—differentiation and integration. Differentiation refers to the segmentation of the organizational design. Integration refers to the coordinating mechanisms in an organization. Coordinating mechanisms serve to tie together the various segments. Systems often have an integrative function associated with their purpose. An increase in integration is also believed to increase complexity and therefore cost. Formalization refers to the degree to which there are standard operating procedures, detailed job descriptions, and other systematic processes or controls in the organization. Centralization refers to the degree to which decision making is concentrated in a relatively few number of personnel.

The dimensions noted above manifest themselves in different organizational structures. The functional organizational design classifies workers into common technical specialization domains. This type of design works best in small to moderately sized enterprises (up to 250 employees) that have standardized practices and a stable external environment. Some advantages of the functional organizational design include professional identity, professional development, and the minimization of redundancy. The major weakness associated with this structure is suboptimization, a condition characterized by competition, coordination, and communication challenges laterally across units at the same level in the hierarchy.

The product or divisional organizational design organizes workers by product cluster. In many organizations, divisions characterize the clusters. At the system level, many complex systems are really "products" in a divisional organizational design. The product variation of the functional design attempts to minimize suboptimization. Instead of focusing on functions, which relate to the mission only indirectly, personnel theoretically identify with a product or system and therefore the product's customer more readily. Another intended advantage with this design is to allow the development and management of profit centers. Each division (or system) can be operated as a business within the business. However, within each product cluster or division, functions typically appear. Thus, the functional units still exist, although at a lower level. Other variations, such as the geographic structure, have comparable strengths and weaknesses.

Since all of the previously mentioned alternatives are variations of the functional design, all have major shortcomings. Specifically, some suboptimization will occur. Thus, enterprise designers derived a new alternative, mostly inspired from a combination of the functional and product structures. The function x product matrix (or the function x project) attempts to integrate the best of functional and product structures. Specifically, the benefits associated with professionalism and lack of redundancy is retained from the functional design. From the product structure, a focus on the customer reduces the possibility of suboptimization.

The major flaws associated with the matrix structure are the potentially confused lines of authority and communication. For example, a complex military or aerospace system that is managed by a matrix structure could have a conflict between a safety manager (functional authority) and a project manager (project authority). Making a launch deadline at the expense of safety could be a dangerous result. One workaround for such a scenario is to determine a priori which axis has more authority or, based on decision type, identify clearly who has final authority.

Figure 6-4 illustrates a product-focused matrix organization for developing BEAST, a high-fidelity aerospace simulation tool (Eichensehr, 2006). This organization creates both advantages and challenges for the group that manages the system. The fact that product area leads (software, payloads, special projects, and large programs) all depend on the same matrix of support engineers and programmers means that goals and efforts are more easily aligned. Pockets of team members function across projects and transfer results from the latest studies and the latest software techniques. The matrix allows superior communication and effective cohesiveness over the BEAST product team (Eichensehr, 2006).

System or organizational scanning involves evaluating the organization's mission, values, history, current change activities, and business environment (Lytle, 1998). It involves defining the workplace in systems terms, including relevant boundaries. The enterprise's mission is detailed in systems terms (i.e., inputs, outputs, processes, suppliers, customers, internal controls, and feedback mechanisms). The system scan also establishes initial boundaries of the work system. As described by Emery and Trist (1978), there are throughput, territorial, social, and time boundaries to consider. Entities outside the boundaries identified during the system scan are part of the external environment which is discussed below.

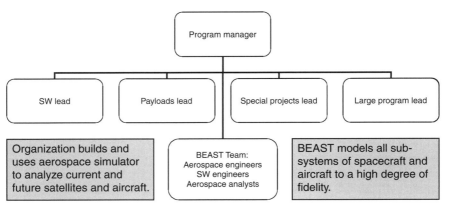

FIGURE 6-4 Example of organizational design (used with permission).

Role Analysis

Role analysis addresses who interacts with whom, about what, and how effective these relationships are. In a role network, the focal role (i.e., the role responsible for controlling key variances) is first identified. With the focal role identified at the center, other roles can be identified and placed on the diagram relative to the focal role. Based upon the frequency and importance of a given relationship or interaction, line length can be varied, where a shorter line represents more or closer interactions. Finally, arrows can be added to indicate the nature of the communication in the interaction. A one-way arrow indicates one-way communication and a two-way arrow indicates two-way interaction. Two one-way arrows in opposite directions indicate asynchronous (different time) communication patterns. To show the content of the interactions between the focal role and other roles and the evaluation of the presence or absence of a set of functional relationships for functional requirements, labels are used to indicate the goal of controlling variances. These labels might be

- adaptation to short-term fluctuations.
- integration of activities to manage internal conflicts and promote smooth interactions among people and tasks.
- long-term development of knowledge, skills, and motivation in workers.

Also the presence or absence of particular relationships is identified as follows:

- vertical hierarchy,
- equal or peer,
- cross-boundary,
- outside, and
- nonhuman.

The relationships in the role network are then evaluated. Internal and external customers of roles can be interviewed or surveyed for their perceptions of role effectiveness as well.

Cultural Analysis

A cultural context is needed for effective system development. While this section cannot be exhaustive, we intend to convey the importance of this often ignored area of system support. Organizational culture is related to the norms, beliefs, unwritten rules, and practices in an organization

(Deal and Kennedy, 1982) and is an area of organization that has been significantly understudied (Schein, 1996). According to Schein (1993), organizational culture is a pattern of shared basic assumptions that a group learned as it solved its problems of external adaptation and internal integration. This apparently has worked well enough to be considered valid and therefore to be taught to new members as the correct way to perceive, think, and feel in relation to those problems (Schein, 1993). The fundamental basis of culture has to do with underlying or foundational values. Culture is different from organizational climate. Culture is much more permanent and pervasive, whereas climate is the temporary reaction to critical incidents and events.

Culture can theoretically be changed in several ways. First, major policy changes or launches of new systems can affect the culture of an enterprise, as change can be mandated by management. Sometimes however, policy and strategic change are invalid reactions to forces from the environment. Second, changing the behaviors of leaders can induce a culture change. Leaders need to model expected behavior if they want enterprise members to modify their own behaviors and attitudes. Third, selection and training can help to change cultures. Finally, when appropriate, a comprehensive work system design change can and often will result in a culture change. Most large-scale system development launches should be conducted as part of a comprehensive work system design change. A work system design change supported by valid changes in policy and leadership and training is likely to be the best approach to achieving desired culture change and effective performance of a new or improved system.

Stakeholder Analysis

In addition to an enterprise context for systems, systems have environments that surround them and the enterprise of which they are a part. The environment is the source of resources (inputs) that are received by systems and enterprises, and it is the stakeholders in the environment that ultimately evaluate the success of the system or enterprise.

An external environment can be further divided into relevant subenvironments. Subenvironment categories typically encompass economic, cultural, technological, educational, political, and other factors. The system itself can be redesigned to align better with external expectations or, conversely, the system owners can attempt to change the expectations of stakeholders to be more consistent with system needs. According to the sociotechnical systems view, the response to variability in part will be a function of whether the environment is viewed by the system owners as a source of provocation or inspiration (Pasmore, 1988). The gaps between system and environmental expectations are often gaps of perception, and communication interfaces need to be developed between subenvironment personnel and the system owners or operators.

Contributions to System Design Phases

As part of developing an understanding of the context of use, it is desirable to understand the organizational context, specifically in terms of organizational structure, roles, culture, and the environment. Thus, analyzing these contexts is most useful at the beginning stages of the system design process. Analysis, design, and implementation that fail to include the perspectives of stakeholders can often lead to systems that fail in functional, organizational, or economic terms. Work-centered approaches attempt to prevent these types of design failures by explicitly grounding the design in the broad context of the work relationship and work practices to be performed and the sociotechnical system in which it is placed. But attention to the organization and the environment does not stop once the system is designed. As Carayon (2006) indicates, the design of sociotechnical systems in collaboration with both the workers and the customers requires increasing attention not only to the design and implementation of systems, but also to the continuous adaptation and improvement of systems in collaboration with customers. Thus, an impact can be made during the design phase, implementation, and operation of sociotechnical systems (Carayon, 2006). Table 6-2 illustrates how variances can be identified and data established for analysis when evaluating gaps between managers' and employees' perceptions.

Strengths, Limitations, and Gaps

The enterprise and the environment will have a major impact on whether a system is successful in meeting its intended mission and is well received. Hendrick and Kleiner (2001) claim that the environment is four times more powerful than other subsystems as a determinant of success. By assessing the enterprise and environmental contexts in the initial design, the likelihood of a successful outcome will be enhanced. There are several frameworks that promote this type of contextual understanding. A challenge is that the entire context cannot be known, and thus it is difficult to decide how much contextual knowledge is *enough*.

TABLE 6-2 Examples of Role Variances

Key Function from Position Description	Perception by Employer	Perception by Employee	Variance Degree	Intensity
1 Ensures that required resources are available for the program(s).	Will supervise cost engineers providing cost estimating and other services.	Only one staff in Northern VA, so doing hands-on cost engineering services (CES).	3	−3
2 Manage one or more very complex programs or portions of larger programs having a lifetime value greater than $50 million.	Will concentrate on business development activities to grow divisional revenue.	Will do business development as necessary to grow CES staff.	1	+1
3 Maintains relationships with customer to satisfy requirements and develop new or additional business opportunities.	Will perform as member of proposal teams for work pursued by other divisions and departments.	Will prepare proposals only for CES department.	3	−2
4 Serves as primary customer contact for government agency or office.	Will attend available seminars, conferences, and engineering society meetings for networking.	Will keep networking activities reasonable so as not to interfere with operations.	1	+1
5 Selects, trains, motivates, and disciplines key staff.	Will assist other program managers with project controls services.	Will assist and mentor other program managers as well as CES staff.	1	+2

FIELD OBSERVATIONS AND ETHNOGRAPHY

Overview

Ethnographic Principles

Ethnographic approaches can provide excellent in-depth reports on conditions of use in specific case studies or at specific locations or sites. These approaches are typically used to build an overall context of use for such specific, in-depth cases. It is therefore crucial to select a broad set of cases, so that the in-depth information provides a good range of what is going on in the domain of interest.

The practice of ethnography involves both a relatively obvious set of procedures and a subtler set of orientations and disciplines; without the latter, the procedures by themselves are unlikely to lead to good-quality data. Nardi (1997) notes that "one of the greatest strengths of ethnography is its flexible research design. The study takes shape as the work progresses" (p. 362). However, this flexibility may also present risks, if the analyst does not know how to make the numerous choices that are always present in field research. More broadly, Blomberg et al. (2003) state, "The ethnographic method is not simply a toolbox of techniques, but a way of looking at a problem" (p. 967). Note that this stance is almost the exact opposite of participatory analysis and design (see below), which tend to be a results-oriented set of methods and practices. We therefore begin with a set of principles of the ethnographic way of looking and then describe the practices. These principles are particularly important in defining an opportunity space.

The first principle is that ethnography is *holistic* (i.e., the assumption that all aspects of the work domain are related to one another, and that no single aspect can be studied in isolation from the others). As Nardi (1997) explains, the quality of the relationship may be complex, including not only relationships of similarity and convergence, but also ones of tension, contradiction, and conflict. This principle of holism is contrary to many experimental laboratory heuristics, which tend to control as many variables as possible, to isolate a small number of variables of interest, and then to manipulate those variables in a systematic manner. By contrast, ethnography may focus on an aspect of interest, but it remains open to discovering how that aspect of interest is related to other aspects, variables, and influences. From the perspective of defining an opportunity space, this orientation can lead to new understandings and syntheses of diverse concepts that might be considered only in isolation in more traditional analytic approaches.

The second principle is that ethnography is *descriptive*, rather than evaluative. Nardi (1997) describes some uses of ethnography for evaluation, occurring relatively late in a product life cycle; however, she agrees with Blomberg et al. (2003) that the principal use of ethnography is early in the life cycle, when evaluation would be premature. It is also the case that ethnography is specialized toward nonjudgmental descriptions, and that there are much more powerful evaluative techniques available when those are needed (see Chapter 8). The purpose of taking a descriptive stance is strategic: ethnography avoids judgment in order to remain open to possibilities, and in order to integrate diverse aspects and concepts into a rich picture of the domain (see Monk and Howard, 1998).

The third principle is that ethnography focuses on—and privileges—the *point of view of the people* whose work or lifeways are being described (the "members," as anthropologists term them). Most ethnographic reports are intended to take the reader into the mind set of the people who are described. Thus, an ethnographic report tends to require a subsequent step of translation or conversion into a set of engineering requirements. Again, this focus on the members' perspectives is an advantage when the goal is to define an opportunity space.

Finally, the fourth principle is that ethnography is usually practiced in the *members' natural setting.* In the field setting, the analyst can see things that have become so commonplace to the members that no one thinks to talk about them. There the analyst can hypothesize new relationships and can use the flexibility of ethnography to test those relationships by turning the analysis in a new direction.

Ethnographic Practices

Ethnography tends to focus on a small number of cases, and to study those cases in depth and detail. It is therefore essential to manage the diversity in those cases, to use that diversity strategically, and exercise caution in generalizing conclusions to other cases that were not studied. There are several strategies and procedures for managing these sampling issues.

As discussed by Blomberg et al. (2003), Bernard (1995) proposed an influential set of disciplined approaches for choosing samples (study sites) for ethnography. In the most controlled quota approach, the team can determine which types of sites are most representative of their application domain, and they have the ability to obtain as many samples (specific sites) of each type to satisfy their sampling requirements. The purposive approach is similar, except that the team cannot control the number of sites of each required type.

But sometimes a team cannot exercise even this much control of where or how they will collect their ethnographic data. In the convenience approach, teams improvise with whatever sites become available. One potential enhancement of this improvisational strategy is the snowball approach, in which each site helps to recruit other sites for the study.

If the analyst cannot prespecify the sites for the study, then what happens to the discipline and systematic sampling advocated by Bernard (1995)? One approach that has gained a strong following is called grounded theory (Glazer and Strauss, 1967), which makes strategic use of the diversity among sites in an ongoing, hypothesis-testing manner. In grounded theory, the analyst begins with a general research question, rather than a specific theory and hypothesis. Each site becomes an opportunity for theory creation and theory refinement concerning the research question, and part of the discipline of grounded theory is to do the hard work of revising the analyst's theory after each site. Subsequent sites are chosen precisely because they provide a strong test of the current revision of the (evolving) theory.

For example, a military ethnographer might study a first site in a flat desert setting, perhaps drawing some tentative conclusions about how warfighters create defensive perimeters based on experiences at that site. However, the terrain is likely to influence those perimeters. More subtly, the terrain might also influence how warfighters construct those perimeters and might even influence the organizational dynamics of who orders the perimeter, who constructs it, and who depends on it (recall the principle of holism described above). Therefore, the analyst would strategically choose a different terrain for the second field site—perhaps a mountainous terrain. Observations at the second site would lead to a more refined theory. The more refined theory might lead to questions that contrast natural obstacles with human-made environments. The analyst might therefore choose a third site that is in a city. And so on.

In this way, grounded theory makes strategic use of the variability that is available in the world, and strives to maximize the variance in the factors of interest. Note that this subtle discipline is quite different from laboratory studies, in which the goal is usually to minimize and control variability. The maximization of variability naturally leads to more opportunities for insights, and thus can contribute powerfully to defining an opportunity space.

Within the bounds of the chosen sampling approach (e.g., quota, purpose, convenience, snowball, or grounded theory), ethnographic practices tend to take a small number of forms. The traditional practices are interviews and observations; however, within ethnography, each of these practices has some important details.

Interviews are typically open, that is, the analyst has a list of topics to ask about, but not a list of specific questions that must be answered before the conclusion of the interview. In contrast to conventional sociological or psychological surveys, ethnographic interviews are not intended to collect a data point on each of a number of preplanned and required dependent measures. Instead, the interview follows the principle of flexibility, aiming to record a rich and holistic description of the members' perceptions of their work and world.

Observations are similarly open-ended. Ethnographers often describe observation practices along a range from observer-participant to participant-observer. The observer-participant attempts to be as unobtrusive as possible, merely recording as much data as possible. By contrast, the participant-observer attempts to join into the activities that she or he is observing and to learn about those activities "from the inside." In some cases, ethnographers supplement the observer-participant approach with recording technologies, both audio and video (e.g., Blomberg et al., 1993). In other cases, ethnographers recruit members (the people being studied) to create their own recordings or diaries (Buur et al., 2000; Wasson, 2000). Most traditional ethnographic observations tend to be broad and holistic.

When appropriate, however, the analyst may modify this breadth into a focus on a particular person, object, event, or activity.

Ethnographers emphasize that the practice of ethnography requires both (a) knowledge of specific practices and (b) a perspective and orientation that come from in-depth study—preferably in the form of an apprenticeship to a practicing ethnographer (Blomberg et al., 1993, 2003; Glazer and Strauss, 1967; Nardi, 1997). As noted above, the vital flexibility of ethnographic practice becomes strength in the discernment of an expert, but a danger in the improvisations of a novice. The practices are frequently valuable for any analyst; however, we encourage newcomers to these methods to seek advice and if possible working collaborations with more experienced practitioners.

Two recent trends are beginning to affect the well-established set of practices in ethnography. First, the Internet itself has become a new influence on culture and cultural practices. Unlike conventional face-to-face ethnographic practice, new practices are required to study people, work, play, collaboration, and spiritual practices on the Internet (e.g., Beaulieu, 2004; see also Hine, 2000; Miller and Slater, 2001; Olsson, 2000; Wittel, 2000). Because our report does not focus on Internet issues, we note this trend but do not describe it in detail.

Second, computer technology has allowed more powerful analytic methods through easy "coding" of field records or transcripts (annotations in terms of a hierarchy of terms and categories of observations) and easy sharing of coding schemes and coded materials. Some of these coding programs may also be used on multimedia field records (e.g., analog or digital video), thus extending the power and utility of those media for ethnographic record-keeping and presentation. Several commercial tools have become de facto standards in this area; see recommendations from the American Anthropology Association for details.[1]

Contributions to the System Design Process

There are major claims of the usefulness of ethnographic work to systems engineering and design (e.g., Hutchins, 1995). For an accessible survey of early success stories, see Hughes et al., (1995). For a more detailed set of accounts, see Button (1992), Luff et al. (2000), and Taylor (2001).

Nardi (1997) and Blomberg et al. (2003) provide detailed discussions of the role of ethnography in system development work. Nardi notes the variety of ways that an ethnographer continually brings users' issues to the

---

[1]For example, http://www.stanford.edu/~davidf/ethnography.html contains an updated list of free and commercial coding products, as a service of the American Anthropological Association; more generally, see http://www.aaanet.org/resinet.htm.

attention of the development team, in both early analysis and even as a proxy for users in early testing.

Blomberg and colleagues note that the interpretation of ethnographic results is a kind of analysis, carried out according to the principles reviewed above. They describe four types of potential contributions from this type of analysis to system development:

1. Propose, inform, enhance, and update the working models that developers use as they think about the end-users (see also Hughes et al., 1997).
2. Provide generative concepts to support innovation and creativity in developers' efforts to define new solutions.
3. Provide a critical lens (elsewhere called a framework) with which to evaluate and prioritize feature ideas and solution alternatives.
4. Serve as a reference for development teams.

Shared Representations

Several types of intermediary products or shared representations may be used between ethnographers and their clients (e.g., systems engineers or developers):

- Experience models are documents or visualizations that help software professionals to understand patterns of human behavior, thought, and communication.
- Opportunity maps are analytic summaries of the relationship of multiple dimensions, such as human activities versus evolutionary changes in attitudes.
- Profiles are similar to personas (discussed later in this chapter).
- Scenarios, as discussed later in this chapter and in Chapter 7.
- Mock-ups and prototypes, as discussed later in this chapter and in Chapter 7.

Strengths, Limitations, and Gaps

Much has been written of the difficulty of translating ethnographic insights into analytic requirements (e.g., Hughes et al., 1992). Crabtree and Rodden (2002) call this relationship a "perennial problem." Ethnographic investigations tend to go into great depth in a small number of sites or cases and to restrict their interpretations to these local settings (Nardi, 1997); it is difficult to generalize reliably from these small samples to the larger risk-reduction questions of what features, functions, or technologies are needed across all relevant users and circumstances (see the powerful theoretical and practical analysis of ethnographers' contextualism and engineers' abstractionism of Potts and Hsi, 1997; see also Hughes et al., 1997). Ethnographers often prefer to provide a wealth of detail, whereas systems professionals often desire a more reductionist summary (Crabtree and Rodden, 2002; Somerville et al., 2003).

One of the hallmarks of ethnography is its ability to change focus and direction when faced with new insights (Nardi, 1997), whereas systems engineering prefers a straightforward process model with known steps, milestones, and completion dates. Ethnographic investigations tend to privilege the perspective of the members (the people being described in the analysis) in rich qualitative terms, whereas systems engineering is often a matter of trading off one perspective against another through the use of common or intertranslatable metrics; these metrics are difficult to apply to a description that is couched entirely in the language of the users' workplace and world (Crabtree et al., 2000).

Much progress has been made more recently in the integration of ethnography into systems engineering. Somerville et al. (2003) provide a thematic analysis and review of issues in this evolving interdisciplinary partnership. They, as well as Hughes et al. (1997), identified three dimensions of the users' work in which ethnographers and systems engineers have been shown to make mutually beneficial knowledge exchanges: (1) distributed coordination, (2) plans and procedures, and (3) awareness of the work of others. Potts and Hsi (1997) used a similar strategy of identifying several key dimensions that can serve as conceptual landmarks for both ethnographers and engineers: (1) decomposition into goals, agents, and objects; (2) analysis of the relationships among goals, agents, and objects in terms of actions and responsibilities; and (3) a set of conceptual, literal, or historical test cases for system robustness, phrased in terms of obstacles and defenses. By contrast, Millen (2000) recommended that applied industrial ethnography be streamlined (in terms of both process and outcome) into a pragmatic set of practices called "rapid ethnography," emphasizing (1) strategically constrained focus and scope, (2) selective work with a small number of key informants, (3) convergence of evidence using multiple field data techniques, and (4) collaborative analysis of qualitative data (for related approaches to collaborative analysis of field data, see Holtzblatt, 2003; Holtzblatt et al., 2004).

The wealth of detail that is available through ethnography is undeniable. The translation of that detail into a form that is useful to systems engineers and designers has been a difficult problem, but there are now both guidelines for how to make that translation and convincing success stories of the effectiveness of the translation in a diversity of system and product environments. In the language of Potts and Hsi (1997), there are now effective ways to bring powerful insights from the contextualism of ethnography into the powerful constructive environment of systems engineering and design.

TASK ANALYSIS

Overview

Suppose you were trying to design a new control room (e.g., for a process control plant or a ship command center). How would you know what displays and controls are needed and how they should be physically laid out? Or suppose you were designing a new web site for an organization (e.g., a corporation, a university, a government agency). How would you know what information to include on the web site and how to organize the information? One of the first things you would need to know is what tasks people will be performing using the system and how those tasks are performed, so that you could design the system and related supports (e.g., procedures, training manuals, tools).

Task analysis refers to any process that identifies and examines the tasks that are performed by users when they interact with systems. Kirwan and Ainsworth (1992) provide a comprehensive review of task analysis methods, covering 25 major task analysis techniques.

Typical task analysis methods are used to understand human-machine and human-human interactions by breaking down tasks or scenarios into component task steps or physical (and sometimes also mental) operations. The result is a detailed description of the sequential and simultaneous activities of a person (or multiple people) as they interact with a device or system to achieve specific objectives. In this section we focus on task analysis methods that are particularly suited for defining tasks and the behavioral sequence of activities necessary to accomplish the task. The next section, on cognitive task analysis, describes specific methods for uncovering and representing the knowledge and mental activities that underlie more cognitive performance (e.g., situation assessment, planning, decision making).

The general task analysis process involves identifying tasks to be analyzed, collecting task data, analyzing the results to produce a detailed task description, and then generating an external shared representation of the analyzed tasks. The output is a description that includes specification of the individual task steps required, the technology used in completing the task (controls, displays, etc.) and the sequence of the task steps involved.

One of the most commonly used task analysis methods is hierarchical task analysis (HTA). HTA involves breaking down the task under analysis into a nested hierarchy of goals, subgoals, plans, and specific (mental or physical) operations (Annett, 2005).

The first step involves data collection to understand the individual(s) performing the task, the equipment or components used to perform the task, and the substeps involved in performing the task, including the stimuli that trigger a task step and the required human response. A variety of methods can be used to collect these data, including

- Observation of actual task performance.
- Task walkthroughs or talkthroughs.
- Verbal protocols.
- Tabletop analyses of expected interaction given design descriptions.
- Interviews with domain practitioners.
- Surveys and questionnaires.
- User-kept diaries and activity logs.
- Automated records (e.g., computer logs of web searches, keystroke capture).

The analysis may be based on examination of video or audio recordings of task performance, detailed notes taken during task performance, or quantitative or qualitative summaries of task performance across individuals.

An interesting example is provided by Ritter, Freed, and Haskett (2005), who performed a task analysis to identify the range of tasks that users of a university department web site might want to accomplish. They used multiple converging techniques to identify these tasks, including analysis of existing web sites, review of web search engine logs to determine typical web site search queries, and interviews of a range of different types of users (e.g., current and prospective students, staff, parents, alumni).

Once the data are collected, it is then analyzed to provide a detailed description of the task steps. In the HTA method, the overall goal of the task under analysis is specified at the top of the hierarchy (e.g., start-up plant, land aircraft, or withdraw money from an ATM machine). Once the overall task goal has been specified, the next step is to break down the overall goal into subgoals (usually four or five) that constitute subelements of the task. For example in the case of withdrawing money from an ATM machine, the substeps might be (1) inserting bank card, (2) specifying account to withdraw funds from, (3) specifying amount to be withdrawn, (4) taking money, and (5) taking bank card back. The subgoals are then further broken down into more detailed subgoals, until specific actions/operations are identified at the lowest nodes in the network. For example, in the case of withdrawing money, the lowest nodes may specify (1) type in digits corresponding to desired amount to be withdrawn, (2) press the enter key, (3) read display, (4) confirm that the amount displayed on the screen confirms to desired amount, and (5) press "yes" key.

Another typical method is a sequential task flow analysis. A flow diagram representation is used to specify the sequence of steps that would be taken under different conditions. This approach was used in the intravenous infusion pump case study described in Chapter 5 (see Figure 5-5).

In the Symbiq™ IV Pump case study, task analysis and contextual inquiry were done through multiple nurse shadowing visits to the most important clinical care areas in several representative hospitals. An important outcome of the task analysis was the foundation of the use-error risk analysis, in the form of a failure modes and effects analysis (FMEA) (see Table 5-3 for an example). Each task statement from the task analysis became a row in the FMEA of possible use errors and their consequences.

Shared Representations

A variety of shared representations are used to depict the output of the task analysis. These can take the form of graphical, tabular, or text descriptions (Stanton et al., 2005b; Kirwan and Ainsworth, 1992). Examples include task description tables, hierarchical network representations, timeline representations, and task flow diagrams. Figure 6-5 shows an example of a graphic representation of the output of a hierarchical task analysis for the simple example of an ATM withdrawal of money. Typically the graphic representation would be supplemented with text providing contextual background and details.

Examples of a task flow diagram and a task description table are provided in the risk analysis section of Chapter 8. The outputs of task analyses

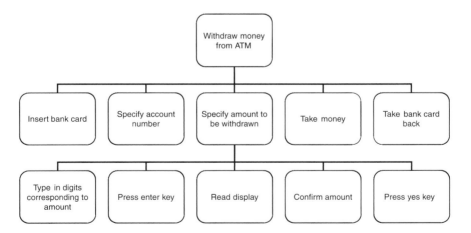

FIGURE 6-5 An example of graphic representation of a portion of a hierarchical task analysis of the "withdraw money from ATM" task. The graphic would be accompanied by textual descriptions that provided contextual background and task details.

can also be expressed as executable simulation models (see models and simulation in Chapter 7).

Uses of Methods

Task analysis methods are widely used to provide a step-by-step description of the activity under analysis. They provide a basis for assessing characteristics of a task, including the number and complexity of task steps, sequential dependencies among task steps, the temporal characteristics of the task (e.g., mean and distribution of time durations for each step and for the task as a whole), the physical and mental task requirements, equipment requirements, mental and physical workload, and potential for error.

Contributions to System Design Phases

The results of a task analysis are relevant to multiple phases in the system design process. The results of task analysis are used to inform

- function allocation.
- staffing and job organization.
- task and interface design and evaluation.
- procedures development.
- training requirements specification.
- physical and mental workload assessment.
- human reliability assessment (i.e., error prediction and analysis).

Strengths, Limitations, and Gaps

Task analysis is one of the most useful and flexible tools available for analyzing and documenting the sequential aspects of task performance. It requires minimal training and is easy to implement. Tasks can be analyzed at different levels of detail, and the output feeds numerous human factors analyses throughout the system development process.

One of the major strengths of task analyses is that they identify when, how, and with what priority information will be needed to perform *expected* tasks for which analyses have been performed. As such they provide a powerful tool for creating displays, procedures, and training to support individuals in performing tasks in the range of situations that have been anticipated and analyzed. They help to reduce the risks of device or task mismatches.

Among the disadvantages that are typically mentioned include that data collection and analysis can be resource intensive to perform thoroughly. Detailed task analyses can be particularly time-consuming to conduct for large, complex tasks (Stanton et al., 2005b). The resource commitment can be amortized if the results of a single task analysis are leveraged to feed into multiple HSI design and analysis activities (e.g., job design, procedure development, training development, human reliability analysis).

Another limitation of sequential task analysis approaches noted by Miller and Vicente (1999) is that they are prone to produce "compiled" procedural knowledge of the steps involved in performing a task, without explicit representation of the deeper rationale for why the task steps work, and how they may need to be adapted to cover situations that were not explicitly analyzed. The results of the task analysis may be narrowly applicable to the specific scenarios analyzed. As a consequence, displays, procedures, and training that exclusively rely on the results of the task analysis may be brittle in the face of unforeseen contingencies (Miller and Vicente, 1999). Work domain analysis, described in Chapter 7, provides a complementary analyses technique, intended to compensate for the potential limitations of task analysis methods.

COGNITIVE TASK ANALYSIS

Overview

Traditional task analysis approaches break tasks down into a series of external, observable behaviors. For tasks that involve few decision-making requirements (e.g., assembly line jobs, interacting with a consumer product that are expected to be easy to operate, such as ATM machines), traditional task analysis methods work well. However many critical jobs (e.g., air traffic control, military command and control, intelligence analysis, electronics troubleshooting, emergency response) involve complex knowledge and cognitive activities that are not observable and cannot be adequately characterized in terms of sequences of task elements. Examples of cognitive activities include monitoring, situation assessment, planning, deciding, anticipating, and prioritizing. Cognitive task analysis (CTA) methods have emerged that are specifically tailored to uncovering the knowledge and cognitive activities that underlie complex performance. CTA methods provide a means to explicitly identify the requirements of cognitive work so as to be able to anticipate contributors to performance problems (e.g., sources of high workload, contributors to error) and specify ways to improve individual and team performance (through new forms of training, user interfaces, or decision aids).

CTA methods provide *knowledge acquisition* techniques for collecting data on the knowledge and strategies that underlie performance as well as methods for *analyzing and representing* the results. A variety of specific techniques for knowledge acquisition have been developed that draw on basic principles and methods of cognitive psychology (Ericsson and Simon, 1993; Hoffman, 1987; Potter et al., 2000; Cooke, 1994; Roth and Patterson, 2005). These include structured interview techniques, such as applied cognitive task analysis (Militello and Hutton, 2000) and goal-directed task analysis (Endsley, Bolte, and Jones, 2003); critical incident analysis methods that investigate actual incidents that have occurred in the past (Flanagan, 1954; Klein, Calderwood, and MacGregor, 1989; Dekker, 2002); cognitive field observation studies that examine performance in actual environments or in high-fidelity simulators (Woods, 1993; Roth and Patterson, 2005; Woods and Hollnagel, 2006, Ch. 5); "think-aloud" protocol analysis methods in which domain practitioners are asked to think aloud as they solve actual or simulated problems (e.g., Gray and Kirschenbaum, 2000); and simulated task methods in which domain practitioners are observed as they solve analog problems under controlled conditions (Patterson, Roth, and Woods, 2001).

Schraagen, Chipman, and Shalin (2000) provide a broad survey of different CTA approaches. Crandall, Klein, and Hoffman (2006) provide an excellent how-to handbook with detailed practical guidance on how to perform a cognitive task analysis. Comprehensive catalogues of CTA methods and additional guidance can also be found on two active web sites: http://www.ctaresource.com maintained by Aptima, Inc., and http://www.mentalmodels.mitre.org/, maintained by MITRE Corp.

Representative Methods

One of the most powerful means of uncovering the cognitive demands inherent in a domain and the knowledge and skills that enable experts to cope with its complexities is to study actual incidents that have occurred in the past to understand what made them challenging and why the individuals who confronted the situation succeeded or failed (Flanagan, 1954; Dekker, 2002). The critical decision method (CDM) is a structured interview technique using that approach (Klein, Calderwood, and MacGregor, 1989; Hoffman, Crandall, and Shadbolt, 1998; Klein and Armstrong, 2005). It is one of the most widely used CTA methods. The CDM approach involves asking domain experts to describe past challenging incidents in which they have participated.

A CDM session includes four interview phases or "sweeps" that examine the incident in successively greater detail. The first sweep identifies a complex incident that has the potential to uncover cognitive and collaborative demands of the domain and the basis of domain expertise. In the second sweep, a detailed incident timeline is developed that shows the sequence of events. The third sweep examines key decision points more deeply using a set of probe questions (e.g., What were you noticing at that point? What was it about the situation that let you know what was going to happen? What were your overriding concerns at that point?). Finally the fourth sweep uses what-if queries to elicit potential expert-novice differences (e.g., someone else, perhaps with less experience might have responded differently). The output is a description of the subtle cues, knowledge, goals, expectancies and expert strategies that domain experts use to handle cognitively challenging situations.

Concept mapping is another interview technique that has been used to uncover and document the knowledge and strategies that underlie expertise (Crandall, Klein, and Hoffman, 2005). In this kind of knowledge elicitation, the CTA analyst helps domain practitioners build up a representation of their domain knowledge using concept maps. Concept maps are directed graphs made up of concept nodes connected by labeled links. They are used to capture the content and structure of domain knowledge that experts employ in problem solving and decision making. Concept mapping are typically conducted in group sessions that include domain experts (e.g., three to five) and two facilitators. One facilitator provides support in the form of suggestions and probe questions, while the second facilitator creates the concept map based on the participants' comments for all to review and modify. The output is a graphic representation of expert domain knowledge that can be used as input to the design of training or decision aids. Figure 6-6 is an example of a concept map that depicts the knowledge of cold fronts in Gulf Coast weather of an expert in meteorology.

Cognitive task analysis techniques have been developed to explore how changes in technology and training are likely to impact practitioner skills, strategies, and performance vulnerabilities. The introduction of new technologies can often have unanticipated effects. This has been referred to as the "envisioned world" problem (Woods and Dekker, 2000). New, unanticipated complexities can arise that create new sources of workload, problem-solving challenges, and coordination requirements. In turn, individuals in the system will adapt, exploiting the new power provided by the technology in unanticipated ways, and creating clever work-arounds to cope with technology limitations, so as to meet the needs of the work and human purposes.

CTA techniques to explore how people are likely to adapt to the envisioned world include using concrete scenarios or simulations to simulate the cognitive demands that are likely to be confronted. Woods and Hollnagel (2006) refer to these methods as "staged world" techniques. One example is a study that used a high-fidelity training simulator to explore how new computerized procedures and advanced alarms were likely to affect the strategies used by nuclear power plant crews to coordinate activities and

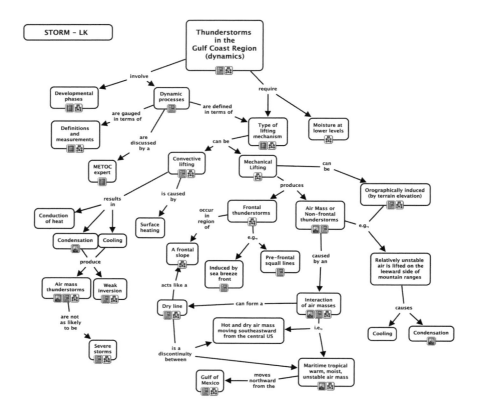

FIGURE 6-6 An example of a concept map that represents expert knowledge of the role of cold fronts in the Gulf Coast (Hoffman et al., 2006). It was created using a software suite called CmapTools. Icons below the nodes provide hyperlinks to other resources (e.g., other cmaps, and digital images of radar and satellite pictures; digital videos of experts). CmapTools was developed at the Institute for Human and Machine Cognition, and is available for free download at http://ihmc.us.

maintain shared situation awareness (Roth and Patterson, 2005). Another example is a study by Dekker and Woods (1999) that used a future incident technique to explore the potential impact of contemplated future air traffic management architectures on the cognitive demands placed on domain practitioners. Controllers, pilots, and dispatchers were presented with a series of future incidents to jointly resolve. Examination of their problem solving and decision making revealed dilemmas, trade-offs, and points of vulnerability in the contemplated architectures, enabling practitioners and developers to think critically about the requirements for effective performance for these envisioned systems.

Relationship to Task Analysis

The boundary between task analysis methods and cognitive task analysis methods is not always clear-cut. While cognitive task analyses focus on cognitive aspects of performance and task analyses have the objective of describing the sequence of activities required to perform a task, there can be overlap in the types of information covered by each approach (Annett, 2000). Task analyses can include information-processing activities as well as external physical activities. In turn, cognitive task analyses will tend to specify the physical activities required to access and integrate the information needed for cognitive tasks (e.g., if a cognitive task requires integrating information across multiple displays, communicating with others, or traversing physically disparate locations, these will be captured in a cognitive task analysis).

A Bootstrap Process

Cognitive task analysis is fundamentally an opportunistic bootstrap process (Potter et al., 2000). The CTA process generally involves the use of multiple converging techniques. In a typical CTA approach, the cognitive analyst might start by reading available documents that provide background on the field of practice (e.g., training manuals, policy and procedure guides). This background knowledge raises new questions and hypotheses that can then be addressed through field observations or interviews with domain practitioners. These in turn may point to complicating factors in the domain that place heavy cognitive demands on the user and create opportunities for user error. The information can be used to create scenarios that illustrate the complexity in the domain. These scenarios can then be used to observe practitioner performance under simulated conditions, comparing the strategies used by experts with those of less experienced domain practitioners. The scenarios can also be used to evaluate the effectiveness of proposed design concepts for supporting performance under challenging conditions.

The particular set of CTA techniques selected will generally depend on the goals of the analysis and the pragmatics of the specific local conditions (e.g., access to domain practitioners, practicality of performing observations in the actual work environment). If the goal of the analysis is to identify leverage points at which new technology could have significant positive impact, then techniques that provide a broad brush overview of cognitive and collaborative requirements and challenges in a domain, such as field observations and structured interviews, can be very effective. If the goal is to develop training programs or to produce assessment protocols to establish practitioner proficiency (e.g., for accreditation purposes) then methods that capture the detailed knowledge and skills (e.g., mental models, declarative and procedural knowledge) that distinguish practitioners at different levels of proficiency (e.g., the CDM and process trace approaches) can be particularly useful. If the goal is to develop a computer model that simulates the detailed mental processes involved in performing a task, then techniques such as the think-aloud verbal protocol methods may be most appropriate.

CTA in the Unmanned Aerial Systems Case Study

The hypothetical case study in Chapter 5 on unmanned aerial systems illustrates the application of cognitive task analysis to the design of an envisioned system. The focus of the cognitive task analysis was workload, but not physical workload. Rather, cognitive or mental workload was examined using a variety of methods, including interviews, observations, accident reports, and event data analysis. The results of the analysis revealed that cognitive workload was not constant but peaked at target areas and when replanning routes. This analysis of the task of operating an unmanned aerial system from a cognitive perspective provided information pertinent to determining the appropriate use of automation for control of multiple unmanned aerial systems. That is, based on these hypothetical results, automation would be most useful at these points of peak cognitive load, as opposed to the en route part of the task.

Shared Representations

The output of a cognitive task analysis can take multiple forms. In some cases, the output is a prose description of critical incidents and the cognitive demands and strategies they reveal. It can also take the form of structured tables that catalogue the decision points that arise, why they are difficult, the knowledge and skill that enable experts to handle the situation, and the typical errors that less experienced personnel make. Other shared representations that are produced from a cognitive task analysis are concept maps that provide graphic depictions of the structure and content of knowledge of domain practitioners (both experts and less experienced individuals) and diagrams that illustrate the problem-solving strategies used by domain practitioners (e.g., contrasting expert versus novice strategies).

The hierarchical task analysis formalism described in the task analysis section can also be used to represent the output of a cognitive task analysis (Annett, 2000). In that case, the goal-subgoal decomposition would include information-processing activities as well as overt physical actions. The GOMS method, which decomposes complex cognitive tasks into goals, operators, methods, and selection rules (Card, Moran, and Newell, 1983) provides another example of a goal decomposition representational approach (see Chapter 7). The goal-directed task analysis method developed by Mica Endsley (Endsley, Bolte, and Jones, 2003) is another example of an approach that produces a goal decomposition representation. In that method, two complementary representations are produced: a goal hierarchy that is similar to a hierarchical task analysis representation and a relational hierarchy that explicitly identifies the decisions related to each goal and subgoal, as well as the information needed to support those decisions.

The output of a cognitive task analysis can sometimes also take the form of a runnable computational model (e.g., an ACT-R model). The section on models and simulation in Chapter 7 provides a number of examples of computational models that have been developed to elucidate cognitive task performance.

Uses of Methods

The output of a cognitive task analysis is used to define the knowledge, skills, problem-solving, and decision strategies that are required for effective performance in the domain. The output can be used to specify requirements for training, procedures, displays, and decision aids. It can also be used to guide personnel selection, manning, and function allocation decisions. The results of cognitive task analysis can also be used as input to workload analysis and human reliability modeling.

Contributions to System Design Phases

Cognitive task analyses are particularly useful as part of early context of use analyses in support of understanding needs and envisioning opportunities. They can be used to help focus further analyses and design efforts on aspects of performance that are most cognitively challenging and error prone and identify leverage points at which the introduction of new technology can have the most positive impact on performance. The output of a cognitive task analysis can also be used to define cognitively demanding scenarios and targets for effective performance that can inform design. The scenarios and performance targets can also be used in later evaluations of the effectiveness of the new design.

Strengths, Limitations, and Gaps

CTA methods are powerful tools for uncovering the complexities in a domain, the knowledge and strategies that underlie expert performance, as well as the contributors to performance difficulty and errors.

CTA methods can be resource intensive. Interviews and observations can be time-consuming to conduct and analyze. They require access to domain experts, which can sometimes be difficult to arrange. Finally, they require analysts who have a background in behavioral sciences and training in CTA methods to conduct and analyze the cognitive task analyses.

While CTA methods can be resource intensive, the CTA tool kit contains a variety of methods that can be tailored to the needs and constraints of the particular application. For example, if access to the actual work environment is not possible, precluding the possibility of conducting field observations, then structured interview techniques can be used. If experts cannot discuss actual cases (e.g., because the information is classified or proprietary) then analyses can be conducted using simulated scenarios or analogous problems. If access to domain experts is not possible, it may be possible to conduct a cognitive task analysis based on review of documented descriptions of past critical incidents (e.g., accident reports).

One of the current gaps that limits CTA productivity is the paucity of computational tools to help in the capture, organization, dissemination, and retrieval of CTA results. Better software tools could improve the efficiency of CTA analyses. They could support the development of a corpus of knowledge that could be updated more easily as new information is learned, communicated to stakeholders more effectively, and accessed and reused more readily across the life cycle of a development project (the same cognitive task analysis could be used to inform design, development of procedures, development of training, and development of safety-case submittals). Such a resource would be especially valuable in complex design projects whose development can span multiple years across multiple organizations. In the current state of practice, organizations are often not aware of cognitive task analyses (or other analyses of context of use) that have been performed previously by others (especially if they have been conducted by other organizations). In cases in which they are aware of prior relevant analyses, the results may not be available to them, or they may be in a form that is difficult to assimilate. At the same time, it can be cost-prohibitive for each new group or organization to conduct a cognitive task analysis from scratch. As a consequence, design efforts are forced to short-circuit the analysis step, even while recognizing its importance because of time and cost constraints. The same difficulty arises for all the context of use methods covered in this chapter. All would benefit equally from improved computational methods for capture, dissemination, and reuse of analysis results.

PARTICIPATORY ANALYSIS

Overview

This section briefly reviews methods in participatory analysis—a field that has been intensely developed since the late 1970s and that we think is ready for use in large systems.

There is evidence that users can participate as insightful and innovative collaborators during all stages of product life cycles. For collections of examples of notable projects and products, see Bjerknes, Ehn, and Kyng (1987), Greenbaum and Kyng (1991), Muller and Kuhn (1993), Noro and Imada (1991), Schuler and Namioka (1993), and the *Proceedings of the Participatory Design Conferences* (even-numbered years from 1990 to 2006; available at http://www.cpsr.org/). For book-length treatments of the users' roles as co-analysts, co-designers, and co-evaluators, see Beyer and Holtzblatt (1998), Carroll (2000), Checkland (1981), Ehn (1988), Mumford and Henshall (1983), and Rosson and Carroll (2002).

Research in participatory analysis and design has tended to focus on three factors for effective user participation. The first is the use of well-tested group or workshop settings that improve the ability of all the stakeholders to participate on an egalitarian basis. The second factor is the establishment of well-understood relationships and project governance structures that include an explicit set of roles and responsibilities for users on the project team (e.g., Bjerknes and Bratteteig, 1987; Bødker et al., 1987; Rector et al., 1992). The third factor is the use of specific methods and practices for participatory analysis, design, or evaluation (for catalogues of over 70 such methods, see Bødker et al., 2004; Ehn and Löwgren, 1997; Muller, Haslwanter, and Dayton, 1997a; Muller, 2007).

The crucial aspect of all of these approaches is the full sharing of diverse expertise and knowledge, as well as an orientation toward mutual learning. Bødker et al. (1988) spoke of the "mutual validation of diverse perspectives." Floyd (1987) wrote of methods as opportunities for learning. Muller et al. (1994) described participatory work as depending on three factors: the sharing of diverse expertise, stakeholder commitment, and democratic practices for knowledge sharing, conflict clarification, problem solving, and the creation of new solutions.

Participatory analysis provides methods for understanding the current state of work, including technologies and work practices. Participatory design provides methods for improving the state of work in various ways, and it is treated in detail in the next chapter. All methods are assumed to be performed in collaboration with users—as co-reporters of the current state of work, as co-analysts of how the work is proceeding, and as co-designers for improved work practices and technologies. In some interpretations, users have had a co-contributor role and also a co-director role (see, e.g., the collective resource approach of Ehn and Kyng, 1987). In North America, it is more common to find users as co-contributors whose work domain knowledge is valued as highly as the more traditional knowledge of technologists, engineers, designers, marketers, trainers, and others (e.g., Beyer and Holtzblatt, 1998; Blomberg et al., 2003; Holtzblatt, 2003; Holtzblatt and Beyer, 1993; Muller et al., 1994; Noro and Imada, 1991; Sanders, 2000; Wixon and Ramey, 1996).

Methods in participatory analysis assist users to describe their work, their work organizations, their work technologies, and their work contexts. Method development in this area has tended to be diverse and creative. We focus on four approaches that have developed a sustained record of experiences and successes.

Participatory Workshops

One strategy for understanding context of use is to leverage directly the knowledge of the workforce (or warfighters in the military)—that is, to work directly with people who are already doing the work that the new system will support, or who are doing related work, or who will be the primary users of the new system. Historically, this approach has been termed participatory design; it is described in Bjerknes, Ehn, and Kyng (1987), Greenbaum and Kyng (1991), Muller and Kuhn (1993), Mumford and Henshall (1983), and Schuler and Namioka (1993). This strategy involves (1) determining crucial knowledge holders and (2) facilitating communication among them so that they can combine their diverse knowledge, expertise, backgrounds, and perspectives to create new and emergent concepts.

At first glance, this appears to be an easy task: get the right people together and ask them to brainstorm. Experience has shown that this simple version of the activity can be surprisingly difficult when the participants come from different disciplines, knowledge traditions, social classes, or power positions in the organization (e.g., officers and enlisted personnel in the military, management and labor in a commercial enterprise). One of the subtle problems is to create a level playing field on which people can contribute on an egalitarian basis, despite the fact that they may have very different power relationships outside the context-of-use activity. A second subtle problem is that diverse groups often need to discover their common ground and to co-create a common language that is synthesized from their diverse backgrounds (Muller, 2003). Over the years, practitioners and researchers in the participatory design tradition have developed specific workshop approaches to resolve these subtle problems. Three workshop approaches are briefly discussed below: future workshops, strategic design workshops, and visual workshops. A comparative review is provided by Muller (2003), as well as a more encyclopedic treatment (Muller, Haslwanter, and Dayton, 1997).

Future workshops.   One of the most effective workshop formats is the future workshop. Originally developed for German civic planning (Jungk and Mullert, 1987), future workshops have been used in diverse software engineering settings and are now included in the emerging participatory information technology methodology of Bødker et al. (2004).

A future workshop proceeds through three phases:

1. Critique the present.
2. Envision the future.
3. Implement the changes to move from the present to the future.

The critique phase allows diverse participants to understand one another's perspectives and experiences, often fostering a co-ownership of the problems that are explained from each stakeholder's point of view. This phase also produces a list of problems to be solved. This list of problems leads to the second phase, in which the group attempts to envision and co-create future solutions to those problems. Those solutions will require implementation, and of course not all solutions *can* be implemented within existing resource limitations. Encountering these kinds of obstacles can send the group back to the phases of envisionment or even critique, before they can develop a proposal for feasible, resource-constrained solutions. Thus, the framework of the future workshop provides minimal structure that has been proven to produce high-quality solution proposals that combine diverse knowledge and experiences, with buy-in and commitment by diverse stakeholders.

Strategic design workshops.   Sanders and colleagues have shown the value of a three-activity workshop protocol called strategic design workshops (Sanders, 2000). These workshops combine methods from market research, ethnography, and participatory design. Activities can include both qualitative, imaginative work (e.g., collages), lay formalization (mapping envisioned work processes on paper), and storytelling. The workshops produce a suite of potential opportunities for further investigation and refinement.

Drawing and other visual workshops.   Several less formal workshop approaches have focused on people's ability to co-analyze, co-create, and co-evaluate ideas using simple graphical communications. Monk and Howard (1998) described freehand collaborative drawing of a conceptual map of the work domain. Dray (1992) provided a more structured approach, in which a group develops a set of related visual concepts through a round-robin brainstorming technique, in which each person spends a few minutes creating an initial diagram, then gives the diagram to another team member for further elaboration, while simultaneously receiving another diagram that had been begun by another team member. Each diagram passes sequentially through the hands of all team members, one at a time. Thus, each diagram becomes one version of a solution, but all versions have received contributions from all team members.

Scenarios in Participatory Analysis

Some participatory analysis methods focus on storytelling to create a level playing field, to put users and technologists on a common footing; in more formal terms, these techniques have been described and analyzed as scenario-based methods (Carroll, 1995, 2000; Carroll, Rosson, and Carroll, 2002, 2003). The scenario-based methods tend to flow smoothly from analysis to design; we make a somewhat arbitrary separation into an "analysis" section in this chapter, and a "design" section in the following chapter.

Low-Technology Representations

One way to document a scenario is through a series of narrative storyboards. Work of Muller and colleagues pursued the level playing field approach through partially structured paper-and-pencil materials to assist users in documenting their own work scenarios in the form of storyboards (Lafrenière, 1996; Muller, 2001; Muller et al., 1995). While these methods were initially conceived as "card games" for participatory analysis, their value emerges more clearly in relation to the scenario methods (described above) and to the generation of engineering requirements (described below).

Earlier work used "cardboard computers" as a means of both describing current working practices and envisioning future working practices (e.g., Ehn and Kyng, 1991; Henderson and Kyng, 1991). Users and other co-analysts act out the current and proposed work practices, using low-tech materials as stage props in informal dramas.

The work with low-technology representations tends to blur the divisions between analysis and design. That is, when people are describing current working practices, they often have profound ideas about how to improve them. Good participatory analysis methods provide a means for capturing and elaborating these design insights and innovations as well.

This blurring of the line between analysis and design can often be powerful, leading to new insights and also to significant savings in time and resources (i.e., combining two life-cycle stages that are often treated as different steps in more formal engineering methods).

Multimedia Documentaries

Other more experimental methods have highlighted documentary materials prepared by users—specifically photo documentaries (Dandavante et al., 2000; Hulkko et al., 2004; Noble and Robinson, 2000) and video documentaries (Björgvinsson and Hillgren, 2004; Mørch et al., 2004). Buur's work (Buur et al., 2000; Pedersen and Buur, 2000; Bødker and Buur, 2002) includes procedures for creating small video clips as starting points in participatory analysis of the working practices shown in those clips (see Ehn and Sjögren, 1991, and Klær and Madsen, 1995, for earlier work using brief textual descriptions as starting points for similar participatory analysis discussions).

Contributions to the System Design Process

The common theme is to find methods that do not require skills or knowledge of technology, but that can instead support users in expressing the knowledge that is uniquely theirs. Formal engineering models are included in scenario-based analysis (see above). Practices have been developed for the other approaches, to translate between the informal, contextual, concrete, rich world of users and usage, and the more formal, decontextualized, abstract, and somewhat impoverished but powerful representations that are tractable for systems analysis. Table 6-3 provides a synopsis of how each participatory method may be of use in the system development process.

Shared Representations

Each category of participatory analysis method produces its own characteristic shared representation.

The scenario-based methods produce stories, storyboards, narratives, and (potentially) use cases and flow charts of users' work. Long stories are problematic for systems engineers, but briefer stories, summarized into the components or elements of systems engineering requirements (e.g., use cases), may be very helpful.

The low-technology representations produce exactly those representations, plus a set of insights, narratives, use cases, and other means of contextualizing those representations in the users' work. The informality

TABLE 6-3 How Participatory Methods Fit into the System Development Process

Method	Role in System Development Process	Shared Representation and Use
Participatory workshop	Understanding context of use Early problem analysis Voice of the user/customer Opportunity analysis	Workshop report (usually informal, except for the following method)
Future workshop	Problem analysis Proposed solutions Opportunity analysis	Structured report (critique, vision, implementation)
Participatory scenarios	Understanding context of use Problem analysis Proposed solutions Pros and cons of solutions	Stories, storyboards, narratives, in-depth experiences by members of the project team
Low-technology representations	Understanding context of use Early designs Design alternatives	Examples of artifacts (current or future) Designs Informal requirements
Documentaries	Understanding context of use Opportunity analysis	In-depth description "Day in the life"

of the materials may make them appear to be less authoritative, but that informality is also a strength, in that it invites interpretation and further refinement. In the more process-oriented methods, such as the collaborative analysis of requirements and the collaborative analysis of requirements and design, it is possible to create a set of materials that correspond to a preexisting high-level, object-oriented analysis of the components of the system, with the result that the outcome is very easy to translate into the language of systems engineering (Muller, 2001; Lafrenière, 1996).

Multimedia documentaries produce various personalized or group-authorized accounts of work. These are somewhat more difficult to integrate directly into the work of systems engineers. These shared representations may thus require a subsequent interpretation or translation into a more consumable information product.

The shared representations and issues related to ethnography are also relevant here.

Strengths, Limitations, and Gaps

Participatory analysis methods are often very fast to execute. Their historic support of democratic work practices may be an advantage in some settings and a disadvantage in others. In any event, they require skilled facilitation. Their openness may lead to a lack of rigor, and their strategic informality (to increase end-user participation) may also become a weakness (they do not look like formal engineering methods).

Addressing the problem of informality, Kensing and Munk-Madsen (1993) described correspondences between a set of concrete, informal end-user-accessible methods and a second set of abstract, formal methods from software engineering. This work was pursued subsequently in a paper to introduce a formal participatory methodology (Kensing et al., 1996) and eventually in a book-length treatment of participatory approaches to information technology (Bødker et al., 2004).

CONTEXTUAL INQUIRY

Overview

Unlike the preceding approaches, contextual inquiry is less concerned with egalitarian contributions by users and analysts and more concerned with structuring users' in-depth contributions to the work of the professional analysts (Beyer and Holtzblatt, 1998; Holtzblatt and Beyer, 1993; Holtzblatt et al., 2004; Wixon and Ramey, 1996). Contextual inquiry is a set of methods for informing analysis with the users' context and working practices, and for interpreting those analyses into engineering requirements. Several systematic book-length treatments of this well-developed methodology exist, so we provide only a brief summary here.

The analytic work of contextual inquiry flows smoothly into the synthetic work of contextual design (e.g., Holtzblatt, 2003). For application to the large-systems work addressed in this report, we separate these two types of endeavor into a section on analysis in this chapter, and a second section on design in the following chapter.

Contextual inquiry pursues three major activities:

1. *Contextual inquiry*—conduct observations and interviews with users (including, in some treatments, a specialized "contextual interview").

2. *Interpretation*—work intensively with members of the development team to understand what was learned in the inquiry step. The interpretation step often focuses on a case study or a single individual at a time, in order to create five relatively formal models of the work.

3. *Affinity analysis*—combine the individualized interpretations and models into a more consolidated view, finding commonalities where appropriate and preserving individual perspectives.

Contextual inquiry begins with investigations in the users' workplace. Interviews and observations are conducted there, with an emphasis on partnership between the investigator and each individual user. The interviews and observations often include a summary statement by the investigator of what was learned, so that the user can correct or elaborate on the investigator's new knowledge and interpretation.

When the investigator returns to her or his team, the entire cross-functional team is convened to discuss the findings and to develop a shared interpretation of those findings. In general, these meetings are strongly participative by team members and produce diverse types of informal and interim representations for team use, largely based on textual notations that are annotated and reconfigured during interpretative meetings. Further such meetings are convened to consolidate data from multiple customers or multiple sites, with the goal of co-constructing affinity diagrams that provide a hierarchical organization of commonalities and differences across sites. More formal models of work and support technologies (see below) begin from these affinity diagrams.

Shared Representations

In the course of these three activities, the contextual inquiry approach creates five analytic models:

1. *Flow model*—a high-level summary of work processes and communication patterns.
2. *Sequence model*—a detailed analysis of the steps required to perform a task.
3. *Physical model*—a literal description of the work context and constraints in terms of objects and spaces.
4. *Cultural model*—a conceptual description of the policies, working practices, attitudes, organizational contexts, and national or group contexts—a second type of "context and constraints."
5. *Artifact model*—a detailed description of the materials and tools involved in the work.

These models are created and elaborated through a series of well-understood methods, such as specific types of brainstorming, diagramming, and so on. The contextual inquiry approach is thus participatory in its initial phases and then is constructed to move from the informal to the formal and from the concrete to the abstract. For further details, see Holtzblatt (2003) and Holtzblatt et al. (2004).

Contributions to the System Design Process

Contextual inquiry produces documents that are strategically designed to be effective inputs to subsequent development stages. The five models described above are written in the language of systems professionals, to inform their design and implementation work.

Strengths, Limitations, and Gaps

Contextual inquiry has been shown to be a highly effective set of practices for designing system context and requirements, as has been demonstrated in numerous commercial engagements. Paradoxically, the thoroughness of its methodology can tend to require more research time and meeting or workshop time than the less formal participatory methods described earlier. The trade-off is obvious: the participatory methods provide less formal, more open outcomes that emphasize the users' unique knowledge, but that may require further interpretation and analysis by systems professionals; the contextual inquiry methods produce more formal, more closed outcomes that are more ready for adoption by systems professionals.

EVENT DATA ANALYSIS

Overview

Human performance in the context of complex systems is often measured in terms of outcome (number of errors, amount of time to complete task). These measures are important, but in most cases, not at a level of detail needed to provide diagnostic information about how to improve system design and overall human-system integration. Many of the methods used in up-front analysis for human-system integration, such as those discussed thus far, produce information that is much richer than number of errors or response time, but they also tend to rely on user introspection, verbal reports, or judgments. For instance, some methods require the user or an observer to make judgments about performance in the context of a system. This could be in the form of a questionnaire, a test, or observer ratings. Although they are a source of rich data, a downside of these methods is that some require the user to provide retrospective data, which may have become stale or poorly remembered over time. If one attempts to correct the problem of retrospective report by asking the users to reply while they are doing a task, then one is certain to disrupt the task itself; the act of self-reporting on the task changes the task. Event data analysis (EDA) offers an alternative that provides output richer than outcome measures, yet it can be less obtrusive and reliant on memory than questionnaires or surveys.

Event data analysis is largely a descriptive approach to the analysis and summary of data that take the form of observations or events that occur over time. The EDA approach incorporates a variety of methods for collecting and reducing data. In the context of human-system integration, it is particularly useful for observations collected via instrumentation (e.g., keystrokes, communication logs) over time. Event data analysis is a bottom-up approach, in that the analyst goes from data, to patterns in the data (often sequential patterns), to general descriptions, and ultimately to theory. Event data analysis has much in common with data mining, although not all data used in event data analysis need to be "mined" (e.g., verbal reports); not all data that are mined take the form of events (e.g., document corpora); and not all event data that are mined are immediately useful for human-system integration (e.g., Google's web crawling to update PageRank[2] algorithms).

The assumption behind event data analysis is that the descriptions of behavior (i.e., patterns of use, collaborative interactions) that result can inform system design or can be used to evaluate the impact of a new tool or system on human performance. The output can be a shared representation, a description (often graphical) of users' behavior in context, as well as quantitative indices associated with that description. The richness of the event data affords a deeper look at the behavior behind effective or ineffective human performance and thus is valuable in reducing uncertainty and guiding human-system integration. Event data analysis is useful for deriving summaries of behavior (system, user, or both) in the context of the existing system. This information is useful, for example, in identifying interface bottlenecks, unused functionality, and patterns of expert or novice actions.

Shared Representations

A set of instrument-collected events typically requires data reduction for meaningful interpretation. Multivariate statistical techniques or sequential data analyses are often applied to these data sets to reduce them to a presumably more meaningful form. Data-reduction methods, such as

---

[2]PageRank is a numerical weighting assigned algorithmically to each element of a set of hyperlinked documents as an indication of its relative importance within the set. The PageRank is typically computed using an analysis of links to and from the documents to calculate document centrality.

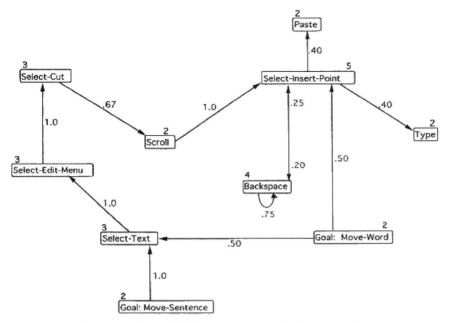

FIGURE 6-7 Example of a Pathfinder network (r = infinite; q = 9) based on conditional transition probabilities between events. Bold numbers on nodes indicate event frequencies. Numbers on links indicate transition probabilities between the two events (adapted from Cooke, Neville, and Rowe, 1996).

multidimensional scaling and Pathfinder network scaling,[3] generate shared representations. For example, in Figure 6-7 the Pathfinder data-reduction procedure (Schvaneveldt, Durso, and Dearholt, 1989) resulted in a graphical representation of word processing events (i.e., keystrokes or mouse clicks) with the most commonly occurring pairs of sequential events being directly linked (Cooke, Neville, and Rowe, 1996). The Pathfinder method takes a set of distance estimates (in this case, probability of transitioning from one function to another in the keystroke sequence) and connects nodes (computer functions in this case) with direct links if they are on the shortest path between two nodes. This kind of description of keystrokes might reveal commonly used functions, unused functions, and common event sequences that should be taken into account in system design.

---

[3]Pathfinder network scaling is a structural modeling technique using algorithms that take estimates of the proximity between pairs of items as input and define a network representation that preserves the most important links.

TABLE 6-4 Examples of Uses of Event Data Analysis

Question	Type of Event Data
What does the operator do from moment to moment? What options are not used? What options precede the request for help? What action sequences occur often enough to be automated or assisted?	Keystrokes, mouse movements, click streams.
What are the service demands made on a shared resource (like a server or a database)? What are critical dates or times of day? How can server/database traffic be anticipated or smoothed?	Hits on a web site. Database accesses. Server traffic. (While conventional server logs provide a very low-level view of these demands, instrumentation can provide a work-oriented account of server demands.)
What are the current issues that the organization is grappling with? What is the organization's current intellectual capital?	User-initiated social-software events and data, like tag creation and tag modification, blog entries, wiki entries, and current searches.
What are people thinking and planning as they work? What confuses them?	Think-aloud reports. Verbal reports. Paired-user testing.
What is the communication network in the organization? Who communicates with whom?	Communications events (email, chat, meeting attendance).
What is the context of critical events? How often do critical events occur and what events preceded and follow them?	Stream of video events (e.g., in an emergency room or air traffic control center). One or more recordings of shared radio frequencies among emergency responders.
How do people use the work space? What communication patterns or traffic patterns occur? How can the space be used more effectively or efficiently?	Movement in an office space.

Uses of Methods

In the context of cognitive work analysis, event data analysis can be especially useful for strategies analysis and social, organization, and cooperation analysis. In the context of organizational analysis, it has specific application in the descriptions of behavior. Overall, event data analysis is a useful approach for systematizing observations and as such, is of value for defining the context of use in the early ICM phase of exploration. For

Type of Data Analysis	Sample Outcomes
Frequency analysis. Lag sequential analysis. ProNet.	Usability data. Frequency of actions and action sequences. Specific sequential dependencies.
Frequency analysis. Time-series analysis. Critical path analysis.	High-frequency and low-frequency service requests. Prediction of server load and potential outages. Redistribution of functionality. Database redesigns.
Lexical analysis. Cluster analysis. Social network analysis.	Identification of new trends. Intelligence analysis. Organizational models.
Protocol analysis.	Descriptions of cognitive processes for that individual. Confusing or error-prone aspects of the user experience.
Social network analysis, via Pathfinder or UCInet.	Network graphs to show frequent communications patterns. Identification of particular communication roles, such as organizer, interorganizational gatekeeper, etc.
Video analysis. Exploratory sequential data analysis of video or audio streams.	Errors and near-misses and events that are temporally related to them; ethnographic interpretation based on video records.
Frequencies. Link analysis. Co-occurrence of individuals in the same space.	Overused and underused areas, traffic patterns. Workspace layout.

example, event data analysis can contribute to the development of system requirements by describing the current context of use. It also can be used to describe behavior in the context of a new design, thereby pitting old design against new, as might be helpful in the development and operation phases.

Event data analysis encompasses a family of methods differing on a variety of dimensions. A sample of possible applications of this approach appears in Table 6-4. Most salient to differentiating these methodologies is the nature of the data or events that are recorded for analysis. Events are discrete slices that occur within an ongoing stream of behavior. Thus the data have temporal properties that lend themselves to sequential data analysis. Some events that are recorded have been used primarily to understand the behavior of a single user interacting within a larger system. Other events take a broader look at the collaboration among multiple users and nonhuman agents, which also occurs in the context of a larger system. Examples of individually oriented event data analysis include verbal protocol analysis (e.g., Ericsson and Simon, 1984), video analysis (e.g., Bødker, 1996), computer event analysis (e.g., Carreira et al., 2004; Cooke, Neville, and Rowe, 1996; Vortac, Edwards, and Manning, 1994), eye-head movement analysis (e.g., Salvucci and Anderson, 2001), as well as physiological measures (Sarter and Sarter, 2003). Event data analysis applied to collaboration includes communication and interaction analysis (e.g., Bowers et al., 1998; Kiekel, Gorman, and Cooke, 2004; Olson, Herbsleb, and Rueter, 1994; Paley, Linegang, and Morley, 2002). The nature of the events collected dictates the intrusiveness of event data analysis (e.g., verbal think-aloud protocol events are more intrusive than logs of text chat). Note, however, that a procedure that is not *behaviorally* intrusive, such as passive screen-recording, may nonetheless have significant privacy problems that make it highly invasive of privacy for at least some users (e.g., Tang et al., 2006).

The application of event data analysis to collaboration is an interesting and fortuitous application for a number of reasons. Just as thinking aloud and the verbal protocol that results is assumed to reflect cognitive processing at the individual level, event data analysis applied to teams is assumed to reflect cognition at the team level (though some assume that it *is* the team-level thinking; Gorman, Cooke, and Winner, in press). Indeed, this is the theoretical basis of distributed cognition (Hutchins, 1995) and of the concept of the collective subject in activity theory (Nardi, 1996). However, the beauty of this general approach applied to groups or teams is that the process that one would like to trace is more readily observed at the group level than at the individual level. That is, one cannot observe individual thought processes and so rely on verbal reports as an indirect measure. But groups communicate, interact, and (some would argue) engage in team-level cognitive processing as a matter of course, making communication events, and therefore team-level thinking, readily observable.

Although EDA methods such as protocol analysis (Ericsson and Simon, 1984) and video analysis (Bødker, 1996) have been around for some time, advances in computing power have made it possible to automate, speed up, and implement in real time many aspects of event data analysis. With this growth in technology, applications have similarly grown beyond user testing applications to problems in collaborative filtering, adaptive user profiles, marketing, communications analysis, and even intelligence analysis. For instance, tools like recording user input (Kukreja, Stevenson, and Ritter, in press) create logs of user interface behavior, ideally suited for event data analysis. In addition, Web 2.0 and the emerging concept of "attention data" (i.e., where does the user spend time and effort?) promise to create enumerable possibilities for rich yet unobtrusive data collection.

The methods and tools associated with event data analysis can be categorized by the methodological step in which each is used. Steps include data collection, data analysis, data representation, and assessment and diagnosis. For some applications it may be sufficient to generate a shared representation, and in others it may be more informative to carry the analysis through to assessment and diagnosis. Each of these steps depends on the intended use or application of event data analysis and is discussed in turn.

Data Collection

Data collected as events range from verbal reports during thinking aloud and video or computer events to eye movements and other physiological measures. Data can also be collected at the group, team, or organizational level. In the spirit of process tracing, the data are not one-time snapshots of individual or group performance (e.g., response time or accuracy) but are indices of a continuous stream of behavior or interactions. Thus, the data recorded for this purpose can include physical interactions among group members (e.g., movement patterns in an office space), events that occur of a certain type that are relevant to the research question (e.g., meetings, phone calls, solitary work, breaks), events that occur strictly over the Internet (emails, text messaging, chat), discourse (written, oral, or gestural), and other kinds of group-level verbal behaviors, such as storytelling and group narratives.

The ultimate success of event data analysis is largely determined by the selection of data to record and the parsing of those data into events. Meaningfulness of the resulting behavioral and collaborative patterns can depend on how data are parsed. Although data collection is relatively straightforward and can be facilitated with tools, decisions about the nature of the data to be collected are not. For example, from whom is data collected? Is it an expert user, a manager, a developer, or a novice? Decisions like these should hinge on the questions that are asked. In addition, these decisions require experienced human intervention and are not well supported by technology.

Data Analysis

Although the rich data needed for this approach can be gathered relatively easily and unobtrusively, there is a downside: that is, the data are rich and qualitative and identifying patterns and high-level descriptions of behavior is a challenge, especially if undertaken manually. Data transcription and coding of the type required to get started on communication analysis can take many more hours than the raw data took to collect. Once the data are in a coded form, then an analytic method is applied to explore the data and look for patterns. Thus, when it comes to event data, one chief goal of the data analysis is to reduce the data in a meaningful way.

Exploratory sequential data analysis (ESDA; Sanderson and Fisher, 1994) is a general approach to this problem that relies heavily on the use of sequential data analysis methods, such as lag sequential analysis or Markov modeling. Although lag sequential analysis and Markov modeling are foundational tools of human factors, custom tools have also been developed (e.g., MacSHAPA; SHAPA) to facilitate the data analysis process. Recognition of statistical patterns in the data has become easier to automate, relieving the human coder of much of the burden. Other foundational data-reduction methods traditionally applied to similarity or relatedness judgments, rather than event data, have also been applied to help simplify event data analysis. Techniques include multidimensional scaling (Shepard, 1962a, 1962b), cluster analysis (Shepard and Arabie, 1979), and Pathfinder (Schvaneveldt, Durso, and Dearholt, 1989). For example, Pathfinder has been adapted for use with event data (i.e., Cooke, Neville, and Rowe, 1996) as well as for the analysis of communication flow data (Kiekel, Gorman, and Cooke, 2004). Furthermore, event data have also been used to derive social networks, although certainly not the typical approach to social network analysis, which has relied more on human judgments regarding relationships (e.g., Tyler, Wilkinson, and Huberman, 2005). These various analytic methods tend to focus on different aspects of the data and thus serve to reduce the data by highlighting different aspects.

Data Representation

The descriptive analytic techniques, such as multidimensional scaling or Pathfinder-based communication analysis routines, often return extremely complex, though rich descriptions of behavior. Patterns are not always easy to detect in the output by visual inspection. In the data representation step, the output from the analysis is presented to the analyst as a shared representation and in this regard is meant to facilitate interpretation. Versions of the Pathfinder routine, for example, return linked nodes in a graphical format that can be spatially manipulated by the analyst. The application of visualization techniques and tools for these complex behavioral and interaction patterns is an area that is ripe for further research.

Assessment and Diagnosis

The preceding three steps result in a qualitative description of individual or collaborative behavior (sequence of eye movements, frequent chains of mouse clicks, who is talking to whom, how often individuals interact, bottlenecks, isolates, etc.), but up to this point there is no value placed on the description. One could imagine postulating the costs and benefits of obvious characteristics of a description, such as an infrequent action, a bottleneck, or an isolate, and indeed these general evaluative interpretations can be made. Metrics from social network analysis can also be adopted for the purpose of evaluating a procedural network representation. However, making the jump from description to some deeper and contextually meaningful interpretation of the description is the most challenging aspect of this process and the most difficult to automate.

One approach is to map (in a very bottom-up way) the descriptions within context onto other criterion measures (e.g., errors, speed, conflict, poor situation awareness, shared mental models). Automation of this process would involve having a machine learn to discriminate behavioral patterns and attach meaning to them. For instance, a series of mouse clicks might be indicative of a specific erroneous mental model. This mental model could then be targeted for intervention. Assessment and diagnosis move event data analysis from its purely descriptive status to serve an additional evaluative function.

Contributions to System Design Phases

Table 6-5 describes how EDA can be applied across the life-cycle phases. It can be used in exploration to gather information about existing conditions, in advance of engineering a new or enhanced system. For ex-

TABLE 6-5 Life-Cycle Phases of the ICM and EDA

Phase	Method	Variation
Exploration	EDA	May help scope problem; can base on expert judgment if no existing system.
Valuation	EDA	Use to describe existing behavior; highlight obvious weaknesses, strengths.
Architecting	EDA	Begin to focus more on future behavioral repertoire; change to existing behavior patterns.
Development	EDA-E	Can collect behavioral data with prototype and evaluate success of new design.
Operation	EDA-E	Given other criterion can collect data from users in beta testing to assess success.

NOTE: EDA-E (Evaluative) includes evaluative steps such as assessment and diagnosis.

ample, capturing a series of keystroke-level events can inform the analyst about the order in which operations are actually carried out, the sequence in which systems are accessed, and the communications (people, frequency, media) that are part of current work. This information can be used to find problems, inefficiencies, and opportunities for improvements. These data can also provide early indications of unanticipated usage patterns, which the alert analyst can "harvest" to create best practices or new product or feature proposals. In a more conservative risk-management perspective, these data can help analysts and their teams to solve problems that are actually occurring in real work, rather than expending resources on problems that are less important.

EDA can also be applied at the early development stages of human-system integration: valuation and architecting. Event data can be collected prior to a prototype if expert judgments are used in lieu of events. Application in the early stages will reduce risk by providing information about typical user behavior or normative patterns of collaboration. Systems developed with the framework of these behavioral patterns will avoid the risk of systems that are incompatible with the user or collaborative behavior, consequently avoiding costly redesign.

Behavioral patterns provide valuable information about ongoing individual behavior and the collaborative process, including strengths, weaknesses, and possible constraints for future design. By relying on expert judgment about behavior through participatory design, for example, rather than actual behavioral observations, these methods also become useful for descriptions of envisioned systems.

Application of EDA in the later stages of system testing will draw attention to possible problems and provide guidance for selecting between two or more design alternatives (based on compatibility with human or collaborative behavior). This guidance also reduces the risk of the need for changes even later in system development or the even greater risk of failures of system productivity or safety.

The more evaluative information, such as which behavioral repertoire is faster or more efficient or best for situation awareness, is useful in later phases of development, in order to test or compare possible designs. The technique in this instance provides a means of assessing individual performance. EDA can similarly be used to assess collaborative performance—often overlooked in favor of more general outcome or system performance. However, it can also provide a deeper, more explanatory level of analysis, regarding the effects of a design on behavior.

Strengths, Limitations, and Gaps

Relative to some of the other methods for human-system integration, EDA has a number of unique advantages and disadvantages that should be considered along with the risk of not using it. One significant advantage is that these data can be collected unobtrusively in the field or operational setting. With more sophisticated tools, much of the processing and analysis of the data can also be done automatically and in real time. This is an advantage because it allows user data to be collected without interrupting users from their routine tasks, consequently avoiding changes in the results due to the interruption and maximizing user time.

There are also costs. The definition of data events and the analysis and interpretation of the rich data collected require some expertise and time. This is particularly true for a new task. The costs incurred in these data definition and interpretation activities should decline as analysts gain experience working with a particular domain and task.

Another cost of this methodology is the associated ethical and privacy concerns when data collection can occur outside an operator's awareness. The collection of much of the data described in this section raises new issues in security, privacy, and ultimately ethics. Some organizations provide guidelines or policies in these areas, but even in those cases, there are many questions for which the researcher/practitioner/engineer must take responsibility. Many systems inform the user that her or his data may be used for research purposes. For large-scale systems, users often form a reasonable assumption that their small use of the system will be "under the radar" of any research program. However, contemporary and near-future quantitative techniques address very large data sets and can easily find individual users who match certain search criteria. Thus, no one can be confidently under the radar any longer, but most users are not aware of this change.

Finally, there are also risks. One obvious risk is that a focus on recordable, quantifiable data may push other phenomena out of focus. For example, measuring the events that occur during a computerized work flow may distract the team from looking at the noncomputerized work-arounds and fix-ups that may also be taking place. Failing to observe these more qualitative, more difficult-to-record events may lead in turn to several types of errors: (1) problems with the work flow may go undetected if all that is measured is the work flow itself and (2) training or education levels may be underestimated if the more demanding work-around activities are not recorded. Thus, event data analysis is one tool in the tool box and should be used in a balanced way with other, more qualitative tools.

A second risk was alluded to earlier in reference to data collection. These techniques will generate results regardless of the quality of the data. Decisions about what data to collect, in what context, for how long, and from whom are critical and nontrivial. Without experienced decision makers, the analyst is in danger of experiencing the "garbage in–garbage out" dilemma and, depending on familiarity with the domain, may never recognize the limits of the data.

7

Defining Requirements and Design

Design is fundamentally an innovative process. The methods discussed in this chapter are intended to support identification and exploration of design alternatives to meet the requirements revealed by analyses of opportunity space and context of use. The methods are not a substitute for creativity or inventiveness. Rather they provide a structure and context in which innovation can take place. We begin with a discussion of the need for and the methods used to establish requirements based on the concept of user-centered design. The types of methods included here are work domain analysis, workload assessment, situation awareness assessment, participatory design; contextual design; physical ergonomics; methods for analyzing and mitigating fatigue, and the use of prototyping, scenarios, persona, and models and simulations. As with the descriptions in Chapter 6, each type of method is described in terms of uses, shared representations, contributions to the system design phases, and strengths, limitations, and gaps. These methods are grouped under design because their major contributions are made in the design phase; however, it is important to note that they are also used in defining the context of use and in evaluating design outcomes as part of system operation. Figure 7-1 provides an overview.

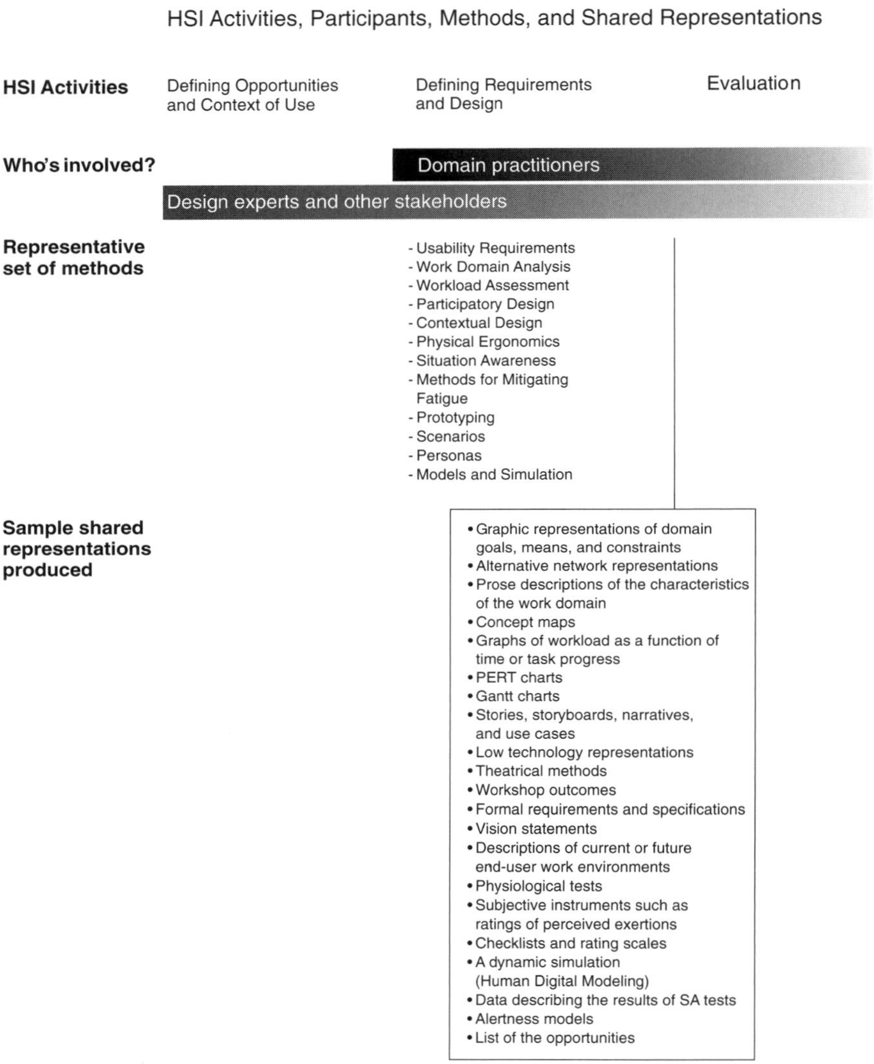

HSI Activities, Participants, Methods, and Shared Representations

HSI Activities	Defining Opportunities and Context of Use	Defining Requirements and Design	Evaluation
Who's involved?		Domain practitioners	
	Design experts and other stakeholders		
Representative set of methods		- Usability Requirements - Work Domain Analysis - Workload Assessment - Participatory Design - Contextual Design - Physical Ergonomics - Situation Awareness - Methods for Mitigating Fatigue - Prototyping - Scenarios - Personas - Models and Simulation	
Sample shared representations produced		• Graphic representations of domain goals, means, and constraints • Alternative network representations • Prose descriptions of the characteristics of the work domain • Concept maps • Graphs of workload as a function of time or task progress • PERT charts • Gantt charts • Stories, storyboards, narratives, and use cases • Low technology representations • Theatrical methods • Workshop outcomes • Formal requirements and specifications • Vision statements • Descriptions of current or future end-user work environments • Physiological tests • Subjective instruments such as ratings of perceived exertions • Checklists and rating scales • A dynamic simulation (Human Digital Modeling) • Data describing the results of SA tests • Alertness models • List of the opportunities	

FIGURE 7-1 Representative methods and sample shared representations for defining requirements and design.

USABILITY REQUIREMENTS

Overview

Inadequate user requirements are a major contributor to project failure. The most recent CHAOS report by the Standish Group (2006), which analyzes the reasons for technology project failure in the United States, found that only 34 percent of projects were successful; 15 percent completely failed and 51 percent were only partially successful.

Five of the eight (highlighted below) most frequently cited causes of failure were poor user requirements:

1. 13.1 percent, incomplete requirements
2. 12.4 percent, lack of user involvement
3. 10.6 percent, inadequate resources
4. 9.9 percent, unrealistic user expectations
5. 9.3 percent, lack of management support
6. 8.7 percent, requirements keep changing
7. 8.1 percent, inadequate planning
8. 7.5 percent, system no longer needed

Among the main reasons for poor user requirements are (1) an inadequate understanding of the intended users and the context of use, and (2) vague usability requirements, such as "the system must be intuitive to use."

Figure 7-2 shows how usability requirements relate to other system requirements. Usability requirements can be seen from two perspectives: characteristics designed into the product and the extent to which the product meets user needs (quality in use requirements).

There are two types of usability requirements. Usability as a product quality characteristic is primarily concerned with ease of use. ISO/IEC 9126-1 (International Organization for Standardization, 2001) defines usability in terms of understandability, learnability, operability, and attractiveness. There are numerous sources of guidance on designing user interface characteristics that achieve these objectives (see the section on guidelines and style guides under usability evaluation). While designing to conform to guidelines will generally improve an interface, usability guidelines are not sufficiently specific to constitute requirements that can be easily verified. Style guides are more precise and are valuable in achieving consistency across screen designs produced by different developers. A style guide tailored to project needs should form part of the detailed usability requirements.

At a more strategic level, usability is the extent to which the product

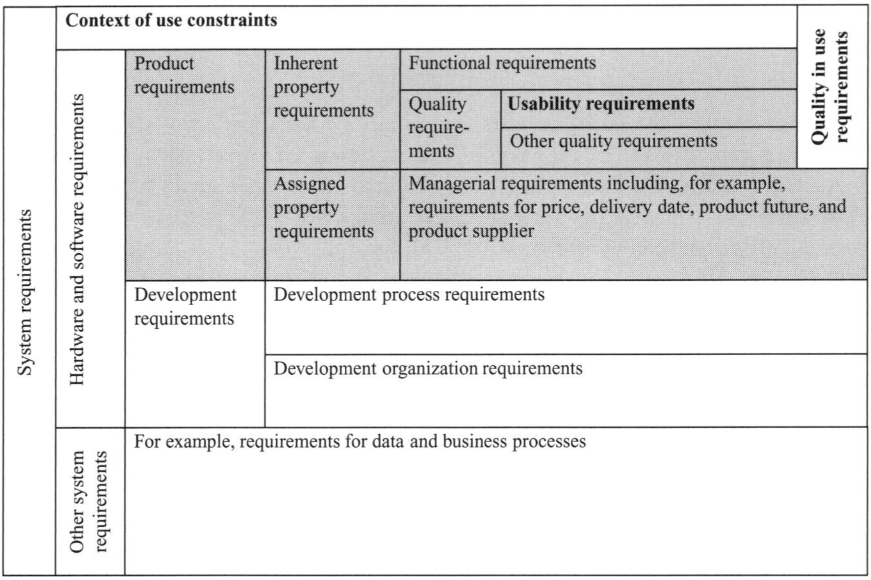

System requirements	Hardware and software requirements	**Context of use constraints**				Quality in use requirements
		Product requirements	Inherent property requirements	Functional requirements		
				Quality requirements	**Usability requirements**	
					Other quality requirements	
			Assigned property requirements	Managerial requirements including, for example, requirements for price, delivery date, product future, and product supplier		
		Development requirements	Development process requirements			
			Development organization requirements			
	Other system requirements	For example, requirements for data and business processes				

FIGURE 7-2 Classification of requirements.
SOURCE: Adapted from ISO/IEC 25030 (International Organization for Standardization, 2007).

meets user needs. ISO 9241-11 (International Organization for Standardization, 1998) defines this as the extent to which a product is effective, efficient, and satisfying in a particular context of use. This high-level requirement is referred to in ISO software quality standards as "quality in use." It is determined not only by the ease of use, but also by the extent to which the functional properties and other quality characteristics meet user needs in a specific context of use.

In these terms, usability requirements are very closely linked to the success of the product.

- Effectiveness is a measure of how well users can perform the job accurately and completely.
- Efficiency is a measure of how quickly a user can perform work and is generally measured as task time, which is critical for productivity.
- Satisfaction is the degree to which users like the product—a subjective response that includes the perceived ease of use and usefulness. Satisfaction is a success factor for any products with discretionary use, and essential to maintain workforce motivation.

Uses of Methods

Measures of effectiveness, efficiency, and satisfaction provide a basis for specifying concrete usability requirements.

Measure the Usability of an Existing System

If in doubt, the figures for an existing comparable system can be used as the minimum requirements for the new system. Evaluate the usability of the current system when carrying out key tasks, to obtain a baseline for the current system. The measures to be taken would typically include

- success rate (percentage of tasks in which all business objectives are met).
- mean time taken for each task.
- mean satisfaction score using a questionnaire.

Specify Usability Requirements for the New System

Define the requirements for the new system, including the type of users, tasks, and working environment. Use the baseline usability results as a basis for establishing usability requirements. A simple requirement would be that when the same types of users carry out the same tasks, the success rate, task time, and user satisfaction should be at least as good as for the current system.

It is useful to establish a range of values, such as

- the minimum to be achieved,
- a realistic objective, and
- the ideal objective (from a business or operational perspective).

It may also be appropriate to establish the usability objectives for learnability, for example, the duration of a course (or use of training materials) and the user performance and satisfaction expected both immediately after training and after a designated length of use.

It is also important to define any additional requirements for user performance and satisfaction related to users with disabilities (accessibility), critical business functions (safety), and use in different environments (universality).

Depending on the development environment, requirements may, for example, either be

- iteratively elaborated as more information is obtained from usability activities, such as paper prototyping during development, or
- agreed by all parties before development commences and subsequently modified only by mutual agreement.

Test Whether the Usability Requirements Have Been Achieved

Summative methods for measuring quality in use (see Chapter 8) can be used to evaluate whether the usability objectives have been achieved. If any of the measures fall below the minimum acceptable values, the potential risks associated with releasing the system before the usability has been improved should be assessed. The results can be used to prioritize future usability work in subsequent releases.

Shared Representations

The Common Industry Specification for Usability Requirements (Theofanos, 2006) provides a checklist and a format that can be used initially to support communication between the parties involved to obtain a better understanding of the usability requirements. When the requirements are more completely defined, it can be used as a formal specification of requirements. These requirements can subsequently be tested and verified.

The specification is in three parts:

1. The context of use: intended users, their goals and tasks, associated equipment, the physical and social environment in which the product will be used, and examples of scenarios of use. An incomplete understanding of the context of use is a frequent reason for partial or complete failure of a system when implemented. The context of use is composed of the characteristics of the users, their task, and the usage environment. There are several methods that can be used to obtain an adequate understanding of this type of information (see Chapter 6).

2. Usability measures: effectiveness, efficiency, and satisfaction measures for the main scenarios of use with target values when feasible.

3. The test method: the procedure to be used to test whether the usability requirements have been met and the context in which the measurements will be made. This provides a basis for testing and verification.

The context of use should always be specified. The importance of specifying criteria for usability measures (and an associated range of acceptable values) will depend on the potential risks and consequences of poor usability.

Communication Among Members of the Development Team

This information facilitates communication among the members of the development or supplier organization. It is important that all concerned groups in the supplier organization understand the usability requirements before design begins. Benefits include the following:

- *Reducing risk of product failure.* Specifying performance and satisfaction criteria derived from existing or competitor systems greatly reduces the risk of product failure as a result of releasing a product that is inferior to existing or competitor systems.
- *Reducing the development effort.* This information provides a mechanism for the various concerned groups in the customer's organization to consider all of the requirements before design begins and reduces later redesign, recoding, and retesting. Review of the requirements specified can reveal misunderstandings and inconsistencies early in the development cycle, when these issues are easier to correct.
- *Providing a basis for controlling costs.* Identifying usability requirements reduces the risk of unplanned rework later in the development process.
- *Tracking evolving requirements by providing a format to document usability requirements.*

Communication Between Customers and Suppliers

A customer organization can specify usability requirements to accurately describe what is needed. In this scenario, the information helps supplier organizations understand what the customer wants and supports the proactive collaboration between a supplier and a customer.

Specification of Requirements

When the product requirements are a matter for agreement between the supplier and the customer, the customer organization can specify one or more of the following:

- intended context of use,
- user performance and satisfaction criteria, and
- test procedure.

The Common Industry Specification for Usability Requirements provides a baseline against which compliance can be measured.

Contributions to System Design Phases

Usability requirements should be integrated with other systems engineering activities. For example, the ISO/IEC 15288 standard (International Organization for Standardization, 2002) for system life-cycle processes includes the user-centered activities in the stakeholder requirements definition process as shown in Box 7-1.

BOX 7-1
User-Centered Activities for Stakeholder Requirements

- Identify the individual stakeholders or stakeholder classes who have a legitimate interest in the system throughout its life cycle.

- Elicit stakeholder requirements. Stakeholder requirements are expressed in terms of the needs, wants, desires, expectations, and perceived constraints of identified stakeholders.

- Scenarios are used to analyze the operation of the system in its intended environment and to identify requirements that may not have been formally specified by any of the stakeholders, for example, legal, regulatory, and social obligations.

- The context of use of the system is identified and analyzed. Included in the context analysis are the activities that users perform to achieve system objectives, the relevant characteristics of the end-users of the system (e.g., expected training, degree of fatigue), the physical environment (e.g., available light, temperature) and any equipment to be used (e.g., protective or communication equipment). The social and organizational influences on users that could affect system use or constrain its design are analyzed when applicable.

- Identify the interaction between users and the system. Usability requirements are determined, establishing, as a minimum, the most effective, efficient, and reliable human performance and human-system interaction. When possible, applicable standards, for example ISO 9241 series, and accepted professional practices are used in order to define (1) physical, mental, and learned capabilities; (2) workplace, environment, and facilities, including other equipment in the context of use; (3) normal, unusual, and emergency conditions; and (4) operator and user recruitment, training, and culture.

- Establish with stakeholders that their requirements are expressed correctly.

- Define each function that the system is required to perform and how well the system, including its operators, is required to perform that function.

- Define technical and quality in use measures that enable the assessment of technical achievement.

Strengths, Limitations, and Gaps

Establishing high-level usability requirements that can be tested provides the foundation for a mature approach to managing usability in the development process. But while procedures for establishing these requirements are relatively well established in standards, they are not widely applied or understood, and there is little guidance on how to establish more detailed user interface design requirements.

With most emphasis in industry on formative evaluation to improve usability, there is often a reluctance to invest in the summative evaluation in the final development of the project. Formal summative evaluation in terms of established usability criteria is needed to determine valid usability.

As much of systems development is carried out on a contractor-supplier basis (even if the supplier is internal to the customer organization), it is for the contractor to judge whether the investment in establishing and validating usability requirements is sufficient to justify the associated risk reduction.

Usability requirements can also provide significant benefits in clarifying user needs and providing explicit user-oriented goals for development, even if they cannot be exhaustively validated. If there are major usability problems, even the results from testing three to five participants would be likely to provide advance warning of a potential problem (for example, if none of the participants can complete the tasks, or if task times are twice as long as expected).

WORK DOMAIN ANALYSIS

Overview

Among the questions that arise when facing the design of a new system are the following: What functions will need to be accomplished? What will be automated, and what will be performed by people? If people will be involved, how many people will it take, and what will be their role? What information and controls should be made available, and how should they be presented to enhance performance? What training is required?

One approach to answering these questions is to start with a list of the tasks to be accomplished and perform task analyses to identify the sequence of actions entailed, the information and controls required to perform those actions, and the implications for number of people and training required. This approach works well when the tasks to be performed and conditions of use can be easily specified a priori (e.g., automated teller machines). However, in the case of highly complex systems (e.g., a process control plant, a military command and control system) unanticipated situations and tasks inevitably arise.

Work domain analysis techniques have been developed to support analysis and design of these more complex systems, in which all possible tasks and situations cannot be defined a priori. Work domain analysis starts with a functional analysis of the work domain to derive the functions to be performed and the factors that can arise to complicate performance (Woods, 2003). The objective is to produce robust systems that enable humans to effectively operate in a variety of situations—both ones that have been anticipated by system designers and ones that are unforeseen (e.g., safely shutting down a process control plant with an unanticipated malfunction).

Work domain analysis methods grew out of an effort to design safer and more reliable nuclear power plants (Rasmussen, 1986; Rasmussen, Pejtersen, and Goodstein, 1994). Analysis of accidents revealed that operators in many cases were faced with situations that were not adequately supported by training, procedures, and displays because they had not been anticipated by the system designers. In those cases, operators had to compensate for information or resources that were inadequate in order to recover and control the system. This led Rasmussen and his colleagues to develop work domain analyses methods to support development of systems that are more resilient in the face of unanticipated situations.

A work domain analysis represents the goals, means, and constraints in a domain that define the boundaries within which people must reason and act. This provides the framework for identifying functions to be performed by humans (or machines) and the cognitive activities those entail. Displays can then be created to support those cognitive activities. The objective is to create displays and controls that support flexible adaptation by revealing domain goals, constraints, and affordances (i.e., allowing the users to "see" what needs to be done and what options are available for doing it).

A work domain analysis is usually conducted by creating an abstraction hierarchy according to the principles outlined by Rasmussen (1986). A multilevel goal-means representation is generated, with abstract system purposes at the top and concrete physical equipment that provides the specific means for achieving these system goals at the bottom. In many instances, the levels of the model include functional purpose (a description of system purposes); abstract function (a description of first principles and priorities); generalized function (a description of processes); physical function (a description of equipment capabilities); and physical form (a description of physical characteristics, such as size, shape, color, and location).

Work domain analyses do not depend on a particular knowledge acquisition method. Any of the knowledge acquisition techniques covered in Chapter 6 can be used to inform a work domain analysis. In turn, the results of the work domain analysis provide the foundation for further analyses to inform human-system integration.

There are a growing number of HSI approaches that are grounded in a work domain analysis. A prominent example is cognitive work analysis (Rasmussen, 1986; Rasmussen et al., 1994; Vicente, 1999) that uses work domain analysis as the foundation for deriving implications for system design and related aspects of human-system integration, including function allocation, display design, team and organization design, and knowledge and skill training requirements. Burns and Hajdukiewicz (2004) provide design principles and examples of creating novel visualizations and support systems based on a work domain analysis.

Applied cognitive work analysis provides a step-by-step approach for performing and linking the results of a work domain analysis to the development of visualizations and decision-aiding concepts (Elm et al., 2003). These include

- using a functional abstraction network to capture domain characteristics that define the problem space confronting domain practitioners.
- overlaying cognitive work requirements on the functional model as a way of identifying the cognitive demands/tasks/decisions that arise in the domain and require support.
- identifying information/relationship requirements needed to support the cognitive work identified in the previous step.
- specifying representation design requirements that define how the information/relationships should be represented to practitioner(s) to most effectively support the cognitive work.
- developing presentation design concepts that provide physical embodiments of the representations specified in the previous step (e.g., rapid prototypes that embody the display concepts).

Each design step produces a design artifact that collectively forms a continuous design thread providing a traceable link from cognitive analysis to design.

Work-centered design (Eggleston, 2003; Eggleston et al., 2005) is another example of an HSI approach that relies on a work domain analysis. Key elements of work-centered design include (a) analysis and modeling of the demands of work, (b) design of displays/visualizations that reveal domain constraints and affordances, and (c) use of work-centered evaluations that probe the ability of the resultant design to support work across a representative range of work context and complexities.

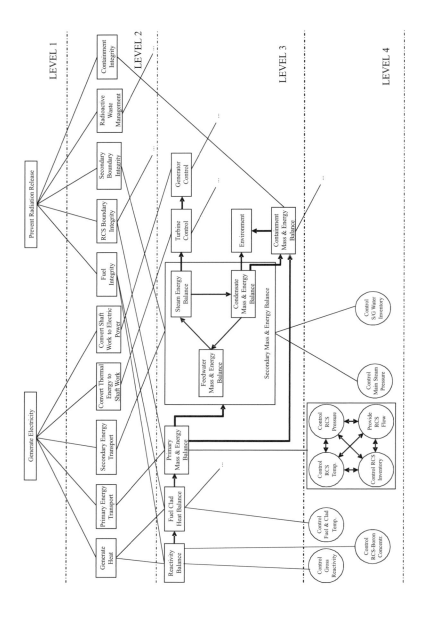

FIGURE 7-3 Selected portions of a work domain representation for a pressurized water reactor nuclear power plant.
SOURCE: Adapted from Roth et al. (2001).

Shared Representations

The shared representation produced as output from a work domain analysis is typically a graphic representation of domain goals, means, and constraints. Figure 7-3 provides an example of a graphic work domain representation that was developed for a nuclear power plant design. The work domain representation specifies the primary goals of the plant (generate electricity and prevent radiation release), the major plant functions in support of those goals (Level 2 functions in the figure) and the plant processes available for performing the plant functions (Levels 3 and 4 in the figure). Level 4 specifies the major engineered control functions available for achieving plant goals. This is the level at which manual and automatic control actions can be specified to affect goal achievement.

While work domain analyses have often adopted Rasmussen's abstraction hierarchy formalism, the results of a work domain analysis can take multiple forms. These include alternative network representations (e.g., Elm et al., 2003), prose descriptions of the characteristics of the work domain, and concept maps.

Uses of Methods

Work domain analyses complement more traditional task analysis approaches. Traditional task analyses model how tasks in a domain are performed or should be performed. Work domain analyses model the problem space in which reasoning and action can take place. The work domain representation provides the basis for deriving the information required to enable domain practitioners to understand and reason about the domain at different levels of abstraction, ranging from domain purposes (e.g., prevent radiation release) all the way down to the particular physical systems (e.g., pumps and valves) available for achieving the domain goals.

The output of a work domain analysis is used to inform further analyses that feed different elements of human-system integration. Table 7-1 provides a summary of the major elements of a cognitive work analysis that provide traceable links between the results of the work domain analysis and implications for system design, including function allocation decisions, team and organization design, design of physical and information systems including displays, personnel selection and training, development of procedures, specification of test cases to drive system evaluation, and conduct of human reliability analyses as part of risk-based analyses.

TABLE 7-1 Analytic Tools Involved in the Cognitive Work Analysis
Methodology

Phases of Cognitive Work Analysis	Description
Work domain analysis	Analyzes the purposes and physical context in which domain practitioners operate. This includes a description of domain goals, means available for achieving those goals, and constraints (e.g., physical constraints, sociopolitical constraints).
Control task analysis	Identifies what needs to be done in a work domain. This includes a description of the work situations that can arise and the work functions that need to be performed, independent of who (person or machine) will perform them or the detailed strategies to be used.
Strategies analysis	Analysis of strategies for making decisions and carrying out tasks, independent of who will carry them out.
Social organization and cooperation analysis	Focuses on who can carry out the work, how it can be distributed or shared, and how it can be coordinated. This includes allocation of work among individuals and/or machines, organization of individuals into teams and larger organizational units, and communication and coordination requirements.
Worker competencies analysis	Analysis of perceptual and cognitive requirements of workers (e.g., skills, knowledge, attitudes) to foster understanding and reduce workload.

Use of Work Domain Analysis in the Port Security Case Study

Work domain analysis has been an integral part of the port security HSI work described in Chapter 5. One recent application involved determining potential technology insertion points for cargo screening at seaports where containers move directly from ship to rail, without exiting through a truck gate. In order to evaluate this domain comprehensively, interviews were conducted with terminal operations managers, physical site maps were collected, and terminal operations walkthroughs were conducted. The information was synthesized into descriptions of current operations at each of the terminals and rail yards, with a focus on identifying common and contrasting operational practices, speed of operations, overall time requirements for ship servicing, dwell time of containers in storage stacks, labor and equipment requirements, potential radiation portal screening choke points, and issues related to the operational impact of screening at these locations. The findings were used to define screening concepts that would maximize threat detection while minimizing impact on commerce.

Other Example Applications

One of the strengths of work domain analysis methods is their ability to drive the design of novel visualizations tailored to the demands of the work (Burns and Hazdukiewicz, 2004). Successful applications range from process control (Roth et al., 2001; Jamieson and Vicente, 2001), to aircraft displays (Dinadis and Vicente, 1999), to medical device applications (Lin, Vicent, and Doyle, 2001), to military command and control (Martinez, Bennett, and Shattuck, 2001; Potter et al., 2002), to network management (Duez and Vicente, 2005; Burns et al., 2000), and to defense against cyber war (Gualtieri and Elm, 2002). In each case, the approach yielded novel decision support concepts that were fine-tuned to the cognitive work requirements of the domain and markedly different from traditional displays in the domain.

One example drawn from a process control application is a large wall-mounted group view display intended to enable power plant control room teams to maintain broad situation awareness of the status of the plant. The goal was to increase the ability of operators to quickly assess plant state and effectively control the plant in both normal and abnormal condition.

The content and organization of the group view display was based on a work domain analysis (see Figure 7-4). The group view display was organized around the major plant functions that need to be achieved to maintain safety and power generation goals, and the physical processes that support them. The objective was to enable operators to rapidly assess whether the major plant functions are being achieved and the state of active plant processes that are supporting those plant functions. In cases of plant disturbances, in which one or more of the plant goals are violated, a functional representation allows them to assess what alternative means are available for achieving the plant goals.

A formal evaluation study demonstrated that the functionally organized overview display was more effective and was preferred by operators over a more conventional overview display that utilized a physical plant mimic as the organizational scheme. Teams performed significantly better with the functionally organized overview display than the more conventional physical mimic display in identifying target events (24-percent improvement) and diagnosing plant disturbances (27-percent improvement) (Roth et al., 2001).

The results illustrate the value of work domain analysis in deriving the critical goals, means, and constraints in the domain that impact decision making and in generating novel displays that effectively communicate these factors to support individuals and teams.

Work domain analyses promote design of novel visualizations that enable practitioners to readily apprehend and assimilate domain information

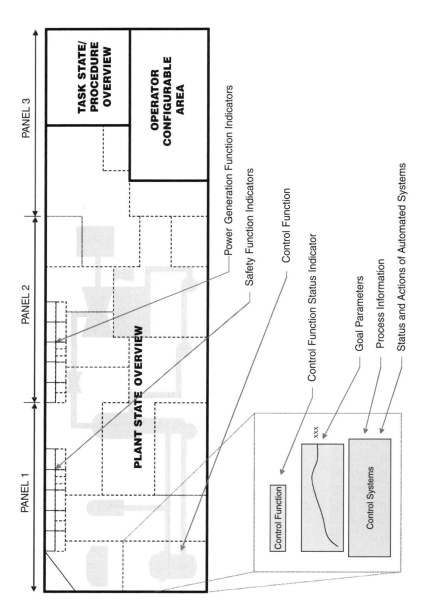

FIGURE 7-4 Schematic representation of a wall-mounted group view display for a compact power plant control room derived from a cognitive work analysis approach.

required to support complex decisions (Burns and Hazdukiewicz, 2004). One recent example is a work-centered support system visualization that was developed to support dynamic mission replanning in a military airlift organization (Roth et al., 2006). A work domain analysis identified domain factors that enter into and complicate airlift mission planning decisions, including the need to match loads to currently available aircraft, obtain diplomatic clearance for landings in and flights over foreign nations, balance competing airlift demands, and conform to airfield and aircrew constraints. Although existing information systems included all the relevant data, operational personnel had to navigate across multiple tabular displays to extract and mentally collate the necessary information. The work domain analysis provided the basis for design of a novel timeline display that enables operational personnel to graphically "see" the relationships between mission plan elements and resource constraints (e.g., airfield operating hours, durations of diplomatic clearances, crew rest requirements) to detect and address violations. A formal evaluation comparing performance with the timeline display to performance with the legacy system established significant improvement in performance with the timeline display (Roth et al., 2006).

Contributions to System Design Phases

A work domain analysis is usually performed at several levels of detail, depending on the stage of system development and complexity of the system being analyzed. A work domain analysis is performed as a preliminary analysis to identify information needs, critical constraints, and information relationships that are necessary for successful action and problem management within the domain. As the design evolves, the work domain analysis can be deepened and used to inform display design, function identification and allocation decisions, team and organization design, as well as identification of knowledge and skills (e.g., accurate system mental models) that are needed to effectively support performance in the domain.

The application of work domain analysis throughout the HSI design cycle has been successfully illustrated by Neelam Nakar and her colleagues, who have been applying work domain analysis and cognitive work analysis methods to the design of a first-of-a-kind Australian AWACS-style air defense platform called the Airborne Early Warning and Control (Naikar and Sanderson, 1999, 2001; Naikar et al., 2003; Naikar and Saunders, 2003; Sanderson et al., 1999; Sanderson, 2003). Their work has demonstrated the usefulness of work domain analysis throughout the system design cycle, including:

- Evaluation of alternative platform design proposals offered by different vendors.

- Determination of the best crew composition for a new platform.
- Definition of training and training simulator needs.
- Assessment of risks associated with upgrading existing defense platforms.

Work domain analyses have been similarly successfully employed to provide early input into the HSI issues in a number of large-scale first-of-a-kind projects, including the design of a next-generation power plant (Roth et al., 2001); a next-generation U.S. navy battleship (Bisantz et al., 2003; Burns, Bisantz, and Roth, 2004), and a next-generation Canadian frigate (Burns, Bryant, and Chalmers, 2000).

Strengths, Limitations, and Gaps

A primary strength of work domain analysis is in emphasizing the importance of uncovering and representing domain characteristics and constraints that impact cognitive and collaborative work, as well as in guiding the design of systems that are fine-tuned to supporting the work demands and enabling domain practitioners to respond adaptively to a broad range of situations. It complements traditional sequential task analyses approaches by providing explicit shared representation of domain goals, characteristics, and constraints (Miller and Vicente, 1999; Bisantz et al., 2003).

A limitation of work domain analysis methods that is often pointed to is that it can be resource-intensive to exhaustively map the characteristics and constraints of a domain. However, as multiple projects have shown, it is not necessary to perform an exhaustive domain analysis to reap the benefits (e.g., Bisantz et al., 2003). A work domain analysis can be performed at different levels of detail, depending on the complexity of the system being analyzed and the phase of analysis. A preliminary, high-level work domain analysis can be performed early in the HSI process to identify information needs, critical constraints, and information relationships that are necessary for successful action and problem management in the domain. As the design evolves, the work domain analysis can be elaborated.

A related strength of work domain analysis methods is that it encourages explicit links between analysis and design via intermediate design artifacts. As the design evolves, these artifacts can be expanded and modified to provide a traceable link between domain demands, cognitive and performance requirements, and system features intended to provide the requisite support.

One of the current gaps that limit the impact of work domain analysis methods is the paucity of computational tools to facilitate analysis and serve as a core living repository of domain knowledge that could be drawn on throughout the system life cycle. While there has been some progress on tool development, such as the work domain analysis workbench (Skilton, Cameron, and Sanderson, 1998) and the cognitive systems engineering tool for analysis tool, more comprehensive and robust tools are needed.

WORKLOAD ASSESSMENT

Overview

One of the most common issues that arise in complex system design is estimating whether the aggregate workload associated with the tasks assigned to system users will result in too much to do in the time available, leading to stress, unreliable performance, or, in some cases, system failure. Workload comes in different varieties and may be assessed from many different perspectives.

For tasks involving significant physical effort, physical workload is an ergonomic issue and in sustained task performance is usually measured in terms of oxygen consumption, or heart rate. Prediction of physical workload depends on having measurement results from other related activities and conditions and estimating the differences between the known results and the postulated activity. Guidelines are available to assess excessive physical workload.

Structurally, the human limbs and eyes can be directed to only one location at a time, and excessive workload can result from a requirement that they be directed to too many places for the time available or that they need to be in different places at the same time. Speech communication is similarly limited. Assessing this kind of structural interference requires estimates or measurements of the time required for the various activities required of the limbs, eyes, and voice in each task, laying them out in sequence, subject to temporal constraints, and evaluating the potential conflicts.

The most challenging evaluation is of mental workload. Humans can generally direct their attention to only one task or activity at a time. That is not to say that one cannot sometimes process, to some level of completeness, multiple streams of information, especially when they are coordinated or relate to the same task. There is a large literature on attention, attention management, and multitasking that is beyond the scope of this report (see, for example, Chaffin, Anderson, and Martin, 1999; Wickens and Hollands, 1999; and Charlton, 2002).

The distinctions among these types may become blurred. Thinking is often accompanied by visual exploration, and it is difficult to distinguish the structural constraint of where the eyes are looking from the mental load of reasoning about what is seen. Demanding physical effort may capture attention that could otherwise be directed to cognitive task performance.

Predicting mental workload has proved daunting, but there are some modeling techniques that have been applied. Most depend on having the results of a detailed task analysis, requiring an understanding of the cognitive components of the task and estimates of the time that will be associated with each task element. McCracken and Aldrich (1984) defined the visual, auditory, cognitive, and perceptual-motor load associated with a collection of common elemental tasks, such as reading an instrument or operating a control. Then, after making corresponding estimates of the time required for each task element in context, they used task analysis results to bring together the elemental components into estimates of the aggregate loads as a function of time on each modality. This basic approach has also been used in a variety of modeling contexts, including network models and more detailed human performance simulations (Laughery and Corker, 1997).

When prediction is not possible or leads to uncertain results, it is necessary to undertake a study to estimate mental workload from actual measurements. There are fundamentally four kinds of measurements and analysis that have been used: (1) varying the task load corresponding to the range of expected task conditions (e.g., pace of input demand, such as air traffic load, or complexity of environment, such as urban versus rural road conditions) and evaluating the functional relation between task performance and task load; (2) introducing independent competing secondary tasks and measuring the quality of performance on the secondary task in the presence of the task under study; (3) asking the user to estimate perceived workload while performing the task or immediately afterward (i.e., subjective assessment, using tools such as the NASA TLX scales; Hart and Staveland, 1988); and (4) employing physiological measures, such as pupil diameter, eye-blink rate, evoked potential responses, or heart rate. There are numerous summary references that document these methods, such as Tsang and Wilson (1997) and Hancock and Desmond (2001).

Uses of Method

When individual tasks are time sensitive or when the system users are subjected to the demands of multitasking, excessive workload is one of the paramount issues that can degrade system performance. Whenever a new system is designed or revised, it is important to consider the impact of the design on user workload. Workload estimates are also needed in job design—the assembly of tasks into jobs. Workload is a key component in preparing estimates of needed manpower or, when there is a mandate to reduce staff, workload estimates are the most important consideration. Ultimately, workload is reflected in the personnel requirements forecast. It is an important area for coordination across the HSI domains.

Shared Representations

The primary shared representations are graphs of workload as a function of time or task progress and PERT charts (a network diagram in which milestones are linked by tasks) or Gantt charts (bar charts that illustrate a project schedule). These shared representations illustrate the timelines of activities, showing where overlaps occur, with highlights showing phases in which the workload exceeds limits. For descriptions of these tools, see Modell (1996).

However, in most cases the output of studies assessing workload is expressed in an experiment report. Whenever possible the estimated workload should be compared with acceptable limits.

Contributions to System Design Phases

In a typical system design, consideration of workload begins with the initial task analysis and context of use assessment. In early stages, the estimates will be largely qualitative. The aspects of the design are identified that may be workload sensitive or where overload presents substantial task completion or safety risk. As the design matures, the workload estimates should become more quantitative, and confidence in the estimates will improve. When designs have reached the stage of completion in which a simulation of the task or of alternative task designs can be built, modeling studies or human-in-the-loop evaluations can be undertaken to estimate the workload of critical phases of the operation or critical elements of the system (see the section below on models and simulations). These studies will contribute to the manpower and personnel domains as well and should be coordinated with specialists in those areas. Measuring workload is also important during summative test and evaluation stages of a project.

Strengths, Limitations, and Gaps

The definition, measurement, and prediction of workload, particularly mental workload, has been on the human factors research agenda for more than 30 years. Measurement protocols and modeling approaches are available. It is much harder to define acceptable limits, because these are dependent on the measures used and there is no standardization of the measures, at least for mental workload. Using them requires the expertise of human factors professionals. All of the methods provide only approximate answers until the full system design is complete and the workload of using the real system can be evaluated.

Objective measures are usually to be preferred, but they require more effort to instrument and apply to simulated or real task performance. Subjective methods have been shown to be reliable if standardized questionnaires are used. Users can report only their perceptions and, under stressful conditions, perceived workload may be more important than objective workload requirements.

There is a need for more collaboration among the specialists of the manpower, personnel, and human factors domains to ensure that the studies that are undertaken meet the requirements of all these stakeholders. Suitable shared representations are not well developed. Workload models can produce PERT chart–like representations that are useful for detailed analysis of operational concepts, but the output of most workload studies is simply an experiment report. New visualizations are required that are grounded in data but that present it in a form that allows all stakeholders to understand not only what the recommendations are, but also how they are supported by the data.

PARTICIPATORY DESIGN

Overview

The preceding sections of this chapter have emphasized design as conducted by professional designers and engineers. This section focuses on design as a hybrid activity (see, e.g., Muller, 2003) conducted by professionals and end-users together, as co-designers. Much of the background for these concepts was provided in the participatory analysis section of Chapter 6. We restrict the discussion here to design-related concepts within that more general framework.

The principal focus of participatory design has been twofold (Blomberg et al., 2003; Bødker et al., 2004; Greenbaum and Kyng, 1991; Kyng and Matthiassen, 1997; Muller, Haslwanter, and Dayton, 1997; Muller and Kuhn, 1993; Schuler and Namioka, 1993):

1. To present design options clearly and understandably to end-users and
2. To provide the means for end-users to make changes in those design options.

This overall philosophy means that end-users are more involved in design and development than is the case in conventional treatments, in which end-users tend to be consulted during requirements elicitation, and again during usability or acceptance testing. By contrast, participatory design typically involves iterative engagements with users as first-class participants at multiple, strategically chosen moments during the specification-design-evaluation processes. When appropriate, this approach supplements the knowledge of engineers and professional designers with the work domain knowledge of the end-users themselves, for a better informed, more efficient development process that typically requires fewer iterations to achieve targeted levels of usability, user satisfaction, and user acceptance.

Participatory design work has focused on issues of theory, context, and practice (for a summary, see Levinger, 1998). In this report, we focus on six sets of practices that have been shown to provide sustained value in system development (for encyclopedic reviews of over 70 participatory practices, see Bødker et al., 2004; Muller, 2003; Muller, Haslwanter, and Dayton, 1997).

Methods and Shared Representations

Scenarios

The analysis phases of scenario-based methods are noted in the previous chapter (Carroll, 1995, 2000; Carroll, Rosson, and Carroll, 2002b, 2003). These activities continue in design. One of the strongest ways to describe a revised or new design is through a story of that design in use. Scenario-based design is based around such stories. Scenario-based design builds on the problem statement through the following steps:

• A set of activity designs (literally, action-oriented scenarios of future use) are constructed and evaluated with end-users. The claims from the previous step (i.e., assertions of value to the end-users) can be used to structure the evaluation.

• An information design is proposed, based on the approved activity designs. Each activity design becomes a reference model for the evaluation of each information design. The information design provides a more detailed perspective on the narrative of the activity design, and is itself a more refined scenario of future use. Again, the claims from the participatory analysis can be used to structure the evaluation.

• A more detailed interaction design is developed, based on a refined and stabilized information design. Each interaction design is an even more refined and developed scenario of future use. The action designs remain the reference models against which the interaction design is evaluated—again with the potential aid of the claims from the participatory analysis.

In these ways, scenario-based design produces a structured series of narratives, each focused on resolving particular questions. The scenarios remain intelligible and accessible to the end-users, who are encouraged to critique and modify them as needed.

Low-Technology Representations

Another powerful way to tell a story about future use is through enactment of that scenario using tangible materials, such as prototypes of the envisioned technology. If the technology has been completed, then this approach becomes a matter of formative or summative usability evaluation (see Chapter 8). However, in participatory design, the prototype is often left strategically incomplete to encourage and even to require users to contribute their ideas directly to the evolving concept.

One of the most powerful forms of strategic incompleteness is to make a nonfunctional prototype out of low-technology materials (Bødker et al., 1987; Ehn and Kyng, 1991; Muller, 1992; Muller et al., 1995). This approach has several advantages. First, it is easy to produce, and that means that it is easy to revise or abandon (an extreme version of the concept of "throwaway prototype"). Second, it is easy to modify in place—a form of user-initiated design.[1] Third, modification of the low-tech representation requires no specialized tools other than domain knowledge. Thus, a low-tech representation becomes another means for leveling the playing field, encouraging end-users to make egalitarian contributions of their knowledge to complement the knowledge of software and design professionals.

Bødker et al. (1987) provided early demonstrations of the value of low-tech mock-ups ("cardboard computers") in critique and redesign of new technologies for newspaper print shops. Muller (1992) provided an evolutionary view of paper-and-pencil materials and associated working practices in the design of user interfaces. Lafrenière (1996) showed a more macroscopic approach involving user-initiated construction of storyboard scenarios through the use of strategically incomplete storyboard frames (see also Muller, 2001). An integration of several of these approaches became a more formal description of proven "bifocal tools" for participatory analysis and design (Muller et al., 1995).

Low-tech representations have the additional advantage of being a form of literal requirements document. That is, the constructed form of the representation is a first approximation of the intended final design of the user interface. In the course of working with the low-tech representation, users and systems professionals usually enact or review one or more

---

[1]Note that the use of low-tech materials for design is quite different from the use of low-tech materials for evaluation, as advocated in contextual inquiry and design (Holtzblatt, 2003; Holtzblatt et al., 2004) and in Snyder's paper prototyping approach (2003). These latter approaches describe the use of a low-tech prototype as a valuable proxy for a functioning system in usability testing. However, by using the materials for usability testing, these approaches effectively reduce the user's input into an acceptance test. In participatory design, the goal is for the users to contribute as peer co-designers, not simply as evaluators.

scenarios of use. The sequence of events in this scenario (often captured in the form of a video recording—e.g., Muller, 1992; Muller et al., 1995) is a first approximation of the user experience and of the user-experienced information design and information architecture that must also be built. In these ways, the simple paper-and-pencil (or cardboard) materials can become powerful engines for explicating and enhancing designs.

Theatrical Approaches

The strategy of acting out a use scenario has been another tool of participatory design. Using the theoretical foundation of Boal's theatre of the oppressed (Boal, 1992), participatory designers have staged dramas to elicit discussion of working practices and technology alternatives. The principal method in information technology (e.g., Ehn and Kyng, 1991; Ehn and Sjögren, 1991) has been Boal's forum theatre, in which the designers present a skit with an undesirable outcome and challenge the end-users to modify the script, the props (i.e., the technology), or the setting, and then to reenact the drama, until the outcome is better. A secondary method in information technology (e.g., Brandt and Grunnet, 2000) has been the practice of "frozen images" or tableaux, in which the actors in a drama are asked to stop ("freeze") while the audience asks each actor what her or his character was trying to achieve, what obstacles she or he faced, and how the situation or circumstances should be improved.

As video technology has become a consumer product, users have also become authors of videos to show current work problems and proposed solutions (Björgvinsson and Hillgren, 2004; Buur et al., 2000; Mørch et al., 2004). An explicit tie-in to scenario-based methods was made by Iacucci and Kuutti (2002) in their work on "performing scenarios" (see also Buur and Bødker, 2000).

Ethnographic Methods

Ethnography has figured prominently in the literature on participatory design (e.g., Blomberg et al., 1993, 2003; Mogensen and Trigg, 1992; Suchman, 1987, 2002; Suchman and Trigg, 1991; Trigg, 2000). The specific methods used by ethnographers in design activities tend to invoke other methods, previously described in the section on participatory design. For broader discussions of ethnography, see Chapter 6.

Workshop Methods

Preceding sections have described the use of stories and scenarios, low-technology representations, and user-produced documentaries as methods and materials for participatory analysis. These and other methods have been integrated in the generative workshops of Sanders and colleagues (Sanders, 2000). Generative workshops consist of methods from market research (e.g., focus groups to elicit users' comments), ethnography (observation of users engaged in work), and participatory design (construction of anticipated or desired future objects through low-technology prototyping). The goal of this conjoint "say-do-make" approach is to triangulate on important user needs, working practices, and innovations.

Contributions to the System Design Process

Each participatory design method produces its own characteristic shared representation and contribution; several of these were reviewed in the preceding chapter on analysis. Table 7-2 provides a summary of contributions and shared representations.

TABLE 7-2 Summary of Contributions and Shared Representations in Participatory Design

Method	Role in System Development Process	Shared Representation and Use
Participatory scenarios	Design in use (actual use or future use) Ongoing opportunity to revisit opportunity analysis and context of use	Layered design documents (activity design, information design, interaction design) Stories, storyboards, narratives
Low-technology representations	Early designs Design alternatives Throwaway prototypes	Designs Artifacts created during the design process Informal requirements
Theatrical approaches	Consequences of designs for work practices Design alternatives	Informal reports Scripts (rare)
Workshops, especially generative workshops	Opportunity to revisit context of use and opportunity analysis Designs Design alternatives Consequences of designs for work practices	Designs Artifacts created during the design process Early marketing insights

Shared Representations

In brief recapitulation, scenario-based methods may produce stories, storyboards, narratives, and use cases; the latter are particularly useful for systems engineering. These materials can become background or reference material for the more detailed work of designers and developers. Alternatively, a more detailed scenario can develop into use cases, which directly inform design and development on an event-by-event (or action-by-action) basis.

Low-technology representations provide first drafts of user interface designs and are suitable inputs to the work of professional designers; the information surrounding them is valuable to resolve questions that designers and implementers might have about why certain features are needed and for what purpose. In addition to the first draft approach, low-technology representations can become detailed design documents, ready for implementation into working hardware or software.

The theatrical methods are similar to the multimedia documentary methods in the preceding chapter. As with the narratives and explanations surrounding a low-technology representation, the additional information in a theatrical method may provide useful contextualization of design recommendations and implementation decisions.

The workshop methods are similar in outcome to the theatrical methods, with the difference that the workshop methods were designed by professional designers to be used by professional designers. Their outcomes are thus structured to be useful inputs to the next, more formalized design steps.

Strengths, Limitations, and Gaps

Strengths and weaknesses of participatory design are similar to those for participatory analysis, as discussed in Chapter 6. A principal strength of the participatory approaches is the collection and use of detailed, in-depth information from the users' perspective. As discussed above, users have access to a different kind of knowledge from that of systems professionals, and the users' knowledge can be very valuable for informing design with the realities of how the work gets done, as well as for defining new opportunities and understanding the context of use (Chapter 6). A second principal strength is the growing body of practices for combining the users' knowledge with the knowledge of design and implementation professionals (and other professionals) through well-understood methodologies.

There are two principal weaknesses of the participatory approaches. The first is a matter of appearance. Participatory approaches involve knowledge holders who have historically been undervalued in systems development, and therefore the participatory design may be required to justify this "unusual" approach to more traditional practitioners and management. Similarly, the strategic informality of the participatory approaches may present an appearance problem—i.e., the use of low-technology, narrative, and expressive media that are so necessary for full and effective communication across disciplinary boundaries.

The second principal weakness of the participatory approaches is that it is sometimes difficult to integrate their informal, open, "soft" outcomes with the kinds of precise knowledge that are typically required as inputs to downstream systems development activities. This problem is rapidly becoming a nonissue, through the integrative methodologies pioneered by Kensing and Madsen (1993), the integrations with formal methods proposed by Muller, Haslwanter, and Dayton (1997), and the development of a participatory information technology methodology (Bødker et al., 2004).

CONTEXTUAL DESIGN

In the participatory analysis section of Chapter 6, we summarized the contextual inquiry process, including the three activities of contextual inquiry, interpretation, and affinity analysis, as well as the construction of the five models characterized, respectively, in flow, sequence, physical, cultural, and artifact terms. Contextual inquiry can lead in turn to contextual design (Holtzblatt, 2003; Holtzblatt et al., 2004), which includes the following activities:

• *Visioning and storyboarding:* Develop new concepts and concretize them in the form of stories ("visions"). Iteratively refine these concepts via storyboards.
• *User environment design:* Develop an abstract version of the structure and function clustering of the system's components and operations independently of the user interface and implementation (Holtzblatt, 2003, p. 943).

It is interesting to note that the stories and storyboards are accessible to end-users, whereas the larger components of the visioning and user environment design activities are explicitly stated to avoid issues of user interfaces or user experiences. Thus, while contextual inquiry involved a major component of user participation in analysis, much of the work of contextual design focuses more on the product team and its professional staff, returning to the users for a more traditional usability evaluation (see Chapter 8).

Contextual design has been designed to be well integrated into a flow of work beginning with contextual inquiry and proceeding into development.

The shared representations of contextual design (see above) are structured and sized for immediate uptake by systems engineers and professional designers.

Contributions to the System Design Process

Contextual design has been developed for effective transfer of knowledge from designers to other systems professionals. The form of storyboarding used in contextual design is intended for rapid uptake (as in use cases), and the structure and function clustering is one of the principal outcomes of a requirements analysis, to assist other systems professionals in making choices in function allocation.

Shared Representations

Contextual design is intended to produce formal requirements and specifications. The vision statements and descriptions of current or future end-user work environments are inputs to those more formal documents.

Strengths, Limitations, and Gaps

As noted in the preceding chapter, the contextual inquiry and design methods involve more research time and more meeting time than some less formal methods, such as participatory design. We proposed in that chapter that there is a straightforward trade-off between the need for informal and open methods that maximize the contributions of end-users (with their own unique knowledge) versus more formal and closed methods that maximize the subsequent uptake by the development team.

PHYSICAL ERGONOMICS

Overview

Physical ergonomics is concerned with human anatomical, anthropometric, physiological and biomechanical characteristics as they relate to physical activity.[2] Complex and simple systems often require both cognitive and physical activities of the user or group of users. Clearly, it is best to design an ergonomically correct system in the early stages of system design (Kroemer, Kroemer, and Kroemer-Elbert, 2001), and ideally a formal

---

[2]In August 2000, the International Ergonomics Association Council adopted an official definition of ergonomics (see http://www.iea.cc/browse.php?contID=what_is_ergonomics [accessed April 2007]).

institutionalized process for incorporating ergonomics into system design preexists. The steps in the overall ergonomic process are (1) organization of the process, (2) identifying the problem, (3) analyzing the problem, (4) developing a solution, (5) implementing the solution, and (6) evaluating the result (Kilbom and Petersson, 2006).

In ergonomics, the philosophy behind the methods is one of prevention and designing the system to minimize risk factors. Without such a proactive, planned approach, the human cost can range from mild discomfort to cumulative trauma or injury and possibly even death. It is therefore a serious matter to consider the human user's physical limitations and capabilities when designing systems. The major ergonomic considerations for healthy, safe, and efficient workplaces and environments are worker task position (reach, grasp, lines of sight, work heights, etc.), posture (seated and standing), clearances (access, movement space, activity space), machine control (visibility, control dimensions), force application (allowable forces), workstation layout (display and control positions and relationships), and physical environment (lighting, noise, climate, vibration, radiation, chemical, psychosocial, spatial, etc.) (Wilson, 1998). Anthropometric (and other) data for ergonomic design in new system design can be found in several published military and civilian guidelines and standards. Human digital modeling is another excellent way to test design alternatives. In addition, controlled testing and laboratory experimentation (e.g., fitting and user testing) can be used to empirically optimize ergonomic design.

In physical ergonomics, concern for the user ranges from perceived discomfort to physical injury. Assessment methods can be used to identify prospective problems in existing systems or for evaluating alternatives in new systems. Using one class of physical ergonomics issues as an example, musculoskeletal injuries often begin with users experiencing discomfort (Hedge, 2005). Left untreated, these perceptions of discomfort can escalate into pain. Untreated pain can then result in musculoskeletal injury (e.g., tendonitis, tenosynovitis, carpal tunnel syndrome) (Hedge, 2005).

Finally, there has been an effort to automate the tools with which physical ergonomics is considered in the design process. Digital human models are ergonomic analysis and design tools that are intended to be used early in the product and system development process to improve the physical design of systems and workstations (see section on models and simulation).

Shared Representations

Shared representations range from physiological tests, such as the measurement of systolic blood pressure, to subjective instruments, such as ratings of perceived exertions (Louhevaara et al., 1998). Physical ergonomics methods that focus on assessing discomfort center around self-report instruments. Such shared representations have the downside of subjectivity. In the assessment of posture, direct observation can be used, with shared representations taking the form of checklists and other data-acquisition and -reduction tools. Fatigue assessments, while attempting to be quantitative, do rely on subjective ratings, and thus shared representations take the form of the output of rating-based instruments. Finally, methods to assess physical risk also tend to rely on shared representations that are at least partially subjective—typically taking the form of checklists and rating scales. With respect to human digital modeling, an avatar or virtual human with specific population attributes is rendered as it dynamically performs tasks in a system. More simply, a dynamic simulation of the human-system interaction is rendered. More detail on the shared representations, including examples, follows in the context of methods.

Uses of Methods

Methods for Assessing Discomfort

In addition to discomfort serving as an early warning sign for injury, discomfort can in and of itself be costly in terms of affecting the quality or quantity of work performed (Hedge, 2005). Since discomfort is not directly assessed and must be perceived by the user, methods for assessment involve self-report instruments. One of the earliest methods to assess a user's degree of musculoskeletal discomfort is a checklist instrument called PLIBEL (Hedge, 2005). This literature-derived instrument allows users to evaluate ergonomics hazards associated with five body regions (see Kemmlert, 1995). The assessment can be applied at the task or system level. In the context of system development within an HSI framework, PLIBEL can help identify specific bodily areas that require attention in design or redesign. For example, if excessive reaches or awkward postures are required by a newly designed jet cockpit "highway in the sky" display, PLIBEL will identify the physical regions of the body at risk.

Another group of discomfort instruments to consider in physical ergonomics assessment is that promoted by the National Institutes for Occupational Safety and Health (NIOSH) (Hedge, 2005). Self-report measures of discomfort are widely accepted by the agency (see Sauter et al., 2005). Most of these instruments share the characteristics of combining body maps with questions and, like PLIBEL, attempt to identify particular body regions at risk.

Additional methods for assessing discomfort include the Dutch Musculoskeletal Survey, the Cornell Musculoskeletal Discomfort Survey, and the Nordic Musculoskeletal Questionnaire (Hedge, 2005).

Methods for Assessing Posture

Workplace posture is a function of the interaction of many factors, including workstation design, equipment design, and methods (Keyserling, 1998). As indicated by Hedge (2005), there are various reasons why self-report instruments are less desirable than unobtrusive observations of, for example, posture. Posture in a sense is a surrogate for musculoskeletal functioning. In system development, users in mock-ups or users in existing systems can be evaluated in real time or through recordings to assess postural risk. The Quick Exposure Checklist involves both observer and user assessments. Its exposures scores are derived (in percentages), and actions ranging from "acceptable" to "investigate and change immediately" are recommended (Li and Buckle, 2005, 1999). The Quick Exposure Checklist can therefore be applied to assessing risks associated with system tasks when evaluating an existing system for redesign or when testing a prototype of a new system.

A widely used method, called rapid upper limb assessment, provides a rating of musculoskeletal loads (McAtamney and Corlett, 1993, 2005). These ratings relate to the posture, force, and movement required by tasks. After postures are selected, they are scored using scoring forms, body part diagrams, and tables. The scores are converted to actions ranging from "acceptable" to "immediate changes required." For tasks that relate to additional body parts, the rapid entire body assessment method can be used. Additional methods include the strain index, the Ovako working posture analysis system, and the portable ergonomics observation method (Hedge, 2005).

Methods for Assessing Fatigue

The previously mentioned methods do not really address the measurement of work effort and fatigue. Methods that attempt to quantify effort and fatigue include the Borg Ratings of Perceived Exertion scale and the Muscle Fatigue Assessment method (Hedge, 2005).

The Borg ratings increase linearly with oxygen consumption, whereby a range of 6-20 was established for healthy, middle-aged people (Borg, 2005). The scale provides a measure of exertion intensity and thus provides quantitative data when evaluating a system or proposed system that requires physical user demands. One limitation is that while quantitative, the scale does rely on perceived exertion.

Strategies for reducing risk can be pursued after defining the level of effort required. The Muscle Fatigue Assessment method works best when applied to production tasks having less than 12-15 repetitions/minute with the same muscle groups and is ideal for team evaluations of a task (Rodgers,

2005). Once tasks are identified, effort intensity levels are determined for each body part. Effort durations and frequencies are determined and a rating system is used to prioritize changes. After strategies are developed for reducing the predicted risk, tasks are rerated to determine the impact of the proposed changes (Rodgers, 2005). Although the technique is partially quantitative, it does rely on subjective input (Rodgers, 2005).

Methods for Assessing Injury Risk

A predictive method for determining back injury risks was developed by NIOSH, known as the NIOSH lifting equation (Hedge, 2005). While the lifting equation does not consider the dynamics of lifting, the lumbar motion monitor (LMM) attempts to account for more realistic task situations. The LMM is a patented triaxial electrogoniometer that is attached to the spine via a hip and shoulder harness (Marras and Allread, 2005). Using potentiometers, the LMM measures the position of the spine relative to the pelvis. Software provides descriptive information about trunk kinematics and, more importantly, the system determines whether a particular worker is at risk, a task is risky, or whether an entire job comprised of several tasks is risky (Marras and Allread, 2005).

The occupational repetitive action (OCRA) methods can be used as the basis for redesign decisions and as an evaluation tool for new designs (Hedge, 2005). The OCRA index is used for the redesign or analysis of workstations and tasks (Occhipinti and Colombini, 2005). The OCRA checklist is generally used for the screening of workstations with repetitive tasks. Both methods assess repetitiveness, force, awkward postures and movements, and lack of adequate recovery periods (Occhipinti and Colombini, 2005). The risk index is the result of a ratio between actual technical actions and the recommended actions.

Human Digital Modeling

Digital human models are ergonomic analysis and design tools that are intended to be used early in the product and system development process to improve the physical design of systems and workstations (Chaffin, 2004, 2005). Software has been developed for human digital modeling (e.g., Jack, Safeworks, Ramsis, SAMMIE, UM 3DSSP, and SANTOS). Digital human models test the capabilities and limitations of humans without the expense and possible risks associated with physical mock-ups. For example, the particular reach limitations or line of sight capabilities of a vehicular driver could be determined (see the section on models and simulation for further discussion).

Contributions to System Design Phases

As noted earlier, failure to account for the user's physical limitations and capabilities when designing systems can result in decreased performance and productivity, discomfort, cumulative trauma or injury, even death. Physical ergonomics is used to identify the physical regions of the body at risk and can help identify specific bodily areas that require attention in design or redesign. The methods can be applied at the task or system level.

To the extent that systems require physical activity, physical ergonomics methods are applicable for defining solutions—that is, to support identification and exploration of design alternatives. More specifically, semiautomated and automated systems will have human users or supervisory controllers operating in workplaces. Design of these workplaces is an iterative process, requiring assessment and support of human user physical needs (Chaffin, 1997).

Physical ergonomics methods can also be used in system evaluation and redesign to compare current and redesigned workstations and to justify funding to decision makers (McAtamney and Corlett, 2005). Physical ergonomics should also be considered in system cost-benefit analysis, since benefits can broadly impact performance (Hendrick, 1998).

Human digital modeling is used early in the product and system development process (construct invent/design) to evaluate proposed new system or workplace designs.

Strengths, Limitations, and Gaps

Attending to the user's physical ergonomics needs improves the likelihood that the human-technology fit will promote better performance and well-being. A limitation of the physical ergonomics approach is that it focuses on "neck down" physiology. Complimentary attention should be placed on "neck up" or cognitive ergonomics. As Vink, Koningsveld, and Molenbroek (2006) suggest, not only can physical ergonomics combat negative issues, but it can also positively impact productivity and comfort. This positive impact is maximized when users and management actively participate in the process. Another historical limitation is that ergonomics has tended to focus on a single user or operator. Some have estimated performance improvement through ergonomics approaches to be in the 10-20 percent range (Hendrick and Kleiner, 2001). With the advent of macroergonomics or systems ergonomics, groups or teams of users can now be considered, as well as broader contextual factors leading to greater performance impact. This broader approach is consistent with the HSI framework. While much research has been conducted and much knowledge has been generated, there is still much to learn. Fundamental issues, such as the actual causes of low back pain, remain. Another gap that is slowly being filled is better integration among physical, cognitive, and macroergonomic approaches in order to consider total human-system integration.

In terms of newer methods, such as human digital modeling, current digital human models are generally static or are not fully dynamic, integrated models. Human motion databases and models are helping to convert existing, static digital human models to dynamic models. Additional research is needed on human motion and biomechanics to help achieve dynamic, complex system modeling.

Current digital human simulation systems are beginning to allow a user to interact with a digital character with full and accurate biomechanics, a complete muscular system, and subject to the laws of physics (Abdel-Malek et al., 2006). Results have been achieved in the areas of dynamic motion prediction, the modeling of clothing, the modeling of muscle activation and loading, and the modeling of human performance measures.

SITUATION AWARENESS

Overview

Situation awareness has become an important ingredient in the analysis of human-system performance, and therefore HSI specialists should include its measurement in the tool box of methods to bring to each new system development (Endsley, Bolte, and Jones, 2003). Tenney and Pew (2006) is a recent review of the state of the art.

In everyday parlance, the term "situation awareness" means the up-to-the-minute cognizance or awareness required to move about, operate equipment, or maintain a system. The automobile driver requires situation awareness in order to safely operate a vehicle in a rapidly changing environment. The driver needs to understand the position of the vehicle in relation to the road and other traffic, the speed limit under which the vehicle is currently operating, the capabilities of the car itself and any special circumstances, such as weather conditions that may influence driver decision making. The driver uses senses—eyes and ears and perhaps nose and touch, to take in information and process it to build a conceptual model of the situation. The process of building up situation awareness is called situation assessment. Operational people in a variety of disciplines, ranging from military planners to hospital operating room staff, find the concept useful because for them it expresses an important but separable element of successful performance—being aware and current about the circumstances surrounding their current state of affairs.

Being involved in every aspect of the job leads to good situation awareness but high workload. Introduction of automation reduces routine workload, but also reduces situation awareness, because it takes the user "out-of-the-loop." Then, when a critical event occurs requiring an operator response, workload again becomes high and situation awareness is inadequate.

Automation also often introduces additional situation awareness requirements to manage the new systems. Human-system integration will be especially important to exploit the information management requirements that will accompany the next generation of automation.

Achieving situation awareness has therefore become a design criterion in addition to more traditional performance measures. However, measuring situation awareness requires more than an everyday understanding of the term. The most widely quoted definition of situation awareness was contributed by Endsley (1988), "Situation awareness is the perception of the elements in the environment within a volume of time and space, the comprehension of their meaning and the projection of their status in the near future" (p. 97). There is general agreement that the term refers to all the sensory, perceptual, and cognitive activity that prepares the user to make a decision, but it does not include the execution of a course of action once a decision is made.

Measuring Situation Awareness

A variety of methods are available that may be used to assess situation awareness. In general they fall into four categories:

1. Direct experimental measures.
2. Measures derived from scenario manipulation.
3. Subjective measures.
4. Think-aloud protocols.

To apply direct experimental measures, the investigator or designer places a user in the context of the task under study, usually by means of exercising a scenario and simulating the operations under study. Then, at various points, the scenario is paused while the user is asked to answer a question about the status of different variables that are relevant to good situation awareness. The measure is the proportion of correct answers to the questions. The most well-known of these techniques is the Situation Awareness Global Assessment Technique (Endsley, 2000).

In order to derive a measure from scenario manipulation, the analyst specifically designs a scenario so that, at one or more points, the participants must make a decision that will reflect how successfully they have assessed the situation. For example, an aircrew is placed in an approach-to-landing situation on the right-most of two parallel runways. Just as they are preparing to land, a second aircraft that was scheduled to land on the left runway suddenly veers over into the airspace appropriate to the right runway. The time it takes the right-runway aircrew to make a decision to go around is a measure of their situation awareness (Pew, 2000).

It is frequently difficult to arrange for collecting these kinds of objective data, and the investigator relies instead on just asking the user to assess their own situation awareness. There are formal scales for doing so, such as the Situation Awareness Rating Technique (Jones, 2000). Again, users are placed in the context of the task under study and then, either during or immediately after completing a trial, they are asked to rate their situation awareness on a predefined scale.

Think-aloud protocols are just what they sound like—users are asked to verbalize what they are thinking while they are working on a task. They are useful early in a system development process to obtain from users their interpretation of what aspects of a situation they are thinking about. They could be applied as soon as candidate stories or scenarios have been developed that reflect the way the system might work. They can help to define the information requirements and understanding required to accomplish the task.

Contributions to System Design Phases

As indicated, think-aloud protocols are useful early, during system development, when they can help elaborate the conceptual structure in which the task will take place. The other methods are most useful when prototype user-interface designs are being considered. Here the data from testing can support the evaluation of the quality of the designs for achieving situation awareness. Evaluation can also be an important part of summative usability testing because situation awareness is such an important part of the success of the application or mission. Data describing the results of situation awareness tests provide useful shared representation with other stakeholders, because it is a concept that, in its everyday meaning, can be widely understood as important to good performance.

Strengths, Limitations, and Gaps

In contrast to overall system performance measures, situation awareness measures provide indices of the way the system is influencing human performance per se, and therefore it is able to provide clues to how to improve the design from the perspective of the user. These measures are more diagnostic, in the sense that they can suggest what is missing from the design or how understanding is inadequate. For some kinds of missions, achieving good situation awareness is the most important aspect of the design.

The main weakness is that they require having an experimental or real system to be available for testing, which limits the assessment of situation awareness until later in the development process than would be desirable.

A significant gap is that one would like to be able to predict situation awareness before anything is built, but good predictive models to assess it are not available, although efforts are under way.

METHODS FOR MITIGATING FATIGUE

Overview

Systems manned by operators need to accommodate the inherent limitations imposed by human circadian rhythms and endurance capacities. This is evident in the establishment of hours-of-service regulations for various industries, particularly transportation, which limit the number of hours in specific periods of time that workers may stay on the job. The basis for these regulations is the need for sufficient time off to permit rest and recovery and, in particular, sufficient sleep. Numerous accident analyses implicate operator fatigue as a proximal cause, and some researchers suggest that certain times during the 24-hour period are a higher risk for accidents regardless of fatigue level (Folkard et al., 1999).

The methods available to the human factors practitioner for defining shift schedule impacts and mitigating them are relatively few and are all based on several factors. These include the basic circadian rhythm, the amount of sleep obtained prior to shift initiation, and the amount of sleep obtained during off-work periods during the shift assignment (e.g., 1 week). It is important to address these issues in the design phase of systems in order to preclude adverse scheduling that may not be covered by hours-of-service regulation and to build in fatigue mitigation elements when schedule impacts cannot be avoided (such as a 24/7 operation or military sustained operations).

Most of the schedule assessment and fatigue mitigation methods come from the transportation sector (Sanquist and McCallum, 2004). The methods with the most general applicability to system design and operation include

- alertness models.
- trip planning.
- strategic napping.
- sleep environment planning and design.

Each of these methods (sometimes referred to as fatigue countermeasures or alertness management) has been shown to have a beneficial impact on reducing or avoiding fatigue in the workplace. Given the potentially lethal impact of fatigue on the job, application of these principles and methods during system design is warranted. The principal risk reduction associated with application of these methods is that of operations, which will lead to excessive fatigue and corresponding degradations in human performance. The following sections briefly describe each method or countermeasure in terms of applicability in a system requirements and design phase of development.

Uses of Methods

Alertness models have been used by researchers for a number of years to predict the likely fatigue level that would result from various shift schedules and the corresponding opportunities for sleep (or lack thereof). Most are based on several key parameters, such as a circadian rhythm component, time of day, preceding amounts of sleep, and availability of a recovery sleep period (Dawson and Fletcher, 2001; Folkard et al., 1999). The models are encoded in specialized software packages that generally require some domain expertise to operate. The outputs consist of fatigue levels before, during, and after a shift, and these values can be used as a guide to schedule construction and assignment. For designers without access to the specific modeling tools, which change fairly rapidly since they are principally a research product, simple heuristics for scheduling and rotation are reasonable substitutes. These include such rules of thumb as providing sufficient time off to permit an 8-hour sleep period, which in practice means at least 10 hours. Similarly, start times prior to 7 am are more likely to be associated with fatigue than later start times.

Trip planning is a method employed in variable ways by transport workers and is highly dependent on the transportation vector, such as air, road, or rail. Both schedulers and individual workers need to plan their trips to provide off-duty breaks of sufficient duration to obtain enough sleep. This applies in particular to workers who need to travel long distances to their work location, such as airline pilots commuting cross-country to start a long-distance flight assignment.

Strategic napping is a fatigue countermeasure that involves short sleep periods of 20-45 minutes duration to provide for recovery during a long-duration shift (Dinges at al., 1991). A number of studies indicate that strategic napping is associated with better job performance following the nap (e.g., landing an airplane). As a consequence, certain international air carriers have sanctioned napping during long-distance flights by one of the crew members, and airplane manufacturers are beginning to build long-haul aircraft with sleeping quarters for crew members. Similarly, rail carriers are beginning to provide napping rooms in their crew turnaround locations.

Sleep environment planning and design (Zarcone, 2000) have entered into the schedule design process for certain air carriers and have also influenced how the carrier-preferred hotels design their facilities. They are now beginning to reserve certain blocks of rooms and floors for day sleepers and to implement other measures, such as blackout shades and additional soundproofing.

Shared Representations

Alertness design methods have a common shared representation in specifying the impact on operator sleep. Alertness models predict how much sleep an operator will get on a certain shift schedule or the likely fatigue level resulting from lack of sleep. Trip planning has a similar output—given a particular duty schedule. What are the opportunities for sleep and how much will be obtained?

Figure 7-5 illustrates a shared representation that is common among alertness designers: a graphic plotting time of day against alertness level. This is a common method of defining time periods that are likely to show fatigue effects that might manifest as accidents.

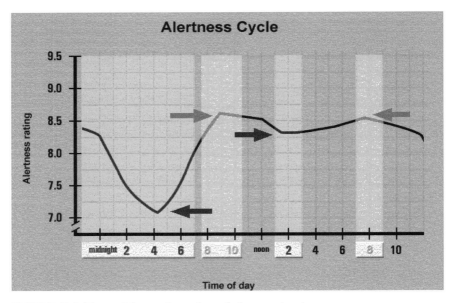

FIGURE 7-5 Time of day and number of alertness level.

Contributions to System Design Phases

Alertness design methods contribute mainly to the architecting phase of the system development process. In any manned system, the elements of staffing, scheduling, and recovery are addressed during the more specific design phases, involving determining how many people will work, doing what tasks, and the nature of the operations (e.g., 24 hour, sustained, or other). Evaluating and designing for alertness management during the architecting phase can prevent unanticipated attrition due to excessive fatigue or more dire consequences, such as accidents.

Strengths, Limitations, and Gaps

The strength of alertness design methods is that they address a problem that is reasonably easy to solve if several key parameters are considered: number of staff, duty periods, recovery time necessary, etc. In their simplest implementation, the methods consist of heuristics designed to assess the adequacy of rest periods. More involved methods, such as nap period design or sleep environment planning, can enhance alertness during long assignments or unusual shift rotations.

A primary limitation of alertness design methods is that they are relatively unknown outside the fatigue research and transportation community. A cultural tradition of work excess in some industries limits the willingness of system designers to consider the basic needs of sleep. A further limitation is that fatigue mitigation and alertness management/design are not often considered in the traditional suite of human factors methods, but they are an important part of the larger HSI domains. This is beginning to change, but the field tends to be dominated by the methods with a more traditional task-oriented focus.

A large gap in alertness design methods is the availability of robust guidelines or processes for addressing fatigue issues in design. Whereas task analysis has many variants and practitioners can learn to apply it rather quickly, alertness design does require some knowledge of biological rhythms and performance effects, and various subtleties of sleep debt accrual and mitigation. The modeling tools developed to date require substantial knowledge in the area for proper application and interpretation, and a simple set of alertness design guidelines, applicable across a wide range of work activities, has yet to be developed.

SCENARIOS

Overview

Scenarios are stories that describe how activities and events unfold over time. They can depict either how the activities currently happen or how the activities might be imagined to happen in the future. Scenarios can be produced at a variety of levels of detail, abstraction, and scale. For example, they can tell a story about how a particular culture might change (big and broad scenario-based planning) or suggest how a new technology can influence a particular process (big and focused). Scenarios can also be produced to suggest how a particular user might interact at the button-push level on a handheld device (small and detailed).

Scenarios can be used by different system stakeholders in different ways. Some design representation methods emphasize the delivery of a formal, integrated concept, embodied in the form of a highly produced and convincing story. By contrast, some participatory analysis methods focus on storytelling to create a level playing field, so as to put users and technologists on a common footing, making scenarios useful as shared representations. In more formal terms, these techniques have been described and analyzed as scenario-based methods (Carroll, 1995, 2000; Rosson and Carroll, 2002, 2003).

Uses of Methods

In using scenarios, researchers play the character's (or persona's) actions forward and are able to share them among themselves and with potential users. The scenarios enable all the participants to critique the assumptions and implications that are made visible. For example, end-users have the potential to see how their work would change in the future. Alternatively, systems professionals may be able to see the implications of changed working practices for new technology opportunities. In this way, scenarios offer participants the opportunity to rewrite or co-construct them until the activities and processes they represent meet all the stakeholders' needs.

Designers create a variety of different types of scenarios depending on the design challenge and where they are in the development life cycle. Scenarios are created to address the needs of specific stakeholders, their environments, technologies, or according to the specific problem that needs to be addressed.

Another consideration in using scenarios is what medium should be used to generate and deliver the scenario. Scenarios can be represented purely verbally, with text and images (in which the images are similar to storyboards used in film and animation), or as fully featured video (see the sections on low-technology representations and multimedia documentaries below). Usually the more informal the medium that is used for the scenarios, the more it invites the viewers to actively participate in modifying or changing them.

Scenarios are typically elicited through a sequence of steps:

• *Root concept:* Beginning with a brief statement of the goal of the project, analysts elaborate a basic rationale for the project, list the crucial stakeholders, and provisionally state some high-level assumptions.
• *Ethnographic inquiry:* Field observations, interviews, and artifact analyses are conducted as needed to understand users' needs and opportunities.
• *Interpretation:* Field observations are then organized and interpreted through a series of affinity analyses (using methods from contextual inquiry).
• *Problem scenarios and claims:* The tentative requirements from the preceding steps are then organized into scenarios of future action that will need to be supported and specific claims (which capture essential or emergent themes and topics) about how the envisioned system will support those scenarios.

Scenario-based work often involves a preliminary coding scheme for the knowledge that is elicited. For example, Rosson and Carroll (2002) note that "Each scenario depicts actors, goals, supporting tools and other artifacts, and a sequence of thoughts, actions, and events, through which goals are achieved, transformed, obstructed, and/or abandoned." These kinds of scenario-based codings had previously been shown to be useful in creating object-oriented designs (Rosson and Carroll, 1996). Under some circumstances, it is useful to provide materials for scenario construction that embody a particular "vocabulary" of events or actions, so that the resulting design has already been precoded into a target set of system components (Muller et al., 1995).

Shared Representations

There are a variety of shared representations that can result from building scenarios. They are, in a conventional time-ordering:

Individual (episodic, vertical) stories from one informant at a time, describing that informant's experience.

Composite stories that are constructed from the individuals' stories; these stories are usually supposed to be accurate summaries and compilations of the individuals' stories and are usually supposed to have a similar "epistemic status" of accuracy and fidelity.

Future-vision stories, which are of necessity fictitious. Typically these early-stage thinking-about-the-future stories tend to be connotative rather than denotative, evocative rather than definitive, open rather than closed, plural rather than singular, and are often deliberately incomplete.

Finally, there is the relatively formal *requirements-related* story, which provides a relatively detailed account of future use for designers and developers. These stories tend to be nearly the opposite of the future-vision stories: denotative, definitive, closed, singular ("we will build this"), and exhaustively complete.

Carroll suggests that scenarios are paradoxically concrete, but rough, tangible, and flexible, encouraging what-if thinking among all parties and pushing designers beyond the expected solutions (Carroll, 2000; see also Erickson, 1995, on the strategic use of roughness in representations). As a shared representation, scenarios permit the articulation of possibilities without undermining innovation, enabling the design team to focus on the systems in the given context. Scenarios can be simultaneously implicit and explicit.

Contributions to System Design Phases

Scenarios can be used in the very early stages of the design process to help explain possible system behavior. They are easy to share because they are in natural language—or in some other conventional representation, such as cartoon frames—and almost anyone can participate in their production (Carroll, 2000). Later on in the process, scenarios enable the collaborative team to begin to immediately synthesize findings from research into situated ideas for the future. They can also be used as an evaluative tool with system users—in other words, the stories and their associated pictures can be shown to end users and other stakeholders before anything is committed to code. According to Rosson and Carroll (2002), "The basic argument behind scenario-based methods is that descriptions of people using technology are essential in discussing and analyzing how the technology is (or could be) used to reshape their activities. A secondary advantage is that scenario descriptions can be created before a system is built and its impacts felt" (Rosson, Maass, and Kellogg, 1989; Weidenhaupt et al., 1998). Finally, later on in the process, scenarios can be translated into use cases or essential use cases and associated with system requirements (Preece, 2002). At this stage, they can also provide the specific task details to support human-in-the-loop simulation experiments and usability evaluation.

Strengths, Limitations, and Gaps

A primary strength of scenarios is that they are easy to make and revise—they are fast and cheap. Nothing has to be coded, and they can even describe system behavior in words alone. When they include storyboards or pictures of the activity, they can help end-users and other stakeholders envision, react, and help shape possible future systems. The limitation of scenarios is that they can never be exhaustive—not every story can be told—so some functionality that could be critical to the design of the system could remain overlooked. Although several treatments have begun to analyze the space of stories (e.g., Carroll, 2000; Muller, 2007; Rosson and Carroll, 2002, 2003), a more extensive cataloging of scenario types, uses, and limitations could be developed to overcome these limitations.

PERSONAS

The personas (or "archetypes") approach has become a very popular technique in applied design activities. Using personas (especially role or segmentation-based archetypes) as actors in scenarios (see following) helps situate the technology in real-life settings. Ever since Alan Cooper described personas in the book *The Inmates Are Running the Asylum*, there has been a great deal of effort spent on understanding why and how personas are useful in the design process and in finding ways to extend the concept beyond their role in bringing scenarios to life (Cooper, 1999, 2004; Pruitt and Grudin, 2003). Personas are useful because they build on people's expectations and natural abilities to anticipate and infer other people's behavior from what is known about that person. Pruitt and Grudin suggest that good personas can be generative and help designers "play forward" or project what they know about a character into new situations. Pruitt, Grudin, and others have extended the use of personas throughout the design process—from prioritizing features, to usability and market research to QA testing.

Shared Representations

While scenarios are concise narrative descriptions, personas are descriptions of one or more people who are (or will be) using a product to achieve specific goals. A persona is specifically designed to become a shared representation of the users of the target system. They are designed to mediate communication about the potential users of the system. A persona is a model or description of a person, ideally based on observed behavior gathered by the up-front analysis team and defined through an intuitive and systematic synthesis of the analysis data. Good personas include descriptions of the character's activities, goals, skills with and without technology, influence on the business, attitudes, and communication strengths and weaknesses (Cooper, 1999; Pruitt and Grudin, 2003; Cooper and Reimann, 2004; Pruitt and Adlin, 2006). Personas become the actors in the stories of current or future use and interaction. In the commercial world, a variety of user types may be modeled. For example, an on-line banking design scenario might include both novice and expert users at different life stages (newlywed, college student, empty nester, etc.). In the military it might include representative enlisted personnel who might be assigned the task and an officer who would use the application in a supervisory role. Although there are significant differences in practice (Adlin et al., 2006), the persona descriptions can also focus more on roles, experience levels, and motivations for the interaction.

Teams are encouraged to make conceptual tests of their design decisions against the persona who represents the users (e.g., "What would Kim think about that feature?"); note, however, that the issue of representativeness is somewhat controversial (Muller et al., 2001). Task analyses can be based, in part or in whole, on the persona description (Redish and Wixon, 2003). Like a method actor who immerses himself or herself in a character, a persona is usually described in considerable personal detail—i.e., with a name, a photograph, a job description, and a variety of personal data that can include pets, favorite foods, make and model of car, and so on in order to support appropriate inference-making on the part of the persona user.

Contributions to the System Design Process

There is little formal research to support the creation of personas as a part of the systems design process. Less formal reports from practitioners are overwhelmingly positive (e.g., Cooper, 2004; Pruitt and Adlin, 2006; Adlin et al., 2006). The principal contribution is within the design or development team—an effective persona can help a team to focus on the experiences and needs of their users, providing a valuable counter balance to the more traditional concerns for systems performance and efficiency. These practitioners have successfully extended their use beyond scenarios all the way up to executive product strategy meetings (Pruitt and Grudin, 2003).

Strengths, Limitations, and Gaps

Personas can play a powerful role in bringing user concerns to the forefront of the development process. When carefully and systematically constructed, they can be an effective shared representation for the development team. A persona is, ideally, created on the basis of information about the population of real users. However, the basis for selecting the relevant attributes of a persona is not agreed on (e.g., Adlin et al., 2006; Grudin and Pruitt, 2002; Muller et al., 2001). A persona might be based on ethnographic research, but most ethnographic accounts are about individuals rather than about group parameters or generalized characteristics, and thus they are too specific to help with the construction of a representation that faithfully represents the relevant attributes of all users. Data from marketing research may be used to select the statistical characteristics of a persona (as suggested by Grudin and Pruitt, 2002, and as partially done by Sinha, 2003), but there remains a wide range of personal characteristics in the persona description whose source is unclear (Adlin et al., 2006).

In a systematic treatment, Pruitt and Adlin (2006) advocate the creation of a "persona-weighted feature matrix" to assist a team in the systematic consideration of multiple personas. These multiple personas might represent users with different responsibilities or even different market segments (Adlin et al., 2006). The feature matrix can then be used to rate the importance (or perhaps market share) of each type of user, and it can be used further for a high-level quantification of the impact of each feature decision on each class of users and thus on the likely overall success of the product.

PROTOTYPING

Overview

Prototyping is a method that can be used at any time during the design process. Prototyping helps teams answer questions, shape, and define the attributes of a desired future state (Schrage, 1996) The word "prototype" refers to a number of different types of things that can be made to express, discuss, critique, or refine a concept or system or product or plan (Beaudouin-Lafon and Mackay, 2003; Tscheligi et al., 1995). What unites the diverse meanings and types of prototypes is that any prototype is a temporary substitute for the real thing that eventually will be (or might be) implemented or constructed. Prototypes are made in different ways, of different materials, by different people, for different purposes (Houde and Hill, 1997). A pen held to one's ear as a stand-in for a cell phone in a design session and the beta release of an application can both be considered prototypes. In the design process, prototypes help teams make the transition from an abstraction of what might be to a concrete notion of what something might be like.

Prototypes are used to reason and communicate—to persuade and argue what ought to be among collaborators (Houde and Hill, 1997; Rith and Dubberly, 2005). Prototyping is a process that brings a desired future to life or makes the design tangible (Wulff, Evenson, and Rheinfrank, 1990;

Coughlan and Prokopoff, 2004), but the role that a prototype plays in facilitating team activities is equally important. As Suchman (2004) notes, a prototype often serves as a means of enactment (i.e., for demonstrating and persuading) as well as the more conventional means of representation—a dynamic dance between the invention of needs and the technologies that support them. A prototype is intended to be a stand-in for the collaborating team's ideas—not just as a version of an eventual or target solution (Boland and Collopy, 2004). Schrage warns that organizations may have a specification-driven culture that may prevent them from innovatively prototyping (1996). In these types of environments, the potential to enact the best possible futures may be stifled. In contrast, in organizations that successfully mediate meaning through prototypes, value is created, communicated, and shared (Schrage, 1994).

Uses of Methods

Prototypes can represent a number of dimensions in the system design. A horizontal prototype may be a reflection or enactment of all activities the system is intended to support at a very high level; a vertical prototype may address a subactivity in the design in complete detail in order to understand the implications of a particular implementation without the cost of prototyping the entire system.

Some prototypes are intended to be thrown away almost immediately, while others are more evolutionary—that is, they are designed to be continually updated throughout the design process. Architectural prototypes are produced in order to provide a representation of the performance and feasibility of a particular attribute of the supporting technology; while a requirements prototype may reflect what the system needs to do to support the activities of users without any implication of technology that will be used to implement a solution. In some situations, wireframes or purely textual prototypes are used to elicit feedback from potential users of a system, while in other situations the representation may be purely visual and a reflection of the final form of an interface (Mannio and Nikula, 2001). The level of finish or degree of roughness of a prototype can also be a consideration (Erickson, 1995). A prototype can be as simple as a few lines on a napkin or as finished as a beta release.

Figure 7-6 shows some examples of different types of prototypes.

Shared Representations

The shared representations produced as output from prototyping may take a variety of forms (Beaudouin-Lafon and Mackay, 2003; Houde and Hill, 1997). What makes the activity of prototyping and the prototypes that

(a)   (b)

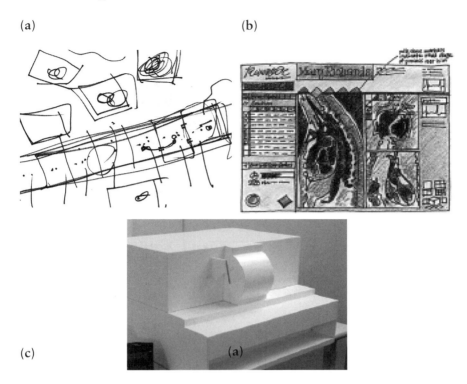

(c)   (a)

FIGURE 7-6 (a) Scribbles on a napkin for prototyping flow across a counter in a service environment. (b) Second round prototype for interface to MRI device. (c) Physical prototype: A foam model of a Blood Analyzer Prototype.

are produced so powerful as shared representations is that they are tangible and can easily be shared and foster communication among team members, stakeholders, and end-users.

Prototypes function to make explicit an aspect of form, fit, or functionality (Boland and Collopy, 2004). Form is the overall structure of the organization, environment, technology, or process. Form can shape interaction and set expectations. Fit describes the resonance (or lack) of the current embodiment to the overall endeavor's objectives. Fit is often subjective but deeply meaningful on levels that are often beyond expression (Gladwell, 2005). Functionality describes whether the design works—that is, whether it is effective, appropriate to human use, and emotionally sustainable; has the potential to be taken up by the organization(s) that it responds to; and is situated in its context (Boland and Collopy, 2004).

Contributions to System Design Phases

Early in the life cycle, a prototype may simply be a placeholder for a real object or system: people use the prototype to show the work or actions that would take place around it (e.g., Buur et al., 2000). Later in the life cycle, a prototype may take the form of a nonfunctional description in concrete materials, such as a physical model of a device (e.g., Bødker et al., 1987, 1988) or a paper-and-pencil mock-up of a user interface (e.g., Ehn and Kyng, 1991; Muller, 2001; Muller et al., 1995); in some cases, the prototype is designed to be modifiable only by experts while in other cases the prototype is designed to be modifiable by anyone, including actual or potential users of the eventual product or system (e.g., Ehn and Kyng, 1991; Muller, 2001; Muller et al., 1994, 1995; Sanders, 2000). Still later in the life cycle, a prototype may be a faithful paper-and-pencil copy of a designed system, used for early user evaluations while the real system is being built (e.g., Snyder, 2003). Houde and Hill (1997) recommend that an integrated prototype be based on the construction of as many as three different types of prototypes (based on the role or function of the target system in people's work, the look and feel of the system, and the implementation technology).

At later phases of the life cycle, prototypes may contain varying levels of functionality. In some cases, the functionality may be complete, but the implementation technology may provide flexibility (to try out new or alternative ideas) in preference to performance. In other cases, the functionality may provide surface fidelity, but with fictitious back-end architectures, data, and communications. In the wizard of Oz style of prototype, the back-end is simulated by a person representing the behavior of the computer. Selecting the appropriate form of prototype depends on the development or communication problem to be solved (or both); see Beaudouin-Lafon and Mackay (2003) and Houde and Hill (1997) for details. At this level, prototypes can support experimentation with alternative designs or formative usability evaluation.

Strengths, Limitations, and Gaps

A primary strength of prototyping and the prototypes that result is the cohesion for the team. According to Kelly (2001), "Good prototypes don't just communicate—they persuade." When discussing ideas or determining direction, having a prototype with which to negotiate makes the process more effective, fosters innovation, and usually reduces development costs (Kelley, 2001).

The greatest feature of prototyping is also its biggest foible. Because prototypes are so real, they make the experience of the product, application, or service so tangible that they can influence teams to fix too quickly on a potential solution. When that happens, people are usually taken in by the level of finish in the prototype and believe that all the qualities and features are set—rather than being open to change. In practice, it is very important to match the level of finish to the stage in the process to avoid early closure on an incomplete solution (Erickson, 1995).

The most frequent use of prototypes has occurred in hardware and software development. However, prototypes have also been used to explore organizational outcomes, and—significantly—to critique and redesign the technologies that might lead to different organizational outcomes. The best-known example is the UTOPIA research project, which dealt with new technologies and their implications for changes in working relations and power balances among two groups of skilled workers (e.g., Ehn and Kyng, 1991; see also Bødker et al., 1987, 1988). Extensions of these methods could be used to explore the interactions of new technologies and new working practices in a variety of home, commercial, and military settings.

Aside from the relatively informal demonstrations of Ehn and Kyng (1991), there is work to be done to understand how physical artifacts—the nonhuman components of the system—interact with the prototypes of the people side of the system. Is there a classification scheme to be developed to include verbal or descriptive concepts and theories, to interactive role-playing, to computational models and simulation? Clearly new methods for visualizing interactions and activities must be developed.

Prototyping organizations (as well as technologies) will help produce and maintain better organizations—because troubling interactions can become visible and refinements can be made before the design is rolled out, saving time, effort, and misunderstanding. By having participants (preferably the intended end-users) contribute to design—and by nature some ownership—the likelihood of adoption and enactment of the goals of the design will be increased (Muller, 1992; Muller et al., 1994). Once the design is implemented, an organization will be better maintained because the prototyping can facilitate (1) changes to accommodate organizational strategy changes and (2) and an ongoing capability for what-if scenario testing for unanticipated outcomes.

Prototyping training systems should not only help produce better trainees early on, but also, as noted above, can enable better system designs that make fewer demands for intensive training later on. Prototyping training also provides an opportunity for early feedback to the systems as well as organizational designers from the target users, providing insightful opportunities for improvement to the developers, as well as potential for early buy-in by the end-users.

MODELS AND SIMULATIONS

Overview

Modeling and simulation have provided important methods and tools to support the system engineering process since the days of analog computers. Models and simulations represent a more formal step in human-system design. They can reduce the time and data gathering required for functional evaluation by screening alternatives and identifying the critical parameter ranges to test. They can also be used for decision making about specifications or the most promising design alternatives. Today the capabilities of computers to support virtual environments, multi-person video games, complex systems and their subsystems, and even human thinking processes makes the potential range of application almost limitless.

The term "computer simulation," or often just "simulation," implies using a computer to mimic the behavior of some physical or conceptual system or environment. It can be used to make concrete the eventual real effects of alternative conditions and courses of action, or it can be used to support training. The term "model" is widely used for everything from fashion design mannequins and physical mock-ups to flow charts and block diagram abstractions. Because simulations are, by definition, abstractions of the real thing, they make use of models. With respect to human-system integration, the kinds of simulations and models of interest are quantitative, usually implemented on a computer, and represent one or more aspects of the characteristics, performance, or behavior of a system, a human, or a human-machine system combination. A simulation of a system also implies a representation of the environment in which it operates. There are many ways to express such models, ranging from closed form mathematical equations to high-fidelity human-system computer simulations.

Types and Uses of Models and Simulations

Human-in-the-Loop Simulation

The Link Trainer is perhaps one of the earliest human-in-the-loop computer simulations. It was an approximate representation of the equations of motion of an airplane and used real aircraft instruments and controls in the cockpit mock-up so that a human could practice the skills of instrument flying. Later, when simulators began to represent the pilot's visual field outside the aircraft, a small-scale physical mock-up of a section of terrain was created and a television camera "flew" over this terrain board to project an image of what the pilot would see. Today very sophisticated human-in-the-loop simulation continues to play an important role, both in operator training, for everything from aircraft operation to physicians practicing medical procedures, and in system development, to evaluate the performance resulting from new technology, concepts of operation, or procedures. The military services, NASA, and the aerospace industry have used human-in-the-loop or mission simulation in research and during system development very successfully over the past 20 years.

For example, NASA has used simulation in its role in research to support the continued improvement and the reduction of human error in the National Aerospace System. They have employed everything from single crew member part-task simulations to full-mission representations of the coordinated behavior of commercial aircraft crews and air traffic controllers in air operations. From 1986 to 2005 the rate of major commercial aircraft accidents per million miles flown in the United States was reduced from 0.401 to 0.103, or 75 percent, while the volume of traffic has increased nearly 100 percent (National Transportation Safety Board, 2006). Similarly, the U.S. Air Force has demonstrated the training value of full-mission human-in-the-loop simulation of air operations involving aircrew and forward air controllers (Schreiber and Bennett, 2006; Schreiber, Bennett, and Gehr, 2006).

Network Models of Human-System Performance

Simulations are usually associated with the representation of systems or subsystems, but there is now a large body of literature on simulation to represent the performance of a person-machine system. Typically, the model is built on the basis of a detailed task analysis, and each subtask is represented as a node in a network of nodes describing the completion of a higher level task. Each node represents, as statistical distributions, the time to complete the subtask and the probability that it will be completed successfully. Tasks can be aggregated into still higher levels of activities, goals, or missions. One can represent contingent branching structures among nodes, and the resulting models can become quite complex. Outcome performance measures are averaged from multiple (often 100-300) Monte Carlo executions of the model, each calculating the aggregate performance time and success probability of the activity or mission. The programming language, Microsaint, is an example of a language, specifically designed and widely used to support this kind of simulation. The most well-known examples of this class of models are the IMPRINT series of models used by the U.S. Army to predict the performance of military systems (Booher and Minninger, 2003; Archer, Headley, and Allender, 2003). IMPRINT has been used to create significant redesigns in many systems, improving performance, saving millions of dollars, and reducing the risk of fielding systems not fit for their purpose.

There is also a long history of the use of models and simulations in psychology to represent aspects of human behavior or performance (or both). Psychologists use them to summarize what they know and to support theories. Some of these models have been shown to be useful for system design to estimate and predict performance or to derive performance measures indicative of human-system performance.

Signal Detection Theory

One such mathematical model is signal detection theory, which was originally developed to quantify the detection of signals in noisy radar returns (Peterson et al., 1954). It is applicable to a wide range of human-system decision problems, including medical diagnosis, weather forecasting, prediction of violent behavior, and air traffic control, and it has been shown to be a robust method for modeling these types of problems (Swets et al., 2000). Signal detection theory has been found to be useful because it provides separate measures of the sensitivity of the human-system combination to discriminate signal from noise distributions on one hand and the decision criterion (the location of the threshold at which people or machines respond with a signal-present/signal-absent decision) on the other. The principal value of applying signal detection theory is to develop metrics for human-system performance and to evaluate design trade-offs between detector sensitivity, base rates of the signals of interest, and overall predictive value of the system output. The method is best employed to model effectiveness of discrete decision processes supported by automated systems. It serves to reduce the risk of picking the wrong operating point for a decision process, resulting in too many false alarms or a nonoptimal number of successful detections.

Models Derived from Human Cognitive Operations

A second, quite different approach is GOMS (Card, Moran, and Newell, 1983). GOMS models represent, for a given task, the user's Goals, Operators (a keystroke, memory retrieval, or mouse move), Methods (to reach a goal, such as using keystrokes or a menu to open a file), and Selection rules (to choose which method to use). These models can be applied as soon as there is an explicit design for a user interface, and they have been used to predict response times, learning times, workload, and to provide a measure of interface consistency and complexity (i.e., similar tasks should use similar methods and operators). These models are now being more widely applied, and there are tools available to support their use (Kieras, 1998; Nichols and Ritter, 1995; Williams, 2000). They provide a sharable representation of the tasks, how they are performed, and how long each will take. GOMS models can support user interface hardware and software design in several ways. They can be used to confirm consistency in the interface, that a method is available for each user goal, that there are ways to recover from errors, and that there are fast methods for frequently occurring goals (Chipman and Kieras, 2004).

The GOMS series of models had their most notable, documented application to predicting the performance of a new design for a telephone information operator's workstation in Project Ernestine (Gray, John, and Atwood, 1993). In this case, a variant of GOMS predicted that performance with a new telephone operator workstation design would be so much slower than that of the existing workstation, which would result in an increased operation cost of about $2.5 million per year. The new workstation was actually built and soon abandoned because the predictions were correct. As another example, preliminary studies suggest that a modeling approach could make cell phone menu use more efficient by reducing interaction time by 30 percent (St. Amant, Horton, and Ritter, 2004). If applied across all cell phones, this would save 28 years of user time per day. Gong and Kieras (1994) describe a GOMS analysis that suggested a redesign of a commercial computer-aided design system would lead to a 40-percent reduction in performance time and a 46-percent reduction in learning time. These time savings were later validated with actual users. Thus, simple GOMS models can reduce the risk of subsequent operational inefficiencies quite early in the system development process.

Models can also provide quantitative evidence for change—they can be used to reject a design that does not perform well enough. Glen Osga (noted in Chipman and Kieras, 2004, pp. 9-10) did a GOMS analysis of a new launch system for the Tomahawk cruise missile system. The analysis predicted that the launch process with the new system would take too long. This was ignored and the system was built as designed. Indeed, the system failed its acceptance test and had to be redesigned. As Chipman and Kieras note, it was costly to ignore this analysis, which could have led to a better design.

Despite their usefulness, GOMS models have not been as widely used by human factors specialists or systems engineers in systems development, particularly in large systems. Although relatively straightforward, they are perceived to be too difficult and time-consuming to apply.

Digital Human Physical Simulations

A third class of models is anthropometric representations of the size, shape, range of motion, and biomechanics of the human body (see also the section on physical ergonomics). Digital human models have been created to predict how humans will fit into physical workspaces, as in ground, aircraft, or space vehicles or to assess operations under the constraints of encumbering protective clothing. Representative of these models are commercial offerings, such as Jack (http://www.ugs.com/products/tecnomatix/human_performance/jack/) (Badler, Erignac, and Liu, 2002), Safeworks, (http://www.motionanalysis.com/applications/industrial/virtualdesign/safeworks.html), and Ramsis (http://www.humansolutions.com/automotive_industry/ramsis_community/index_en.php). They are available as computer programs that represent the static physical dimensions of human bodies, and they are increasingly able to represent the dynamics and static stresses for ergonomic analyses (Chaffin, 2004). They are primarily used for checking that the range of motion and accessibility are feasible, consistent with safe ergonomic standards, and efficient. They typically contain an anthropometric database that enables them to perform these evaluations for a range of types and sizes of users.

Dynamic anthropometric models are thus routinely used to reduce the risks of creating unusable or unsafe systems. The resulting models and analyses can be shared between designers and across design phases. Having a concrete computer mannequin that confirms the success or failure of accommodation at a workplace is a very useful shared representation. There is beginning to be interest in integrating these models with human behavior representations to integrate the physical and cognitive performance of tasks. MIDAS provided an early demonstration of this concept, and new developments are being introduced regularly (e.g., Carruth and Duffy, 2005).

Models that Mimic Human Cognitive and Perceptual-Motor Behavior

A fourth class, human performance and information processing models, simulates the sensory, perceptual, cognitive, and motor behavior of a human operator. They are referred to by some as integrated models of cognitive systems and by the military as human behavior representations. They interact with a system or a simulation and represent human behavior in enough detail to execute the required tasks in the simulation as a human would, mimicking the results of a human-in-the-loop simulation without the human.

Some of these models are based on ad hoc theories of human performance, such as the semiautonomous forces in simulations, such as the military ModSAF and JSAF. Others are built on cognitive architectures that represent theories of human performance. Examples of cognitive architectures include COGNET/iGEN (Zachary, 2000), created specifically for engineering applications; Soar (Laird, Newell, and Rosenbloom, 1987), an artificial intelligence–based architecture used for modeling learning, interruptability, and problem solving; ACT-R (Anderson et al., 2004), used to model learning, memory effects, and accurate reaction time performance;

EPIC (Kieras, Wood, and Meyer, 1997), used to model the interaction between thinking, perception, and action; and D-OMAR (Deutsch, 1998), used to model teamwork. Available reviews note further examples that have been developed for specific purposes (Morrison, 2003; National Research Council, 1998; Ritter et al., 2003).

These human behavior representations are more detailed because they actually mimic the information processing activities that generate behavior. They require a substantial initial investment, and each new application requires additional effort to characterize the task content to be performed. However, once developed, they can be used, modified, and reused throughout the system development life cycle, including to support conceptual design, to evaluate early design prototypes, to exercise system interfaces, and to support the development of operational procedures. They offer the ability to make strong predictions about human behavior. Because they provide not only what the descriptive models provide, but also the details of the information processing, they can be used to support applications in which it is useful to have models stand in for users for such things as systems analyses, or in training games and synthetic environments as colleagues and opponents. Models in this class have been used extensively in research and demonstration, but they have not, as yet, been widely used in system design (Gluck and Pew, 2005).

In some cases, models of human performance are represented only implicitly in a design tool that takes account of human performance capacities and limitations in making design recommendations. Automatic web site testing software is an example of this. Guidelines and style guides that suggest good practice in interface design are increasingly being implemented in design tools and guideline testing tools. A review of these types of testing tools shows their ease of use and increasing range (Ivory and Hearst, 2001). For example, "Bobby" (http://www.watchfire.com/products/webxm/bobby. aspx) is one of many tools to test web sites. Bobby notes what parts of a web site are barriers to accessibility by people with disabilities and checks for compliance with existing accessibility guidelines (e.g., from Section 508 of the U.S. Rehabilitation Act). Bobby does this by checking objects on a web page in a recursive manner against these guidelines (e.g., that captions for pictures are also provided to support blind users, that fonts are large enough).

While the developers of these systems may not have thought specifically about developing a model of the user, the guidelines and tools make assumptions about users. For example, Bobby makes assumptions about the text-to-speech software used by blind users, as well as about the range of visual acuity of sighted users. The implementation often hides the details of these models, creating human performance models that are implicit with the shared representation being only the results of the test, not the assumptions supporting the test. On one hand, to their credit, these tools represent methods of incorporating consideration of human characteristics into designs that are very easy to use. On the other hand, just as with using statistics programs without understanding the computations they implement, using these tools without understanding the limitations of their implicit user models and performance specifications creates risks of inappropriate application or overreliance on the results.

Contributions to System Design Phases

Human-system simulation can play an important role in system design across the development life cycle to reduce the development risk. Human-in-the-loop simulation is widely accepted and has been applied successfully in all of the life-cycle phases discussed below. In this section, we focus on applications of human-system modeling because this kind of modeling has been less widely applied and has the potential to make significant contributions. In research labs routinely and increasingly in applied settings, the use of explicit computer models representing human performance has been demonstrated for a variety of uses, including testing prototypes of systems and their interfaces; testing full interfaces to predict usage time and errors; providing surrogate users to act as colleagues in teamwork situations; and validating interfaces as meeting a standard for operator performance time, workload, and error probability. They can also be used to evaluate the ability to meet user requirements and the interface consistency in a common system or a system of systems. Further reviews on models in system design are available (e.g., Beevis, 1999; Howes, 1995; National Research Council, 1998; Vicente, 1999).

Exploration and Valuation

Human-system models can be useful in exploratory design, because they can range from back-of-the-envelope calculations to formal models that reflect, at a detailed level, the costs and benefits of alternative approaches to a new or revised system. If one is working in air traffic control, for example, models of traffic flow in the U.S. airspace could be modified to postulate the impact of introducing alternative forms of automation. Analysis and network models will be particularly helpful in this stage because they are more flexible and can be performed earlier in the design process. In many cases, the model's impact in the elaboration phase may be derived from design lessons learned from previous designs—they will help the designer choose better designs in what can be a very volatile design period.

An important contribution of a model, especially in the early development stages, is that the model's development forces the analyst to think very deeply and concretely about the human performance requirements, about the user-system interactions, and about the assumptions that must be made for a particular design to be successful. For example, a network model can help make explicit the tasks that must be supported, providing a way for development teams to see the breadth of applicability and potential requirements of a system.

Architecting and Design

During the system's construction period, models help describe and show the critical features of human performance in the system. A human-system performance model can serve as a shared representation that supports envisioning the HSI implications of a design. As such, they can help guide design, suggesting and documenting potential improvements. Most model types can be used to predict a variety of user performance measures with a proposed system. These measures, including the time to use, time to learn, potential error types, and predicted error frequency, can provide predicted usability measures before the system is built. The models do not themselves tell how to change the system, but they enable alternative designs to be compared. As designers incorporate the implications of a representation in their own thinking, the models also suggest ways to improve the design. In addition, experience with models reflecting multiple design alternative provides a powerful way to help designers understand how the capacities and limitations of their users constrain system performance. Booher and Minninger (2003) provide numerous examples in which redesign was performed, sometimes with initial reluctance but with long-term payoff based on model-based evaluations at this and later stages of design.

In a previous section, the usefulness of prototypes was highlighted. Prototypes can be represented at many different levels of specificity. When the design has progressed to the point at which concrete prototype simulations can be developed, it can be very useful to exercise the simulation with a human behavior representation. The development of the human behavior representation itself will be illuminating because it will make the tasks and human performance concrete, but it will also be useful for exploring alternative operational concepts, refining the procedures of use, and identifying the user interface requirements. Again, the human-system simulation can serve as a very useful shared representation that brings the development team together.

Evaluation

Models can be very helpful in evaluating prototype system and user-interface designs. That is, using a model of the user to evaluate how the interface presents information or provides functionality.

Refining and testing offer perhaps the canonical application of user models in system design. The same or refined versions of models applied earlier in the design process can be reused to support system evaluation. A human model can exercise the interface and compute a variety of usability and system performance measures. While the system is still evolving, evaluation is formative—that is, supporting refinement and improvement. In the later stages of test and evaluation, the evaluation is summative, providing estimates of how the system will perform in the field. Many examples of refining systems using models are now are available (Booher and Minninger, 2003; Kieras, 2003; St. Amant, Freed, and Ritter, 2005).

Also, all types of models have been used to help create system documentation or for developing training materials. As the model specifies what knowledge is required to perform a task, the model's knowledge can also serve as a set of information to include in training and operations documentation, either as a manual or within a help system.

Operation

The designs of a complex system are never complete because they continually evolve. Human-system simulations can continue to be applied to guide the evolution as experience is gained from the system in the field. Potential changes can be tried out in the simulated world and compared with the existing performance. This has frequently been done in the space program, in which engineers on the ground try out solutions with simulation to find the best one to communicate to the actual flight crew. It should be noted that simulations are less successful as complexity grows and for dealing with conditions such as boundary conditions and anomalies.

Strengths, Limitations, and Gaps

Strengths

Simulations, particularly human-in-the-loop simulations, and human-system models are especially valuable because they make concrete, explicit, and quantitative the role of users in task execution and their impact on the characteristics of the systems to be controlled. They provide concrete examples of how a system will operate, not only how the equipment will operate, but also what human-system performance will result. Another aspect of the use of models and simulations in design is the cumulative learning that occurs in the designer as a result of a simulation-based design and evaluation process. When using a model or simulation to design an interface, the designer receives feedback about users, their behavior, and how they interact with systems. In their next design task, if the feedback was explicit and heeded, designers have a richer model of the user and of the system, their joint behavior, and the roles users play. Having the knowledge in the designer's head supports the creative process and makes the knowledge easier to apply than through an external tool.

Limitations

Ease of use. If the models are more challenging and costly in time and effort than practitioners are willing to use, then one cannot expect them to be used to reduce risk during development. Full-mission human-in-the-loop simulation is costly and time-consuming to apply and should be used only when the potential risks and opportunities justify it. Part-task simulation is a less costly alternative in which only the elements that bear critically on the questions to be answered are simulated. Human-system models range widely in their scope and the effort required to apply them. While the keystroke-level model version of GOMS can be taught fairly quickly, other modeling approaches all appear to be more difficult to use than they should be and more difficult than practitioners currently are willing to use routinely. Even IMPRINT, a well-developed and popular collection of models, is considered too difficult for the average practitioner to use. This may be inherent in the tools; it may be due to inadequate instructional materials or to inadequacies in the quality of the tools and environments to support model development and use. It may also result from the lack of education or experience about how valuable the investment in models can be—that the investment is worth the cost in time and effort. Few people now note how expensive it is to design and test a computer chip, a bridge, or a ship or bemoan the knowledge required to perform these tasks. And yet humans and their interactions are even more complex; designing for and with them requires expertise, time, and support. Further work is needed to improve the usability of the model development process and the ease of use of the resulting models.

In order for human-system models to be credible as shared representations, they must make their characteristics and predictions explicit in a way that can be understood by the range of stakeholders for whom they are relevant. There is a range of questions that people ask about models including what their structure is, how they "work," and why they did or did not take a particular action (Councill, Haynes, and Ritter, 2003). This problem is more acute for the more complex models, particularly the information-processing models. Unclear or obtuse models risk not being used or being ignored if they are not understood. Promoting the understanding of models will increase trust in understanding where the system risks are. Future models will need to support explanations of their structure, predictions, and the source of the predictions.

How models are developed will be important to how models will be used in system design. Using models across the design process from initial conception to test and evaluation will require adapting the level of depth and completeness to each task. Right now, model developers are at times still struggling with building user models once, let alone for reuse and across designers and across design tasks.

There have been several efforts to make models more easily used. For human behavior representations, these include Amadeus (e.g., Young, Green, and Simon, 1989), Apex (Freed et al., 2003), CogTool (John et al., 2004), Herbal (Cohen, Ritter, and Haynes, 2005), and G2A (St. Amant, Freed, and Ritter, 2005). At their best, these tools have offered, in limited cases, a 3 to 100 times reduction in development time, demonstrating that progress can be made in ease of use.

While promising, these tools are not yet complete enough to support a wide range of design or a wide range of interfaces, tasks, and analyses. For example, CogTool is useful and supports a full cycle of model, test, revise interface. It cannot model problem solving or real-time interactive behavior, but it starts to illustrate what such an easy-to-use system would look like. Research programs have been sponsored by the U.K. Ministry of Defence ("Reducing the Cost of Acquiring Behaviours") and by the U.S. Office of Naval Research ("Affordable Human Behavior Modeling") to make models more affordable and are sources of further examples and systems in this area.

Integration.   There are gaps in integrating user models within and across design phases as well as connecting them to the systems themselves. As models get used in more steps in the design process, they will serve as boundary objects, representing shared understanding about users' performance in the systems under evaluation—their goals, their capabilities to execute tasks, and their behavior. IMPRINT has often been used this way. Once widely used, there will be a need to integrate models to ensure that designers and workers at each stage are talking about the same user-system characteristics. The models might usefully be elaborated together, for example, starting with a GOMS model and moving to a human behavior representation model to exercise an interface. This kind of graceful elaboration has been started by several groups (Lebiere et al., 2002; Ritter et al., 2005, 2006; Urbas and Leuchter, 2005) but is certainly not yet routine.

The models will also have to be more mutable so that multiple views of their performance can be used by participants in different stages of the design process. Some designers will need high-level views and summaries of behavior and the knowledge required by users to perform the task, and other designers may need detailed time predictions and how these can be improved.

It is especially valuable for models of users to interact with systems and their interfaces. Models that interact with systems are easiest for designers to apply, most general, and easiest to validate. Eventually it could allow models' performance to serve as acceptance tests, and it may lead to new approaches, such as visual inspection of operational mock-ups rather than extensive testing. Currently, connecting models to system or interface simulations is not routine. The military has shown that the high-level architecture connection approach can be successful when the software supporting the models and systems to be connected is open and available for inspection and modification. However, much commercial software is proprietary and not available for modification to support model interaction (Ritter et al., 2000). In the long term, we think that the approach of having models of human behavior representations interacting directly with an unmodified or instrumented interface software will become the dominant design approach, which can also include automatic testing with explicit models. Models that use SegMan represent steps toward this approach of automatic testing of unmodified interfaces (Ritter et al., 2006; St. Amant, Horton, and Ritter, 2004).

High-level languages. Currently, many models, particularly human behavior representation models, require detailed specifications. Creating these models for realistic tasks can be daunting. For example, there are at least 95 tasks to include in a university department web site design (Ritter, Freed, and Haskett, 2005). One way to reduce the risk that human behavior models will be unused is to provide a high-level language that is similar to that used in network models. Interface designers will need a textual or graphical language to create models that are higher level than most of the current human behavior representation languages, and analysts will need libraries of tasks (or the ability to read models as if they were libraries), and they will need to be able to make it easy to program new and modified tasks. More complete lists of requirements for this approach are available (e.g., Kieras et al., 1995; Ritter, Van Rooy, and St. Amant, 2002).

Cultural, team, and emotional models. Models of individual task performance have rarely included social knowledge about working in groups or cultural differences. Users are increasingly affected by social processes, including culture and emotion. As one better understands the role of these effects on systems, models will need to be extended to include what is known about these characteristics as a further element of risk reduction. For a mundane but sometimes catastrophic example, consider the interpretation of switches in different cultures. Some cultures flip switches up to be on, and some switch them down. The design, and implementation, of safety-critical switches, such as aircraft circuit breakers or power plant controls, needs to take account of these cultural differences.

Social knowledge, cultural knowledge, theories of emotions, and task knowledge have been developed by different communities: models of social processes will need to be adapted if they are to be incorporated in models of task execution (like human behavior representation models, Hudlicka, 2002). Understanding and applying this knowledge to design is of increasing interest as a result of a desire to improve the quality of models performance and an acknowledgment that cultural, team, and emotional effects influence each other and task performance. For example, there is a forthcoming National Academies study on organizational models (National Research Council, 2007) and there is also recent work on including social knowledge in models of human behavior representation (e.g., Sun, 2006).

8

Methods for Evaluation

This chapter presents two classes of methods for evaluating human performance and the interaction between humans and systems. The first class of methods, risk analysis, discusses the approaches to identifying and addressing business risks and safety and survivability risks. The second class of methods, usability evaluation, describes the range of experimental and observational approaches used to determine the usability of system features in all stages of the system development life cycle. Figure 8-1 provides an overview. This figure lists the foundational methods (e.g., surveys, interviews, experiment design) noted in the Introduction to Part II because they play a central role in evaluation.

RISK ANALYSIS

Overview

This section describes some commonly used tools for risk management, including failure modes and effects analysis (FMEA) and fault tree analysis (FTA). These tools are flexible and can be used to assess, manage, and mitigate

- business risk due to faults in the development process, including failed steps to consider human-system integration (HSI).
- failed usability outcomes (e.g., failure to meet customer usability objectives, which results in product failure in the marketplace).

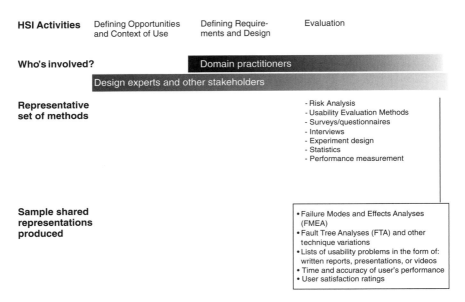

FIGURE 8-1 Representative methods and sample shared representations for evaluation.

- use-error faults that result in harm to product users (e.g., medical devices, failed mission objectives, such as failure to destroy enemy targets in a military system).

The emphasis is on use of these tools to evaluate and control negative outcomes related to use error or errors resulting from defects in the user interface element of human-system integration. By simple extensions, they can also be used to evaluate and control business risk related to the development cycle. Most of the following text is focused on use errors, but we make the case for the relative ease of using the philosophy behind these tools for many other purposes, including assessing and controlling business risk. In the military, the analysis of use error is especially relevant to the HSI domains of human factors, safety and occupational health, and survivability.

As noted, these tools and related methods are frequently applied to understanding use errors made with medical and other commercial devices.

Use errors are defined as predictable patterns of human errors that can be attributable to inadequate or improper design. Use errors can be predicted through analytical task walkthrough techniques and via empirically based usability testing. Here we explain and discuss the special methodology of use-error focused risk analysis and some of its history. Examples are presented that illustrate the methods of use-error risk analysis such as FTA and FMEA and some pitfalls to be avoided. These methods are widely used in safety engineering. The concepts are illustrated with a medical device case study using an automatic external defibrillator and a business risk example.

Risk-Management Techniques

Risk analysis in the context of use errors in products and processes has received increasing attention in recent years, particularly for medical devices. These techniques have been used for decades to assess the effect of human behavior on critical systems, such as in aerospace, defense systems, and nuclear power applications. Use errors are defined as a pattern of predictable human errors that can be attributable to inadequate or improper design. Use error can also produce faults that create failures for many types of systems and products, including

- *E-commerce web sites*—the user fails to complete the checkout process and revenue from orders is lost.
- *Weapons systems*—the user fails to arm and deploy the weapons system and a critical enemy target survives and goes on to destroy combat systems and personnel.
- *Energy systems*—the operator fails to detect and isolate a component failure and the entire energy plant fails.
- *Transportation system*—the driver fails to avoid another approaching vehicle and all occupants of both vehicles are killed in the subsequent collision.

Defining Use Error

Use error is characterized by a repetitive pattern of failure that indicates that a failure mode is likely to occur with use and thus has a reasonable possibility of predictability of occurrence. Use error can be addressed and minimized by the device designer and proactively identified through the use of such techniques as usability testing and hazard analysis. An important point is that, in the area of medical products, regulator and standards bodies make a clear distinction between the common terms "human error" and "user error" in comparison to "use error." The term "use error" attempts to remove the blame from the user and open up the analyst to consider other causes, including the following

- Poor user interface design (e.g., poor usability).
- Organizational elements (e.g., inadequate training or support structure).
- Use environment not properly anticipated in the design.
- Not understanding the user's tasks and task flow.
- Not understanding the user profile in terms of individual differences in training, experience, task performance, incentives, and motivation.

ANALYSIS OF HUMAN ERROR

The analysis of human error has played a central role in risk analysis since the 1950s. Initially in nuclear weapons assembly, then in the nuclear power industry and in industry more generally, particularly after the Three Mile Island accident in 1979. Although in this chapter, risk analysis focuses on safety critical systems, the risk of human error is relevant to human-system integration more generally because errors can also result in inefficiencies, excessive cost of operations, and wasted resources.

Reason (1990) provides a comprehensive classification of errors as shown in Figure 8-2. This classification makes clear that even though every error is identified by an action, the source of the error can be a much wider set of alternative failures. The category of knowledge-based mistakes can be expanded to include the many additional psychological sources of mistakes, including the following:

- Situation awareness.
- Decision making.
- Estimation.
- Computation.

Embry (1987) summarizes approaches to human reliability assessment—that is, assessment of the risk of human error. The oldest and most well-known technique is the technique for human error rate prediction (THERP) (Swain, 1963; Swain and Guttman, 1983). This approach is based on probabilistic risk analysis and fault tree task decomposition methods, and it has been applied extensively in nuclear power plant design and procedure assessment. The techniques described in this chapter are the basic building blocks of quantitative methods, such as THERP; the degree to which complex models involving estimates of error probability are necessary depends largely on the application and extent to which quantifica-

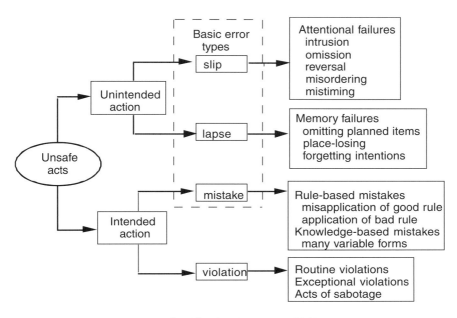

FIGURE 8-2 Reason's error classification (Reason, 1990).

tion is necessary. However, basic error risk analysis as described in this chapter is relatively straightforward and is warranted in virtually all HSI applications.

Identification of Hazards and When Risk Management Is Conducted

An important first step in risk management is to understand and cata-logue the hazards and possible resulting harms that might be caused by a product or system. Sometimes this is called hazard analysis. Others use the term in a more general way as a synonym for risk-management. Hazard analysis is often accomplished as an iterative process, with a first draft be-ing updated and expanded as additional risk management methods (e.g., FMEA, FTA) are used. Medical experts and those in quality control and product development, among other commercial product disciplines, can brainstorm on harms and hazards. Technically, hazards are the potential for harms. Harms are defined as physical injury or damage to the health of people or damage to property or the environment. Box 8-1 shows examples

---

BOX 8-1
Possible Harms and Hazards
from the Use of Medical Equipment

Use of an Automatic Needle Injection Device
- Bleeding, bruising, or tearing of skin, leading to a possible infection
- Incomplete injection that may lead to giving another injection, leading to overmedication
  - Undermedication
  - Delay in therapy
  - Failed therapy due to unsuccessful injection
  - Pain on injection
  - Increased bleeding, due to the presence of alcohol
  - Nondelivery, wasted dose
  - Delivery intramuscularly instead of subcutaneously
  - Possible infection from microorganisms present on skin

Use of an Automatic External Defibrillator
- Nondelivery of defibrillating shock
- Delay in delivery of defibrillating shock
- Administration of shock when not needed
- Bystander shocked when touching patient during delivery
- Set victim on fire
- Delivery of weak noneffective shock
- Ignoring subsequent second episode of cardiac fibrillation
- Burns caused by delivery of electrodes touching each other

---

of harms from hazards for a penlike automatic needle injector device and shows similar harms and hazards from an automatic external defibrillator. Box 8-2 extends the notion of harm to negative business outcomes resulting from HSI faults.

Below we describe the most commonly used tools involved in user error risk analysis, FMEA, and FTA. These tools can also be used to assess and control business risk. The shared representations typically resulting from these methods are reports containing graphical portrayals of the fault trees or tabular descriptions of the failure modes. The FTA representations show cumulative probabilities of logically combined fault events demonstrating the overall risk levels. The tabular shared representations documented with FMEA tables show calculated risk levels associated with different business or operational hazard outcomes.

BOX 8-2
Negative Business Outcomes Resulting from HSI Faults

- Product cannot be developed. All development costs are sunk costs with no return on investment (ROI).

- Product introduction is delayed and market window is missed. Reduced net present value (NPV) of product revenue stream.

- Substandard product is introduced and support costs become very high.

- Manufacturing costs of the product exceed estimates in business case and margins are drastically reduced.

- Not all desired features can be delivered and product fails to meet revenue plan in business case.

- Product is faulty and needs to be recalled. Recall costs are enormous.

- Product is unsafe and subsequent liability claims become very large and threaten the financial viability of the development organization.

- Product fails to meet the target market needs (not developed for the most important user profiles) and misses revenue plans.

Shared Representations

FMEA

The recommended steps for conducting a use-error risk analysis are the same as for traditional risk analysis with one significant addition, namely the need to perform a task analysis. Possible use errors are then deduced from the tasks (Israelski and Muto, 2006). Each of the use errors or faults is rated in terms of the severity of its effects and the probability of its occurrence. A risk index is calculated by combining these two elements and can then be used for risk prioritization. For each of the high-priority items, modes (or methods) of control are assumed for the system or subsystem and reassessed in terms of risk. The process is iterated until all higher level risks are eliminated and any residual risk is as low as reasonably practicable (sometimes referred to as ALARP).

Among the most widely used of the risk analysis tools is FMEA and its close relative, failure modes, effects, and criticality analysis (FMECA).[1]

---

[1]FMECA is an extension of FMEA that starts with FMEA elements and further considers ratings of criticality and probability of occurrence. Because of their common basis, FMEA and FMECA are commonly referred to as FMEA. Likewise, in this section FMEA and FMECA will be referred to as FMEA.

FMEA is a design evaluation technique used to define, identify, and eliminate known or potential failures, problems, and errors from the system. The basic approach of FMEA from an engineering perspective is to answer the question: If a system component fails, what is the effect on system performance or safety? Similarly, from a human factors perspective, FMEA addresses the question, "If a user commits an error, what is the effect on system performance from a safety or financial perspective?" A human factors risk analysis has several components that help define and prioritize such faults: (1) the identified fault or use error, (2) occurrence (frequency of failure), (3) severity (seriousness of the hazard and harm resulting from the failure), (4) selection of controls to mitigate the failure before it has an adverse effect, and (5) an assessment of the risk after controls are applied.

A use-error risk analysis is not substantially different from a conventional design FMEA. The main difference is that, rather than focusing on component or system-level faults, it focuses on user actions that deviate from expected or ideal user performance. For business risk, the development faults would include the items shown in Box 8-2. Table 8-1 summarizes the steps in performing FMEA.

FTA and Other Technique Variations

Other commonly used tools for analyzing and predicting failure and consequences are fault tree and event tree analysis. FTA is a top-down deductive method used to determine overall system reliability and safety (Stamatis, 1995). A fault tree, depicted graphically, starts with a single undesired event (failure) at the top of an inverted tree, and the branches show the faults that can lead to the undesired event—the root causes are shown at the bottom of the tree. For human factors and safety applications, FTA can be a useful tool for visualizing the effects of human error combined with device faults or normal conditions on the overall system. Furthermore, by assigning probability estimates to the faults, combinatorial probabilistic rules can be used to calculate an estimated probability of the top-level event or hazard.

An event tree is a visual representation of all the events that can occur in a system. As the number of events increases, the picture fans out like the branches of a tree. Event trees can be used to analyze systems that involve sequential operational logic and switching. Whereas fault trees trace the precursors or root causes of events, event trees trace the alternative consequences of events. The starting point (referred to as the initiating event) disrupts normal system operation. The event tree displays the sequences of events involving success and/or failure of the system components. In human factors analysis the events that are traced are the contingent sequences of human operator actions (Swain and Guttman, 1983).

TABLE 8-1 Steps in Performing FMEA

Steps	Description
1. Form a team	The most effective risk analyses are performed by a team of stakeholders.
2. Perform a task analysis	A task analysis is a detailed sequential description (in graphic, tabular, or narrative form) of tasks performed while operating a devise or system. The analysis should cover the major task flows performed by users.
3. Start a worksheet	There are a variety of FMEA worksheets for documenting use errors. Computer spreadsheets can be useful.
4. Brainstorm potential use errors (failure modes)	Brainstorming involves identifying possible operator errors and actions that deviate from the expected or optimal behavior for each task identified in the task analysis (step 2 above).
5. List potential effects of each failure mode/ operator error	The team identifies potential harms associated with each failure mode. This step is important for subsequent determination of risk ratings.
6. Assign severity ratings to the harm or negative outcomes	A severity rating determines the seriousness of the effects of a given fault if it occurs. Severity can be assigned a numeric value or a qualitative descriptive rating.
7. Assign occurrence ratings	Occurrence ratings are estimates of the predicted frequency or likelihood of the occurrence of a fault. These ratings should be based on existing data such as customer complaints or usability test results.
8. Derive risk index	A numeric risk index is calculated by multiplying the severity rating by the occurrence rating. A qualitative risk rating requires the development of criteria establishing risk levels based on combinations of severity and occurrence ratings.
9. Prioritize risks	Risks are prioritized to determine how, when, and whether identified failure modes should be addressed.
10. Take actions to eliminate or reduce high-priority failure modes	Organized problem-solving approaches are used by the team to select modes of control for each high-priority failure. The most desirable mode of control is design; training and warnings may also be considered.
11. Assign effectiveness ratings	Effectiveness ratings are assigned to each mode of control selected/identified in step 10 above. Depending on the stage in the development life cycle, these ratings may be based on either formative or summative evaluation data.
12. Revise risk priorities	When modes of control are in place, numerical or qualitative risk indices are revised or recomputed.

As with FMEAs, fault trees and event trees can be developed by teams or by individuals with team review. For more information, refer to the literature in reliability engineering or systems safety engineering (e.g., Nuclear Regulatory Commission, 1981).

In recent years, graphical software programs have been made available for personal computers that enable users to rapidly assemble fault trees by "dragging and dropping" standard logic symbols onto a drawing area and connections are made (and maintained) automatically. These tools automatically calculate branch and top-level probabilities based on the estimated event probabilities entered. Such tools make FTAs much more accessible and much less labor intensive. Figure 8-3 is an example of a fault tree diagram for an automatic external defibrillator. Table 8-2 shows a summary of the steps in creating an FTA.

Contributions to System Design Phases

Use-error-focused risk analyses including FMEA and FTA are particular methods in the user-centered or human factors design process. It is the analytical complement to empirical usability assessment, commonly called usability testing. Risk analysis, evaluation, and control starts early in any development process (e.g., the incremental commitment model development process) and is iterated and reassessed as the development process progresses and the system design matures. For human-system integration, risk is assessed for usability, systems safety, and survivability issues. There are opportunities to develop single analyses that would serve all of these purposes, with the proper coordination across these development teams.

Strengths, Limitations, and Gaps

These risk-management techniques can be powerful analytic tools. Tables 8-3 and 8-4 list advantages and disadvantages of both FMEAs and FTAs.

The limitations for FTAs and FMEAs are similar:

• Achieving group consensus is difficult. Research is needed on more effective and reliable techniques, such as modifications of the Delphi group decision-making technique. Groups can be dominated by individuals based on their rank, power, or personality, and the final ratings may not really reflect the group opinion.
• Estimating likelihood of occurrence is very unreliable. Better probability modeling is needed.
• Better tools are needed to integrate FTAs and FMEAs to make them easier to modify and apply.

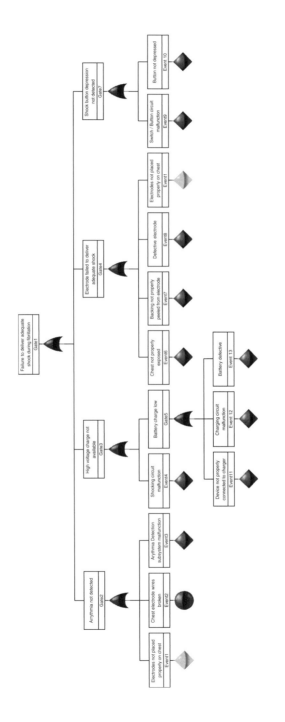

FIGURE 8-3 Example FTA for a hypothetical automatic external defibrillator.
SOURCE: Israelski and Muto (2006).

TABLE 8-2 Steps in Performing an FTA

Steps	Description
1. Identify the top-level hazards.	The team will brainstorm to identify the top-level hazards (undesired events) to be addressed. A fault tree will be developed for each of these hazards.
2. Identify fault tree events.	Identify faults and other events (including normal events) that could result in the top-level undesired event. These can be documented in a list or on notes posted on a wall.
3. Identify the conditions under which the events can lead to failure.	These include events that may lead directly to harm (single-point failure) or cause another fault without other events occurring; events that must happen in conjunction with other events to cause failure; and events that must happen in sequence to cause a failure.
4. Combine the above events into a fault tree.	A fault tree is constructed using symbols that represent individual events and the most significant logic symbols, the "OR gate" and the "AND gate."
5. Assign probabilities to each event.	If the fault tree does not sufficiently characterize the system and human interactions, the team will assign probabilities to each of the events based on quantitative data or estimates based on expert judgment.
6. Calculate the probability of each of the branches leading to the top-level hazard.	Fault tree probabilities propagate upward from the individual events. The probability of the individual gates and the overall fault tree probability are computed by using numerical combinatorial rules for various logic gates.

TABLE 8-3 Advantages and Disadvantages of FMEA

Advantages	Disadvantages
Risk index /RPN enable prioritization of faults.	Difficult to assess combination of events complex interactions (unless explicitly documented).
Explicitly documents modes of control/mitigation.	Large documents can be difficult to manage: minimize inconsistencies and redundant items.
Format useful for tracking action items.	Severity and occurrence ratings are often difficult for individuals or teams to estimate. Much time can be spent in discussions.
Easily constructed using hand-written spreadsheets or computer-based software tools: spreadsheets/word processing tables specialized FMEA tools.	Sometimes can be overly conservative. With each fault isolated, failure to consider combinatorial events (as do fault trees) may lead to the false conclusion that every item requires explicit mitigation.

TABLE 8-4 Advantages and Disadvantages of FTA

Advantages	Disadvantages
Graphical format enables visualization of combination of events.	Drawings can become large and unwieldy in complex systems.
Enables estimation of overall probability of failure based on estimates of root causes.	Modes of control are not always explicit.
Small fault trees can be developed using common flowchart drawing tools.	Requires more training than FMEA.
	Special software required for rapid development of fault trees.

USABILITY EVALUATION METHODS

Overview

This section explains how usability evaluation methods can contribute to systems development by providing feedback on usability problems and validating the usability of a system. These methods not only help improve the user interface, but also often provide insight into the extent to which the product will meet user requirements.

There are four broad approaches to ensuring the usability of a product or system:

1. Evaluation of the user's performance and satisfaction when using the product or system in a real or simulated working environment. Also called evaluation of "quality in use" or "human in the loop."

2. Evaluation of the characteristics of the interactive system, tasks, users, and the working environment to identify any obstacles to usability.

3. Evaluation of the process used for systems development to assess whether appropriate HSI methods and techniques were used.

4. Evaluation of the capability of an organization to routinely employ appropriate HSI methods and techniques.

Thus, an organization needs the capability to apply human-system integration in the development process in order to be able to design a product or interactive system with characteristics that will enable adequate user performance and satisfaction in the intended contexts of use (Figure 8-4).

Evaluation of the usability of a product provides feedback on the extent to which a design meets user needs, and thus it is central to a user-centered design process. Feedback from usability evaluation is particularly important because developers seldom have an intimate understanding of the user's per-

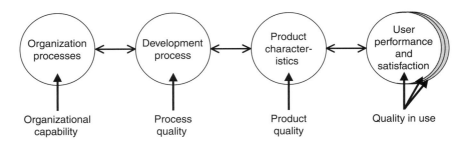

FIGURE 8-4 Approaches to ensuring usability. The quality in use is determined by the quality of the product, which is determined by the quality of the development process, which is determined by the organizational capability.

spective and work practices. In the collective experience of the committee, initial designs therefore very rarely fully meet user requirements. The cost of rectifying any divergence between the design and user needs increases rapidly as development proceeds, which means that user feedback should be obtained as early as possible.

Without proper usability evaluation, a project runs a high risk of expensive rework to adapt a system to actual user needs or of potential rejection of the product or system. Usability evaluation can be used to assess the magnitude of these. For more information on evaluating the development process and organizational capability, see Earthy, Sherwood Jones, and Bevan (2001).

Uses and Types of Methods

Usability is determined not only by the characteristics of the interactive product or system, but also by the whole context of use, including the nature of the users, tasks, and operational environment (see Chapter 6). In the broadest context, usability is concerned with optimizing all the factors that determine effective interaction between users and systems in a working environment. But in some cases, the scope of the evaluation is more limited, for example to support the design of a particular interactive component in an otherwise predetermined system. The word "product" is used below to refer to the component or system being evaluated.

Evaluations of user behavior and product characteristics are complementary. Although a user-based evaluation is the ultimate test of usability, it is not usually practical to evaluate all permutations of user type, task, and operational conditions. Evaluation of the characteristics of the product or interactive system can anticipate and explain potential usability problems, and it can be carried out before there is a working system. However, evaluation of detailed characteristics alone can never be sufficient, as this does not provide enough information to accurately predict the eventual user behavior.

Uses of Methods: Formative and Summative Evaluation

The most common type of usability evaluation is formative: to improve a product by identifying and fixing usability problems. Formative evaluation of early mock-ups can also be used to obtain a better understanding of user needs and to refine requirements. An iterative process of repeated formative evaluation of prototypes can be used to monitor how closely the prototype designs match user needs. The feedback can be used to improve the design for further testing. Early formative evaluation reduces the risk of expensive rework. Formative evaluation is most effective when it involves a combination of expert and user-based methods.

Some examples of prototypes that can be evaluated are

- paper-based, low-fidelity simulations for exploratory testing.
- computer simulations (typically screen-based, e.g., Flash™, Macromedia Director™, Visual Basic™, Java, HTML). This can simulate the user interface while sacrificing full fidelity.
- working early prototypes of the actual product.

Prototypes are discussed in more detail in Chapter 7.

In a more mature design process, formative evaluation should be complemented by establishing usability requirements (see Chapter 7) and testing whether these have been achieved by using a more formal summative evaluation process. Summative testing reduces the risk of delivering a product that fails as a result of poor user performance. Usability has also been incorporated into six sigma quality methods (Sauro and Kindlund, 2005).

Summative usability testing of an existing system can be used to provide baseline measures that can form the basis for usability requirements (i.e., objectives for human performance and user satisfaction ratings) for the next modification or release. A Common Industry Specification for Usability Requirements (Theofanos, 2006) has been developed to support iterative development and the sharing of such requirements.

Summative tests at the end of development should have formal acceptance criteria derived from the usability requirements. Summative methods can also be elaborated to identify usability problems, but if prior iterative rounds of formative usability testing are performed, then typically there will be few usability surprises uncovered during this late-stage testing (Theofanos, 2006).

Types of Methods

The remainder of this section describes methods in the following categories:

User Behavior Evaluation Methods

- Methods based on observing users of a real or simulated system.
- Methods that collect data from usage of an existing system.
- Methods based on models and simulation.

Product Usability Characteristics Evaluation Methods

- Methods based on expert assessment of the characteristics of a system.
- Automated methods based on rules and guidelines.

All the methods can provide formative information about usability problems. The first two types of user behavior methods can also provide summative data. Other more informal techniques (such as a focus group) often do not provide reliable information for evaluation.

Methods based on observing users of a real or simulated system.   Methods in this category are used

- at all stages of development if possible.
- to provide evidence for management.
- in observing user trials, as a good way of providing incontrovertible evidence to developers.

In these user-based methods, users step through the design attempting to complete a task with the minimum of assistance. There are different types of user-based methods adapted specifically for formative testing or to also provide summative data (see Table 8-5).

- Formative methods focus on understanding the user's behavior, intentions, and expectations and typically employ a think-aloud protocol.
- Summative methods measure the quality in use of a product and can be used to establish and test usability requirements. Summative usability testing, normally based on the principles of ISO 9241-11 (International Organization for Standardization, 1998), obtains quality in use measures for

TABLE 8-5 Types of User-Based Evaluation Method

Type	Description	When in Design Cycle	Typical Sample Size (per group)	Considerations
Formative Usability Testing				
Exploratory	High-level test of users performing tasks	Conceptual design	5-8	Simulate early concepts, for example, with very low-fidelity paper prototypes or foam core models.
Diagnostic	Give representative users real tasks to perform	Iterative throughout the design cycle	5-8	Early designs or computer simulations. Used to identify usability problems.
Comparison	Identify strengths and weaknesses of an existing design	Early in design	5-8	Can be combined with benchmarking.
Summative Usability Testing				
Benchmarking Competitive	Real users and real tasks are tested with existing design	Prior to design	8-30	To provide a basis for setting usability criteria. Can be combined with competitive comparison.
Validation	Real users and real tasks are tested with final design	End of design cycle	8-30	To validate the design by having usability objectives as acceptance criteria and should include any training and documentation.

–*Effectiveness*—"the accuracy and completeness." Error-free completion of tasks is important in both business and military applications.
–*Efficiency*—"the resources expended." How quickly a user can perform work is critical for productivity.
–*Satisfaction*—"positive attitudes toward the use of the product." Satisfaction is a success factor for any products with discretionary use and essential to maintain workforce motivation.

Each type of measure is usually regarded as an independent factor with a relative importance that depends on the context of use (e.g., efficiency may be paramount for employers, while satisfaction is essential for public users of a web site).

These measures can also be used to assess accessibility (the performance and satisfaction of users with disabilities), and learnability (e.g., the duration of a course or use of training materials), and the user performance and satisfaction expected immediately after training and after a designated length of use. In summative testing, the system to be evaluated may be a functioning prototype (e.g., in alpha or beta testing) or controlled trials of an existing system.

Methods that collect data from usage of an existing system. This category of methods is used when planning to improve an existing system. They include

• *Satisfaction surveys:* Satisfaction questionnaires distributed to a sample of existing users can provide an economical way of obtaining feedback on the usability of an existing product or system.
• *Web metrics:* A web site can be instrumented to provide information on entrance and exit pages, frequency of particular paths through the site, and the extent to which search is successful. If combined with pop-up questions, the results can be related to particular user groups and tasks.
• *Application instrumentation:* Data points can be built into code that "count" when an event occurs (e.g., in Microsoft Office—Harris, 2005). This could be the frequency with which commands are used or the number of times a sequence results in a particular type of error. The data are sent anonymously to the development organization. This real-world data from large populations can help guide future design decisions.

For more information, see the section on event data analysis in Chapter 6.

Methods based on models and simulation. This category of methods is used when models can be constructed economically, particularly if user testing is not practical. Model-based evaluation methods can predict such measures as the time to complete a task or the difficulty of learning to use an interface. Some models have the potential advantage that they can be used without the need for any prototype. However, setting up a model usually requires a detailed task analysis, so model-based methods are most cost-effective in situations in which other methods are impracticable, or the information provided by the model is a cost-effective means of managing particular risks. See Chapter 7 for more information on modeling.

Methods based on expert assessment of the characteristics of a system. These methods are used for the following purposes:

- To provide breadth that complements the depth of user-based testing.
- When there are too many tasks to include all of them in a usability test.
- Before user-based testing.
- When it is not possible to obtain users.
- When there is little time.
- To train developers.

The several approaches to expert-based evaluation are discussed briefly in the paragraphs below:

Guidelines and style guides. Conformance to detailed user interface guidelines or style guides is an important prerequisite for usability, as it can impose consistency and conformance with good practice. But as published sources typically contain several hundred guidelines (e.g., ISO 9241 series), they are difficult to apply or assess unless simplified and customized to project needs.

Interfaces can be assessed for conformance with general guidelines, such as the usability heuristics recommended by Nielsen (Nielsen and Mack, 1994) and the ISO-9241-10 dialogue principles (International Organization for Standardization, 1996). Checking conformance with ISO 9241-10 forms part of the usability test procedure approved by DATech in Germany (Dzida, Geis, and Freitag, 2001).

Parts 12-17 of the ISO 9241 series of standards contain very detailed user interface guidelines. Although these are an excellent source of reference, they are very time-consuming to employ in testing. Further information on standards can be found in Bevan (2005).

Detailed guidelines for web design have proved more useful to both usability specialists and web designers. The most comprehensive, well-researched, and easy-to-use set has been produced by the U.S. Department of Health and Human Services (2006).

Following guidelines usually improves an interface, but they are only generalizations so there may be particular circumstances in which guidelines conflict or do not apply—for example, because of the use of new features not anticipated by the guideline.

Heuristic evaluation. Heuristic evaluation assesses whether each dialogue element follows established heuristics. Although heuristic evaluation (Nielsen and Mack, 1994) is a popular technique and research has shown that heuristics are a useful training aid (Cockton et al., 2003), using heuristics in the context of a task-based walkthrough is usually more effective.

Usability walkthrough. Usability walkthrough identifies usability problems while attempting to achieve tasks in the same way as a user, making use of the expert's knowledge and experience with relevant usability research. A variation is pluralistic walkthrough, in which a group of users, developers, and human factors people step through a scenario, discussing each dialogue element.

Cognitive walkthrough. This originally referred to a detailed process of analyzing the cognitive processes of a user carrying out a task, although it is now also sometimes used to refer to a usability walkthrough. The distinctions are summarized in Table 8-6.

Methods such as a usability walkthrough that employ task scenarios are generally the most cost-effective and can be combined with using heuristic principles or checking conformance to guidelines.

Expert evaluation is simpler and quicker to carry out than user-based evaluation and can, in principle, take account of a wider range of users and tasks than user-based evaluation, but it tends to emphasize more superficial problems (Jeffries and Desurvire, 1992) and may not scale well for complex interfaces (Slavkovic and Cross, 1999). To obtain results comparable to user-based evaluation, the assessment of several experts must be combined. The greater the difference between the knowledge and experience of the experts and the real users, the less reliable are the results.

Automated methods based on rules and guidelines. This category of methods is used primarily for basic screening. There are some automated tools (such as WebSAT, LIFT, and Bobby) that automatically test for conformance with some basic usability and accessibility rules. Although these are useful for screening for basic problems, they only test a very limited scope of issues (Ivory and Hearst, 2001).

TABLE 8-6 Types of Expert-Based Evaluation Methods

Guidelines	Task Scenarios	
	No	Yes
None	Expert review	Usability walkthrough Pluralistic walkthrough
General guidelines	Heuristic inspection	Heuristic walkthrough
Detailed usability guidelines	Guidelines inspection	Guidelines walkthrough
Information processing view	N/A	Cognitive walkthrough

SOURCE: Adapted from Gray and Salzman (1998).

Shared Representations

All evaluations result in a list of usability problems, and these may be reported to the stakeholders in a written report, a presentation, or a video. While the people responsible for sponsoring the usability work may be quite receptive, those who have to act on the results may be less sympathetic. So it is good practice to praise the strengths of the system from a user perspective before listing the problems.

The list of problems can be categorized (typically by task or screen) and prioritized, either from a user perspective or by the estimated costs and benefits of fixing the problem. It may make sense to ignore very low-priority issues, although they are worth reporting if they are easy to fix.

For maximum impact, stakeholders should be invited to view user-based evaluations. If this is not practical, edited videos of major issues have a much higher impact than other types of report or presentation.

If the evaluation results are being used to validate requirements, they will probably be incorporated into an existing quality control process.

Contributions to System Design Phases

Evaluation from a user perspective should be an integral part of systems development. In a risk-driven development process, the question is not whether to evaluate, but how to evaluate and how often. Early expert or user-based evaluation of mock-ups of new designs is essential to clarify requirements and to assess the viability of design concepts.

Evaluation of working prototypes can assess both their ease of use and whether they support the needs and tasks of real users. Late evaluation can validate whether a system has met the usability requirements.

Strengths, Limitations, and Gaps

There is a long history of research into the usefulness of different types of usability evaluation, resulting in broad agreement on the value and importance of including it in any system development for human-intensive systems.

While the costs and benefits of usability evaluation are well established (Bias and Mayhew, 2005), there is no way to be sure that all the important problems have been found. With some complex applications like an e-commerce web site, 15 or more users may be required to identify all the serious problems (Spool and Schroeder, 2001). In some situations, this number or more test participants will be cost-effective.

There have been several reports of different teams identifying different usability issues for the same system (Molich et al., 2004; Molich and

Dumas, 2006). Optimizing the evaluation procedures to obtain maximum value and consistency is still a research issue.

There may also be a temptation to apply the same evaluation procedure to every project, although the most effective approach will depend on a wide range of issues, including the availability and diversity of users, the range of tasks, and the potential risks of poor usability (see Chapter 4 and the first section of this chapter). An experienced usability practitioner will tailor the evaluation to the needs of the situation. Appropriate tools could be developed to support this process and would be of particular assistance to the less experienced practitioner.

Part III

The Future: Scenarios, Conclusions, and Recommendations

9

Scenarios for the Future

In this report, we have outlined a systems engineering view of the life cycle of development activities, a human-system integration (HSI) view, and an overview of how the two should be fit together seamlessly. We have emphasized that these development processes should be risk-driven, iterative, incrementally growing, and providing a basis for agreement among all stakeholders. There are a variety of tools and methodologies that the systems analyst can apply to meet these challenges; and new and revised tools are constantly under development. We have summarized the kinds of methods, tools, and shared representations that are available to support the HSI development process. Although our summary is not exhaustive, we think it is representative of the state of the art. We have indicated where there are gaps in the currently available methodologies and some needed new tools and methodologies.

There are tools and methods for investigating and documenting the task requirements and the context of use. Contemporary forms of simulation and virtual environments can support rapid prototyping, visualization, and human-in-the-loop testing. Human performance models and related analytic tools are often used, sometimes in conjunction with engineering models, to evaluate alternative designs early, eliminate impractical alternatives, and to narrow the choices and set parameter bounds on alternatives to be tested. Product and usability evaluation methodologies are widely used.

In this chapter we advance the clock 5 to 10 years into the future to envision new directions for how, with the addition of new supporting technology, the HSI discipline, including this collection of HSI system development tools and processes, could play out. In the following sections we present scenarios for the future. The first describes the bases for an integrated methodology. The second focuses on HSI-led system development and the need for the development of a formal HSI discipline. The third scenario suggests a set of knowledge-based planning aids that would support HSI activities in the larger systems engineering context. The fourth scenario features a new perspective on active user participation in system design.

AN INTEGRATED METHODOLOGY

We think that there are many advantages to streamlining and supporting the HSI process with advanced technology in the ways proposed here. It can reduce the development risk, cycle time, and cost by ensuring that products developed early can be expanded and reused throughout the development cycle. It can support the visualization of how the system will function and be used before it is fully committed to hardware and software, leading to fewer unforeseen difficulties and required retrofits. Finally, it should contribute to the creation of systems that can continue to evolve as experience with their operation is accumulated.

We think that such an integrative methodology is becoming feasible because of continued advances in semantic web technology (Shadbolt, Berners-Lee, and Hall, 2006), virtual environment technology, simulation, modeling and gaming technology, multimedia technology, and collaboration technology.

Here we provide an overview of such a methodology in terms of four of the main HSI activity categories in Figure 2-3 and Table 2-1:

1. Defining opportunities and requirements.
2. Defining the context of use.
3. Designing solutions.
4. Evaluating.

As Figure 2-3 illustrates, these activity categories are not to be confused with life-cycle phases. They comprise the steps that are taken repeatedly, in some cases concurrently, and iteratively as the life-cycle phases and milestones are met. However, when defining an integrative methodology, it is these activities that provide the basis for integration that can result in cost savings and more efficient development as a design is formalized, extended in depth, implemented, and tested throughout the life cycle.

Generating a Baseline

Most system developments are undertaken to replace and improve an existing system or set of procedures. It is important to begin the process by ensuring that there is documentation supporting the understanding and performance of the prior implementation. Such baselines often do not exist and have to be produced. The more quantitative these baselines can be the better. They are important in order to understand the basis for improvement and to develop a quantitative business case for undertaking the new development.

Defining Opportunities and Requirements and Defining the Context of Use

We take these two categories together because they are the most open-ended of the HSI development activities and are similar in terms of the methods used and representations that result. It is here that exploration and evaluation of high-level opportunities take place. These activities require information collection and representation. As we project these processes into the future, we would not propose to change the methods of information collection from those described in Part II, with the caveat of incorporating the new developments and improvements suggested there and in our recommendations.

The integration emphasis in these activities focuses on incorporating the documentation of the baseline, when it is relevant, and improved representation of the results. Their goal in the future should be to produce shared representations or artifacts that are linked associatively to each other. It is to be expected that, early in the process, these representations will be incomplete. As the initial steps in designing solutions are undertaken, there will be much iteration of the initial representations. Also, it should be noted that the choice, scope, and completeness of these representations will be in scale with the size and complexity of the enterprise. Below are some examples intended to survey the alternatives applicable to the most complex project:

- Personas representative of the potential individual users of the system.
- Goal/task decompositions reflecting the activities required.
- A catalog of information required to accomplish these activities.
- A description of the anticipated work environment that ultimately can be populated with product or workstation descriptions.
- Scenarios representative of the domain and activities to be performed.
- Situations in which the current system does not fully meet user requirements.
- Time lines or Gantt charts visualizing the potential sequences of overlapping activities implied by the scenarios.
- A risk analysis identifying potential development risks.

- A risk analysis identifying HSI risks, including safety risks and potential for human error.
- Stakeholder success criteria.
- The business case for undertaking the development.
- System requirements specifications (at varying levels of detail) derived from the information gathering and representation activities.

There may be other intermediate representations that are produced prior to these, such as storyboards, artifacts from the field, workshop reports, etc., but ultimately those artifacts will be used to produce the representation on which integration will be based.

In the early phases, these will be static descriptions represented in a set of associative databases. They must be interlinked because an important feature of the representations should be that a stakeholder could ask questions and trace audit trails through them. For example, the information requirements should be linked to the goal decomposition, the Gantt chart, or to a scenario so that one could ask where and when that information is needed, or a requirement could be traced to the source that generated it. Having these representations in interactive form makes it possible for stakeholders to study, explore, and review the state of the development in more depth so that they do not have to rely solely on the presentations at the milestone reviews.

This early phase of investigation and analysis provides a crucial moment of flexibility, in which new ideas can be explored and compared at low cost to the project and its stakeholders. Project teams can engage in various types of what-if analyses, assuming for example the consequences of using certain types of new technologies or exploring the consequences of potential new threats. The interlinkage of descriptions should include the ability for any stakeholder to make annotations and recommendations, which can then be analyzed by the team when it is time to move from exploration to stakeholder commitment.

Design Solutions

As design is initiated and alternative function allocations between human and system considered, the representations described above will continue to be enriched and, in some cases transformed into more quantitative representations. Priorities for which activities to consider first should be based on the risk analyses suggesting where the greatest uncertainties and HSI risks lie. System components will be enumerated and prototypes of the user interfaces will be sketched out as facades, with the functionality only implied. Implications of the tentative design solutions may be explored by high-level simulation before committing resources to a particular solution.

At this point, the beginnings of a formal system simulation that will embody the growing richness of the system representation should be kicked off. The previously static descriptive scenarios will become executable in the context of the simulation so that the operational concepts can be envisioned as a part of the system representation. The Gantt charts can become time-based and synchronized with the scenarios guided by GOMS (goals-operators-methods-selection rules) analysis. The personas may be implemented as human performance models of those roles. The simple facades will become working prototypes, but much of the system backing it up may still be scripted. At this stage, it becomes possible to postulate alternative system designs that can be quantitatively evaluated, either in a modeling framework or as human-in-the-loop simulations. Gradually, as the design is committed, the scripted modules will be fleshed out in hardware and software and those modules substituted for the scripted versions. In the prototyping languages of today and tomorrow, it should be possible to move seamlessly from early prototypes to production-quality software. The goal is that at each stage there will artifacts that represent the current state of development that may be examined and used by relevant stakeholders. These artifacts become the basis for visualization of the operational concepts and how they might play out.

Evaluation

Evaluation is ongoing throughout the development life cycle, with peaks at the incremental commitment milestones, as illustrated in Figure 2-3. As the modeling and human-in-the-loop simulation efforts progress, a measurement module is added that makes it possible to generate performance measures appropriate to the current state of system development. At different stages in development, the measurement may consist of video recording of simulated or real interactions, keystroke-level monitoring of model users or real users' activity, eye-movement recording, and higher level derivation of human and system performance measures. As mentioned in Part II, the ability to coordinate, interleave, and annotate these data records will also be important. Early in the development, the formative evaluations may be nothing more than written critiques produced by various stakeholders—or user-informed critiques from the participatory design or contextual design traditions—but when simulations become available, then more systematic and quantitative evaluation becomes possible. Model results must be validated with human-in-the-loop simulations. As detailed design and implementation are completed, the simulation transitions to actual system hardware and software, and evaluation of actual system components in use is undertaken. The evaluation culminates in a formal, summative evaluation—field test and evaluation in the case of the military; early deployment to a restricted number of field sites in the case of commercial software. Evaluation reports become shared representations that are useful at each life-cycle milestone and are linked with the configurations tested.

The Meaning of Integration

There are several senses in which this postulated development process is integrated. First, it is integrated in the sense that the products of each activity are manifest in representations that may be shared across the development community. Second, it is integrated in the sense that each product builds on the reusable components of previous ones. Common threads are provided by storyboards, use cases, scenarios, timelines, models, and system simulations. Documents, such as the business case, are elaborated, not reinitiated from scratch. Third, it is integrated in the sense that achieving the goals described requires, even demands, the cooperation of many stakeholders serving as an integrated team. Finally, the successful resulting design will accomplish much of system integration before implementation begins, and the result will represent a system that is truly responsive to the needs of its users, the ultimate goal of human-system integration.

HSI-Led System Development

Currently human-system integration is viewed as a support discipline, when it is engaged at all. This scenario for the future envisions it as the lead discipline in the system development life cycle. Current development practice tends to be dominated by the technical disciplines that are most salient for the particular system being built: software for information-processing-intensive systems, and various electrical, mechanical, and physical sciences for systems heavily dominated by electronics, structures, or sensors, respectively. In these instances, it is often the case that technical performance overrides human factors and operational considerations, these being considered secondary to, for example, sensor system optimization. Indeed, the system development process can become dominated by technical functionality that is later unused or, worse, gets in the way of the task at hand—that is, generates risk.

The ultimate goal of our vision for HSI-led systems is that an HSI professional with a system engineering background and training will be responsible for overall program management for new, complex systems, especially systems in which people play a significant role. The program manager with an HSI background and experience will speak the language of developers and understands their constraints, while also being properly attuned to business case issues, such as schedule and resources. At the same time, the specialist will ensure that human-system integration is appropriately addressed by the HSI specialty team. This assignment will lead to the proper balance for ensuring that systems meet (satisfice) stakeholder requirements, especially operational stakeholders, while delivering a product within the schedule and budget constraints.

We have emphasized the ways in which the hierarchical decomposition of the work domain should take precedence over the engineering decomposition of functional modules, because work domain factors are the ultimate contributors to operational system effectiveness and success. It is the HSI professional who has the broadest perspective on these factors. Such a person, when also endowed with systems engineering training and expertise, becomes the strongest candidate for program manager.

The HSI specialist–program manager will provide a leadership and management culture that understands, embraces, and promotes the importance of human-system integration in system development. There is no need for education or salesmanship on the part of human-system integration, because, with an HSI-knowledgeable program manager, the culture sees it as integral to good design as well as cost-effective. Human-system integration becomes the glue that pulls all the system components together in a way that emphasizes human use. This leads to a supportive environment and appropriate levels of resources to carry out the HSI functions. Human-system integration is viewed as an important component of overall risk reduction in complex development, and the specialty is always an integral element of system development from the earliest stages.

As the program manager for complex systems involving people, the HSI specialist-systems engineer would lead the program management team. Cross-functional and multidisciplinary interaction is critical to the success of large programs and can be accomplished through use of integrated product teams (IPTs), as advocated by Rouse (2005). The program manager's assignment of resources will be based on risk-opportunity analyses, but separate IPTs would be established to coordinate the most critical risks. One such team, if warranted, would be an HSI IPT. Some large projects are already using an HSI IPT. This team is responsible for the aspects of system concept definition involving end-users, further defining requirements associated with the concept, communicating those requirements in appropriate shared representations to affiliated IPTs, such as software development or structural design, and working with those teams to develop specifications for aspects of the system affecting end-users, such as displays, operational processes, and communications. The HSI IPT would also have representation from individuals representing planning for operations support, such as manpower and personnel domains and training developers. A typical IPT structure is shown in Figure 9-1.

A key element of the implementation of the HSI IPT process is the application of the various methods described in this book. During the

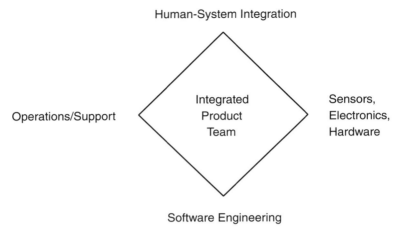

FIGURE 9-1 IPT structure for HSI-led system development.

early phases of development, methods for defining context of use and requirements are applied. Design methods are used to develop solutions, and evaluation approaches are applied to characterize performance. During each phase, the HSI IPT produces appropriate shared representations, such as display concepts and behavior specifications, facility drawings, and process descriptions, to communicate design-relevant information to other specialties.

Developing Human-System Integration as a Discipline

The committee envisions a new educational perspective on the specialties associated with HSI design and implementation, perhaps eventually leading to a new engineering discipline. As described in Chapter 2, the committee uses the following definition of human-system integration:

> A comprehensive management and technical program that focuses on the integration of human considerations into the system acquisition and development process to enhance human-system design, reduce life-cycle ownership cost, and optimize total system performance.

Furthermore, a key element of the HSI approach is the coordination and integration of the HSI domains at each system life-cycle phase.

The vision of human-system integration as a discipline will require new educational programs that cover the HSI disciplines but also include training in systems engineering. It will also provide linking interfaces to such disciplines as computer science, software engineering, and acquisition management, rather than create additional wedges with these functions. Many current academic programs have certain components of human-system integration. The Naval Postgraduate School is in the process of initiating such a curriculum, but no other known programs have all the necessary components and focus on their integration. The traditional recruiting ground for HSI personnel has been the academic discipline of experimental psychology, reflecting the origins of the field. Industrial engineering programs often have an ergonomics and human factors specialty. More recently, usability professionals have been developed from the academic tradition of information sciences and technical writing. Although these types of background serve important functions in human-system integration as a support discipline, they are to be too narrowly focused to integrate effectively with other engineering personnel or program management constraints. Similarly, traditional systems engineering without HSI perspectives does not, by itself, meet the needs of this new discipline.

This perspective asserts that human-system integration is fundamentally an engineering discipline. It can emerge as a recognized discipline in its own right, within an engineering program supported by the appropriate academic curricula and programs.

We think that a market study would demonstrate that there is demand for this kind of HSI professional. This demand would presumably be derived from an increasing recognition among acquisition, program, and project managers of the important role of humans in systems and that effective human-system integration can significantly reduce risk.

We envision meeting these increased demands through HSI courses and curricula. At the undergraduate level, this content would be likely to be covered to track with a chapter in a text. At the graduate level, assuming that demand can be demonstrated, masters and Ph.D. programs will emerge. The domain lends itself particularly well to satellite campus or distance-learning technologies to support the part-time student working professionally in industry or government. Similar integrative academic programs have begun to emerge to meet integration demands for cognitive science and social science, in the new "schools for information," and more broadly in programs that grant a combination degree in human-computer interaction and business.

It is expected that these educational programs will convince prospective students that successful careers can be pursued through the study of human-system integration. Career ladders in both industry and government will be created to legitimize human-system integration and to emphasize HSI knowledgeability in promotion criteria. Workshops and continuing education programs for working professionals will emerge, including programs for making non-HSI people HSI knowledgeable. The definition of the domain and the currency of methods and tools will need to be maintained to have long-term success and impact as well. Kleiner and Booher (2003) provide some initial thinking on levels of HSI competency for different functional assignments ranging from entry level to HSI manager. They discuss both the core competencies needed at all career levels and the specific knowledge, skills, and aptitudes needed for each specific level.

Since human-system integration is a project-oriented discipline, it would be beneficial in the future to create a "practicum" environment out of existing, complex projects in which undergraduate students who are on a work-study program or graduate students could have available applied experiences. In addition to developing processes by which HSI projects can make use of graduate and undergraduate interns and assistants, it is envisioned that there would be opportunities for which federal HSI specialists could be involved in interagency or industry projects. Such assignments would be rewarded and recognized and should not be perceived as detrimental to career development.

Finally, our vision includes HSI tracks at professional conferences and special editions of relevant journals.

KNOWLEDGE-BASED PLANNING FOR HUMAN-SYSTEM INTEGRATION

Many complex system development efforts begin with a core team of managers and systems engineers who may know that getting the HSI aspects right is important, but who have little knowledge of which HSI techniques work best in different situations, or of when such HSI techniques are no longer cost-effective.

In helping such managers and systems engineers, another scenario for what may be achievable in the next 10 years with sustained investment in HSI support technology is the development, usage, and growth of a family of domain-specific tools for helping projects to assess their risks and to suggest what HSI skills, methods, and tools they would need to identify, analyze, prioritize, and mitigate HSI risks.

Here is an example future scenario of the use of such a capability in the domains of command and control (C2) for defense or emergency services. An IPT consisting of operational stakeholders representing the major C2 functions of observation, orientation, decision, and action management, as well as development stakeholders representing human-system integration, hardware engineering, software engineering, and C2 system acquisition management functions is convened for the purpose of a scoping and planning project to develop a new C2 system. As part of their team building, scoping, and planning activity, they interact with a C2-domain, knowledge-based planning aid for an HSI tool.

The tool input requires the IPT to provide a set of project descriptors addressing the project and system as a whole and its C2 functions. The system or project specifications would include such descriptors as:

•   Size in terms of the number of people, information sources, and assets in need of C2.
•   Organizational complexity in terms of the number of independently managed organizations involved in providing the services being commanded and controlled, as well as the degree of interorganizational coupling involved in providing the services.
•   Precedents for this team in terms of the past history of developing similar systems, of having the organizations work together, of C2 development experience of the organizations, and the need for new C2 doctrine, organization, training, material, logistics, personnel, and facilities.
•   Criticality in terms of the risk to human life and the value of the assets at stake.
•   Technical and human factors complexity of the functions involved in providing the C2 services and of the need for such additional system functions as security, instant response, rapid adaptation to change, and degraded mode operation.
•   Available expertise among organizations for system engineering, developing, and acquiring similar C2 systems.

Drawing on its knowledge base of related successful and unsuccessful C2 development projects, the C2 knowledge-based tool provides the IPT with the following:

•   A summary of the most significant acquisition and operational risks needing to be managed.
•   Recommended development timelines and staffing profiles.
•   Necessary levels of system acquisition, human-system integration, hardware engineering, software engineering, and C2 subject matter expert staffing required during the system life-cycle phases.
•   The likely most relevant methods and tools to be used during the various phases, along the lines of Appendix Table 3-A1.

These tool capabilities would enable the IPT to perform sensitivity analyses of differences in tool inputs in order to better identify, avoid, and manage risks; to avoid the late rework and project overruns; and to deliver more cost-effective C2 system performance.

USER PARTICIPATION

Our state-of-the-art review has emphasized the importance of grounding design in a deep understanding of work domain activities and the context of use. We have also argued for the importance of including domain practitioners who are the intended users of the system as active partners in the design endeavor. While we have argued for the importance of these activities to successful design, we acknowledge that many of the current approaches for analysis of context of use can be time and labor intensive, require expertise to employ, and produce results that are not always packaged in a way that can readily be assimilated in the system development process. These factors combine to slow their adoption and limit their effectiveness. A related consideration is that user activities and context of use are not fixed elements that can be captured once and for all. The activities that people engage in and the physical, social, and organizational environment in which they take place are constantly evolving. It is important to develop efficient techniques that can dynamically capture changes in work context and requirements and to create systems that can be readily adapted to meet changing demands (e.g., Woods and Dekker, 2000; Hoffman and Elm, 2006; Roth et al., 2006).

These points highlight the importance of developing new approaches to capturing user activities and context of use in ways that are less obtrusive, less resource intensive, more continuous, and more readily assimilated into the system development (and update) process.

Approaches to Capturing User Input

In Chapter 6 we pointed to some promising directions for streamlining the capture and analysis of context of use knowledge, such as event data analysis methods that are intended to collect information on context of use unobtrusively. In this section we point to an emerging confluence of activities and technologies that promise to help end-users learn more about their activities, reflect on their actions, and provide useful contributions to the system development and evolution processes.

In the past, system designers often assumed that users received their technologies in a finished state then went on to use those technologies as intended by the designers. Numerous studies have now shown that users often have to modify the technology or its usage extensively (see, e.g., Bikson and Eveland, 1996; Dourish, 2001, 2003; Muller et al., 2003; Pipek, 2005; more broadly, see Darrah, 1995; Eglash et al., 2004). In military terms, the practice of "field modification" is another example of users' needs to change and reinvent the technologies that they receive.

Developments in Web 2.0 have accelerated this process (O'Reilly, 2005).

In the new networks, it is common to interface one application or service with another, to create new functionalities and new value propositions. Each application provides a standardized interface (typically XML) to other applications, and new services can be created through simple interfaces among these existing applications (making a "call" between applications, similar to a subroutine call in a conventional program architecture). The standardization of data formats among these services allows very rapid prototyping and testing of new service concepts, and these integrations can lead to user experiences that appear to be entirely new concepts and functionalities. Each such web site or module uses these standardized formats to offer "services" that can be called from other web sites or modules—hence the more formal description as "service-oriented architectures" or SOAs (Erl, 2005; SOA Technical Committee, 2006). We describe five classes of new services here.

The first class of such services are the examples of combining list-based advertising entries from one system with map-based visualizations from a second system, using standardized address data representations as the common service-calling protocol, to provide interactive geographic summaries of opportunities that change dynamically with new textual entries to the original list.[1] These quickly assembled services have been called "mash-ups" to emphasize that they have been constructed by bringing together two different data sets.

These technology-centric developments have enabled new forms of shared usage and collaboration-at-a-distance, often on a massive scale, and often involving users who have no knowledge of one another other than through these new systems and forms of collaboration. These developments have been generally described as "social software" (Allen, 2004; IBM, n.d.; Teton and Allen, 2007; see also Chi et al., 2007). The remaining four classes of new services fall into this general area.

A second class of such services provides awareness services in the form of "feeds" of information via the RSS protocol.[2] Each feed is provided in the form of updates on a specified page at a web site—a "weblog" or "blog." These blogs can be read and aggregated by a user via one of many "feedreaders," leading to increasingly integrated lists of updates from selected web sites. Commercial uses range from financial awareness to competitive intelligence. Military uses could include situational awareness.

A third class of such services involves the collection within a web site of shared references (e.g., "bookmarks") to entities at other web sites, in which each reference includes keyword descriptors called "tags" (Golder

---

[1]See http://www.craigslist.org.
[2]See http://www.rssprotocol.com, http://www.rssboard.org/rss-specification.

and Huberman, 2006). These references may refer to documents,[3] pictures,[4] recorded music, and many other types of data and are created independently by thousands of users, and each such reference is generally shared with all other users of the original web site. Searches can thus be conducted by tag or by user, resulting in a powerful and low-maintenance alternative to complex directories or organizational taxonomies (classification schemes). Significantly, people have begun to aggregate these emergent "folksonomies" (i.e., bottom-up, user-co-constructed alternatives to taxonomies) across web sites and services, and there is a trend toward linking selected types of references to commercial sites (e.g., user-constructed references to books at LibraryThing are often linked to book product descriptions at Amazon.com).

A fourth class of such services is much more person-oriented and involves the posting of information by a user about herself or himself.[5] Some of the information may be relatively static, while some of the information may be frequently updated, including in the form of a blog (see above). In addition, information about each person may be aggregated from other web sites through mash-up or SOA-based technologies.

A fifth class of such services involves the co-creation of knowledge resources by many users, with the expectation that the knowledge will be accessed by many more users—a group-constructed encyclopedia, of which Wikipedia[6] is the most well known of many instances.

The pace of development using these new technologies is so swift that there are web sites dedicated to providing daily updates about the status of various Web 2.0 experiments, beta tests, and business propositions.[7] Key characteristics of these developments are the reuse of technologies and services for new offerings, the diffuse and bottom-up nature of both the development effort, and the data accumulation through the contributions and negotiations of thousands of users. Users are rapidly becoming designers and data providers in these new web services.

In a related trend, networked technologies have empowered people to "cache" their lives. Users—especially young users—are integrating text, video, photos, and audio to produce moment-by-moment descriptions of their daily activities, using commonly available end-user web technologies. These young users are beginning to enter the civilian and military workforce and are bringing their familiarity and expectations of these technologies

---

[3]See http://del.icio.us/.
[4]See http://www.flickr.com/.
[5]See http://www.facebook.com.
[6]See http://www.wikipedia.org.
[7]See http://www.momb.socio-kybernetics.net/, the Museum of Modern Betas.

into work cultures. These technologies are likely to be transformed for self-reflection in most any situation.

The tools enable things such as auto-uploading, tagging by association, dynamic views of tag clouds and—crucially—the "mash-up" technologies of Web 2.0 to integrate these diverse media into coherent new services. In the future, additional information will be gathered from sensors in objects in the world and digital tagging of locations in the environment.

We see these tools as a means to end-user empowerment in much the same way that desktop publishing on personal computers transformed business communication in the workplace. Recently, Bradley Horwitz, vice president of Yahoo!'s product strategy group, explained that only a small number of people needs to leverage the tools in order for the resulting information to become useful for the masses (see also discussions of the "long tail,"—a statistical analysis of the influence of a small number of high-frequency contributors on a much larger community of low-frequency contributors and readers—Anderson, 2006).[8] We suspect that the same will be true in this context. Not all users will have to be actively reflecting on their activities and environment, but those who do will help positively transform the environment for everyone. McKinsey describes this as a new model of knowledge production, access, and distribution. He goes on to suggest that communities, not individuals, become the sources of innovation in a world of open-source approaches to knowledge development (Davis and Stephenson, 2006). In this vein, the following vision of the future is presented.

Systems Engineering for User Participation

In 5 to 10 years, HSI professionals are still focused on identifying HSI needs, translating their findings into opportunities, developing prototypes, requirements, and ultimately designing solutions that respond to those needs. But the world has fundamentally changed and systems engineering and HSI professionals have anticipated these changes and are working in new ways.

Some activities look the same, but others look radically different. HSI professionals are gathering their information with some of the methods they used in the past (such as cognitive task analysis or through observation) but they also have new ways to uncover opportunities, understand users and their contexts, and define solutions—they are constantly sensing and responding and have the skills to create not only solutions—but also wholly new ways of doing things from the data they are collecting and through the collaborative efforts of the real end-users.

---

[8]See also http://www.thelongtail.com.

So what is different? Data about the users, the environment, and objects in the environment are being continuously collected in real time and then re-presented for users to comment and learn from. Nearly every object in the user's system has been "spime"-enabled. A spime is a currently theoretical object with embedded sensing and responding capabilities that enable tracking through space and time (Sterling, 2004). The geospatial web has enabled the environment to constantly update people with location-based services and location-aware applications. Information will be integrated with the historical, cultural, and other relevant information of the specific place or setting or from smart dust distributed among places (Liebhold, 2004). This technological development is a logical maturation of some of the technologies reviewed in sections about event data analysis in previous chapters.

At the same time, end-users are becoming increasingly sophisticated producers and distributors of interlinked media. Collections of users have the ability to form reporting communities. Best practices in one community can easily be shared across the network. Events produce dynamic blogs, too, in which participants can see the activity of people, objects, and the interaction with the environment as it happens. The histories are then mined to look for patterns that can be used to build models, and then the models are trained to make better predictions about future events. Users are monitoring and contributing to their own "moblogs" that compile information about their activities into views that are meaningful to them. People post to these blogs through mobile cellular or other input devices. The algorithms are constantly updated and made better through the analysis of the behavior of real people in real settings and the commentary users provide through their blogging activities.

Why are the users participating? There are several reasons. It is easy to comment and re-present information. Wearable technologies have made "in the action" collection automatic or nearly so. Another reason is that there are widgets embedded in the interfaces that enable users to build and create their own ways to track data based on what they think they really need. As individuals become recognized by their community for their contributions—we can anticipate more and more participation in much the same way bloggers today do. Eventually the "best of the best" contribute to design efforts and trainers—of the systems, the other users, and the developers.

In the meantime, HSI professionals have also been able to study what has happened even without users' annotations. They have studied how different people have appropriated the technologies in the moment. They have watched, in real-time, how people have built new applications out of old technology, what used to be a work-around is now a "work as."

HSI staffs for their part are now building the tools that others formerly built for themselves. For a system to remain work-centered over time, it must not only support the elements of work identified at the design stage, but it must also be able to accommodate elements that the initial design did not appropriately capture and be adaptable to meet the changing nature of the work (Roth et al., 2006). Systems need to explicitly incorporate mechanisms to enable users to adapt the system to evolving requirements. The development of these modular systems place even greater demands on HSI professionals.

Similar calls have been made in the computer-human interaction community to move toward end-user development systems (Fischer et al., 2004). The goal of end-user development is to develop tools to enable end-users to adapt and further develop applications to meet evolving requirements. It has its roots in early calls to enable users to create customizations, extensions, and applications so as to address unanticipated requirements (Mackay, 1990; Nardi, 1993). Fischer and his colleagues (2004) have argued for the importance of developing meta-design approaches that create open systems that can be modified by their users and evolve over time. End-user development systems range from systems that provide for modest user modifiability to systems that have end-user programming features (e.g., open source code).

These new evolvable, work-centered systems are consistent with a growing recognition in the sociotechnical literature that software system requirements should not be viewed as fixed but rather as emergent over time as changes arise in the context of work (Floyd, 1987; Truex, Baskerville, and Klein, 1999; Scacchi, 2004). As Truex et al. (1999) have argued, this implies a need for ongoing analysis, negotiated requirements among system stakeholders, and an ongoing investment in software maintenance activities.

Another change that can be anticipated is that HSI personnel become the experts in issue tracking and resolution as systems are now never finished—but more dynamically evolving—and in continuous beta mode. Their experience in requirements gathering and documentation has been successfully leveraged in this new role of keeper of the desired future state of the systems.

Together, these trends have sharply reduced a number of system integration risks. The greater participation by end-users in the design of systems has led to technologies that are finally ready for use as delivered to end users. From a military perspective, ready for use translates into reduced training and user assistance requirements, faster learning, more effective use, and fewer accidents. From a consumer products perspective, ready for use translates into reductions in use errors or other problems with unanticipated uses. From a business-to-business perspective, ready for use translates into immediate return on investment and reduced total cost of ownership.

A second area of risk reduction occurs because of the richer, more immediate, and more broadly based sources of data. Spimes promise to provide nearly instantaneous awareness of changing conditions, and the data-participative trends of Web 2.0 bring many users' knowledge to bear on collaborative problems (e.g., the "wisdom of crowds").

The third area of risk reduction occurs in the rarer cases in which a system is delivered that does not meet the users' requirements—or in cases in which the users' environment has changed so quickly (due to changing threats or new business challenges) that the original design has been made obsolete by changing conditions. In these cases, the abilities of users to modify and enhance the technologies (e.g., through the mash-up capabilities in Web 2.0 technologies) allow users to make rapid changes that can provide new functionality to an obsolete technology so that it remains a worthwhile investment or a valuable part of defensive or offensive capability.

In this chapter we have envisioned a future in which knowledge acquisition will no longer be a laborious manual process but will instead leverage the collective knowledge that naturally emerges as domain practitioners act in the world, reflecting on their own practices and on the ability of their tools to support their work, engage in collaborative knowledge sharing, and appropriate and adapt their software tools to accommodate dynamically changing needs. Already today we see evidence of users embracing new technologies to share experiences and lessons learned and build shared knowledge bases (e.g., specialized blogs, discussion groups, and tag-based sharing cites have emerged in multiple domains, including military groups). We also see evidence in virtually every domain of users creatively extending and adapting software tools (e.g., creating new visualizations, local databases, and home-grown software support systems) to meet the constantly changing demands of work. We think this is an important positive trend that needs to be fostered and facilitated through design methods that acknowledge and accommodate evolving requirements, as well as software systems that are designed with expectation of user appropriation and adaptation. As Hoffman and Elm (2006) have pointed out, there is a need to rethink the assumption that system requirements can be fixed in a world that is not fixed (see also Floyd, 1987). To them, "'Requirements creep' is not a nasty thing to eradicate, but an empirical inevitability to accommodate and understand empirically" (Hoffman and Elm, 2006, p. 76).

Having sketched out the broad vision, we want to acknowledge that there are technical challenges to be overcome and to diffuse some potential misconceptions. First, we want to make clear that, while we envision that knowledge of user practices and use contexts will naturally emerge and that software systems will be appropriated and adapted, we do not intend to suggest that explicit analysis of users and context of use will no longer be needed. Nor do we mean to suggest that users will evolve their own software so that explicit systems analysis and software design will no longer be required. Human factors analysts will still be needed to synthesize and interpret the domain knowledge gleaned; they will simply be able to do their job more efficiently and comprehensively than has been possible in the past. Similarly, systems, software, and hardware engineers will still need to analyze requirements and architect solutions, but with more explicit awareness of the need to develop solutions that accommodate change. This is especially true in safety-critical domains, such as the military and the transportation and health care industries and systems of systems more generally, in which explicit consideration of unanticipated side effects and risk consequences of design decisions are critical.

Finally, we want to make clear that our vision of a more automated means of collecting information on user goals, needs, and activities is not intended as a substitute for including users as explicit stakeholders and equal partners in the design endeavor. Effective design will continue to require active dialogue and discovery among a variety of stakeholders, including users, human factors specialists, systems engineers, and software developers.

10

Conclusions and Recommendations

In this chapter, we report our broad conclusions related to each of the themes we introduced at the start of the report. These conclusions reflect detailed consideration of (1) our research into current views of systems engineering, (2) what the committee learned is needed to meet the requirements for adequate support for the role of humans in systems, (3) our survey of the methods and tools available to support what is needed, and (4) our assessment of the state of the art in human-system integration (HSI).

Our most fundamental conclusion is that human performance and human-system integration will never be most effective in system design unless it is seen by all stakeholders as an integral part of the entire systems engineering process, from initial exploration and concept evaluation through operational use, reengineering, and retirement. Many systems have failed because the role of humans was considered only after design problems were identified—when it was too late to make the kind of changes that were required to produce systems responsive to users' needs. We conclude that the definition of user requirements should begin when the system is first being conceived, and those requirements should continue to provide important evaluation criteria right up to the time the system is placed in use.

The military services are recognizing the need for more emphasis on human considerations in design through the introduction of MANPRINT, SEAPRINT, and, most recently, AIRPRINT requirements. More and more commercial software, hardware, and service industries are beginning to realize that commercial success requires attention to the customer's needs and that achieving that success has implications for the product engineering team, not just the marketing and sales teams. It begins with product conceptualization and continues throughout the product development cycle.

As a process for integrating human considerations into the systems engineering process, the committee has built on the strengths of existing systems engineering process models (waterfall, V-model, concurrent, incremental, spiral, evolutionary, agile) to synthesize an incremental commitment model (ICM) that helps to situate HSI activities within a system's life cycle. As described in the introduction, this model is based on five critical success factor principles: (1) negotiation to "satisfice" system stakeholders' (e.g., users, acquirers, developers) requirements; (2) incremental growth of system definition and stakeholder commitment; (3) concurrent system definition and development; (4) iterative system definition and development; and (5) risk management. Incremental commitment model is consistent with current approaches to systems engineering, including the U.S. Department of Defense (DoD) 5000 series of system acquisition policies and guidelines, and provides the kind of emphasis that the committee considers important to achieving human-system integration. Although it is not the only model that could be used on future human-intensive systems, it has served as a reasonably robust framework for explaining the study's HSI concepts, and for evaluating these via the case studies in Chapter 5. However, there are ways to extend or reinterpret existing process models to accommodate the five critical success factor principles and HSI activities.

In the paragraphs below we build on the six themes first mentioned in the introduction, and highlight features based on them that require special attention from the perspective of human-system integration.

Begin HSI contributions to development early and continue them throughout the development life cycle. If there were a single message to communicate to program managers and developers, it would be to understand that HSI expertise is important from the very beginning of the life cycle, when systems are first being conceived. HSI specialists are trained to explore and understand the environment in which a system will be used. In order to develop an operational concept, full understanding of the context of use is required. These factors need to be assessed even before a conceptual design is put forward. Human factors specialists have a collection of methods and tools for efficiently understanding the system environment and context of use. Consideration of these factors early can have orders-of-magnitude impacts on system performance. If human factors and other HSI input are left until the test and evaluation stage, only small-percentage improvements can be realized under the best of circumstances, and there is a risk that the system will not satisfy the original goals. We have also emphasized that system development needs to be an iterative process, and that there are human-system design considerations that evolve and need to be iterated along with every other aspect of system development.

Integrate across human-system domains as well as across the system life cycle. The domains identified in the MANPRINT methodology—human factors, manpower, personnel, training, system safety and health, habitability, and survivability, the first five of which are potentially as relevant to commercial products as to military systems—are not independent, and consideration of them must not be treated separately (i.e., "stove-piped"). While each has its own methods, there are many areas in which the methodologies we describe in Part II can serve multiple purposes across the domains and do not have to be analyzed for each. For example, task analysis, risk analyses, and workload analysis can support human factors, manpower, training, and safety. Ergonomic analysis can support human factors, training safety, and health hazards. For it to do so requires that the individual specialists in each area cooperate up front to ensure that the resulting shared representations meet the requirements of all the domains. This is a critical aspect of negotiation to "satisfice" system stakeholders' requirements.

Adopt a risk- and opportunity-driven approach to determining needs for HSI activity. At each of the system development milestones, the systems engineering team undertakes an analysis of the development risk and opportunities before proceeding to the next milestone. It is essential that the HSI team contribute an evaluation of HSI risks and opportunities to be considered in collaboration with the rest of the system engineering team. It is through the risk analysis that the argument may be made for assigning resources to evaluate particular risks further or to find ways to mitigate the risks that the system will fail, for example, because of safety risk, risk that it will be too costly to train the personnel in its use, or risk that it will be maladapted to the people who must use it. In addition, considering opportunities may allow the HSI team to improve program execution and system capabilities.

There is often a tendency for the HSI team to insist on a complete HSI analysis. The purpose of the risk and opportunity analysis is to focus attention on the risks whose likelihood and seriousness are both appreciable, as well as the opportunities with the greatest payoffs. It will also serve to identify the areas of development in which the risks are minimal and do not need further attention. HSI risk and opportunity analysis becomes a component of the overall system development risk analyses and is given equal importance to other system risk factors. The use of human-sensitive mission effectiveness models, simulations, and exercises can be highly effective in this regard.

If there are integrated product teams (IPT) for which HSI issues are relevant, there should be at least one HSI representative on each such team, and that person should be responsible for ensuring that the HSI risks and opportunities are considered.

Tailor methods to time and budget constraints. Every system development takes place under time and budget constraints. It is not possible to undertake full-scale HSI evaluation of every aspect of a system development. Early in the life cycle, as a part of the iterative system definition and development, it is important to evolve the human-system requirements, prepare the HSI part of the business case for designing and fielding the system, and undertake the risk and opportunity analysis. The business case should include quantitative performance objectives based on human capacities and limitations. From that point on, it is important that the HSI team, driven by its risk, opportunity, and requirements analyses, focus further attention on the critical issues and requirements identified in the risk/opportunity analysis only. With respect to each identified issue, they should evaluate the analysis requirements carefully, consider alternative approaches to achieving them, and select the methods and tools that are most cost-effective for answering the questions at hand. The proposed budget should be based on a careful but realistic analysis of what needs to be done to satisfy the critical and most risky requirements. Doing so will gain the respect and confidence of the program manager and will improve the chances that adequate budget will be provided.

Ensure communication among stakeholders of HSI outputs. Many of the contributions of the HSI team—especially those that are developed early in the development process—tend to be based on observation, interview, and questionnaire methods. The individuals who collect the data become the most knowledgeable about the characteristics of the system environment and context of use. Similarly, the knowledge acquisition associated with developing task and process analysis results in very rich information in the heads of the analysts. However, much of this information is needed by all the system stakeholders, from the funders and program managers to the detail designers and developers. In following the principle of negotiating to satisfice all stakeholders' requirements, it is very important that the HSI team provide outputs and deliverables that capture the information and its interpretation in forms that are understandable and usable by these stakeholders—we have called them shared representations. We have discussed the kinds of methods to be used for generating the needed information and, for each method, suggested that the kinds of shared representations we recommend should be developed as the outputs. Effort should be made to create these shared representations in a form that is readily assimilated into the engineering process, that is, expressed in terms that are compatible with other engineering outputs. This might be accomplished through the generation of scenarios of use, models and/or simulations based on the task analysis output, or analyses of the context of use. Effective shared representations can be very helpful in smoothing the flow of information among team members and in ensuring that the HSI team output is influential.

Design to accommodate changing conditions and requirement in the workplace. There have been and are continuing to be significant changes in many factors that influence the way that work gets accomplished and the nature and complexity of the systems that are developed. Personnel costs are a significant percentage of the operational cost of systems, and everywhere there is pressure to reduce the numbers of personnel. Technology is often seen as the panacea to reduce personnel costs, increase efficiency, and improve safety. Technological evolution has become much more rapid, and the systems developed last year may be already out of date.

It is impossible to capture all the requirements up front, so it is valuable to develop systems that can be more easily adapted or modified in order to continue to provide support as the work context changes. The ultimate ideal is to create evolvable systems that can be "appropriated" (or reinvented) by the users and tailored to meet the inevitable changes that will arise. This argument is consistent with the principles of incremental growth of system definition and concurrent system definition and development—the idea that requirements should not be assumed to be fixed but instead expected to evolve over the life cycle of the system.

The design of systems of systems involves a level of complexity and challenge much greater than the design of individual complex systems themselves. For example, the military is designing command and control systems that span the activities of many logistics, battlefield operations, manned and unmanned aerial systems, and multinational forces. Telephone companies are now faced with integrating digital phone systems with cell phones, Internet access, and television delivery systems. Hospital information systems must be integrated with the accounting, nursing unit, pharmacy, and individual physician's workstations, not to mention supply systems and inventory control, and they must do it in a way that promotes patient safety.

Complex systems of systems demand new approaches to uncover the multiple points of interdependency across systems and anticipate their impacts on the people operating in those environments. New envisioning methods and modeling tools are needed to predict the kinds of challenging situations that are likely to arise, the kinds of adaptations that will be required of people to cope with new complexities, and the kinds of errors and failures that may emerge in the future (Woods and Dekker, 2000; Woods, 2002; Winograd and Flores, 1987; Feltovich et al., 2004). The ability to anticipate likely reverberations of technology insertions early in the design process can contribute substantively to the design of complex systems and systems of systems that are resilient in the face of a wide range of operational perturbations (Hollnagel, Woods, and Leveson, 2006).

The emergence of systems of systems further emphasizes the importance of considering human-system integration as an integral part of the development process. We have highlighted the value of iterative design and the role that shared representations and especially models and simulations can play in ensuring that all stakeholders remain informed about the current state of development. In this kind of very dynamic development environment, it is important to keep in mind the potential for changes after the system is implemented. Information currency is likely to be a very important consideration, since design requirements can change with each new iteration. In Chapter 2, we described a procedure for accommodating rapid change and high assurance through incremental development. Design for evolvable systems requires anticipating the scope of changes that might take place, making the design modular, leaving appropriate entry points for the changes, providing thorough software documentation, and providing scalable service-oriented architectures.

RESEARCH AND POLICY RECOMMENDATIONS

These recommendations identify further critical steps to facilitate the kind of integration into systems engineering that we consider of paramount importance. Our intent is to provide sufficient detail to guide the development of a research plan and the formulation of policy initiatives for the DoD and other government and private organizations. The recommendations are organized into four areas: (1) realizing the full integration of human systems and systems engineering; (2) methods for defining opportunities and the context of use; (3) methods for defining requirements and design; (4) and methods for evaluation. Accomplishing these steps will provide needed support to realize the future scenarios outlined in Chapter 9. The committee was not able to prioritize these research recommendations as they cover diverse areas of equal importance. We believe work in these areas should proceed concurrently.

Realizing the Full Integration of Human Systems and Systems Engineering

This report presents the incremental commitment model as an example framework for system development activities and discusses how human-system integration fits within this framework. Here we present our policy and research recommendations regarding the principal areas of research, development, and policy initiatives needed to facilitate integration throughout the development life cycle and across HSI disciplines. These areas include

- Institutionalizing the success factors associated with the incremental commitment model.
- Accommodating the emergence of HSI requirements.

- Ensuring that HSI operational requirements are included in the initial system development contract and acquisition documents.
- Managing integrated system development.
- Providing traceability of HSI objectives, decision points, and the rationale for decisions across life-cycle design phases.
- Developing approaches to human-system integration and systems of systems research.
- Sizing the HSI effort.
- Designing shared representations to facilitate communication across disciplines and life-cycle phases.
- Creating knowledge-based planning aids for providing HSI information.
- Developing human-system integration as a discipline and as a lead for the IPT.
- Fostering more synergy between research and practice.

Institutionalizing a System Development Process Based on the Success Factors

Through our analyses of more and less successful HSI projects, our evaluation of alternative HSI process models, and our case studies, the committee makes the case that a model like the incremental commitment model better enables the kind of human-system integration that will be needed for the complex, human-intensive systems of the future. It embodies the success factor principles of stakeholder satisficing, incremental growth of system definition and stakeholder commitment, iterative system development and definition, concurrent system definition and development, and risk-driven activity levels, product levels of detail, and anchor point milestones. However, it does this in clearer ways than the spiral model, particularly for HSI considerations, and it does so in a manner compatible with the DoD acquisition milestones and the commercial IBM/Rational Unified Process and the Eclipse Process Framework OpenUP milestones. It provides a process framework for the top-level recommendation of realizing the full integration of human engineering and systems engineering.

> **Recommendation:** The U.S. Department of Defense and other government and private organizations should refine and coordinate the definition and adoption of a system development process that incorporates the principles embodied in the incremental commitment model. It should be adopted as the recommended approach for realizing the full integration of human-related design considerations with systems engineering in organizational policies and process standards, such as the DoD 5000 series and the ISO systems engineering standards.

Accommodating the Emergence of HSI Requirements

Particularly for complex systems of systems and for collaboration-intensive systems, human-system interface states, modes, and functional requirements are not known at the time of program initiation. Many current system acquisition policies and standards require these human considerations to be fully defined before proceeding into development.

Although it is risky to leave HSI requirements completely undefined, it is equally risky to insist on defining them before they are fully understood or allowed to emerge through experience. A reasonable middle approach is to use incremental and evolutionary development processes and to define HSI requirements in terms of capabilities, with more detail provided for later increments, but sufficient detail provided for earlier increments to ensure proper preparation for the later increments. This approach is consistent with the principle of risk-driven levels of product detail.

> **Recommendation:** The U.S. Department of Defense and other government and private organizations should revise current system acquisition policies and standards to enable incremental, evolutionary, capabilities-based system acquisition that includes HSI requirements and uses risk-driven levels of requirements detail, particularly for complex systems of systems and for collaboration-intensive systems.

HSI Operational Requirements in Contracts and Acquisition Documents

In discussing risk management, we have alluded to the importance of considering HSI aspects when negotiating baseline metrics for program execution. This negotiation is a critical phase in product development, when estimates and assumptions are formulated and agreed on by all stakeholders. Customer requirements and value propositions, technical performance measures that measure compliance with technical requirements, schedule milestones, and requisite resources all contribute to that negotiation. Involving HSI practitioners in the negotiation process ensures that their perspective and knowledge are accounted for, increasing the likelihood that HSI risks and issues will not arise during program execution. This recommendation focuses on policy, rather than research, and addresses the need to have human-system integration considered in establishing program execution baselines. Key to successful contract execution, resulting in an end product that fills a specified role and meets operational needs, are crisp requirements that have been properly vetted.

Recommendation: The U.S. Department of Defense and other government and private organizations should put the operational requirements of human-system integration on a par with traditional engineering requirements at the beginning of initial *requirements analyse*s to determine which requirements have priority and provide an opportunity for negotiation.

Recommendation: When developing system acquisition programs, the U.S. Department of Defense and other government and private organizations should define potential means for verifying and validating HSI requirements to enable supplier program managers to establish clearly specifiable HSI technical performance measures for contracts.

The procuring agency has the ability to drive contractor HSI efforts by seeding the extent to which HSI considerations are accounted for contractually and their degree of importance. Without the inclusion of HSI considerations throughout program definition efforts, contractors have limited basis for addressing HSI considerations in their business offer.

Recommendation: The U.S. Department of Defense and other government and private organizations should account for HSI considerations in developing the technical, cost, and schedule parameters in the business offer. In particular, contracts need to reflect an understanding of how human-system integration affects the ability to reuse existing technical solutions or the feasibility of inserting new technologies, as well as an appreciation of how anticipated HSI risks may affect meeting program award fee criteria. It is also important that the contractor understand how HSI elements in their product offering contribute to achieving market capture goals and subsequently the viability of their business case.

Overall, the procuring agencies are able to directly influence the extent to which HSI elements are addressed in contracts by establishing well-articulated HSI requirements reflective of end-user needs and working with the contractor to establish verification and validation methods that overcome program management concerns about the typically subjective nature of HSI elements. The contractors or suppliers should take the time to involve HSI practitioners in their business development efforts to account for HSI elements in the business offer, thereby mitigating a portion of potential HSI risks and issues that may arise during program execution.

Managing Integrated System Development so That All Representations Are Kept in Synchronization

In our vision for an integrated system development methodology, a serious concern is configuration control of the various entities that are being developed in order to support it. It is likely that new developments in web technology will be able to support some of these requirements.

> **Recommendation:** Explore the usefulness of the technologies associated with Web 2.0 and related web developments for providing support for configuration control and synchronization of the component representations in a large system development project as they evolve and become more quantitatively defined.

> **Recommendation:** Support a research program to explore how to provide flexible and open systems with appropriate security protections. The apparent conflict between openness and protection is not a matter of balance or trade-off, but rather of providing strong forms of both attributes.

Traceability and Requirements

The committee has argued for the importance of capturing the context of use in a form that can inform later phases of design. This is important to ensure that operational objectives and constraints and their design implications are taken into account in the system design process, so that the final "as-built" system meets the support objectives and constraints identified in earlier phases. This goal can be met only if methods and tools facilitate capture and traceability of HSI design objectives, decision points (together with the rationale for those decisions) and constraints across design phases.

Our vision is to adapt existing tools or to develop new software tools to facilitate the traceability of HSI design objective implications and how they are being met to ensure that they are preserved across design phases. This includes traceability across multiple intermediate human-system integration shared representations, starting with (1) outputs of context of use analyses that specify domain demands, stakeholder objectives, human performance needs, and design implications; through (2) the products of intermediate design phases, such as scenarios, personas, models, and prototypes; through (3) the decision rationale and system hardware and software design specifications intended to reflect the support objectives embodied in the design concepts; through (4) the final as-built system. Traceability across design phases is important to ensure that HSI objectives and constraints are preserved across design phases or when modification or redesign is undertaken. It also makes it easier to assess whether the as-built system meets the operational and support objectives and design implications uncovered by earlier design phases.

> **Recommendation:** Adapt existing or develop new methods and tools that facilitate capture and traceability of HSI design objectives, design rationale, and constraints across design phases. Specifically:
>
> 1. Develop shared representations that effectively communicate how the output of one design activity meets the objectives, design rationale, constraints, and design implications uncovered in the prior design phase.
> 2. Develop shared representations that effectively communicate essential design characteristics and their rationale that can be interpreted and used by multiple system development stakeholders—including individuals that did not participate in earlier design activities (see Wampler et al., 2006, for an example of an effort toward this goal).
> 3. Adapt existing and develop new software tools to support traceability and update as changes arise in later design phases that require updates to outputs of earlier design phases.
> 4. Adapt existing and develop new tools and techniques for explicitly connecting HSI objectives and design implications to higher level system requirements tracked in formal system requirements tracking systems. This is important to ensure explicit links between HSI design objectives and system-level requirements that reflect contractual commitments.
> 5. Adapt existing and develop new methods for generating scenarios that reflect the range of complexities uncovered by context of use analyses. This corpus of scenarios can be used to support development and evaluation of designs, procedures, and training, including human reliability and safety analyses. They could also be used to exercise models and simulations as part of the system development process. The goal would be to ensure that the systems have been explicitly designed and tested to support performance across a comprehensive range of representative situations, as identified by context of use analyses. Context of use scenarios are also essential to the meaningful definition of such key performance parameters as response time, reliability, and accuracy.
> 6. Develop methods to identify meaningful human (and joint person-computer system) performance metrics that can provide the basis for objective system acceptance criteria. This is important to encourage incorporating HSI objectives as part of formal contractual

requirements that are established early in the systems acquisition process. Steps include

a. Developing methods for identifying individual, team, organization, and joint person-computer system (as well as systems of systems) performance metrics that provide objective measures of factors that are key to successful performance of tasks, of system design, and of accepted systems.

b. Developing methods for establishing objective acceptance criteria that accurately reflect human-system integration and context of use goals while being straightforward to evaluate.

Shared Representations

The committee has argued for the importance of shared representations, sometimes referred to as boundary objects. They can serve an important role in fostering communication across the various systems engineering disciplines. Focusing explicitly on representations that communicate across discipline boundaries is novel. Although we have provided many examples of artifacts that could serve as shared representations, research is needed to understand just what this means and how best to achieve it. We identified a specific issue concerning shared representations for task analysis among the specialists supporting the various MANPRINT domains, especially the domains of human factors, staffing requirements, training, and safety. Each tends to undertake its own task analysis, resulting in substantial duplication of effort.

Recommendation: Conduct research to identify characteristics of shared representations that communicate effectively across HSI domains and engineering disciplines. We recommend the following steps:

1. Identify characteristics of a useful shared representation:
   a. Define what it means to share an understanding.
   b. Characterize the mental models and representations associated with design used by various stakeholders, such as flow charts, blueprints, wiring charts, or Gantt charts, as well as more work-oriented representations, such as prototypes and mock-ups.
   c. Define the areas of overlap between those who are practitioners in HSI domains and other stakeholders that represent fruitful areas in which to develop shared representations.
2. Consider a specific area, such as cognitive task analysis or risk analysis:
   a. Review and evaluate existing and proposed representations.

   b. Identify common aspects and differences.
   c. Synthesize representations that have the potential for improving communication across stakeholders.
3. Assemble an IPT representing the MANPRINT domains with the assignment to reach agreement on a single set of generic specifications for what needs to be included in shared representations for task analysis.
4. Design a multimedia database format and tool, including coordinated video, as a shared representation derived from HSI evaluations. Build on multimedia software and tools used for documenting usability evaluations.

Systems of Systems

There is a gap in the arsenal of HSI methodologies in that many of them (perhaps most of them) fail to scale up to the systems of systems level. For example, usability methods are typically suited to the single user–single interface scenario: How can these methods be adapted to complex systems of systems, and how can organizational modeling approaches (National Research Council, 1998) be applied to human-system integration? Similarly, how can other HSI methods, such as cognitive task analysis and participatory design, be adapted for this complexity? Is cognitive work analysis as suited for network-centric command and control environments as it is for process control systems (Cummings, 2006)? Other methodological issues, such as envisioned worlds (i.e., systems that do not yet exist in any form and may even be revolutionary, resulting in the need for methods that are not anchored in existing systems) and tailorability to the situation, are exacerbated by the complexity of systems.

Recommendation: Conduct research and development on HSI methods for systems of systems in the following manner:

1. Develop a test-bed that provides a research environment simulating systems of systems in the context of a domain by working closely with domain users, experts, and developers to design the test-bed, and to ensure transition of work in the test-bed to the real world.
2. Select methods and identify potential ways to adapt them for complex systems. Include state-of-the art methods and technologies, such as data mining, wikis, social software applications such as blogs and tagging systems, and virtual collaboration and envisioned worlds.
3. Apply the methods in the context of the test-bed to test reliability and validity, compare methods with each other, and identify meth-

ods that scale up and aspects of methods that seem to scale better than others.

4. Feed back scalable methods and methods for envisioning new systems to system developers.

In addition to a gap in metrics applicable to systems of systems, there are other problems that arise in regard to human-system integration and systems of systems. For example, the human capability for understanding or developing a mental model of a system of system stretches the limits, raising issues for training, operations, and maintenance of these systems, as well as for determining risks or degree of system resilience (Feltovich et al., 2004; Hollnagel, Woods, and Leveson, 2006). Furthermore, systems of systems inherit potentially incompatible human-system interfaces from the best suppliers and legacy systems. Systems of systems also bring together stakeholders with different linguistic, cultural, and technical backgrounds who must effectively collaborate but have a wider range of linguistic, cultural, and technical backgrounds than those involved in smaller systems. Finally, systems of systems must support multiple missions with different objectives, constraints, and success-critical stakeholders.

Recommendation: Conduct research and development studies to

1. Develop mental models and system transparency as applied to large and complex systems of systems.
2. Undertake efforts toward envisioning methods and models to uncover the sources of complexity and points of interdependency across systems and anticipate their impacts on the people operating in those environments.
3. Undertake studies to develop methods and tools for identifying and reconciling incompatibilities inherited from the best suppliers and legacy systems.
4. Undertake studies to develop methods and tools for analyzing and synthesizing candidate multimission solutions and supporting stakeholders' convergence on a mutually satisfactory solution.
5. Undertake studies to develop methods and tools for analysis and design of *resilient systems* that foster adaptability to cope with unanticipated disturbances and change (Hollnagel, Woods, and Leveson, 2006).

Sizing the HSI Effort

Systems engineering maturity models, such as the capability maturity model integration, require organizations to have objective and experience-based methods for estimating systems engineering effort, but in practice the methods for estimating HSI effort are largely ad hoc. In general, the estimation community has a number of methods for estimating effort, but their relative applicability to HSI effort estimation is not well understood.

Major relevant classes of effort estimation include (1) bottom-up or activity-based methods in which individual performers estimate their needed amount of effort and the results are summed up; (2) top-down or system-based methods that involve various forms of analogy-based estimation (using comparisons with the effort expended on similar previous systems); (3) unit-cost methods that involve counting the number of work units (operational threads or scenarios, transaction types, etc.), perhaps weighted by complexity, volatility, and reuse, and multiplying the number of work units of each type by the average effort for each type; (4) expert consensus methods that involve IPTs or consensus-determination techniques such as Delphi to converge on an effort estimate; (5) parametric models that attempt to characterize and parameterize the factors that cause variations in effort per work unit and to develop parametric models that account for the variations; and (6) risk-based "how much is enough" models that involve balancing the risk of expending too little HSI effort (operational shortfalls, expensive rework, project overruns) with the risk of doing too much HSI effort (critical path delays in making project progress; nonvalue-adding effort). Each of these approaches has strengths and weaknesses.

> **Recommendation:** Conduct research to develop, experimentally apply, evaluate, and refine versions of these methods for HSI effort estimation.

Knowledge-Based Planning Aids for Human-System Integration

As described in our vision for knowledge-based planning, currently human-system integration most often takes place as stand-alone activities that are not well integrated with the mainstream system development processes. Research is needed to develop a framework for integrating and adapting HSI methods and techniques into complex system development environments, supported by a tool implementing the framework that can be used to select the most cost-effective methods and techniques based on operational, business, organizational, and project needs. Human-system integration and systems engineering activities rely on different methods, techniques, languages, and tools.

The basis for integration exists in ISO/IEC 15288 (systems engineering—system life-cycle processes), ISO/TR 18529 (human-centered life-cycle process descriptions), and ISO/PAS 18152 (specification of the process assessment of human-system issues), as well as in approaches to human-system integration. See International Organization for Standardization (2000b, 2002, 2003). Schaffer (2004) has published an example of how to institutionalize usability.

Some example planning tools that could be leveraged to support this kind of development are

• Logistics planning tools, such as DART and Cougaar in the Defense Advanced Research Projects Agency.
• Hardware, software, and systems engineering resource estimation tools, such as the Price Systems, Galorath, SEER/SEM, and USC COCOMO/COSYSMO tool suites.
• Risk assessment tools, such as Active Risk Management, @Risk, the Software Technology Risk Advisor (Toth, 1995), and Expert COCOMO/COCOTS (Madachy, 1995; Yang et al., 2006).
• Experience base management systems, such as those at the NASA–University of Maryland's Software Engineering Lab and the Mitre Corporation's risk repository.

Recommendation: Develop a framework for integrating and adapting HSI methods and techniques into complex system development environments.

Recommendation: Establish a top-down framework for integrating human-system integration with contrasting development environments to provide the common ground to leverage the integration of HSI methods, languages, and techniques into systems development.

Recommendation: Develop a tool for selecting the most cost-effective methods and techniques for human-system integration based on business, organizational, and project needs and for integrating them with system engineering processes. There is currently little agreement in textbooks or the literature on appropriate methods and techniques, with conflicting advice from different sources.

Recommendation: Based on the framework outlined above, develop a set of criteria for selecting methods and techniques derived top-down from specific organizational, project, and life-cycle needs. The criteria will promote effective integration with mainstream system development processes.

1. Provide estimates of the relative costs and benefits that would be obtained by using different combinations of HSI methods and techniques.
2. Develop support tools incorporating the criteria.

Developing Human-System Integration as a Discipline

This report makes the case that improved system performance and reduced development and operational risk would result from proper attention to the human user's capacities and limitations and from better integration among user requirements and technical specifications, especially concerning the introduction of computer support and automation. The committee has established a vision for human-system integration to emerge as a distinct discipline. Such a discipline would be made up from components of systems engineering, occupational health and safety, human factors and ergonomics, manpower, personnel and training, as well as business economics. It would provide specialists who could serve as the lead on HSI IPTs, as the HSI representative on multidisciplinary IPTs and, with the appropriate experience, could be selected as system development program managers. As systems and systems of systems become increasingly complex, the kind of expertise associated with this discipline will be a requirement.

Recommendation: Human-system integration should be developed as a distinct discipline. Several questions and actions are posed in reaching this goal:

1. What is HSI expertise?
   a. Building on the work of Booher (2003a, 2003b), develop a consensus-based taxonomy of skills, knowledge, and abilities by surveying leading HSI subject matter experts in both commercial and military domains. Use the definitions and assumptions from Booher (2003a, 2003b) and from this report to define human-system integration and to design the survey instrument.
   b. Perform a market study that quantifies the benefits and costs associated with formalizing HSI curricula and continuing education programs in current or emergent academic departments. Kleiner and Booher (2003) provide a template and details for such a curriculum. Experience gained thus far with the Naval Postgraduate School HSI program can be benchmarked for additional education programs. There is a need to serve both the military and nonmilitary communities.

2. What does it mean to be proficient at human-system integration?
   a. Benchmark current best practices and requirements derived from this report; create a standardized HSI program management job description (knowledge-skills-abilities expectations).
   b. Assuming the results of the market study are suggestive of further development, fund a number of pilot HSI graduate programs. The details of curricula and proficiency requirements will be established by the academicians in these departments, with input from HSI subject matter experts.
3. What is the rationale for selecting alternative HSI methods for different purposes?
   a. Research is needed to establish the reliability, validity, and scalability of HSI methods, as well as the knowledge, skills, and abilities required to carry them out. These results are needed so that contractors can justify their selection of methods and procuring organizations can evaluate their selections.
4. How can the discipline grow internationally?
   a. Establish a source of HSI research funding that requires cross-cultural or international teams. This can be funded by a single agency (e.g., the National Science Foundation or DoD) or can be multiagency (e.g., Department of Commerce/European Union).
   b. Establish international HSI symposia within recognized professional conferences (e.g., International Ergonomics Association, North Atlantic Treaty Organization).
   c. Establish dedicated international HSI meetings and conferences.
   d. Establish or reinforce HSI technical groups in relevant professional organizations, such as the Human Factors and Ergonomics Society that has a systems development technical group, and the International Council on Systems Engineering, which has an HSI working group that can help promote the recommendations in this report.
   e. Establish an *International Journal of Human System Integration* to disseminate applied research and appropriately evaluated case studies related to human-system integration. Ideally, a relevant government agency or university with appropriate funding would host such a journal. The objective of the journal would be to serve as a repository of applied research, including appropriately designed and evaluated case studies that will expand the depth and breadth of knowledge, skills, and abilities associated with human-system integration worldwide, across application domains and sectors.

Fostering More Synergy Between Research and Practice

One factor that has hampered the advancement of human-system integration as a discipline is the chasm that exists between research and practice. Practitioners are not sufficiently aware of relevant research, and research is not sufficiently informed by the insights and body of knowledge gained from practice (Norman, 1995; Woods and Christoffersen, 2002). There is a need to develop more effective ways to abstract knowledge and models from individual application contexts in a form that can be readily transferred to new application domains. While there are many examples of excellent HSI designs, their successes rely heavily on local knowledge and expertise. There is a need to develop methods and tools to more effectively leverage the knowledge and insights gained from practice and improve the cross-dialogue between research and practice.

> **Recommendation:** Develop methods and tools to facilitate knowledge generalization and transfer across application domains and improve cross-fertilization between research and practice.

- Develop methods and tools for extracting abstract descriptions of behavioral patterns and the conditions that shape them that can be generalized across specific application domains (e.g., conditions that lead to specific error forms or foster specific types of expertise).
- Develop abstract reusable design patterns that embody specific aiding principles and can be transferred across application domains;
- Create publication vehicles for presenting field studies and design case studies that offer generalizable insights (the new *Journal of Cognitive Engineering and Decision-Making* is one such example).
- Encourage practitioner-oriented publications that synthesize research results in a form that can be readily assimilated and applied by HSI practitioners.

Methods for Defining Opportunities and Context of Use

We make research and development recommendations in two major areas. First, we recommend the development of software tools to capture and disseminate the results of context of use analyses so that they can more easily by applied in various phases of system life-cycle development. Second, we make a series of recommendations concerning the active participation of users in engineering design, the future of unobtrusive, passive data collection, and the ethical considerations of both.

Tools to Support Capture and Dissemination of Results of Context of Use Analyses

The committee has argued for the importance of capturing the context of use in a form that can be more readily communicated and used throughout the HSI design life cycle. Improved software tools are needed to support capture, organization, dissemination, update, and retrieval of results of context of use analyses. This includes capture of the results of task and cognitive task analyses, field observations, participatory analysis and design activities, contextual inquiry, and work domain analyses. The research objective is to provide a suite of software tools to enable analysts to build and maintain a core corpus of work domain and context of use knowledge that can be updated easily as new information is learned, communicated to stakeholders effectively, and accessed and reused more readily across the life cycle of a development project. This core corpus of knowledge would then be available to inform design, the development of procedures, the development of training, the development of safety case submittals, etc. Such a resource would be especially valuable in complex design projects whose development can span multiple years and multiple organizations. Some promising research efforts toward developing core multimedia knowledge repositories include the work domain analysis workbench developed by Sanderson and her colleagues (Skilton, Cameron, and Sanderson, 1998) and the CmapTools software suite created at the Institute for Human and Machine Cognition. More research is needed to produce more robust systems with broader applicability.

> **Recommendation:** Conduct research to provide a suite of software tools to enable analysts to build and maintain a core corpus of work domain and context of use knowledge. Specific steps include

1. Identify characteristics of a core corpus of work domain and context of use knowledge required to support a variety of stakeholders across the system life cycle. This would include HSI system designers, individuals responsible for system verification and validation, individuals responsible for development of risk analyses and safety case submittals, and individuals responsible for personnel selection, personnel training, and procedure and document development for system operation and maintenance.

2. Explore multimedia databases and software architectures to support development and retrieval of a variety of shared representations derived from context of use analyses. This would include graphic representations of domain and context of use knowledge, such as concept maps and abstraction hierarchies, and multimedia

capture of elements of the work context and proposed design concepts (e.g., videos illustrating expert strategies, still images of work environments illustrating user-generated artifacts and workarounds compensating for poor system designs, sketches of design concepts generated during participant design sessions).

3. Identify and develop a demonstration project that would exercise and evaluate the approach in a particular complex application—ideally one that involves system of systems design challenges.

User Participation in Systems Engineering and Event Data Analysis and Their Ethical Implications

In the vision for systems engineering for user participation scenarios, we have argued for new ways to understand conditions in the field, as well as the work practices of the end-users that involve unobtrusive, passive logging and interpretation of these activities. We have also argued that the new technologies of Web 2.0 and related web development will allow end-users to modify, create, and revise systems that are already in use, thus providing a significantly greater role for end-users in designing the systems that they will use. Finally, we have argued for greater use of what we called event data analysis, to collect users' actions and other occurrences in the field and to find emergent patterns from the data. These trends converge into three related sets of recommendations.

Recommendation: Conduct a research program with the goal of revolutionizing the role of end-users in designing the system they will use.

1. Conduct lab and field studies to understand current practices in server-log data extraction and analysis and develop tools to efficiently generate logs whose format is more useful to analysis than server logs.
2. Develop tools to facilitate re-representing automatically generated data, such as server logs, reflecting users' perspectives on their work, their tools, and their experiences. We note that some of these issues may also involve issues of credit or payment or digital rights management of the users' ideas (intellectual property). Specific research and development activities include
   a. Conduct research (lab and field studies) and develop designs and technology to support user control or influence over the online display of the user's identity, i.e., impression management (Goffman, 1956) and reputation management (Beard, 1996).
   b. Conduct research (lab and field studies) and develop designs

and technology to support user control or influence over descriptions and representations of the user's experience (individually or collectively with other users).

c. Conduct research (lab and field studies) and develop designs and technology to support users in developing shared representations that effectively communicate the users' needs, goals, intentions, strategies, and user-generated solutions to problems (individually or collectively with other users).

d. Conduct research (lab and field studies) exploring the usefulness of collaborative communication technologies for accomplishing the goals of improved user participation in system development.

3. Conduct research (lab and field studies) and develop designs and technology to support users in transforming existing technologies and systems into modified or new systems that meet their needs. This process has variously been described as "re-invention," "evolution," and "evolvability," "appropriation," and "field-modification." Specifically:

a. Identify, develop, or refine (as necessary) new software architectures that make it easier for users to modify systems or tailor configurations to support new uses, for subsequent use by other users or for subsequent "harvesting" by organizations.

b. Develop tools to support users in maintaining credit or ownership for their innovations.

4. Conduct research on the interactions of the new technologies— such as the introduction of sensors in objects (spimes) and locations (geospatial web), in the targeted contexts. Specifically:

a. Determine what the introduction of spontaneously communicating ubiquitous devices will do to the work. Develop methods for users to reform or reshape those technologies to change those interactions, as needed.

b. Determine how users will understand the functionality and security or privacy challenges of the new sensing and data integration technologies. Determine effective ways of presenting these new technologies and new challenges to end-users.

c. Identify the users' mental models of the technologies. Determine how the technologies should be changed or packaged to match these mental models. Determine what education or training will be needed on the part of end-users.

d. Determine how these new technologies can be made useful and usable by end-users in offices, homes, and military theatres through reinvention or field modification and other practices.

The first set of recommendations in this section explored the use of these data and technologies for end-users' recording of data and experiences, harvesting of insights, communication of lessons learned, and expression of needs and recommendations. By contrast, the second set of recommendations in this section explores the analyst's role in the use of such data for somewhat different purposes. In these recommendations, we focus on a more analytic approach to real-time data collection, with an emphasis on data collection that does not intrude on the users' consciousness and therefore may provide a more traditional view on time and motion and other quantitative measures of how users do their work. Data such as keystrokes, communications, emails, and web sites visited can be logged unobtrusively over the course of a day, weeks, or years as the user performs the task and potentially serve as a rich source of ethnographic and usability data for human-system integration. In addition, Web 2.0 and the emerging concept of "attention data" (i.e., Where does the user spend time and effort?) promise to create enumerable possibilities for rich yet unobtrusive data collection.

Recommendation: Refine event data analysis methods and develop new methods in line with the following series of interrelated activities:

1. Explore the data sources described above for types of data that can be collected without interfering with the users' ongoing work (e.g., keystroke analysis, observational cameras, and transportation data).
2. Instrument a setting (real or test-bed) for collection of event data of a targeted variety to understand the practical implications for obtaining these kinds of data.
3. Collect other indices of performance/usability/cognition as well to serve as criterion measures.
4. Request users to provide their own perspective on their work (e.g., according to selected methods in the first set of recommendations in this section).
5. Apply, adapt, and develop data-mining or pattern recognition algorithms to identify regularities, anomalies, and changes in the data.
6. Map the patterns onto meaningful outcomes by associating them with other criteria.
7. Derive a small number of data structure standards for the records of such a behavioral instrumentation log, to facilitate quick analysis, searchable storage, and (when appropriate) data exchange of behavioral instrumentation logs in a (secured) group of collaborators or analysts.

The collection of these kinds of data raises new issues in security, privacy, and (ultimately) ethics. Some organizations provide guidelines or policies in these areas, but even in those cases, there are many questions for which the researcher/practitioner/engineer must take responsibility. Many systems inform the user that her or his data may be used for research purposes. For large-scale systems, users often form a reasonable assumption that their limited use of the system will be under the radar of any research program. However, contemporary and near-future quantitative techniques address very large data sets and can easily find individual users who match certain search criteria. Indeed, many of the commercial applications of attention data operate on just such a basis. Thus, no one can be confidently under the radar any longer, but most users are not aware of this change.

Convergently, there have been major advances in data mining and data extraction by several communities whose interests are not necessarily aligned with the interests of the users, such as advertisers, fraud artists, and intelligence agencies (e.g., legitimate agencies as well as competitive agencies in the commercial space and enemy agencies in the military intelligence space). Various low-visibility industries exist for the purpose of understanding users' interests and habits from the perspective of manipulating or taking advantage of them. When researchers or engineers compile large data sets, they are producing targets of high value for this shadowy industry.

A third set of issues arises in different national policies. In the United States, most users consider their data privacy to be their own responsibility. By contrast, countries in the European Union are more likely to have rules that govern the privacy of personal data, in which personal data can in some cases include not only private records created by an individual, but also private and public records that make reference to that individual.

Recommendation: Conduct research on technologies to protect privacy and security and on the broader ethical and legal issues surrounding privacy and security.

1. Develop a graduated scale of data privacy. Some data about users should be generally available; other data should have greater protection. What models of data protection are technically feasible? What options for user privacy and permission should be provided, beyond the current two approaches that have been summarized as

"opt-in" and "opt-out"?[1] How can the available privacy options be effectively presented and explained to the users? What technology and user experience are required to allow users to define and implement their own data protection and security policies?

2. Examine the programs of nonprofit organizations that have proposed to store users' data in a protected repository, so that users can negotiate for some benefit in exchange for allowing other organizations to access and use their data.[2] How can these options be implemented technically on a large-scale (market) basis? How can these options be effectively presented and explained to the users? What commercial models of benefit for personal data access transactions should be available? What fraud protections are possible? What are effective mechanisms through which users can (a) make their personal data available to third parties and then, upon need, (b) withdraw both their permission and their data from those third parties?

3. Explore ways in which large data sets of user information could be made available to authorized users and yet be protected from unauthorized users. Determine ways to (a) detect unauthorized access, (b) record the extent of unauthorized access to data stores, and (c) automatically notify affected users, so they can know what kinds of self-protection to invoke following such unauthorized access.

Methods for Defining Requirements and Design

The committee makes recommendations concerning the research and development needs related to human-system development and to developing prototypes of organizations and training programs.

Human-System Model Development

Human-system models have been shown already to be useful in the system acquisition and development process as a means to reduce uncertainty and development risk; however, they are not employed to the extent that even the current state of development would justify. There is a perception that models that reflect human performance characteristics are too hard to

---

[1]In an opt-in approach, the user's permission (e.g., to store or share data) is explicitly requested, and no action is taken unless the user takes an action to permit storage or sharing of data. In an opt-out approach, the user is informed that storage and/or sharing will be done *unless* the user takes action to prevent it or to revoke permission. In this latter case, the burden is on the user to prevent the storage or sharing of her or his data. In general, users prefer opt-in approaches, whereas merchants prefer opt-out approaches.

[2]See http://www.attentiontrust.org.

use or understand. Potential users focus on the limitations and not on the advantages. In fact, models exist at all levels of complexity from simple mathematical expressions to complex computer programs. That said, it is true that the more sophisticated models, particularly those derived from discrete event simulators and cognitive architectures, are often brittle, costly, and time-consuming to develop and are not yet well validated for all uses in design. There is a wide variety of both research developments and policy changes that have the potential to impact the usefulness and usability of human-system models.

> **Recommendation:** Conduct an in-depth study of how human-system models are created, used, and shared, together with their strengths and limitations. The study should consider not only the various structures and architectures in which to build models, but also how data are acquired and represented in these models. What makes a model easy or difficult to use? To what extent are models reusable? Why aren't they reused more often? Such a study would support improved education about how to develop models as well as provide recommendations for improving the quality, robustness, usefulness, and usability of the models that are developed. The study should include a retrospective review of a range of models, such as Fitts's law, signal detection theory, GOMS, Micro-Saint-based models, to complex cognitive architectures, such as ACT-R and EPIC.

> **Recommendation:** Pick, as a case study, a class of models at an intermediate level of complexity and invent a high-level human-system model development language, having as its goal to make building such models as simple as customizing an Excel spreadsheet to a specific application.

> **Recommendation:** Explore the applicability of computer learning and adaptation algorithms for growing more robust models.

Currently, in models such as IMPRINT, the user models included in the systems are useful, but the theories from which they are derived often lead to a basically linear, single thread model of human attention to tasks. Increasingly, multiple task management, the impact of interruptions, and the role of situation awareness for decision making and planning are important in complex system analysis.

> **Recommendation:** Expand the fidelity of the user representations to include these aspects of behavior and how these aspects change with time on task, workload, heat, stress, and other behavior moderators.

Recommendation: Expand models, particularly human behavior representation and cognitive models, to include the effects of culture, social processes, and emotion. This will also require gathering additional data, as many studies in these areas are not performed with the application to models in mind.

There is much research on validating models, and it is recognized as a very complex and difficult problem. The consensus is that face validity is inadequate, but that achieving "application validity" is realistic and should be required. Application validity is defined as the degree to which a model or simulation is a faithful representation of the real world from the perspective of the intended users. Models are developed for specific purposes, and it is validation with respect to those purposes that is important.

Policy Recommendation: Require all human-system performance models that are to be used in system acquisition risk reduction to meet the standards of application validity.

Recommendation: At a research level, better validation criteria need to be created. How good is good enough? Better model validation criteria are needed for specific model types and for models in general. Currently, when models are applicable, how much risk they reduce, or how valid they need to be to reduce risk is not well defined or even well explored.

Models and simulations have the potential to serve as effective shared representations for communicating the state of system development across the range of stakeholders. Their major uses will be to support coordination and integration of multiple viewpoints, to provide shared envisioning of operational concepts and predicted performance characteristics, and for system integration. Current examples fall short of achieving required goals and require further development.

Recommendation: Conduct research on how to make the design rationale and the relationships among model and simulation assumptions, execution, and derived performance measures more transparent and understandable.

Prototyping Training and Organizational Design

The committee has explained the role of prototyping in the systems development process. One of the challenges in developing integrated systems is that of the balance of prototyping elements of the proposed system in isolation (in order to support parallel development and validation of the elements) and prototyping the collection of subsystems (in order to evaluate the overall behavior of the linked subsystems and trade-offs among them). In conventional systems engineering practice, both are done. The real challenge comes when the human operator, team, or organization must be considered in a more inclusive HSI design effort. It is clear from increasingly complex system development efforts that the earlier HSI issues can be addressed, the better.

One way of addressing the challenge early is to create—like the early machine system prototypes—early prototypes of the people organization that will be interacting with the mediating technology or system hardware and software components. Organizational prototypes could take many forms. They could be simply verbal or descriptive concepts and theories, involving walkthroughs or talkthroughs with hypothetical organizational structures. Or the rules defining the relationships between organizational elements could be defined and individuals could stand in for each organizational element, a kind of interactive role-playing, and carry out prototypical interorganizational operations (i.e., follow predefined scenarios), while observing these rules and constraints (for summaries of successful applications of these types of approaches, see Bjerknes, Ehn, and Kyng, 1987; Bødker et al., 2004; Muller, 2007; Muller et al., 1997). Alternatively, organizational elements could be represented by computational models and simulations, including the rules and constraints for interacting with each other (National Research Council, 1998). For example, a synthetic teammate based on a computational model could serve as a training or operational aid, as well as a component prototype for system design (Gluck et al., 2006). It will mean that one has to know not only about all the interrelationships or links involved (human to human, human to machine, and machine to machine interactions) but also the nonmachine elements or nodes. Like any prototyping problem, the appropriate level of resolution (person, team, organization) will become even more critical as person-machine coproduction defines the success or failure of the teams, organization, and system involved.

Similarly, it is important to consider prototyping the training program of potential team members as early in the design process as possible. This involves postulating alternative ways the training could be accomplished and testing their usefulness at varying levels of specificity as the design matures. Success in this approach will mean that the system design, organization, and training program all co-influence each other. This kind of work is at such an early stage of development that there are many unanswered questions:

1. What does it mean to prototype an organization—what is the cur-

rent state of the art? Are there differences with prototyping formal versus informal organizations? What are the implications for prototyping static versus dynamic teams and organizations? And how are artifacts—the non-human components of the system—accounted for?

2.   Are the prototyping issues different for individual, team, and organizational prototypes? What disciplines should be involved in supporting prototyping at an individual (cognitive psychology), team (social psychology), and organizational level (sociology, economics, anthropology, political science)?

> **Recommendation:** Undertake a review of the current state of the art in prototyping organizations. Define a set of requirements that effective prototyping methods should meet. Select a candidate relatively complex domain, perhaps a system of systems domain, and define alternative organizational structures that might be effective in this domain. Define alternative prototyping methods designed to span the range from very abstract to very specific. Apply the different methods to evaluate the different possible organizations for this domain and revise the methods until they meet the requirements proposed.

> **Recommendation:** Undertake a review of the current state of the art in prototyping training systems. Define a set of operational domains and compare training requirements. Examine use of synthetic agents in the development of training prototypes.

Methods for Evaluation

We have discussed two classes of evaluation methods: risk usability evaluation and risk analysis. Here the committee provides research and development objectives in both areas.

Improve the Use of Usability Objectives

The quantification of usability goals through the use of usability objectives is a recognized human factors and HSI best practice for many kinds of systems. But their use is not employed very often or consistently. The main goal of specifying usability objectives (also known as usability requirements, usability goals, performance goals, human factors requirements) is to create a metric that can be applied during usability testing as a way of having quantitative acceptance criteria for the test. Usability objectives are one way to create a quantitative quality-related goal and avoid qualitative conclusions that are sometimes claimed about devices (e.g., "This device is user-friendly"). Typically, quantified usability objectives include

- Human performance goals (objective goals), such as task completion time, success rate or error rate and type, learning time, and accuracy.
- Efficiency (number of total steps and missteps), such as number of references to instructions or online help.
- User satisfaction (subjective goals) using such approaches as rating scales (Likert, e.g., agree or disagree or comparative ratings) and semantic differential (pick rating between two opposite adjectives).

In systems in which usability objectives are relevant, they should be validated as part of customer requirements (using common market research techniques, such as interviews, surveys, and focus groups) and compared with competitive benchmarks (usually obtained from published studies or from comparative usability testing of best-in-class competitor's products). Only a few critical task-related usability objectives typically are necessary. Examples of quantitative usability objectives or goals are

- 90 percent of experienced nurses will be able to insert the infusion pump tubing set on the first try with no instructions. And 100 percent will be able to correct any insertion errors.
- 90 percent of experienced anesthesiologists will be able to calibrate the cardiac monitor within 2 minutes with no errors.
- Experienced operators working in port security will be able to detect potential dangerous substances with a sensitivity of d' = 3 or greater.
- Unmanned aerial vehicle operators will be able to fly 3 planes at the same time in level flight and be able to land the 3 planes within 15 minutes, with no more than a 5-percent failure rate.
- 80 percent of experienced maintenance technicians will rate their satisfaction with the usability of device X as 7 or higher on a 10-point satisfaction scale.
- After reading the quick reference card, 90 percent of experienced clinicians will be able to properly configure the display on the first try to show the two ECG lead traces.
- 80 percent of experienced intensive care unit nurses will prefer the readability of the display for the latest generation ventilator monitor compared with the existing monitors.
- 95 percent of technicians with no prior experience with this type of network management system will achieve the target mastery level in 2 or fewer hours of use.

Recommendation: For cases in which usability objectives have been shown to be useful, conduct research to develop better ways to investigate, set, and use them as acceptance criteria. This research would specifically show the value and limitations of usability objectives in achieving overall project goals. Specifically:

1. Improve methods for demonstrating when usability objectives are valuable by surveying DoD and commercial projects on their successes and failures in using usability objectives and collecting examples of usability objectives from surveys and literature reviews; create a taxonomy of usability objectives.

2. Improve methods for creating and setting usability objectives by surveying methods that have been used and their strengths and weaknesses; conducting experimental research on the relationship of using risk-management techniques, like failure mode and effects analysis and fault tree analysis, to set utility objectives and whether these projects are successful and meet project/mission goals; and searching the literature in other domains, such as software, electrical engineering, and the like and how they have used quantifiable performance objectives and how they set and validate them.

3. Improve methods for validating usability objectives by surveying validation methods that have been used and their strengths and weaknesses and conducting literature reviews of techniques in other domains, such as marketing research, used to validate their objectives.

4. Improve methods for using usability objectives as a subset of project acceptance criteria by surveying techniques (including their strengths and weaknesses) for using usability objectives as acceptance criteria, including hypothesis testing and appropriate statistical techniques that have been used.

Maximize the Cost-Effectiveness of Usability Evaluation

Although usability evaluation methods are widely used, no systematic and generalizable research has been carried out on the study size, scope, or protocols that cost-effectively identify the most important usability problems. Nielsen et al. (1994) analyzed the results of usability studies in the early 1990s to produce a formula to relate the number of test participants to the proportion of usability problems identified. This has been criticized as being applicable to only a limited class of products. Molich and Nielsen (1990) have shown that different usability evaluation procedures identify different subsets of problems; however, there is not good matching of problems with evaluation procedures. Furthermore, it is rarely cost-effective to evaluate every permutation of user type and task.

There is little applied research evidence and few practices to assist a practitioner in deciding what number of studies to reduce the risk of human system mismatches are cost-effective in a particular development environment, or to determine which groups or strata of users to include. Market researchers have developed efficient methods from sociology for defining and using segmented or stratified samples, and there has been a small amount of research in human-computer interaction (principally by Siegel and Dray, 2001) to integrate these market-oriented methods with traditional methods.

> **Recommendation:** Conduct research to generalize the sample size formula developed by Nielson so that it can be applied to a wider range of products and systems, including such factors as system complexity, job function diversity, end-user demographics, and other relevant factors.

> **Recommendation:** Conduct research to understand which evaluation procedures are most appropriate for different types of products and systems, and how the evaluation procedure can be refined to maximize the number of problems identified most cost-effectively while producing valid and reliable results.

> **Recommendation:** Conduct research to understand how to choose culturally appropriate evaluation methods, how to treat each method as a lens on a potentially larger set of usability problems, and how to translate from the constraints of a particular evaluation method into a more general or canonical description of the usability problems that were discovered and clarified by that particular method.

> **Recommendation:** There is often a shortage of skilled personnel to carry out usability evaluations. Conduct research to establish whether members of a development team without a formal human factors background could be trained to carry out simple usability evaluations that produce valid and reliable results or, failing that, to understand the trade-offs in data collection and quality when HSI methods are carried out by untrained practitioners.

> **Recommendation:** Conduct research to establish how precisely the evaluation procedure needs to be specified to ensure that two organizations will produce acceptably similar usability measures for summative evaluation.

Identify and Assess HSI Risks

It is often stated in the HSI discipline that usability or human factors risks that are not addressed in the engineering design process are the basis for catastrophic errors. The profession tends to fall back on the history of well-known events, such as Three Mile Island, Bhopal, and the *Vincennes* downing, to illustrate the perils of failing to address human-system issues in design. While these examples can be compelling, they do not provide a rigorous basis for understanding risks in developing systems or for analyzing potentially catastrophic error conditions that may result from human operation. There are many human error classification schemes, but they tend to be locally focused and do not scale up to system-wide implications.

We envision the initial research activity resulting from this recommendation to be developing a comprehensive database of HSI risks that are described at multiple levels and from multiple perspectives, from the initiating activity (e.g., cognitive error) to a system or society-wide result (e.g., melting the core of a power plant). This is both a theoretical and a practical research activity, requiring the integration and extension of various error classification schemes, with larger scale systems impacts, such as costs, malfunctions, rework, among others, and multiple theoretical and even political frameworks. We see this research activity as going well beyond the typical cost justification exercise for human factors engineering and resulting in a systems model of HSI risks.

> **Recommendation:** Conduct research to develop a robust HSI risk taxonomy and a set of methodologies for analyzing and comparing relevant risk representations and conflicting values.

The general nature of the problem is to define the confluence of human and system factors that may align to create operational problems that exceed the design basis of the system or result in operations that were totally unanticipated (Reason, 1990, 1997). Such features have been referred to as "emergent" in discussions of systems of systems, and that is really the principal focus of this research—linking the human and hardware and software systems with analytic techniques that can better identify extreme situations. Incorporating the concepts of the relatively new domain called *resilience engineering* (Hollnagel, Woods, and Leveson, 2006) will help to move this approach forward.

> **Recommendation:** Extend traditional fault tree and risk analysis techniques to better identify the "boundary cases" that may lead to extreme operational consequences.

The benefit to the HSI field of conducting this research will be to establish a more robust basis for risk analysis and design than currently exists today. The error taxonomies are a start, but they tend to leave off where theoreticians stop—well before examining the linkages in complex systems during the design process. The overall vision of this research recommendation is that the results will place HSI risk analysis on a more even footing with well-accepted risk methods, such as the probabilistic risk analysis work performed in designing complex process plants, and they will extend the traditional fault analysis techniques to identifying and addressing situations that are beyond the typical design basis faults.

Improve the Communication of Risk

The analysis of risk must be done systematically, with great attention to use error or operational risk, business risk and mission risk, and (when appropriate) societal risk. In this report, the theme of risk reduction is mentioned quite often. Techniques such as failure modes effect criticality analysis and fault tree analysis are recommended to analyze and control risk. These methods have been in use for many years, but they suffer from methodological problems, mostly involving how to make reliable estimates of risk parameters such as fault likelihood and severity of the consequences. Another major issue concerns the weaknesses in the ways these project and user risks are communicated to decision makers and other stakeholders, as well as the political processes that may required to reconcile and integrate views of risks across multiple constituencies that may have different perspectives on systems and their implications (e.g., to achieve a satisficed solution).

> **Recommendation:** Conduct research studies to show the value of improved assessment and shared representations that quantify the risk level for improved communication of business and operational risks to management and development team stakeholders. Specifically:
>
> 1. Survey communication techniques in other domains, such as advertising, sales, and news, and categorize success factors that could apply to business and operational risk communications.
> 2. Conduct literature searches and analysis of successful communication techniques used in other domains that might be applicable to risk-management communication stakeholders.
> 3. Conduct experiments comparing different risk communication techniques, for example, do risk estimation calibration exercises to improve risk communication as measured by changes in operator or decision-maker behavior.

> **Recommendation:** Support applied interdisciplinary investigations into the communication, representation, and negotiation of risks and related

issues, with the goal of assisting conflicting parties in mutual under-standing and satisficed decision making.

Identify and Assess HSI Contributors to System Adaptability and Resilience

While humans are often viewed as the "weak-links" in systems that contribute to errors and risk, there is a growing body of literature that has shown that people in fact play a critical role in system resilience—the ability of systems to operative effectively in the face of unanticipated disturbances. Individuals, teams and organizations contribute to system resilience by planning for, recognizing and adapting to perturbations and surprises—especially ones that fall outside of the range of situations that the system was designed to handle (e.g., Carthey, deLeval and Reason, 2001; Weick and Sutcliffe, 2001). Alternatively, the individuals and management poli-cies can be the detriments to resilience. This has led to a newly emerging area called Resilience Engineering that attempts to advance the study and design of systems that exhibit resilience (Hollnagel, Woods, and Leveson, 2006; Woods and Hollnagel, 2006). More research is needed to understand the role people play in contributing to or inhibiting system resilience, and how new tools and technologies can be deployed to enhance people in the former role.

Recommendation: Conduct research to understand the factors that contribute to system resilience, the role of people in resilient systems and how to design more resilient systems. Some of the key questions that need to be addressed include the following:

- What kinds of knowledge and strategies enable people (particularly experts) to catch and recover from error and adapt to unantici-pated situations?
- What methods can be used to analyze, measure, and monitor the resilience of organizations, systems and systems of systems?
- What traits and metrics enable systems to be developed and evalu-ated according to their adaptability and resilience?
- What methods can be used to model and predict the short and long-term effects of change on adaptability and resilience?

References

Abdel-Malek, K., Arora, J., Yang, J., Marler, T., Beck, S., Swan, C., Frey-Law, L., Mathai, A., Murphy, C., Rahmatalla, S., and Patrick, A. (2006). *Santos: A physics-based digital human simulation environment.* Presentation and demonstration at the 50th annual meeting of the Human Factors and Ergonomics Society, October 16-20, San Francisco, CA.

Adlin, T., Hynes, C., Pruitt, J., McGrane, K., Goodwin, K., Rosenstein, A., and Muller, M.J. (2006). *Putting personas to work.* Panel discussion at the Conference on Human Factors in Computing Systems (CHI 2006), April 22-27, Quebec, Canada.

Allen, C. (2004). *Life with alacrity: Tracing the evolution of social software.* Available: http://www.lifewithalacrity.com/2004/10/tracing_the_evo.html [accessed March 2007].

Allender, L. (2000). Modeling human performance: Impacting system design, performance, and cost. In M. Chini (Ed.), *Proceedings of the military, government, and aerospace simulation symposium, Advanced simulation technologies conference* (pp. 139-144). San Diego, CA: The Society for Computer Simulation International.

Amram, M., and Kulatilaka, N. (1999). *Real options: Managing strategic investment in an uncertain world.* Boston: Harvard Business School Press.

Anderson, C. (2006). *The long tail: Why the future of business is selling less of more.* New York: Hyperion.

Anderson, J.R., Bothell, D., Byrne, M.D., Douglass, S., Lebiere, C., and Qin, Y. (2004). An integrated theory of the mind. *Psychological Review*, 111, 1036-1060.

Annett, J. (2000). Theoretical and pragmatic influences on task analysis methods. In J.M. Schraagen, S.F. Chipman, and V.L. Shalin (Eds.), *Cognitive task analysis* (pp. 25-40). Mahwah, NJ: Erlbaum.

Annett, J. (2005). Hierarchical task analysis (HTA). In N. Stanton, A. Hedge, K. Brookhuis, E. Salas, and H. Hendrick (Eds.), *Handbook of human factors and ergonomics methods* (pp. 33-1–33-7). Boca Raton, FL: CRC Press.

Archer, S., Headley, D., and Allender, L. (2003). Manpower, personnel, and training integration methods and tools. Chapter 11 in H.R. Booher (Ed.), *Handbook of human systems integration* (pp. 379-432). Hoboken, NJ: Wiley.

Badler, N.I., Erignac, C.A., and Liu, Y. (2002). Virtual humans for validating maintenance procedures. *Communications of the ACM, 45*(7), 56-63.

Beard, J.W. (Ed.). (1996). *Impression management and information technology.* Greenwood, CT: Quorum.

Beaudouin-Lafon, M., and Mackay, W. (2003). Prototyping tools and techniques. In J.A. Jacko and A. Sears (Eds.), *The human-computer interaction handbook: Fundamentals, evolving technologies, and emerging applications* (pp. 1006-1031). Mahwah, NJ: Erlbaum.

Beaulieu, A. (2004). Mediating ethnography: Objectivity and the making of ethnographies of the internet. *Social Epistemology, 18*(2-3), 139-163. Available: http://www.virtual-knowledgestudio.nl/staff/anne-beaulieu/documents/mediating-ethnography.pdf [accessed Feb. 2007].

Beck, K. (1999). *Extreme programming explained: Embrace change.* Boston: Addison-Wesley.

Beevis, D. (Ed.). (1999). *Analysis techniques for human-machine systems design: A report produced under the auspices of NATO Defense Research Group Panel 8.* Wright-Patterson Air Force Base, OH: Crew Systems Ergonomics/Human Systems Technology Information Analysis Center.

Bernard, H.R. (1995). *Research methods in anthropology: Qualitative and quantitative approaches* (2nd ed.). Thousand Oaks, CA: Sage.

Bevan, N. (2005). International standards for HCI. In C. Ghaoui (Ed.), *Encyclopedia of human computer interaction* (pp. 362-372). Hershey, PA: Idea Group.

Beyer, H., and Holtzblatt, K. (1998). *Contextual design: Defining customer-centered systems.* San Francisco: Morgan Kaufmann.

Bias, R.G., and Mayhew, D.J. (Eds.). (2005). *Cost-justifying usability: An update for the internet age.* San Francisco: Morgan Kaufmann.

Bikson, T.K., and Eveland, J.D. (1996). Groupware implementation: Reinvention in the socio-technical frame. In *Proceedings of the Conference on Computer Supported Cooperative Work (CSCS 96)* (pp. 428-437), Nov. 16-20, Boston, MA. New York: Association for Computing Machinery Press.

Bisantz, A.M., Roth, E.M., Brickman, B., Gosbee, L., Hettinger, L. and McKinney, J. (2003). Integrating cognitive analyses in a large-scale system design process. *International Journal of Human Computer Studies, 58*, 177-206.

Bjerknes, G., and Bratteteig, T. (1987). Florence in wonderland: System development with nurses. In G. Bjerknes, P. Ehn, and M. Kyng (Eds.), *Computers and democracy: A Scandinavian challenge* (pp. 279-295). Brookfield, VT: Gower.

Bjerknes, G., Ehn, P., and Kyng, M. (Eds.). (1987). *Computers and democracy: A Scandinavian challenge.* Brookfield, VT: Gower.

Björgvinsson, E., and Hillgren, P.A. (2004). On the spot experiments within healthcare. In *Proceedings of the Participatory Design Conference (PDC 2004)*, vol. 1, track 2, Methodological Considerations. Available: http://trout.cpsr.org/conferences/pdc2004/proceedings/vol_1/p93_Bjorgvinsson.pdf [accessed March 2007].

Black, F., and Scholes, M. (1973). The pricing of options and corporate liabilities. *Journal of Political Economy, 81*, 637-659.

Blomberg, J., Burrell, M., and Guest, G. (2003). An ethnographic approach to design. In J.A. Jacko and A. Sears (Eds.), *The human-computer interaction handbook: Fundamentals, evolving technologies, and emerging applications* (pp. 964-986). Mahwah, NJ: Erlbaum.

Blomberg, J., Giacomi, J., Mosher, A., and Swenton-Wall, P. (1993). Ethnographic field methods and their relation to design. In D. Schuler, and A. Namioka (Eds.), *Participatory design: Principles and practices* (pp. 123-155). Hillsdale, NJ: Erlbaum.

Boal, A. (1992). *Games for actors and non-actors* (A. Jackson, Trans.). London, England: Routledge.

Bødker, K., Kensing, F., and Simonsen, J. (2004). *Participatory IT design: Designing for business and workplace realities.* Cambridge, MA: MIT Press.

Bødker, S. (1996). Applying activity theory to video analysis: How to make sense of video data in HCI. In B. Nardi (Ed.), *Context and consciousness: Activity theory and human-computer interaction* (pp. 147-174). Cambridge, MA: MIT Press.

Bødker, S., and Buur, J. (2002). The design collaboratorium—A place for usability design. *Transactions on Computer-Human Interaction, 9*(2), 152-169.

Bødker, S., Ehn, P., Kammersgaard, J., Kyng, M., and Sundblad, Y. (1987). A UTOPIAN experience: On design of powerful computer-based tools for skilled graphical workers. In G. Bjerknes, P. Ehn, and M. Kyng (Eds.), *Computers and democracy: A Scandinavian challenge* (pp. 251-278). Brookfield, VT: Gower.

Bødker, S., Knudsen, J.L., Kyng, M., Ehn, P., and Madsen, K.H. (1988). Computer support for cooperative design. In I. Grief, and L. Suchman (Eds.), *Proceedings of the Conference on Computer-Supported Cooperative Work* (CSCW 88), Sept. 26-28, Portland, OR. New York: Association for Computing Machinery Press.

Boehm, B. (1991). Software risk management: Principles and practices. *IEEE Software, 8*(1), 32-41.

Boehm, B. (1996). Anchoring the software process. *Software*, July, 73-82.

Boehm, B. (2000). Unifying software engineering and systems engineering. *Computer*, March, 114-116.

Boehm, B. (2006). Some future trends and implications for systems and software engineering processes. *Systems Engineering*, spring, 1-19.

Boehm, B., Brown, A.W., Basili, V., and Turner, R. (2004). Spiral acquisition of software-intensive systems of systems. *CrossTalk*, May. Available: http://www.stsc.hill.af.mil/Crosstalk/2004/05/index.html [accessed March 2007].

Boehm, B., Egyed, A., Kwan, J., Port, D., Shah, A., and Madachy, R. (1998). Using the winwin spiral model: A case study. *Computer*, July, 33-44.

Boehm, B., and Hansen, W. (2001). The spiral model as a tool for evolutionary acquisition. *CrossTalk*, May, 4-11.

Boehm, B., and Jain, A. (2005). An initial theory of value-based software engineering. In S. Biffl, A. Aurum, B. Boehm, H. Erdogmus, and P. Grünbacher (Eds.), *Value-based software engineering* (pp. 15-37). Berlin, Germany: Springer-Verlag.

Boehm, B., and Lane, J. (2006). 21st century processes for acquiring 21st century systems of systems. *CrossTalk*, May. Available: http://www.stsc.hill.af.mil/crosstalk/2006/05/index.html [accessed March 2007].

Boland, R.J., and Collopy, F. (2004). Toward a design vocabulary for management. In R.J. Boland and F. Collopy (Eds.), *Managing as designing* (pp. 265-276). Palo Alto, CA: Stanford University Press.

Booher, H.R. (2003a). Introduction: Human systems integration. In H.R. Booher (Ed.), *Handbook of human systems integration* (pp. 1-30). Hoboken, NJ: Wiley.

Booher, H.R. (Ed.). (2003b). *Handbook of human systems integration.* Hoboken, NJ: Wiley.

Booher, H.R., and Minninger, J. (2003). Human systems integration in army systems acquisition. In H.R. Booher (Ed.), *Handbook of human systems integration* (pp. 663-698). Hoboken, NJ: Wiley.

Borg, G. (2005). Scaling experiences during work: Perceived exertion and difficulty. In N. Stanton, A. Hedge, K. Brookhuis, E. Salas, and H. Hendrick (Eds.), *Handbook of human factors and ergonomics methods* (pp. 11-1–11-7). Boca Raton, FL: CRC Press.

Bowers, C.A., Jentsch, F., Salas, E., and Baun, C.C. (1998). Analyzing communication sequences for team training needs assessment. *Human Factors, 40*, 672-679.

Brandt, E., and Grunnet, C. (2000). Evoking the future: Drama and props in user centered design. In *Proceedings of the Participatory Design Conference* (PDC 2000). Available: http://intranet.dkds.dk/postnukephoenix/images/imageUpload/305/files/PDC00_evoking_ the_future_FINAL.pdf [accessed March 2007].

Bucciarelli, L.L. (1988). An ethnographic perspective on engineering design. *Design Studies,* 9(3), 159-168.

Burns, C.M., Barsalou, E., Handler, C., Kuo, J., and Harrigan, K. (2000). A work domain analysis for network management. In *Proceedings of the International Ergonomics Association/ Human Factors and Ergonomics Society* (IEA 2000/HFES 2000 Congress) (vol. 1, pp. 469-471). Santa Monica, CA: Human Factors and Ergonomics Society.

Burns, C.M., Bisantz, A.M., and Roth, E.M. (2004). Lessons from a comparison of work domain models: Representational choices and their implications. *Human Factors,* 46(4), 711-727.

Burns, C.M., Bryant, D., and Chalmers, B. (2000). A work domain model to support shipboard command and control. In *Proceedings of the 2000 IEEE International Conference on Systems, Man and Cybernetics* (vol. 3, pp. 2228-2233). Piscataway, NJ: IEEE.

Burns, C.M., and Hajdukiewicz, J.R. (2004). *Ecological interface design.* Boca Raton, FL: CRC Press.

Button, G. (Ed.). (1992). *Technology in working order: Studies of work, interaction, and technology.* London, England: Routledge.

Buur, J., Binder, T., and Brandt, E. (2000). Taking video beyond "hard data" in user centered design. In *Proceedings of the Participatory Design Conference* (PDC 2000). Available: http:// www.sdu.dk/Nat/MCI/m/Research/Publications/UCD/VIDEOBEYONDHARDDATA. PDF [accessed March 2007].

Buur, J., and Bødker, S. (2000). From usability lab to "design collaboratorium": Reframing usability practice. In *Proceedings of the Conference on Designing Interactive Systems: Processes, Practices, Methods, and Techniques* (DIS 2000), pp. 297-307, Aug. 17-19, New York City.

Carayon, P. (2006). Human factors of complex socio-technical systems. *Applied Ergonomics,* 37, 525-535.

Card, S.K., Moran, T.P., and Newell, A. (1983). *The psychology of human-computer interaction.* Hillsdale, NJ: Erlbaum.

Carlile, P.R. (2002). A pragmatic view of knowledge and boundaries. *Organization Science,* 13(4), 442-455.

Carreira, R., Crato, J.M., Goncalves, D., and Jorge, J.A. (2004). Evaluating adaptive user profiles for news classification. In *Proceedings of the 9th International Conference on Intelligent User Interface* (IUI 04), Jan. 13-16, Funchal, Madeira, Portugal (pp. 206-212). New York: Association for Computing Machinery Press.

Carroll, J.M. (Ed.). (1995). *Scenario-based design: Envisioning work and technology in system development.* New York: Wiley.

Carroll, J.M. (2000). *Making use: Scenario-based design of human-computer interactions.* Cambridge, MA: MIT Press.

Carroll, J.M. (2002). Dimensions of participation: Elaborating Herbert H. Simon's "science of design." In J. Perrin (Ed.), *Les sciences de la conception [science of design].* Presented at the International Conference in Honour of Herbert Simon, March 15-16, INSA de Lyon.

Carruth, D., and Duffy, V.G. (2005). Towards integrating cognitive models and digital human models. In *Proceedings of the 11th International Conference on Human-Computer Interaction,* July 22-27, Las Vegas, NV. Mahwah, NJ: Erlbaum.

Chaffin, D.B. (1997). Biomechanical aspects of workplace design. In G. Salvendy (Ed.), *Handbook of human factors and ergonomics* (2nd ed., pp. 772-789). New York: Wiley.

Chaffin, D.B. (2004). Human motion simulation for vehicle and workplace design. In *Proceedings of 10th International Conference on Human Aspects of Advanced Manufacturing: Agility and Hybrid Automation*, Aug. 24-27, Galway, Ireland.

Chaffin, D.B. (2005). Improving digital human modeling for proactive ergonomics in design. *Ergonomics*, *48*(5), 478-491.

Chaffin, D.B., Anderson, G.B., and Martin, B.J. (1999). *Occupational biomechanics* (3rd ed.). New York: Wiley.

Charlton, S.G. (2002). Mental workload test and evaluation. In S.G. Charlton and T.G. O'Brien (Eds.), *Handbook of human factors testing and evaluation* (2nd ed.). Mahwah NJ: Erlbaum.

Charlton, S.G., and O'Brien, T.G. (Eds.). (2002). *Handbook of human factors testing and evaluation* (2nd ed.). Mahwah, NJ: Erlbaum.

Checkland, P. (1981). *Systems thinking, systems practice.* New York: Wiley.

Chi, E., Kittur, A., Mytkowicz, T., Pendleton, B., and Suh, B. (2007). *Augmented social cognition: Understanding social foraging and social sensemaking.* Plenary presentation at Human Computer Interaction Consortium, Feb., Winter Park, CO.

Chipman, S.F., and Kieras, D.E. (2004). Operator centered design of ship systems. In American Society of Naval Engineers, *Engineering the total ship symposium 2004.* Alexandria, VA: American Society of Naval Engineers.

Cockton, G., Woolrych, A., Hall, L. and Hindmarch, M. (2003). Changing analysts' tunes: The surprising impact of a new instrument for usability inspection method assessment. In P. Palanque, P. Johnson, and E. O'Neill (Eds.), *People and computers XVII: Designing for society* (Proceedings of HCI 2003, pp. 145-162). Berlin, Germany: Springer-Verlag.

Cohen, M.A., Ritter, F.E., and Haynes, S.R. (2005). Herbal: A high-level language and development environment for developing cognitive models in Soar. In L. Allender and T. Kelley (Eds.), *Proceedings of the 14th Conference on Behavior Representation in Modeling and Simulation* (pp. 133-140). Orlando: University of Central Florida.

Conrow, E.H. (1995). The use of ordinal risk scales in defense systems engineering. In *Proceedings of the Acquisition Research Symposium (16th)—Acquisition Reform: A Mandate for Change—Reengineering the Acquisition Process.* Fort Belvoir, VA: Defense Systems Management College.

Cook, J., and Brown, J.S. (1999). Bridging epistemologies: The generative dance between organizational knowledge and organizational knowing. *Organization Science*, *10*(4).

Cook, T.D., and Campbell, D.T. (1979). *Quasi-experimentation: Design and analysis issues for field settings.* Chicago, IL: Rand McNally.

Cooke, N.J. (1994). Varieties of knowledge elicitation techniques. *International Journal of Human-Computer Studies*, *41*(6), 801-849.

Cooke, N.J., Neville, K.J., and Rowe, A.L. (1996). Procedural network representations of sequential data. *Human-Computer Interaction*, *11*, 29-68.

Coolican, H. (2004). *Research methods and statistics in psychology (*4th ed.). London, England: Hodder and Stoughton.

Cooper, A. (1999). *The inmates are running the asylum: Why high tech products drive us crazy and how to restore the sanity* (1st ed.). Indianapolis, IN: Sams.

Cooper, A. (2004). *The inmates are running the asylum: Why high tech products drive us crazy and how to restore the sanity* (2nd ed.). Indianapolis, IN: Sams.

Cooper, A., and Reimann, R. (2003). *About face 2.0: The essentials of interaction design.* New York: Wiley.

Coughlan, P., and Prokopoff, I. (2004). Managing change, by design. In R.J. Boland and F. Collopy (Eds.), *Managing as designing* (pp. 188-192). Palo Alto, CA: Stanford University Press.

Councill, I.G., Haynes, S.R., and Ritter, F.E. (2003). Explaining Soar: Analysis of existing tools and user information requirements. In F. Detje, D. Dörner, and H. Schaub (Eds.), *Proceedings of the Fifth International Conference on Cognitive Modeling* (pp. 63-68). Bamberg, Germany: Universitäts-Verlag Bamberg.

Crabtree, A., O'Brien, J., Nichols, D., Rouncefield, M., and Twidale, M. (2000). Ethnomethodologically informed ethnography and information systems design. *Journal of the American Society for Information Science and Technology, 51*(7), 666-682.

Crabtree, A., and Rodden, T. (2002). Ethnography and design? In *Proceedings of the International Workshop on 'Interpretive' Approaches to Information Systems and Computing Research* (pp. 70-74). West London, England: Brunel University.

Crandall, B., Klein, G., and Hoffman, R.R. (2006). *Working minds: A practitioner's guide to cognitive task analysis.* Cambridge MA: MIT Press.

Crisp, H. (2006). *Systems engineering vision 2020, version 2.0.* Presentation to the Washington Metropolitan Area Chapter International Council on Systems Engineering (INCOSE), May 9.

Cummings, M.L. (2006). *Can CWA inform the design of networked intelligent systems?* Paper presented at the Moving Autonomy Forward Conference, June 21-23, Grantham, England.

Curtis, B., Krasner, H., and Iscoe, N.A. (1988). Field study of the software design process for large systems. *Communications of the ACM, 31,* 1268-1287.

Dandavante, U., Steiner, D., and William, C. (2000). Working anywhere: Co-design through participation. In *Proceedings of CoDesigning 2000.* London, England: Springer.

Darrah, C.N. (1995). *Techno-Guanxi: Connecting relationships and icons through technology.* Paper presented at the American Anthropological Association annual meeting, Washington, DC.

D'Astous, P., Détienne, F., Visser, W., and Robillard, P.N. (2004). Changing our view on design evaluation meetings methodology: A study of software technical review meetings. *Design Studies, 25,* 625-655.

Davis, I., and Stephenson, E. (2006). Ten trends to watch in 2006. *McKinsey Quarterly.* Available: http://www.mckinseyquarterly.com/article_abstract_visitor.aspx?ar=1734&l2=21&l3=33&srid=17&gp=0#registerNow [accessed March 2007].

Dawson, D., and Fletcher, A. (2001). A quantitative model of work-related fatigue: Background and definition. *Ergonomics, 44,* 144-163.

Deal, T.E., and Kennedy, A.A. (1982). *Corporate cultures: The rites and rituals of corporate life.* Harmondsworth, England: Penguin.

Dekker, S. (2002). *The field guide to human error investigations.* Burlington, VT: Ashgate.

Dekker, S., and Woods, D.D. (1999). Extracting data from the future: Assessment and certification of envisioned systems. In S. Dekker and E. Hollnagel (Eds.), *Coping with computers in the cockpit* (pp. 7-27). Burlington, VT: Ashgate.

Deming, W.E. (2000). *Out of the crisis.* Cambridge, MA: MIT Press.

Détienne, F. (2006). Collaborative design: Managing task interdependencies and multiple perspectives. *Interacting with Computers, 18*(1), 1-20.

Deutsch, S.E. (1998). Interdisciplinary foundations for multiple-task human performance modeling in OMAR. In *Proceedings of the Twentieth Annual Meeting of the Cognitive Science Society,* Madison, WI. Mahwah, NJ: Erlbaum. Also available: http://omar.bbn.com/ [accessed March 2007].

Dinadis, N., and Vicente, K.J. (1999). Designing functional visualizations for aircraft system status displays. *International Journal of Aviation Psychology, 9,* 241-269.

Dinges, D.F., Connell, L.J., Rosekind, M.R., Gillen, K.A., Kribbs, N.B., and Graeber, R.C. (1991). Effects of cockpit naps and 24-hour layovers on sleep debt in long-haul transmeridian flight crews. *Sleep Research, 20,* 406.

Dourish, P. (2001). *Process descriptions as organizational accounting devices: The dual use of workflow technologies.* Available: http://www.informatik.uni-trier.de/%7Eley/db/conf/group/group2001.html#Dourish01. [accessed March 2007].

Dray, S.M. (1992). Understanding and supporting successful group work in software design: Lessons from IDS. In *Proceedings of the Computer Supported Cooperative Work (CSCW '92) Conference.* New York: Association for Computing Machinery Press.

Duez, P., and Vicente, K.J. (2005). Ecological interface design and computer network management: The effects of network size and fault frequency. *International Journal of Human-Computer Studies, 63,* 565-586.

Dzida, W., Geis, T., and Freitag, R. (2001). The DATech usability-engineering and testing process based on ISO 13407. In *Proceedings of the 6th Congress on Software Quality Management,* Cologne, Germany.

Earthy J., Sherwood Jones B., and Bevan N. (2001). The improvement of human-centred processes—Facing the challenge and reaping the benefit of ISO 13407. *International Journal of Human-Computer Studies, 55*(4), 553-585.

Eggleston, R.G. (2003). Work-centered design: a cognitive engineering approach to system design. In *Proceedings of the Human Factors and Ergonomics Society 47th Annual Meeting* (pp. 263-267). Santa Monica, CA: Human Factors and Ergonomics Society.

Eggleston, R.G., Roth, E., Whitaker, R., and Scott, R. (2005). Conveying work-centered design specifications to the software designer: A retrospective case analysis. In *Proceedings of the Human Factors and Ergonomics Society 49th Annual Meeting* (pp. 332-336). Santa Monica, CA: Human Factors and Ergonomics Society.

Eglash, R., Crossiant, J., Di Chiro, G., and Fouché, R. (2004). *Appropriating technology: Vernacular science and social power.* Minneapolis: University of Minnesota Press.

Ehn, P. (1988). *Work-oriented design of computer artifacts.* Falköping, Sweden: Almqvist and Wiksell International.

Ehn, P., and Kyng, M. (1987). The collective resource approach to systems design. In G. Bjerknes, P. Ehn, and M. Kyng (Eds.), *Computers and democracy: A Scandinavian challenge* (pp. 17-57). Brookfield, VT: Gower.

Ehn, P., and Kyng, M. (1991). Cardboard computers: Mocking-it-up or hands-on the future. In J. Greenbaum and M. Kyng (Eds.), *Design at work: Cooperative design of computer systems* (pp. 169-195). Hillsdale, NJ: Erlbaum.

Ehn, P., and Löwgren, J. (1997). Design for quality-in-use: Human-computer interaction meets information systems development. In M. Helander, T.K. Landauer, and P.V. Prabhu (Eds.), *Handbook of human-computer interaction* (2nd ed., pp. 299-313). Amsterdam, Netherlands: Elsevier.

Ehn, P., and Sjögren, D. (1991). From system descriptions to scripts for action. In J. Greenbaum and M. Kyng (Eds.), *Design at work: Cooperative design of computer systems* (pp. 241-268). Hillsdale, NJ: Erlbaum.

Eichensehr, P. (2006). Knowledge Application Module. Macroergonomics. Virginia Tech.

Elm, W.C., Potter, S.S., Gualtieri, J.W., Easter, J.R., and Roth, E.M. (2003). Applied cognitive work analysis: A pragmatic methodology for designing revolutionary cognitive affordances. In E. Hollnagel (Ed.), *Handbook for cognitive task design* (pp. 357-382). Mahwah, NJ: Erlbaum.

Embry, D.E. (1987). Human reliability. In R. Anthony (Ed.) *Human reliability in nuclear power.* London, England: IBC Technical Services.

Emery, F.E., and Trist, E.L. (1978). Analytical model for sociotechnical systems. In W.A. Pasmore and J.J. Sherwood (Eds.), *Sociotechnical systems: A sourcebook* (pp. 120-133). LaJolla, CA: University Associates.

Endsley, M.R. (1988). Design and evaluation for situation awareness enhancement. In *Proceedings of the Human Factors Society 32nd Annual Meeting* (vol. 1). Santa Monica, CA: Human Factors Society.

Endsley, M.R. (2000). Direct measurement of situation awareness: Validity and use of SAGAT. In M.R. Endsley and D.J. Garland (Eds.), *Situation awareness analysis and measurement* (pp. 147-174). Mahwah, NJ: Erlbaum.

Endsley, M.R., Bolté, B., and Jones, D.G. (2003). *Designing for situation awareness: An approach to user-centered design.* London, England: Taylor and Francis.

Erickson, T. (1995). Notes on design practice: Stories and prototypes as catalysts for communication. In J.M. Carroll (Ed.), *Scenario-based design: Envisioning work and technology in system development* (pp. 37-58). New York: Wiley.

Erickson, T. (1996). Design as story-telling. *Interactions, 3*(4), 30-35.

Ericsson, K.A., and Simon, H.A. (1984). *Protocol analysis: Verbal reports as data.* Cambridge, MA: MIT Press.

Ericsson, K.A., and Simon, H.A. (1993). *Protocol analysis: Verbal reports as data* (rev. ed.). Cambridge, MA: MIT Press.

Erl, T. (2005). *Service-oriented architecture: Concepts, technology, and design.* Upper Saddle River, NJ: Prentice Hall.

Evenson, S. (2005). *Designing design: Establishing a new common ground for collaboration.* Presented at the 11th International Conference on Human-Computer Interaction: Interaction Design Education and Research: Current and Future Trends, July 22-27, Las Vegas, NV.

Federal Republic of Germany. (2004). *V-Modell XT.* Available: http://www.v-modell-xt.de [accessed March 2007].

Feltovich, P.J., Hoffman, R.R., Woods, D.D., and Roesler, A. (2004). Keeping it too simple: How the reductive tendency affects cognitive engineering. *IEEE Intelligent Systems, 19*(3), May/June, 90-94.

Fischer, G., Giaccardi, E., Ye, Y., Sutcliffe, A.G., and Mehandjiev, N. (2004). Meta-design: A manifesto for end-user development. *Communications of the ACM, 47*(9), 33-37.

Fisher, R., and Ury, W. (1981). *Getting to yes: Negotiating agreement without giving in.* Boston: Houghton-Mifflin.

Flanagan, J.C. (1954). The critical incident technique. *Psychological Bulletin, 51,* 327-358.

Floyd, C. (1987). Outline of a paradigm change in software engineering. In G. Bjerknes, P. Ehn, and M. Kyng (Eds.), *Computers and democracy: A Scandinavian challenge* (pp. 191-210). Brookfield, VT: Gower.

Folkard, S., Akerstedt, T., Macdonald, I., Tucker, P., and Spencer, M.B. (1999). Beyond the three-process model of alertness: Estimating phase, time on shift and successive night effects. *Journal of Biological Rhythms, 14,* 579-587.

Fowler, F.J., Jr. (2002). *Survey research methods* (3rd ed.). Thousand Oaks, CA: Sage.

Freed, M., Matessa, M., Remington, R., and Vera, A. (2003). How Apex automates CPM-GOMS. In F. Detje, D. Dörner, and H. Schaub (Eds.), *Proceedings of the Fifth International Conference on Cognitive Modeling* (pp. 93-98). Bamberg, Germany: Universitäts-Verlag Bamberg.

Garvey, P.R., and Lansdowne, Z.F. (1998). Risk matrix: An approach for identifying, assessing, and ranking program risks. *Air Force Journal of Logistics, 25*(1), 16-19.

Gasson, S. (2005). The dynamics of sensemaking, knowledge and expertise in collaborative boundary-spanning design. *Journal of Computer-Mediated Communication, 10*(4), 14.

Gladwell, M. (2005). *Blink: The power of thinking without thinking.* New York: Little, Brown and Company.

Glaser, B.G., and Strauss, A.L. (1967). *The discovery of grounded theory: Strategies for qualitative research.* New York: Aldine.

Gluck, K.A., Ball, J.T., Gunzelmann, G., Krusmark, M.A., Lyon, D.R., and Cooke, N.J. (2006). *A synthetic teammate for UAV applications: A prospective look: Final report.* Mesa, AZ: Air Force Research Laboratory. Available: http://handle.dtic.mil/100.2/ADA452642 [accessed March 2007].

Gluck, K.A., and Pew, R.W. (Eds.). (2005). *Modeling human behavior with integrated cognitive architectures.* Mahwah, NJ: Erlbaum.

Goffman, E. (1956). *Presentation of self in everyday life.* Garden City, NY: Doubleday.

Golder, S.A., and Huberman, B.A. (2006). *Structure of collaborative tagging systems.* Available: http://www.hpl.hp.com/research/idl/papers/tags/tags.pdf [accessed March 2007].

Gong, R., and Kieras, D.E. (1994). A validation of the GOMS model methodology in the development of a specialized, commercial software application. In *Proceedings of the Conference on Human Factors in Computing Systems* (CHI 1994) (pp. 351-357). New York: Association for Computing Machinery Press.

Gorman, J.C., Cooke, N.J., and Winner, J.L. (in press). *Measuring team situation awareness in decentralised command and control systems.* Submitted to *Ergonomics* for special issue on command and control.

Gray, W.D., John, B.E., and Atwood, M.E. (1993). Project Ernestine: Validating a GOMS analysis for predicting and explaining real-world task performance. *Human-Computer Interaction, 8*(3), 237-309.

Gray, W.D., and Kirschenbaum, S.S. (2000). Analyzing a novel expertise: An unmarked road. In J.M. Schraagen, S.F. Chipman, and V.L. Shalin (Eds.), *Cognitive task analysis* (pp. 275-290). Mahwah, NJ: Erlbaum.

Gray, W.D., and Salzman, M.C. (1998). Damaged merchandise? A review of experiments that compare usability evaluation methods. *Human-Computer Interaction, 13*(3), 203-261.

Greenbaum, J., and Kyng, M. (1991). *Design at work: Cooperative design of computer systems.* Hillsdale, NJ: Erlbaum.

Grudin, J., and Pruitt, J. (2002). Personas, participatory design, and product development: An infrastructure for engagement. In *Proceedings of the Participatory Design Conference Participation and Design: Inquiring into the Politics, Contexts and Practices of Collaborative Design Work* (pp. 144-161). Palo Alto, CA: Computer Professionals for Social Responsibility.

Gualtieri, J.W., and Elm, W.C. (2002). Power tool for countering cyberwar: Visualizations for information assurance and computer network defense. In *Proceedings of the Human Factors and Ergonomics Society 46th Annual Meeting* (pp. 463-467). Santa Monica, CA: Human Factors and Ergonomics Society.

Hall, E.M. (1998). *Managing risk: Methods for software systems development.* Reading, MA: Addison-Wesley.

Hancock, P.A., and Desmond, P.A. (2001). *Stress, workload, and fatigue.* Mahwah, NJ: Erlbaum.

Harris, J. (2005) *An office user interface blog.* Available: http://blogs.msdn.com/jensenh/archive/2005/10/31/487247.aspx. [accessed July 2006].

Hart, S.G., and Staveland, L.E. (1988). Development of NASA-TLX (Task Load Index): Results of empirical and theoretical research. In P.A. Hancock and N. Meshkati (Eds.) *Human mental workload* (pp. 139-183). Amsterdam, Netherlands: Elsevier.

Hedge, A. (2005). Physical methods. In N. Stanton, A. Hedge, K. Brookhuis, E. Salas, and H. Hendrick (Eds.), *Handbook of human factors and ergonomics methods* (pp. 2-1–2-4). Boca Raton, FL: CRC Press.

Henderson, A., and Kyng, M. (1991). There's no place like home: Continuing design in use. In J. Greenbaum and M. Kyng (Eds.), *Design at work: Cooperative design of computer systems* (pp. 219-240). Hillsdale, NJ: Erlbaum.

Hendrick, H.A., and Kleiner, B.M. (2001). *Macroergonomics: An introduction to work system design.* Santa Monica, CA: Human Factors and Ergonomics Society.

Hendrick, H.W. (1998). Lowering costs through ergonomics. In W. Karwowski, and G. Salvendy (Eds.). *Ergonomics in manufacturing: Raising productivity through workplace improvement* (pp. 29-42). Dearborn, MI: Society of Manufacturing Engineers.

Highsmith, J. (2000). *Adaptive software development: A collaborative approach to managing complex systems.* New York: Dorset House.

Hine, C.M. (2000). *Virtual ethnography.* Thousand Oaks, CA: Sage.

Hoffman, R. (1987). The problem of extracting the knowledge of experts from the perspective of experimental psychology. *AI Magazine, 8*(summer), 53-67.

Hoffman, R., Coffey, J.W., Ford, K.M., and Novak, J.D. (2006). A method for eliciting, preserving, and sharing the knowledge of forecasters. *Weather and Forecasting, 21,* 416-428.

Hoffman, R., Crandall, B.W., and Shadbolt, N.R. (1998). Use of the critical decision method to elicit expert knowledge: A case study in cognitive task analysis methodology. *Human Factors, 40,* 254-276.

Hoffman, R., and Elm, W.C. (2006). HCC implications for the procurement process. *IEEE Intelligent Systems, 21*(1), 74-81.

Hollnagel, E., Woods, D.D., and Leveson, N. (2006). *Resilience engineering: Concepts and precepts.* Burlington, VT: Ashgate.

Holtzblatt, K. (2003). Contextual design. In J.A. Jacko and A. Sears (Eds.), *The human-computer interaction handbook: Fundamentals, evolving technologies, and emerging applications* (pp. 941-963). Mahwah, NJ: Erlbaum.

Holtzblatt, K., and Beyer, H. (1993). Making customer-centered design work for teams. *Communications of the ACM, 36*(10), 92-103.

Holtzblatt, K., Wendell, J.B., and Wood, S. (2004). *Rapid contextual design: A how-to guide to key technologies for user-centered design.* San Francisco, CA: Morgan Kaufmann.

Houde, S., and Hill, C. (1997) What do prototypes prototype? In M. Helander, T.K. Landauer, and P.V. Prabhu (Eds.), *Handbook of human-computer interaction* (2nd ed., pp. 367-381). Amsterdam, Netherlands: Elsevier.

Howes, A. (1995). Cognitive modelling in HCI. In A. Monk and N. Gilbert (Eds.), *Perspectives on HCI: Diverse approaches* (pp. 97-119). London, England: Academic Press.

Hudlicka, E. (2002). Increasing socially-intelligent architecture realism by modeling and adapting to affect and personality. In K. Dautenhahn, A.H. Bond, L. Canamero, and B. Edmonds (Eds.), *Multiagent systems, artificial societies, and simulated organizations.* Dordrecht, Netherlands: Kluwer Academic.

Hughes, J., King, V., Rodden, T., and Anderson, H. (1995). The role of ethnography in interactive systems design. *Interactions,* 56-65.

Hughes, J.A., O'Brien, J., Rodden, T., Rouncefield, J., and Blythin, S. (1997). Designing with ethnography: A presentation framework for design. In *Proceedings of Designing Interactive Systems: Processes, Practices, Methods, and Techniques (DIS 97).* New York: Association for Computing Machinery Press.

Hughes, J.A., Randall, D., and Shapiro, D. (1992). Faltering from ethnography to design. In *Proceedings of the Computer Supported Cooperative Work (CSCW '92) Conference.* New York: Association for Computing Machinery Press.

Hulkko, S., Mattelmäki, T., Virtanen, K., and Keinonen, T. (2004). *Mobile probes.* Presented at the Nordic Conference on Computer-Human Interaction (NordiCHI 2004), Oct. 23-27, Tampere, Finland.

Hutchins, E. (1995). *Cognition in the wild.* Cambridge, MA: MIT Press.

Iacucci, G., and Kuutti, K. (2002). Everyday life as a stage in creating and performing scenarios for wireless devices. *Personal and Ubiquitous Computing, 6,* 299-306.

IBM (n.d.). *Social software for business.* Available: http://www-142.ibm.com/software/sw-lotus/products/product3.nsf/wdocs/connections [accessed Feb. 2007].

Institute of Medicine. (2000). *To err is human. Building a safer health system.* L.T. Kohn, J. M. Corrigan, and M.S. Donaldson, Eds. Committee on Quality of Health Care in America. Washington, DC: National Academy Press.

International Organization for Standardization. (1996). *ISO 9241-10. Ergonomic requirements for office work with visual display terminals (VDTs)óPart 10: Dialogue principles.* Available: http://www.iso.org/iso/en/CatalogueDetailPage.CatalogueDetail?CSNUMBER =16882 [accessed April 2007].

International Organization for Standardization. (1998). ISO 9241-11. *Ergonomic requirements for office work with visual display terminals (VDTs)—Part 11: Guidance on usability.* Available: http://www.iso.org/iso/en/CatalogueDetailPage.CatalogueDetail?CS NUMBER=16883&ICS1=13&ICS2=180&ICS3= [accessed April 2007].

International Organization for Standardization. (2000a). ISO 14971. *Medical devices—Application of risk management to medical devices.* Available: http://www.iso.org/iso/en/CatalogueDetailPage.CatalogueDetail?CSNUMBER=31550 [accessed April 2007].

International Organization for Standardization. (2000b). *ISO/TR 18529. Ergonomics of human-system interaction—Human-centered lifecycle process descriptions.* Available: http://www.iso.ch/iso/en/CatalogueDetailPage.CatalogueDetail?CSNUMBER=33499&s copelist= [accessed April 2007].

International Organization for Standardization. (2001). *ISO/IEC 9126-1. Software engineering-Product quality—Part 1: Quality model.* Available: http://www.iso.org/iso/en/CatalogueDetailPage.CatalogueDetail?CSNUMBER=22749&ICS1=35&ICS2=80&ICS3= [accessed April 2007].

International Organization for Standardization. (2002). *ISO/IEC 15288. Systems engineering—System life cycle processes.* Available: http://www.iso.org/iso/en/CatalogueDetailPage.CatalogueDetail?CSNUMBER=27166&ICS1=35&ICS2=80&ICS3= [accessed March 2007].

International Organization for Standardization. (2003). *ISO/PAS 18152. Ergonomics of human-system interaction—Specification for the process assessment of human-system issues.* Available: http://www.iso.org/iso/en/CatalogueDetailPage.CatalogueDetail?CSN UMBER=38596 [accessed April 2007].

International Organization for Standardization. (2006). *ISO/IEC 25062. Software engineering—Software product quality requirements and evaluation (SQuaRE)-Common industry format (CIF) for usability test reports.* Available: http://www.iso.org/iso/en/CatalogueDetailPage.CatalogueDetail?CSNUMBER=43046&ICS1=35&ICS2=80&ICS3= [accessed March 2007].

International Organization for Standardization. (2007). *IS0/IEC 25030. Software engineering—Software product quality requirements and evaluation (SQuaRE)-Quality requirements.* Available: http://www.iso.org/iso/en/CatalogueDetailPage.CatalogueDeta il?CSNUMBER=35755&scopelist=PROGRAMME [accessed April 2007].

Israelski, E.W., and Muto, W.H. (2006). Human factors engineering and the design risk management in medical devices. In P. Carayon (Ed.), *Handbook of human factors and ergonomics in healthcare and patient safety* (Part V, Technology). Mahwah, NJ: Erlbaum.

Ivory, M.Y., and Hearst, M.A. (2001). The state of the art in automating usability evaluation of user interfaces. *ACM Computing Surveys, 33*(4), 470-516.1-47. Available: http://webtango.berkeley.edu/papers/ue-survey/p470-ivory.Pdf. [accessed April 2007].

Jamieson, G.A., and Vicente, K.J. (2001). Ecological interface design for petrochemical applications: Supporting operator adaptation, continuous learning, and distributed, collaborative work. *Computers and Chemical Engineering, 25,* 1055-1074.

Jamshidi, M. (2005). System-of-systems engineering—A definition. *IEEE Transactions. System, Man, Cybernetics,* (Oct.).

Jeffries, R., and Desurvire, H. (1992). Usability testing vs. heuristic evaluation: Was there a contest? *SIGCHI Bulletin, 24*(4), 39-41.

John, B.E., Prevas, K., Salvucci, D.D., and Koedinger, K. (2004). Predictive human performance modeling made easy. In *Proceedings of the Conference on Human Factors in Computing Systems (CHI 2004)* (pp. 455-462), April, Vienna, Austria. New York: Association for Computing Machinery Press.

Jones, D.G. (2000). Subjective measures of situation awareness. In M.R. Endsley and D.J. Garland (Eds.), *Situation awareness analysis and measurement* (pp. 113-128). Mahwah, NJ: Erlbaum.

Jungk, R., and Müllert, N. (1987). *Future workshops: How to create desirable futures.* London, England: Institute for Social Inventions.

Kelley, T. (2001). Prototyping is the shorthand of innovation. *Design Management Journal, 12*(3), 35-42.

Kemmlert, K. (1995). A method assigned for the identification of ergonomic hazards–PLIBEL. *Applied Ergonomics, 126,* 199-211.

Kensing, F., and Madsen, A. (1993). PD: Structure in the toolbox. *Communications of the ACM 36*(6), 78-85.

Kensing, F., and Munk-Madsen, K.H. (1991). Generating visions: Future workshops and metaphorical design. In J. Greenbaum and M. Kyng (Eds.), *Design at work: Cooperative design of computer systems* (pp. 155-168). Hillsdale, NJ: Erlbaum.

Kensing, F., Simonsen, J., and Bødker, K. (1996). MUST—A method for participatory design. In *Proceedings of the Participatory Design Conference* (PDC 1996), Nov. 13-15, Cambridge, MA. San Francisco: Computer Professionals for Social Responsibility.

Keyserling, W.M. (1998). Methods for evaluating postural workload. In W. Karwowski and G. Salvendy (Eds). *Ergonomics in manufacturing* (pp. 167-188). Dearborn, MI: Society of Manufacturing Engineers.

Kiekel, P.A., Gorman, J.C., and Cooke, N.J. (2004). Measuring speech flow of co-located and distributed command and control teams during a communication channel glitch. In *Proceedings of the Human Factors and Ergonomics Society 48th Annual Meeting,* Sept. 20-24, New Orleans, LA. Santa Monica, CA: Human Factors and Ergonomics Society.

Kieras, D.E. (1998). A guide to GOMS model usability evaluation using NGOMSL. In M. Helander (Ed.), *Handbook of human-computer interaction* (vol. 12, pp. 391-438). Amsterdam, Netherlands: Elsevier.

Kieras, D.E. (2003). Model-based evaluation. In J.A. Jacko and A. Sears (Eds.), *The human-computer interaction handbook: Fundamentals, evolving technologies, and emerging applications* (pp. 1139-1151). Mahwah, NJ: Erlbaum.

Kieras, D.E., Wood, S.D., Abotel, K., and Hornof, A. (1995). GLEAN: A computer-based tool for rapid GOMS model usability evaluation of user interface designs. Paper presented at the ACM Symposium on User Interface Software and Technology (UIST'95), New York.

Kieras, D.E., Wood, S.D., and Meyer, D.E. (1997). Predictive engineering models based on the EPIC architecture for a multimodal high-performance human-computer interaction task. *Transactions on Computer-Human Interaction, 4*(3), 230-275.

Kilbom, Å., and Petersson, N.F. (2006). Elements of the ergonomic process. In W.S. Marras and W. Karwowski (Eds.), *Occupational ergonomics handbook: Interventions, controls, and applications in occupational ergonomics* (2nd ed., pp. 1-1–1-6). Boca Raton, FL: CRC Press.

Kirwan, B., and Ainsworth, L.K. (Eds.). (1992). *A guide to task analysis.* London, England: Taylor and Francis.

Klær, A., and Madsen, K.H. (1995). Participatory analysis of flexibility. *Communications of the ACM, 38*(5), 53-60.

Klein, G., and Armstrong, A.A. (2005). Critical decision method. In N. Stanton, A. Hedge, K. Brookhuis, E. Salas, and H. Hendrick (Eds.), *Handbook of human factors and ergonomics methods* (pp. 35-1–35-8). Boca Raton, FL: CRC Press.

Klein, G., Calderwood, R., and MacGregor, D. (1989). Critical decision method for eliciting knowledge. *IEEE Transactions. System, Man, Cybernetics, 19*, 462-472.

Kleiner, B.M. (1997). An integrative framework for measuring and evaluating information management performance. *International Journal of Computers and Industrial Engineering, 32*(3), 545-555.

Kleiner, B.M., and H.R. Booher (2003). Human systems integration education and training. In H.R. Booher (Ed.), *Handbook of human systems integration* (pp. 121-163). Hoboken, NJ: Wiley.

Kleiner, B.M., Drury, C.G., and Palepu, P. (1998). A computer-based productivity and quality management system for cellular manufacturing. *Computers and Industrial Engineering, 34*(1), 207-217.

Kroemer, K.H.E., Kroemer, H.B., and Kroemer-Elbert, K.E. (2001). *Ergonomics: How to design for ease and efficiency* (2nd ed.). Upper Saddle River, NJ: Prentice Hall.

Kruchten, P. (1999). *The rational unified process: An introduction.* Boston: Addison Wesley.

Kukreja, U., Stenson, W.E., and Ritter, F.E. (in press). RUI—Recoding user input from interfaces under Windows and Mac OS X. Submitted to *Behavior Research Methods, Instruments, and Computers, 2.*

Kyng, M., and Matthiassen, L. (Eds.). (1997). *Computers in design and context.* Cambridge MA: MIT Press.

Lafrenière, D. (1996). CUTA: A simple, practical, low-cost approach to task analysis. *Interactions, 3*(5), 35-39.

Laird, J.E., Newell, A., and Rosenbloom, P.S. (1987). Soar: An architecture for general intelligence. *Artificial Intelligence, 33*(1), 1-64.

Lane, J., and Valerdi, R. (2005). Synthesizing systems-of-systems concepts for use in cost estimation. In *Proceedings of the 2005 IEEE International Conference on Systems, Man, and Cybernetics (SMC 2005),* Oct. 10-12, Waikoloa, HI. Piscataway, NJ: IEEE.

Laughery, K.R., Jr., and Corker, K.M. (1997). Computer modeling and simulation of human/system performance. In G. Salvendy (Ed.), *Handbook of human factors* (2nd ed., pp. 1375-1408). New York: Wiley.

Lebiere, C., Biefeld, E., Archer, R., Archer, S., Allender, L., and Kelley, T.D. (2002). IMPRINT/ACT-R: Integration of a task network modeling architecture with a cognitive architecture and its application to human error modeling. In *Proceedings of the Advanced Technologies Simulation Conference.* San Diego, CA.

Levinger, D. (1998). *Participatory design history.* Available: http://www.cpsr.org/prevsite/conferences/pdc98/history.html [accessed July 2006].

Levis, A. (2006). Private presentation to the committee.

Li, G., and Buckle, P. (1999). Current techniques for assessing physical exposure to work-related musculoskeletal risks, with emphasis on posture-based methods. *Ergonomics, 42*, 674-695.

Li, G., and Buckle, P. (2005). Quick exposure checklist (QEC) for the assessment of workplace risks for work-related musculoskeletal disorders (WMSDs). In N. Stanton, A. Hedge, K. Brookhuis, E. Salas, and H. Hendrick (Eds.), *Handbook of human factors and ergonomics methods* (pp. 6-1–6-10). Boca Raton, FL: CRC Press.

Liebhold, M. (2004). *Infrastructure for the new geography.* Menlo Park, CA: Institute for the Future.

Lin, L., Vicente, K.J., and Doyle, D.J. (2001) Patient safety, potential adverse drug events, and medical device design: A human factors engineering approach. *Journal of Biomedical Informatics, 34*, 274-284.

Louhevaara, V., Smolander, J., Aminoff, T., and Ilmarinen, J. (1998). Assessing physical work load. In W. Karwowski, and G. Salvendy (Eds.). *Ergonomics in manufacturing: Raising productivity through workplace improvement* (pp. 121-134). Dearborn, MI: Society of Manufacturing Engineers.

Luff, P., Hindmarsh, J., and Heath, C. (Eds.). (2000). *Workplace studies: Recovering work practice and informing system design.* Cambridge, England: Cambridge University Press.

Lytle, W.O. (1998). *Designing a high performance organization: A guide to the whole-systems approach.* Clark, NJ: Block Petrella Weisbord.

Mackay, W.E. (1990). *Users and customizable software: A co-adaptive phenomenon.* Doctoral Dissertation. Cambridge, MA: Sloan School for Management, Massachusetts Institute of Technology.

Madachy, R. (1995). Knowledge-based risk assessment and cost estimation. *Automated Software Engineering, 2*(3), 219-230.

Maier, M. (1998). Architecting principles for systems-of-systems. *Systems Engineering, 1*(4), 267-284.

Mannio, M., and Nikula, U. (2001). *Requirements elicitation using a combination of prototypes and scenarios.* Lappeenranta, Finland: Lappeenranta University of Technology.

Marenzano, J.F., Rozsypal, S.A., Zimmerman, G.H., Warnken, G.W., Wirth, P.E., and Weiss, D.M. (2005). Architecture reviews: Practice and experience. *IEEE Software*, March/April, 34-43.

Marras, W.S., and Allread, W.G. (2005). Lumbar motion monitor. In N. Stanton, A. Hedge, K. Brookhuis, E. Salas, and H. Hendrick (Eds.), *Handbook of human factors and ergonomics methods* (pp. 14-1–14-7). Boca Raton, FL: CRC Press.

Martinez, S.G., Bennett, K.B., and Shattuck, L., 2001. Cognitive systems engineering analyses for army tactical operations. In *Proceedings of the Human Factors and Ergonomics Society 44th Annual Meeting* (pp. 523-526). Santa Monica, CA: Human Factors and Ergonomics Society.

Mayer, D. (2005). Falconer AOC weapon system achieves IOC. *The Integrator, 1*(27). Available: http://integrator.hanscom.af.mil./2005/June/06232005/06232005.htm [accessed April 2007].

McAtamney, L., and Corlett, N. (1993). RULA: A survey method for the investigation of work-related upper limb disorders. *Applied Ergonomics*, 24, 91-99.

McAtamney, L., and Corlett, N. (2005). Rapid upper limb assessment (RULA). In N. Stanton, A. Hedge, K. Brookhuis, E. Salas, and H. Hendrick (Eds.), *Handbook of human factors and ergonomics methods* (pp. 7-1–7-11). Boca Raton, FL: CRC Press.

McCracken J.H., and Aldrich, T.B. (1984). *Analyses of selected LHS mission functions: Implications for operator workload and system automation goals.* [Technical Note ASI 497-024084(B)]. Fort Rucker, AL: Anacapa Sciences.

Militello, L.G., and Hutton, R.J.B. (2000). Applied cognitive task analysis (ACTA): A practitioner's toolkit for understanding cognitive task demands. In J. Annett and N.A. Stanton (Eds.), *Task analysis* (pp. 90-113). London, England: Taylor and Francis.

Millen, D.R., (2000). Rapid ethnography: Time deepening strategies for HCI field research. In *Proceedings of the Conference on Designing Interactive Systems: Processes, Practices, Methods, and Techniques* (DIS 2000), pp. 280-286, August 17-19, New York City.

Miller, C.A., and Vicente, K.J. (1999). Task 'versus' work domain analysis techniques: A Comparative Analysis. In _Proceedings of the Human Factors and Ergonomics Society 43rd Annual Meeting_ (pp. 328-332). Santa Monica, CA: Human Factors and Ergonomics Society.

Miller, D., and Slater, D. (2001). _The internet: An ethnographic approach._ Oxford, England: Berg.

Miller, R.B. (1953). _A method for man-machine task analysis._ (Report #53-137). Dayton, OH: Wright Air Development Center, Wright-Patterson Air Force Base.

Modell, S. (1996). Management accounting and control in services: structural and behavioural perspectives. _International Journal of Service Industry Management, 7_(2), 57-80.

Mogensen, P., and Trigg, R. (1992). Artifacts as triggers for participatory analysis. In _Proceedings of the Participatory Design Conference (PDC'92),_ Nov. 6-7, Cambridge, MA. San Francisco: Computer Professionals for Social Responsibility.

Molich, R., and Dumas, J.S. (2006). Comparative usability evaluation (CUE-4). _Behaviour and Information Technology, 25._

Molich, R., Ede, M.R., Kaasgaard, K., and Karyukin, B. (2004) Comparative usability evaluation. _Behaviour and Information Technology, 23_(1), 65-74.

Molich, R., and Nielsen, J. (1990). Improving a human-computer dialogue. _Communications of the ACM, 33,_ 338-348.

Monge, P.R., and Contractor, N.S. (1999). Emergence of communication networks. In F.M. Jablin and L.L. Putnam (Eds.), _Handbook of organizational communication_ (2nd ed.). Thousand Oaks, CA: Sage.

Monk, A., and Howard, S. (1998). The rich picture: A tool for reasoning about work context. _Interactions, 2,_ 21-30.

Mørch, A.I., Engen, B.K., and Åsand, H.-R.H. (2004). The workplace as a learning laboratory: The winding road to e-learning in a Norwegian service company. In _Proceedings of the Participatory Design Conference (PDC 2004)_ (pp. 142-151). New York: Association for Computing Machinery Press.

Morrison, J.E. (2003). _A review of computer-based human behavior representations and their relation to military simulations._ (IDA paper #P-3845). Alexandria, VA: Institute for Defense Analyses.

Muller, M.J. (1992). Retrospective on a year of participatory design using the PICTIVE technique. In _Proceedings of the Conference on Human Factors in Computing Systems (CHI '92)_ (pp. 455-462). New York: Association for Computing Machinery Press.

Muller, M.J. (2001). Layered participatory analysis: New developments in the CARD technique. In _Proceedings of the Conference on Human Factors in Computing Systems (CHI 2001),_ (pp. 90-97), March 31-April 5, Seattle, WA. New York: Association for Computing Machinery Press.

Muller, M.J. (2003). Participatory design: The third space in HCI. In J.A. Jacko and A. Sears (Eds.), _The human-computer interaction handbook: Fundamentals, evolving technologies, and emerging applications_ (pp. 1051-1068). Mahwah, NJ: Erlbaum.

Muller, M.J. (2007). Participatory design: The third space in HCI (revised). In J.A. Jacko and A. Sears (Eds.), _The human-computer interaction handbook_ (2nd ed.). Mahwah, NJ: Erlbaum.

Muller, M.J., Haslwanter, J.H., and Dayton, T. (1997). Participatory practices in the software lifecycle. In M. Helander, T.K. Landauer, and P.V. Prabhu (Eds.), _Handbook of human-computer interaction_ (2nd ed., pp. 255-297). Amsterdam, Netherlands: Elsevier.

Muller, M.J., and Kuhn, S. (Eds.). (1993). Special issue on participatory design. _Communications of the ACM, 36_(6).

Muller, M.J., Millen, D.R., and Strohecker, C. (2001). What makes a representative user representative? A participatory poster. In *Proceedings of the Conference on Human Factors in Computing Systems (CHI 2001)*, extended abstracts, March 31-April 5, Seattle, WA. New York: Association for Computing Machinery Press.

Muller, M.J., Raven, M.E., Kogan, S., Millen, D.R., and Carey, K. (2003). Introducing chat into business organizations: Toward an instant messaging maturity model. In *Proceedings of GROUP 2003 International Conference on Supporting Group Work*, Nov. 9-12, Sanibel Island, FL. New York: Association for Computing Machinery Press.

Muller, M.J., Tudor, L.G., Wildman, D.M., White, E.A., Root, R.W., Dayton, T., Carr, R., Diekmann, B., and Dykstra-Erickson, E. (1995). Bifocal tools for scenarios and representations in participatory activities with users. In J.M. Carroll (Ed.), *Scenario-based design: Envisioning work and technology in system development* (pp. 135-163). New York: Wiley.

Muller, M.J., Wharton, C., Laux, L., and Mciver, W., Jr. (1997). Toward an HCI research and practice agenda based on human needs and social responsibility. In *Proceedings of the Conference on Human Factors in Computing Systems (CHI '97)*, April 18-23, Atlanta GA. New York: Association for Computing Machinery Press.

Muller, M.J., Wildman, D.M., and White, E.A. (1994). Participatory design through games and other group exercises. In *Proceedings of the Conference on Human Factors in Computing Systems (CHI '94)*, April, Boston, MA. New York: Association for Computing Machinery Press.

Mumford, E., and Henshall, D. (1983). *Designing participatively: A participative approach to computer systems design: A case study of the introduction of a new computer system.* Manchester, England: Manchester Business School. (Original work published in 1979).

Naikar, N., Pearce, B., Drumm, D. and Sanderson, P.M. (2003). Designing teams for first-of-a-kind, complex systems using the initial phases of cognitive work analysis: Case study. *Human Factors, 45*(2), 202-217.

Naikar, N., and Sanderson, P.M. (1999). Work domain analysis for training-system definition and acquisition, *International Journal of Aviation Psychology, 9*(3), 271-290.

Naikar, N., and Sanderson, P.M. (2001). Evaluating design proposals for complex systems with work domain analysis, *Human Factors, 43*(4), 529-542.

Naikar, N., and Saunders, A. (2003). Crossing the boundaries of safe operation: An approach for training technical skills in error management, *Cognition, Technology and Work, 5*, 171-180.

Nardi, B. (1993). *A small matter of programming: Perspectives on end user computing.* Cambridge, MA: MIT Press.

Nardi, B. (Ed.). (1996). *Context and consciousness: Activity theory and human-computer interaction.* Cambridge, MA: MIT Press.

Nardi, B. (1997). The use of ethnographic methods in design and evaluation. In M. Helander, T.K. Landauer, and P.V. Prabhu (Eds.), *Handbook of human-computer interaction* (2nd ed., pp. 361-366). Amsterdam, Netherlands: Elsevier.

National Research Council. (1997). *More than screen deep: Toward an every-citizen interface to the nation's information infrastructure.* Toward an Every-Citizen Interface to the Nation's Information Infrastructure Steering Committee. Computer Science and Telecommunications Board. Commission on Physical Sciences, Mathematics, and Applications. Washington, DC: National Academy Press.

National Research Council. (1998). *Modeling human and organizational behavior: Application to military simulations.* R.W. Pew and A.S. Mavor (Eds.). Panel on Modeling Human Behavior and Command Decision Making: Representations for Military Simulations, Commission on Behavioral and Social Sciences and Education. Washington, DC: National Academy Press. Also available: http://www.nap.edu/catalog.php?record_id=6173 [accessed March 2007].

National Transportation Safety Board. (2006). *Aviation accident statistics, Table 2.* Accidents and Accident Rates by NTSB Classification, 1986 through 2005, for U.S. Air Carriers Operating Under 14 CFR 121. Available: http://www.ntsb.gov/aviation/Stats.htm [accessed March 2007].

Nemeth, C.P. (2004). *Human factors methods for design: making systems human-centered.* Boca Raton, FL: CRC Press.

Nichols, S., and Ritter, F.E. (1995). A theoretically motivated tool for automatically generating command aliases. In *Proceedings of the Conference on Human Factors in Computer Systems (CHI '95),* (pp. 393-400), May 7-11, Denver, CO. New York: Association for Computing Machinery Press.

Nielsen, J., and Mack, R.L. (Eds.). (1994). *Usability inspection methods.* New York: Wiley.

Nightingale, D.J., and Rhodes, D.H. (2004). *Enterprise systems architecting: Emerging art and science within engineering systems.* Paper presented at the MIT Engineering Systems Symposium, Session VI, March 31, Cambridge, MA. Available: http://esd.mit.edu/symposium/pdfs/papers/nightingale.pdf [accessed March 2007].

Noble, A., and Robinson, C. (2000). For the love of the people: Participatory design in a community context. In *Proceedings of CoDesigning 2000* (pp. 81-91). London, England: Springer.

Norman, D. (1993). *Things that make us smart: Defending human attributes in the age of the machine.* Cambridge, MA: Perseus.

Norman, D. (1995). *On the difference between research and practice: Ergonomics in design.* Santa Monica, CA: Human Factors and Ergonomics Society.

Noro, K., and Imada, A.S. (Eds.). (1991). *Participatory ergonomics.* London, England: Taylor and Francis.

Nuclear Regulatory Commission. (1981). *Fault tree handbook.* W.E. Vesely, F.F Goldberg, N.H. Roberts, and D.F. Haasl, Eds. Washington, DC: Author.

Occhipinti, E., and Colombini, D. (2005). The occupational repetitive action (OCRA) methods: OCRA index and OCRA checklist. In N. Stanton, A. Hedge, K. Brookhuis, E. Salas, and H. Hendrick (Eds.), *Handbook of human factors and ergonomics methods* (pp. 15-1–15-14). Boca Raton, FL: CRC Press.

O'Hara, J.M. and Roth, E.M. (2005). Operational concepts, teamwork, and technology in commercial nuclear power stations. In C.A. Bowers, E. Salas, and F. Jentsch (Eds.), *Creating high-tech teams: Practical guidance on work performance and technology* (pp. 139-159).Washington, DC: American Psychological Association.

Olson, J.S., Olson, G.M., Storrøsten, M., and Carter, M. (1992). How a group editor changes the character of a design meeting as well as its outcome. In *Proceedings of the Conference on Computer-Supported Cooperative Work* (CSCW '92) (pp. 91-98), Nov. 1-4, Toronto, Ontario, Canada. New York: Association for Computing Machinery Press.

Olson, G.M., Herbsleb, J., and Rueter, H. (1994). Characterizing the sequential structure of interactive behaviors through statistical and grammatical techniques. *Human-Computer Interaction, 9,* 427-472.

Olsson, S. (2000). *Ethnography and internet: Differences in doing ethnography in real and virtual environments.* Paper presented at the Conference on Information Research Seminar in Scandinavia (IRIS 23) Doing IT Together, Aug. 12-15, Uddevalla, Sweden. Available: http://citeseer.ist.psu.edu/cache/papers/cs/20350/http:zSzzSziris23.htu.sezSzproceeding-szSzPDFzSz102final.PDF/olsson00ethnography.pdf [accessed Feb. 2007].

O'Reilly, T. (2005). *What is web 2.0? Design patterns and business models for the next generation of software.* Available: http://www.oreillynet.com/pub/a/oreilly/tim/news/2005/09/30/what-is-web-20.html [accessed March 2007].

Paley, M.J., Linegang, M.P., and Morley, R.M. (2002). Using communication data to assess organizational and system effectiveness in future combat systems. In *Proceedings of the Human Factors and Ergonomics Society 46th Annual Meeting*, Baltimore, MD. Santa Monica, CA: Human Factors and Ergonomics Society.

Pasmore, W.A. (1988). *Designing effective organizations: The sociotechnical systems perspective.* New York: Wiley.

Pasztory, E. (2005). *Thinking with things: Toward a new vision of art.* Austin: University of Texas Press.

Patterson, F. (1999). System engineering life cycles: life cycles for research, development, test, and evaluation; acquisition; and planning and marketing. In A. Sage and W. Rouse (Ed.), *Handbook of systems engineering and management* (pp. 59-111). New York: Wiley.

Patterson, E.S., Cook, R.I., and Render, M.L. (2002). Improving patient safety by identifying side effects from introducing bar coding in medication administration. *Journal of the American Medical Informatics Association, 9*(5), 540-553.

Patterson, E.S., Roth, E.M., and Woods, D.D. (2001). Predicting vulnerabilities in computer-supported inferential analysis under data overload. *Cognition, Technology and Work, 3*, 224-237.

Pedersen, J., and Buur, J. (2000). Games and moves: towards innovative codesign with users. In *Proceedings of CoDesigning 2000*. London, England: Springer.

Peterson, W.W., Birdsall, T.G., and Fox, W.C. (1954). The theory of signal detectability. *IRE Professional Group on Information Theory, 4*, 171-212.

Pew, R.W. (2000). The state of situation awareness measurement: Heading toward the next century. In M.R. Endsley and D.J. Garland (Eds.), *Situation awareness analysis and measurement* (pp. 33-50). Mahwah, NJ: Erlbaum.

Pipek, V. (2005). *From tailoring to appropriation support: Negotiating groupware usage.* PhD thesis, Oulu University, Finland. Available: http://herkules.oulu.fi/isbn9514276302/ [accessed June 2005].

Potter, S.S., Elm, W.C., Roth, E.M., Gualtieri, and Easter, J. (2002). Bridging the gap between cognitive analysis and effective decision aiding. In M.D. McNeese and M.A. Vidulich (Eds), *State of the art report (SOAR): Cognitive systems engineering in military aviation environments: Avoiding cogminutia fragmentosa!* (pp. 137-168). Dayton, OH: Human Systems Information Analysis Center, Wright-Patterson Air Force Base. Available: http://iac.dtic.mil/hsiac/.

Potter, S.S., Roth, E.M., Woods, D.D. and Elm, W.C. (2000). Bootstrapping multiple converging cognitive task analysis techniques for system design. In J.M. Schraagen, S.F. Chipman, and V.L. Shalin (Eds.), *Cognitive task analysis* (pp. 317-340). Mahwah, NJ: Erlbaum.

Potts, C., and Hsi, I. (1997). Abstraction and context in requirements engineering: A synthesis of goal refinement and ethnography. *Annals of Software Engineering, 3*, 23-61.

Preece, J. (2002). Supporting community and building social capital—Introduction. *Communications of the ACM, 45*(4), 37-39.

Price, H.E. (1985). The allocation of functions in systems. *Human Factors, 27*(1), 33-45.

Pruitt, J., and Adlin, T. (2006). *The persona lifecycle: Keeping people in mind throughout product design.* San Francisco, CA: Morgan Kaufmann.

Pruitt, J., and Grudin, J. (2003). *Personas: Theory and practice.* Presented at the Conference on Designing for User eXperience (DUX2003), June 5-7, San Francisco, CA.

Raiffa, H. (1982). *The art and science of negotiation.* Cambridge, MA: Harvard University Press.

Rasmussen, J. (1986). *Information processing and human-machine interaction: An approach to cognitive engineering.* New York: North-Holland.

Rasmussen, J., Pejtersen, A.M., and Goodstein, L.P. (1994). *Cognitive systems engineering.* New York: Wiley.

Reason, J.T. (1990). *Human error.* Cambridge, England: Cambridge University Press.

Reason, J.T. (1997). *Managing the risks of organizational accidents.* Brookfield, VT: Ashgate.

Rector, A. L., Horan, B., Fitter, M., Kay, S., Newton, P.D., Nowlan, W.A., Robinson, D., and Wilson, A. (1992). User centered development of a general practice medical workstation: The PEN&PAD experience. In *Proceedings of the Conference on Human Factors in Computing Systems* (CHI 1992). New York: Association for Computing Machinery Press.

Redish, J., and Wixon, D. (2003). Task analysis. In J.A. Jacko and A. Sears (Eds.), *The human-computer interaction handbook: Fundamentals, evolving technologies, and emerging applications* (pp. 922-940). Mahwah, NJ: Erlbaum.

Rheinfrank, J., and Welker, K. (1994). Working from the border. *Human-Computer Interaction, 9*(1), 111-114.

Rith, C., and Dubberly, H. (2005). *Horst Rittel: A definitive bibliography.* San Francisco, CA: Dubberly Design.

Ritter, F.E., Baxter, G.D., Jones, G., and Young, R.M. (2000). Supporting cognitive models as users. *ACM Transactions on Computer-Human Interaction, 7*(2), 141-173.

Ritter, F.E., Freed, A.R., and Haskett, O.L. (2005). User information needs: The case of university department web sites. *ACM interactions, 12*(5), 19-27.

Ritter, F. E., Haynes, S. R., Cohen, M., Howes, A., John, B., and Best, B. (2006). High-level behavior representation languages revisited. In D. Fum, F. del Missier, and A. Stocco (Eds.), *Proceedings of ICCM-2006 Seventh International Conference on Cognitive Modeling* (pp. 404-407). Trieste, Italy: Edizioni Goliardiche.

Ritter, F.E., Van Rooy, D., and St. Amant, R. (2002). A user modeling design tool based on a cognitive architecture for comparing interfaces. In C. Kolski and J. Vanderdonckt (Eds.), *Computer-Aided Design of User Interfaces III, Proceedings of the 4th International Conference on Computer-Aided Design of User Interfaces (CADUI 2002)* (pp. 111-118). Dordrecht, Netherlands: Kluwer Academic.

Ritter, F.E., Shadbolt, N.R., Elliman, D., Young, R.M., Gobet, F., and Baxter, G.D. (2003). *Techniques for modeling human performance in synthetic environments: A supplementary review.* Dayton, OH: Human Systems Information Analysis Center, Wright-Patterson Air Force Base.

Rodgers, S. (2005). Muscle fatigue assessment: Functional job analysis technique. In N. Stanton, A. Hedge, K. Brookhuis, E. Salas, and H. Hendrick (Eds.), *Handbook of human factors and ergonomics methods* (pp. 12-1–12-10). Boca Raton, FL: CRC Press.

Rosson, M., and Carroll, J.M. (1996). *Object-oriented design from user scenarios.* Available: http://sigchi.org/chi96/proceedings/tutorial/Rosson/mbr_txt.htm [accessed July 2006].

Rosson, M., and Carroll, J.M. (2002). *Usability engineering: Scenario-based development of human-computer interaction.* San Francisco, CA: Morgan Kaufmann.

Rosson, M. and Carroll, J.M. (2003). Scenario-based design. In J.A. Jacko and A. Sears (Eds.), *The human-computer interaction handbook: Fundamentals, evolving technologies, and emerging applications* (pp. 1032-1050). Mahwah, NJ: Erlbaum.

Rosson, M., Maass, S., and Kellogg, W. (1989). The designer as user: Building requirements for design tools from design practice. *Communications of the ACM, 31*(11), 1288-1297.

Roth, E.M., Lin, L., Kerch, S., Kenney, S.J., and Sugibayashi, N. (2001). Designing a first-of-a-kind group view display for team decision making: A case study. In E. Salas and G. Klein (Eds.), *Linking expertise and naturalistic decision making* (pp. 113-135). Mahwah, NJ: Erlbaum.

Roth, E.M., and Patterson, E.S. (2005). Using observational study as a tool for discovery: Uncovering cognitive and collaborative demands and adaptive strategies. In H. Montgomery, R. Lipshitz, and B. Brehmer (Eds.), *How professionals make decisions* (pp. 379-393). Mahwah, NJ: Erlbaum.

Roth, E.M., Scott, R., Deutsch, S., Kuper, S., Schmidt, V., Stilson, M. and Wampler J. (in press). Evolvable work-centered support systems for command and control: Creating systems users can adapt to meet changing demands. Submitted to *Ergonomics*.

Roth, E.M., Stilson, M., Scott, R., Whitaker, R., Kazmierczak, T., Thomas-Meyers, G., and Wampler, J. (2006). Work-centered design and evaluation of a C2 visualization aid. In *Proceedings of the Human Factors and Ergonomics Society 49th Annual Meeting* (pp. 332-336). Santa Monica, CA: Human Factors and Ergonomics Society.

Rouse, W.B. (2003). Human systems integration and new product development. In H.R. Booher (Ed.), *Handbook of human systems integration* (pp. 877-903). Hoboken, NJ: Wiley.

Royce, W.E. (1998). *Software project management*. Boston: Addison Wesley.

Royce, W.W. (1970). Managing the development of large software systems: Concepts and techniques. *Proceedings of IEEE WESCON*, 26(August), 1-9. Available: http://www.cs.umd.edu/class/spring2003/cmsc838p/Process/waterfall.pdf [accessed March 2007].

Sage, A., and Cuppan, C. (2001). On the systems engineering and management of systems of systems and federations of systems. *Information, Knowledge, and Systems Management*, 2, 325-345.

Sage, A., and Rouse, W. (Eds.) (in press). *Handbook of systems engineering and management* (revised edition). New York: Wiley.

Sage, A., and Rouse, W. (1999a). An introduction to systems engineering and systems management. In A. Sage and W. Rouse (Ed.), *Handbook of systems engineering and management* (pp. 1-58). New York: Wiley.

Sage, A., and Rouse, W. (Eds.) (1999b). *Handbook of systems engineering and management*. New York: Wiley.

Sager, L., and Grier, R.A. (2005). *Identifying and measuring the value of human factors to an acquisition project*. Presented at the Human Systems Integration Symposium. Available: http://www.aptima.com/publications/2005_Sager_Grier.pdf [accessed March 2007].

Salvendy, G. (2006). *Handbook of human factors and ergonomics* (3rd ed.). Hoboken, NJ: Wiley.

Salvucci, D.D., and Anderson, J.R. (2001). Automated eye-movement protocol analysis. *Human-Computer Interaction*, 16, 39-86.

Sanders, E.B.-N. (2000). Generative tools for co-designing. In *Proceedings of CoDesigning 2000*. London, England: Springer.

Sanderson, P. (2003). Cognitive work analysis. In J.M. Carroll (Ed.), *HCI models, theories, and frameworks: Toward a multidisciplinary science* (pp. 225-264). San Francisco: Morgan Kaufmann.

Sanderson, P., and Fisher, C. (1994). Exploratory sequential data analysis: foundations. *Human-Computer Interaction*, 9, 251-317.

Sanderson, P., Naikar, N., Lintern, G., and Goss, S. (1999). Use of cognitive work analysis across the system life cycle: Requirements to decommissioning. In *Proceedings of the 43rd Annual meeting of the Human Factors and Ergonomics Society* (pp. 318-322). Santa Monica, CA: Human Factors and Ergonomics Society.

Sanquist, T.F., and McCallum, M.C. (2004). A comprehensive evaluation and classification of fatigue countermeasures for transportation operators. In *Proceedings of the Human Factors Society Annual Meeting*. Santa Monica, CA: Human and Ergonomics Society.

Sarter, N., and Sarter, M. (2003). Neuroergonomics: Opportunities and challenges of merging cognitive neuroscience with cognitive ergonomics. *Theoretical Issues in Ergonomics Science*, 4, 142-150.

Sauro, J., and Kindlund, E. (2005). *Making sense of usability metrics: Usability and Six Sigma.* Presented at the Usability Professionals' Association Meeting (UPA 2005), June 27-July 1, Montreal, Quebec, Canada. Available: http://www.measuringusability.com/ [accessed March 2007].

Sauter, S.L., Swanson, N.G., Waters, T.R., Hales, T.R. and Dunkin-Chadwick, R. (2005). Musculoskeletal discomfort surveys used at NIOSH. In N. Stanton, A. Hedge, K. Brookhuis, E. Salas, and H. Hendrick (Eds.), *Handbook of human factors and ergonomics methods* (pp. 4–1–10). Boca Raton, FL: CRC Press.

Scacchi, W. (2004). Socio-technical design. In W.S. Bainbridge (Ed.), *The encyclopedia of human-computer interaction* (pp. 656-659). Great Barrington, MA: Berkshire.

Schaffer, E. (2004). *Institutionalization of usability: A step-by-step guide.* Boston: Addison-Wesley.

Schein, E. (1996). Culture: The missing concept in organizational studies. *Administrative Science Quarterly, 41*, 229-240.

Schraagen, J.M., Chipman, S.F., and Shalin, V.L. (Eds.). (2000). *Cognitive task analysis.* Mahwah, NJ: Erlbaum.

Schrage, M. (1994). Peeking from the periphery: Does the document metaphor inspire (re)designs? *Human-Computer Interaction, 9*(1), 115-118.

Schrage, M. (1996). Cultures of prototyping. In T. Winograd (Ed.), *Bringing design to software* (pp. 191-205). New York: Association for Computing Machinery Press.

Schreiber, B.T., and Bennett, W., Jr. (2006). *Distributed mission operations within-simulator training effectiveness baseline study. Volume I: Summary report* (AFRL-HE-AZ-TR-2006-0015). Mesa, AZ: Warfighter Training Research Division, Air Force Research Laboratory.

Schreiber, B.T., Bennett, W., Jr., and Gehr, S.E. (2006). Fidelity trade-offs for deployable training and rehearsal. In *Proceedings of the Interservice/Industry Training, Simulation and Education Conference (I/ITSEC).* Orlando, FL: National Security Industrial Association.

Schuler, D., and Namioka, A. (Eds.). (1993). *Participatory design: Principles and practices.* Hillsdale, NJ: Erlbaum.

Schvaneveldt, R.W., Durso, F.T., and Dearholt, D.W. (1989). Network structures in proximity data. In G.H. Bower (Ed.), *The psychology of learning and motivation: Advances in research and theory* (vol. 24, pp. 249-284). New York: Academic Press.

Shadbolt, N., Berners-Lee, T., and Hall, W. (2006). The semantic web revisited. *IEEE Intelligent Systems, 21*(3), 96-101.

Shepard, R.N. (1962a). Analysis of proximities: Multidimensional scaling with an unknown distance function. *I Psychometrika, 27*, 125-140.

Shepard, R.N. (1962b). Analysis of proximities: Multidimensional scaling with an unknown distance function. *II Psychometrika, 27*, 219-246.

Shepard, R.N., and Arabie, P. (1979). Additive clustering: Representation of similarities as combinations of discrete overlapping properties. *Psychological Review, 86*, 87-123.

Shneiderman, B. (2002). *Leonardo's laptop: Human needs and the new computing technologies.* Cambridge, MA: MIT Press.

Siegel, D., and Dray, S. (2001). New kid on the block: Marketing organizations and interaction design. *Interactions, 8*(2), 19-24.

Sinha, R. (2003). Persona development for information-rich domains. In *Proceedings of the Conference on Human Factors in Computing Systems (CHI 2003)*, extended abstracts, (pp. 830-831), April 5-10, Ft. Lauderdale, FL. New York: Association for Computing Machinery Press.

Skilton, W., Cameron, S., and Sanderson (1998). Supporting cognitive work analysis with the work domain analysis workbench (WDAW). In *Proceedings of the Computer Human Interaction Conference* (pp. 260-267), Nov. 30-Dec. 4. Piscataway, NJ: IEEE.

Slavkovic, A., and Cross, K. (1999). Novice heuristic evaluations of a complex interface. In *Proceedings of the Conference on Human Factors in Computing Systems: The CHI is the Limit (CHI '99)*, extended abstracts, May 15-20, Pittsburgh, PA. New York: Association for Computing Machinery Press.

Snyder, C. (2003). *Paper prototyping: The fast and easy way to design and refine user interfaces.* San Francisco: Morgan Kaufmann.

Somerville, I., Martin, D., and Rouncefield, M. (2003). Informing the requirements engineering process with patterns of cooperative interaction. *International Arab Journal of Information Technology, 1*(1).

Special issue on collaboration, cooperation, and conflict in dialogue systems. (2000). *International Journal of Human-Computer Studies 53*(6).

Spool, J., and Schroeder, W. (2001) Testing web sites: Five users is nowhere near enough. In *Proceedings of the Conference on Human Factors in Computing Systems* (CHI '01) (pp. 285-286), extended abstracts, March 31-April 5, Seattle, WA. New York: Association for Computing Machinery Press.

St. Amant, R., Freed, A.R., and Ritter, F.E. (2005). Specifying ACT-R models of user interaction with a GOMS language. *Cognitive Systems Research, 6*(1), 71-88.

St. Amant, R., Horton, T.E., and Ritter, F.E. (2004). Model-based evaluation of cell phone menu interaction. In *Proceedings of the Conference on Human Factors in Computing Systems (CHI '04),* (pp. 343-350), April 24-29, Vienna, Austria. New York: Association for Computing Machinery Press.

Stamatis, D.H. (1995). *Failure mode and effect analysis: FMEA from theory to execution.* Milwaukee, WI: ASQC Quality Press.

Standish Group. (2006). *The Standish store.* Available: https://secure.standishgroup.com/reports/reports.php [accessed March 2007].

Stanton, N.A., Hedge, A., Brookhuis, K., Salas, E., and Hendrick, H. (Eds.) (2005a). *Handbook of human factors and ergonomics methods.* Boca Raton, FL: CRC Press.

Stanton, N.A., Salmon, P.M., Walker, G.H., Baber, C., and Jenkins, D.P. (200b5). *Human factors methods: A practical guide for engineering and design.* Burlington, VT: Ashgate.

Star, S.L. (1989). The structure of ill-structured solutions: Boundary objects and heterogeneous distributed problems solving. In L. Gasser and M.N. Huhns (Eds.), *Distributed artificial intelligence (*vol. II, pp. 37-54). San Francisco: Morgan Kaufmann.

Sterling, B. (2004). *When blobjects rule the earth.* Keynote address presented at the 31st International Conference on Computer Graphics and Interactive Techniques (SIGGRAPH 2004), Aug., Los Angeles. Available: http://www.boingboing.net/images/blobjects.htm [accessed March 2007].

Suchman, L.A. (1987). *Plans and situated actions: The problem of human-machine communication.* Cambridge, England: Cambridge University Press.

Suchman, L.A. (2002). Located accountabilities in technology production. *Scandinavian Journal of Information Systems, 14*(2), 91-105.

Suchman, LA. (2004). Decentering the manager/designer. In R.J. Boland and F. Collopy (Eds.), *Managing as designing* (pp. 169-173). Palo Alto, CA: Stanford University Press.

Suchman, L., and Trigg, R. (1991). Understanding practice: Video as a medium for reflection and design. In J. Greenbaum and M. Kyng (Eds.), *Design at work: Cooperative design of computer systems* (pp. 65-90). Hillsdale, NJ: Erlbaum.

Sun, R. (Ed.). (2006). *Cognition and multi-agent interaction: From cognitive modeling to social simulation.* Cambridge, England: Cambridge University Press.

Suthers, D.D. (2005). Collaborative knowledge construction through shared representations. In *Proceedings of the 38th Annual Hawaii International Conference on System Sciences (HICSS '05)*. Washington, DC: IEEE Computer Society.

Suwa, M., and Tversky B. (2002). External representations contribute to the dynamic construction of ideas. In *Proceedings of the Diagrammatic Representation and Inference: Second International Conference, Diagrams 2002*, Callaway Gardens, GA, April 18-20 (p. 341). Berlin, Germany: Springer-Verlag.

Swain, A.D. (1963). *A method for performing a human factors reliability analysis.* (Monograph #SCR-685). Albuquerque, NM: Sandia National Laboratories.

Swain, A.D., and Guttmann, H.E. (1983). *Handbook of human reliability analysis with emphasis on nuclear power plant applications.* (NUREG/CR 1278). Albuquerque, NM: Sandia National Laboratories.

Swets, J.A., Dawes, R.M., and Monahan, J. (2000). Psychological science can improve diagnostic decisions. *Psychological Science in the Public Interest, 1*, 1-26.

Tang, J.C., Liu, S.B., Muller, M.J., Drews, C., and Lin, J. (2006). Unobtrusive but invasive: Using screen recording to collect field data on computer-mediated interaction. In *Proceedings of the 20th Anniversary Conference on Computer Supported Cooperative Work (CSCW 2006)* (pp. 479-482), Nov. 4-8, Alberta, Canada. New York: Association for Computing Machinery Press.

Taylor, S. (Ed.). (2001). *Ethnographic research: A reader.* London, England: Sage.

Tenney, Y.J., and Pew, R.W. (2006). Situation awareness catches on: What? So what? Now what? In R.C. Williges (Ed), *Reviews of human factors and ergonomics.* Santa Monica, CA: Human Factors and Ergonomics Society.

Teton, D., and Allen, S. (2007). *The growth of social software.* Available: http://www.fastcompany.com/resources/networking/teten-allen/120606.html [accessed Feb. 2007].

Theofanos, M. (2006). A practical guide to the CIF: Usability measurements. *Interactions, 13*(6), 34-37.

Thorp, J. (1998). *The information paradox: Realizing the business benefits of information technology.* Toronto, Canada: McGraw Hill.

Toth, G. (1995). Automated method for identifying and prioritizing project risk factors. *Automated Software Engineering, 2*(3), 231-248.

Trigg, R.H. (2000). From sandbox to "fundbox": Weaving participatory design into the fabric of a busy non-profit. In *Proceedings of the Participatory Design Conference* (PDC 2000) (pp. 174-182). New York: Computer Professionals for Social Responsibility.

Truex, D., Baskerville, R., and Klein, H. (1999). Growing systems in an emergent organization. *Communications of the ACM, 42*(8), 117-123.

Tsang, P.S., and Wilson, G.F. (1997). Mental workload. In G. Salvendy (Ed.), *Handbook of human factors and ergonomics* (2nd ed., pp. 417-449). New York: Wiley.

Tscheligi, M., Houde, S., Marcus, A., Mullet, K., Muller, M.J., and Kolli, R. (1995). Creative prototyping tools: What interaction designers really need to produce advanced user interface concepts. In *Proceedings of the Conference on Human Factors in Computer Systems (CHI '95)*, (pp. 170-171), May 7-11, Denver, CO. New York: Association for Computing Machinery Press.

Tversky, B, Morrison, J.B., and Betrancourt, M. (2002). Animation: Can it facilitate? *International Journal of Human-Computer Studies, 57*(4), 247-262.

Tyler, J.R, Wilkinson, D.M., and Huberman, B.A. (2005). E-mail as spectroscopy: Automated discovery of community structure within organizations. *The Information Society, 21*, 1443-1453.

Urbas, L., and Leuchter, S. (2005). Model-based analysis and design of human-machine dialogues through displays. *KI–Zeitschrift für künstliche Intelligenz [AI-Journal for AI]*, 45-51.

United States Army. (2000). *MANPRINT history*. Available: http://www.manprint.army.mil/manprint/mp-history.asp. [accessed March 2007].

United States Department of Defense. (1999). *Department of Defense handbook: Human engineering program process and procedures*. (MIL-HDBK-46855A). Available: http://hfetag.dtic.mil/docs-hfs/mil-hdbk-46855a.pdf. [accessed March 2007].

United States Department of Defense. (2003a). *Department of Defense instruction 5000.2: Operation of the defense acquisition system*. Available: http://akss.dau.mil/dag/DoD5000.asp?view=document [accessed April 2007].

United States Department of Defense. (2003b). *Risk management guide for DOD acquisition*. Fort Belvoir, VA: Defense Acquisition University Press.

United States Department of Health and Human Services. (2006). *Research-based web design and usability guidelines*. Available: http://www.usability.gov/pdfs/guidelines.html. [accessed March 2007].

United States Navy. (2005). *Human performance center, SEAPRINT*. Available: https://www.spider.hpc.navy.mil/index.cfm?RID=WEB_OT_1001399 [accessed March 2007].

Vicente, K.J. (1999). *Cognitive work analysis: Toward safe, productive, and healthy computer-based work*. Mahwah, NJ: Erlbaum.

Vink, P., Koningsveld, E.A.P., and Molenbroek, J.F. (2006). Positive outcomes of participatory ergonomics in terms of greater comfort and higher productivity. *Applied Ergonomics, 37*(4), 537-546.

Wampler, J., Roth, E., Whitaker, R., Conrad, K., Stilson, M., Thomas-Meyers, G., and Scott, R. (2006). *Defining a work-centered specification: An approach to integrate cognitive requirements into the software development of complex work systems*. Presented at the Human Factors and Ergonomics Society (HFES) 50th Annual Meeting, Oct. 16-20, San Francisco, CA.

Wasson, C. (2000). Ethnography in the field of design. *Human Organization, 59*(4), 377-388.

Weick, K.E., and Sutcliffe, K.M. (2001). *Managing the unexpected: Assuring high performance in an age of complexity*. San Francisco: Jossey Bass.

Weidenhaupt, K., Pohl, K., Jarke, M., and Haumer, P. (1998). Scenarios in system development: Current practice. *IEEE Software, 15*(2), 34-45.

White, B.E. (2005). *A complementary approach to enterprise systems engineering*. Presented at the National Defense Industrial Association 8th Annual Systems Engineering Conference Focusing on Mission Areas, Net-Centric Operations and Supportability of Defense Systems, Oct. 24-27, San Diego, CA.

Wickens, C.D., and Hollands, J.G. (1999). *Engineering psychology and human performance* (3rd ed.) New York: Harper-Collins.

Williams, K.E. (2000). An automated aid for modeling human-computer interaction. In J.M. Schraagen, S.F. Chipman, and V.L. Shalin (Eds.), *Cognitive task analysis* (pp. 165-180). Mahwah, NJ: Erlbaum.

Wilson, J.R., and Corlett, E.N. (1998). *Evaluation of human work: A practical ergonomics methodology*. London, England: Taylor and Francis.

Winograd, T., and Flores, F. (1987). *Understanding computers and cognition: A new foundation for design*. Boston: Addison-Wesley.

Wittel, A. (2000). Ethnography on the move: From field to internet. *Forum: Qualitative Social Research, 1*(1). Available: http://www.qualitative-research.net/fqs-texte/1-00/1-00wittel-e.pdf [accessed Feb. 2007].

Wixon, D., and Ramey, J. (Eds.). (1996). *Field methods casebook for software design*. New York: Wiley.

Womack, J.P., and Jones, D.T. (1996). *Lean thinking: Banish waste and create wealth in your corporation*. New York: Simon and Schuster.

Woods, D.D. (1993). Process-tracing methods for the study of cognition outside of the experimental psychology laboratory. In G. Klein, J. Orasanu, R. Calderwood, and C.E. Zsambok (Eds), *Decision making in action: Models and methods*. Norwood, NJ: Ablex.

Woods, D.D. (2002). Steering the reverberations of technology change on fields of practice: Laws that govern cognitive work. Plenary address in *Proceedings of the 24th Annual Meeting of the Cognitive Science Society Aug, 10-12, Fairfax, VA*. Austin, TX: Cognitive Science Society.

Woods, D.D. (2003). Discovering how distributed cognitive systems work. In E. Hollnagel (Ed.), *Handbook of cognitive task design* (pp. 37-53). Mahwah, NJ: Erlbaum.

Woods, D.D. (2006). Resilience engineering: Redefining the culture of safety and risk management. *HFES Bulletin*, 49(12), 1-3.

Woods, D.D., and Christoffersen, K. (2002). Balancing practice-centered research and design. In M.D. McNeese and M.A. Vidulich (Eds.), *Cognitive systems engineering in military aviation environments: Avoiding cogminutia fragmentosa. State of the art report* (pp. 121-134). Dayton, OH: Human Systems Information Analysis Center, Wright-Patterson Air Force Base.

Woods, D.D., and Dekker, S. (2000). Anticipating the effects of technological change: A new era of dynamics for human factors. *Theoretical Issues in Ergonomics Science*, 1(3), 272-282.

Woods, D.D., and Hollnagel, E. (2006). *Joint cognitive systems: Patterns in cognitive systems engineering*. Boca Raton, FL: CRC Press.

Wulff, W., Evenson, S., and Rheinfrank, J. (1990). Animating interfaces. In *Proceedings of the Conference on Computer-Supported Cooperative Work (CSCW '90)*, Oct. 7-10, Los Angeles. New York: Association for Computing Machinery Press.

Yang, Y., Boehm, B., and Clark, B. (2006). Assessing COTS integration risk using cost estimation inputs. In *Proceedings of the ACM/IEEE 28th International Conference on Software Engineering* (pp. 431-438), May 20-28, Shanghai, China.

Yin, R.K. (2003). *Case study research: Design and methods* (3rd ed.). Thousand Oaks, CA: Sage.

Young, R.M., Green, T.R.G., and Simon, T. (1989). Programmable user models for predictive evaluation of interface designs. In *Proceedings of the Conference on Human Factors in Computing Systems (CHI'89)* (pp. 15-19). New York: Association for Computing Machinery Press.

Zachary, W. (2000). *COGNET tutorial and overheads*. Presentation at the Third International Conference on Cognitive Modeling (ICCM-2000), March 23-25, Groningen, Netherlands.

Zarcone, V.P. (2000). Sleep hygiene. In M.H. Kryger, T. Roth, and W.C. Dement (Eds.), *Principles and practices of sleep medicine* (3rd ed., pp. 657-662). New York: W.B. Saunders.

Appendix A

Sponsors and Contributors

SPONSORS

John Lockett, Army Research Laboratory
Ed Martin, Air Force Research Laboratory
Maris Vikmanis, Air Force Research Laboratory

CONTRIBUTORS

Britt Bray, Dynamics Research Corporation
Nancy Dolan, HSI Office, U.S. Navy
Rick Drawbaugh, U.S. Air Force
Michael Drillings, Director of MANPRINT, U.S. Army
Jonathan Earthy, Lloyd's Register
John Hawley, U.S. Army Research Laboratory, Human Resources and
    Engineering Directorate
Randall Hill, Institute for Creative Technologies
Andrew Jones, Institute for Creative Technologies
Taylor Jones, MANPRINT Acquisition Liaison, U.S. Army
Alex Levis, George Mason University
John Owen, U.S. Navy
Bill Swartout, Institute for Creative Technologies
Harvey Weintraub, Abbott Laboratories
Greg Zacharias, Committee on Human Factors

Appendix B

Biographical Sketches of Committee Members and Staff

Richard W. Pew (*Chair*) has been a principal scientist at BBN Technologies in Cambridge, Massachusetts, since 1974 and is currently working part-time there. He has 35 years of experience in human factors, human performance, and experimental psychology as they relate to systems design and development. Throughout his career, he has been involved in the development and use of human performance models and in the conduct of experimental and field studies of human performance in applied settings. Before BBN, he spent 11 years on the faculty of the Psychology Department at the University of Michigan, where he was involved in human performance teaching, research, and consulting. The university has recently created a collegiate chair in his name. He was the first chair of the National Research Council's Committee on Human Factors. He has been president of the Human Factors Society and of Division 21 of the American Psychological Association. He has a bachelor's degree in electrical engineering from Cornell University (1956), a master of arts degree in psychology from Harvard University (1960), and a Ph.D. in psychology with a specialization in engineering psychology from the University of Michigan (1963).

Nigel Bevan is an independent usability consultant with wide industrial and research experience. He provides consultancy and training in usability and user-centered design. He was technical coordinator of the EU MUSiC (measurement of usability in context), a project that produced methods for usability measurement, which have since been widely applied commercially. He was manager of the INUSE and RESPECT projects, which set up a network of usability support centers around Europe; the TRUMP project, which incorporated user-centered design into the development processes of two large organizations; the PRUE project, which trialed use of the common industry format for usability test reports; and the UsabilityNet project, which established a web site of usability resources. He participates in several international standards groups in which he has introduced the concept of quality in use. He contributed to ISO 13407 and the common industry format and edited ISO 9241-11 (guidance on usability), ISO/IEC 14598-1 (evaluation of software quality—general guide), ISO/IEC 9126-1 (software product quality model), and ISO/IEC 9126-4 (quality in use metrics). He currently edits ISO/IEC 25030 (quality requirements), ISO 20282-2 (usability of everyday products), and the new common industry format for usability requirements. He has a B.Sc. in physics and in psychology from London University, and a Ph.D. in man-machine interaction from the Council for National Academic Awards (CNAA).

Barry W. Boehm is TRW professor of software engineering and director of the Center for Software Engineering at the University of Southern California. Between 1989 and 1992, he served in the U.S. Department of Defense as director of the DARPA Information Science and Technology Office and as director of the DDR&E Software and Computer Technology Office. His current research interests focus on value-based software engineering, including a method for integrating a software system's process models, product models, property models, and success models, called model-based (system) architecting and software engineering (MBASE). His contributions to the field include the constructive cost model (COCOMO), the spiral model of the software process, the theory W (win-win) approach to software management and requirements determination, the foundations for the areas of software risk management and software quality factor analysis, and two advanced software engineering environments: the TRW software productivity system and quantum leap environment. He is a member of the National Academy of Engineering. He has a B.A. from Harvard University (1957) and an M.S. (1961) and a Ph.D. (1964) from the University of California, Los Angeles, all in mathematics. He also received an honorary Sc.D. in computer science from the University of Massachusetts in 2000.

Kristen A. Butler (*research assistant*) joined the National Academies in 2005. She is currently the research assistant for the Committee on Human-System Design Support for Changing Technology, the Committee on Human Factors, and the Committee on Organizational Modeling from Individuals to Societies. Prior to working at the National Research Council, she worked as a student co-op in the human factors division of the Volpe National Transportation Systems Center of the U.S. Department of Transportation. She has a B.S. in engineering psychology and biomedical engineering from the Tufts University School of Engineering.

Nancy J. Cooke is professor in the Applied Psychology Unit at Arizona State University and is science director and on the board of directors of the Cognitive Engineering Research Institute in Mesa, Arizona. Currently, she supervises graduate and undergraduate research in the Laboratory for Cognitive Engineering Research on Team Tasks. Her research interests include the study of knowledge and its application to the development of cognitive and knowledge engineering methodologies, as well as to expertise, intelligent tutors, human-computer interfaces, and team performance. In particular, she specializes in the development, application, and evaluation of methodologies to elicit and assess individual and team cognition. Her most recent work includes the development and validation of methods to measure shared knowledge and team situation awareness and research on the impact of cross training, distributed mission environments, and workload on team knowledge, process, and performance. She is editor-in-chief of *Human Factors*. She has a B.A. in psychology from George Mason University and M.A. (1983) and Ph.D. (1987) degrees in cognitive psychology from New Mexico State University.

Shelley Evenson is currently associate professor in the area of interaction design in the School of Design at Carnegie Mellon University. She has worked for more than 25 years in multidisciplinary consulting practices, working closely with users to develop products that are aesthetically pleasing and usable to them. Her clients include Apple Computer, the Bank of Montreal, Diamond Technologies, Kodak, Texas Instruments, the Williamsburg Institute, and Xerox. She uses rapid prototyping to iteratively reshape solutions and present them to users for interactive evaluation. These prototypes incorporate business strategy and new technologies and are used to transform the users' experiences of the product and increase product adoption and loyalty. Evenson was cofounder of seeSpace and chief experience strategist for Scient. She served as a board member for the American Center for Design. Her current interests include design languages and strategies, organizational interfaces, design, and the study of what lies beyond user-centered design. She has a B.S. in industrial design from the Ohio State University.

Dave Graeber is a human factors engineer at Boeing Phantom Works in Seattle. He has a background that has afforded application of human factors skills, techniques, and concepts to a diverse array of projects spanning complex systems design, business development, project management, and bringing technologies to new markets. Working within a mix of systems engineering and business development environments, his focus centers on the trade space of system design to support end-users and the pragmatic realities of program management. He has a Ph.D. in industrial engineering from the University of Central Florida.

Edmond W. Israelski is a human factors program manager at Abbott Laboratories in Abbott Park, Illinois. He has worked as a systems engineer, product manager, market researcher, and industrial/organizational psychologist as well as a human factors engineer. He was technical manager of the human factors systems group at Lucent Technologies—Bell Labs, formerly AT&T. Later he was director of human factors for SBC/Ameritech, where his organization supported the design and evaluation of user interfaces for telecommunications products and services. In 2000, he became chief technology officer at Human Factors International, a user interface design and consulting firm. He joined Abbott Laboratories, a medical device and pharmaceutical company, as program manager of human factors in 2001, where he leads a cross-division team to embed best-practice human factors design methods into all of Abbott's products to ensure safety and usability. He is a fellow of the Human Factors and Ergonomics Society and cochair of the human factors engineering standards development committee for the Association for the Advancement of Medical Instrumentation. He has a B.S. in electrical engineering from the New Jersey Institute of Technology, an M.S. in operations research from Columbia University, and a Ph.D. in industrial and engineering psychology from the Stevens Institute of Technology.

Brian M. Kleiner is a professor of industrial and systems engineering at Virginia Polytechnic Institute and State University. He also directs the Center for Innovation in Construction Safety and Health. His research interests focus on sociotechnical systems, health and safety and on the analysis and design of work systems and work system interfaces (macroergonomics). This includes function allocation in automation and system design, training/communication/information system, support system design, design of collaborative and distributed work environments, safety and health, and human reliability and decision making in quality control. He has an M.S. (1983) in human factors concentration and a Ph.D. (1990) in industrial engineering (human factors concentration) from the State University of New York at Buffalo.

Anne S. Mavor (*study director*) is the staff director for the Committee on Human Factors and the Committee on Human-System Design Support for Changing Technology. Her previous National Research Council work has included studies on occupational analysis and the enhancement of human performance, modeling human behavior and command decision making, human factors in air traffic control automation, human factors considerations in tactical display for soldiers, scientific and technological challenges of virtual reality, emerging needs and opportunities for human factors research, and modeling cost and performance for purposes of military enlistment. For the past 35 years, her work has concentrated on human factors, cognitive psychology, and information system design. She has an M.S. in experimental psychology from Purdue University.

Michael Muller is a research scientist in the Collaborative User Experience group at IBM Research in Cambridge, Massachusetts. His expertise is in participatory design, having codeveloped participatory practices, such as PICTIVE, CARD, and Participatory Heuristic Evaluation. His current work analyzes knowledge sharing and knowledge management through social software applications in organizations. He has worked in research and practice in usability, user-centered design, and work analysis at Microsoft, U.S. West Advanced Technologies, and Bellcore, and serves on IBM's Collaboration Invention Development Team. He has a Ph.D. in cognitive psychology from Rutgers University.

Frank E. Ritter is associate professor of information sciences and technology, of psychology, and of computer science and engineering at the Pennsylvania State University. He has received study fellowships from the Air Force Office of Scientific Research, the European Science Foundation's Program on Learning in Humans and Machines, and the Fulbright Commission. He has developed software, tutorials, and methodology for cognitive modeling, particularly with Soar and ACT-R, creating models that have tested human-robot interfaces, sample and real telephones, and complex interfaces. He has published widely in the area of cognitive modeling, artificial intelligence, and psychology. He is on the editorial board of *Human Factors*, *AISB Journal*, and *AISB Quarterly*, and is the editor for Oxford University Press' series on *Cognitive Models and Architectures*. He has a B.S.E.E. (with honors) from the University of Illinois at Urbana-Champaign as well as an M.S. in psychology and a Ph.D. in artificial intelligence and psychology from Carnegie Mellon University.

Emilie Roth is president of Roth Cognitive Engineering. Her work has involved analysis of human problem solving and decision making in real-world environments (e.g., military command and control, intelligence analysis, monitoring and control of internet networks, nuclear power plant operations, railroad operations, surgery), and the impact of support systems (e.g., computerized procedures, alarm systems, advanced graphical displays, new forms of automation) on performance. She has conducted empirical studies of naturalistic decision making, developed and applied cognitive task analysis and cognitive work analysis techniques for understanding the cognitive demands imposed by work environments, and developed principles for effective decision support for individuals and teams. She has served as part of multidisciplinary design teams developing first-of-a-kind systems, including design and manning of the command center for a next-generation

Navy ship, design of a next-generation nuclear power plant control room, and design of work-centered support systems for flight planning and monitoring for an Air Force organization. She is currently serving as editor of the Design of Complex and Joint Cognitive Systems track of the *Journal of Cognitive Engineering and Decision Making*. She has a Ph.D. in cognitive psychology from the University of Illinois at Urbana-Champaign.

Thomas F. Sanquist is a research scientist with the Pacific Northwest Laboratory in Seattle. His research focuses on the use of analytic and field research methods for designing and evaluating user interfaces for complex systems. Application areas include intelligence analysis, security systems, transportation, imaging devices, satellite control systems, nuclear power plants, and military command and control. He has experience in both the research and practice of human factors engineering, having designed and implemented significant large-scale systems such as the Air Force satellite control network user interface and seaport radiation portal monitoring for Customs and Border Protection. He has a B.A. from the University of Michigan (1974) and a Ph.D. in cognitive and physiological psychology from the University of California, Los Angeles (1980).

Index

A

Abstraction hierarchies, 198
Accidents
    Bhopal, 328
    Chernobyl, 1
    in large-scale systems, 1
    at power plants, 198
    Three Mile Island, 1, 256, 328
    by *Vincennes*, 328
ACR. *See* Architecture commitment review
ACT-R model, 167, 244, 321
Active Risk Management, 311
Activity view, concurrent levels of, 41–44
ACWA. *See* Applied cognitive work
    analysis method
Adaptability, 6, 26
Adjustable methods, 24
Advanced spectroscopic portals (ASPs),
    105
Advocacy. *See also* Nonadvocate technical
    experts
    for consideration of HSI, 15
Affinity analysis, 175
Afghanistan, current needs in, 93
AFQT. *See* Armed Forces Qualification Test
Aggregation, of features, 26
Agile methods, 35, 37
Air Force Falconer Air Operations Center,
    16

Air Force Research Laboratory, 2
Air traffic control systems, 13, 21
AIRPRINT, 296
Alarms, with melodies, 111–112
ALARP. *See* As low as reasonably
    practicable
Alertness level, 227–228
Ambiguity, 63
American Anthropology Association,
    154n. 1
Anchor point milestone reviews, 23, 25,
    37, 44
    development commitment, 44–46
Anthropometric models, 244
Applied cognitive work analysis (ACWA)
    method, 62
Applied Physics Lab, 144
Applied Psychology Research Unit, 10
Aptima, Inc., 162
Archetypes, composite user, 65
Architecting phase, 3
    and design, 247
    point-solution, 33
Architectural prototypes, 236
Architecture commitment review (ACR), 44
    procedures, 46
Architectures, back-end, 238
Armed Forces Aptitude Test Battery
    (ASVAB), 19–20

Armed Forces Qualification Test (AFQT), 19
Army Comanche Helicopter program, 13
Army Human Engineering Directorate, 19
Army Research Laboratory, 2
Artifact models, 50, 176, 280
As low as reasonably practicable (ALARP), 259
ASPs. *See* Advanced spectroscopic portals
Assessment of HSI
    of contributors to system adaptability and resilience, 330
    of risks, 327–329
ASVAB. *See* Armed Forces Aptitude Test Battery
Asynchronous communication patterns, 147
ATM machine withdrawals, 197
    hierarchical task analysis of, 158–159, 161
AT&T Architecture Review Board procedures, 46
Attention management, 207, 318
Automated methods, based on rules and guidelines, 272
Automatic external defibrillator, example FTA for a hypothetical, 263
Automation, 11

B

Back-end architectures, 238
Baselines, generating, 278–279
BDUF. *See* Big design up front activities
BEAST. *See* Boeing Engineering Aerospace Simulation Tool program
Behavioral patterns, 186
Bell Laboratories, 10
Best-effort definitions, 49
Best practices
    for HSI, 57
    for risk mitigation, 67–74
    tables of, 44
Bhopal accident, 328
"Bifocal tools," 212
Big design up front (BDUF) activities, 39
"Blogs," 22, 289–290, 292
"Bobby" tool, 245, 272
Boeing Engineering Aerospace Simulation Tool (BEAST) program, 146

Bootstrap process, 165–166
Borg Ratings of Perceived Exertion, 220
Budget constraints, 23
    tailoring methods to, 24
Business case, 77
    viability of, 4
Business Week, 1

C

CAIV. *See* Cost as an independent variable
Cameras, reconceptualizing, 65
"Cardboard computers," 172, 212–213
Case studies, 91–125
    "next-generation" intravenous infusion pump, 105–125
    port security, 97–105
    unmanned aerial systems, 92–97
Cassette loading, semiautomatic, 112–113
Cause-effect relationships, 50
CBP. *See* Customs and border protection
CDM. *See* Critical decision method
Centralization, 145
Change. *See also* Rapid change
    in conditions and requirements
        in the workplace, designing to accommodate, 26, 300–301
CHAOS report, 191
Chernobyl accident, 1
Child safety, concerns about, 10
Choke points, identifying, 103, 202
Circadian rhythm, 227
Cmap Tools software suite, 315
COGNET/iGEN model, 244
Cognitive task analysis (CTA), 161–169
    a bootstrap process, 165–166
    contributions to system design phases, 167
    overview, 161–166
    relationship to task analysis, 165
    representative methods, 162–165
    shared representations, 166–167
    strengths, limitations, and gaps, 168–169
    in the unmanned aerial systems case study, 166
    uses of methods, 167
Cognitive walkthroughs, 272
Cognitive work analysis methodology, 199
    analytic tools involved in, 202

Collaboration-at-a-distance, 289
Collaboration failures, 5
Collaboration-intensive systems, 4, 25
Color touch screens, large, 111
Colors, stoplight, 83
Command and control (C2), 286–287, 300
Command and control vehicles, 12
Committee on Human Factors, 2
Committee on Human-System Design
  Support for Changing Technology, 2
  charge and scope of, 16–17
  report organization, 27–28
Common ground, 61
Common Industry Specification for
  Usability Requirements, 194–195,
  267
Communication. *See also* Shared
  representations for communication
  among members of the development
  team, 195
  creating shared representations for, 25
  between customers and suppliers, 195
  of risk, improving, 329–330
Compatibility, evidence of, 45
Complexity of systems, 1, 144–145, 308
Composite stories, 231
Composite user archetypes, 65
Computational tools, paucity of, 206
Computer simulations, 25, 106, 240, 267
Concept mapping, 163
  of the role of cold fronts in the Gulf
    Coast, 164
Concurrent engineering process models, 34,
  37, 48, 51
Concurrent systems, definition and
  development, 32, 105
Conditions, accommodation to changing,
  101–102
Consensus building, 2n. 1
Consequence levels, assessing, 82–83
Consumer Product Safety Commission, 10
Context of use analysis methods, 136–138
  cognitive task analysis, 161–169
  contextual inquiry, 175–177
  defining opportunities and, 55, 129,
    135–188, 279–280
  event data analysis, 177–188
  field observations and ethnography,
    150–157
  organizational and environmental
    context, 139–150

participatory analysis, 169–175
task analysis, 157–161
Contexts, 18–22
  military sector, 18–20
  private sector, 20–22
  of use, 138
Contextual design, 216–217
  contributions to the system design
    process, 217
  shared representations, 217
  strengths, limitations, and gaps, 217
Contextual inquiries, 114–115, 149,
  175–177
  affinity analysis, 175
  contributions to the system design
    process, 139, 177
  interpretation, 175
  overview, 175–176
  shared representations, 176
  strengths, limitations, and gaps, 177
Control, of information, 22
Control rooms, 157
  for power plants, 139
Cornell Musculoskeletal Discomfort
  Survey, 219
Cost as an independent variable (CAIV),
  76
Cost-competitive contracts, 33
Cost-effective systems, 23
Costs, providing a basis for controlling,
  195
Cougaar, 311
Crisis response systems, 15
Critical decision method (CDM), 162
Critical success factor (CSF) aspects of top
  five software projects, 52
CTA. *See* Cognitive task analysis
Cultural analysis, 147–148
Cultural models, 144, 176, 251–252
Current-point-in-time shapshot
  requirements, 33
Customer observations, negative, 13–14,
  112–113
Customs and border protection (CBP), 98,
  104

D

D-OMAR model, 245
DART, 311

Data
  analysis, 183–184
  collection, 6, 183, 187, 319
  mining, 178, 318–319
  privacy of, 319
  rate of change of, 22
  representation, 184
Data-reduction methods, 178
DATech, 271
DCR. See Development commitment
    review
Decentralization, of information, 22
Decompositions
  goal/task, 279–280
  hierarchical, 283
Defense Advanced Research Projects
    Agency, 311
Defense systems, 24
Defibrillators, automatic external, 263
Defining requirements and design, 56, 129,
    189–252
  contextual design, 216–217
  methods for mitigating fatigue,
    226–229
  models and simulations, 240–252
  participatory design, 210–216
  personas, 233–235
  physical ergonomics, 217–223
  prototyping, 235–239
  scenarios, 230–233
  situation awareness, 223–226
  usability requirements, 191–197
  work domain analysis, 197–207
  workload assessment, 207–210
Delphi group decision-making technique,
    262
Descriptive methods, in ethnography, 151
Design
  as an innovative process, 189
  as a socially constructed process, 61
Design cycle time, pressure to reduce, 12
Design issues
  decisions, 109
  meaning, 63
  and methods used, 124–125
  opportunities and constraints, 5
  solutions, 56, 280–281
Design team members, 11
Development commitment review (DCR),
    44, 47, 49
  procedures, 46

Development phase, 3
  risk of destabilizing, 50
DHS. See U.S. Department of Homeland
    Security
Diagrams, 25
Differentiation, 144–145
Digital human physical simulations,
    243–244
Disuse, operational stage risk of, 59
Diversity, managing, 152
Documentaries, multimedia, 173
DoD. See U.S. Department of Defense
Domain knowledge, repository of, 206
Drawing workshops, 171–172
Dutch Musculoskeletal Survey, 219

E

E-commerce web sites, 255
Ease of use, 249–250
Eclipse Process Framework OpenUP, 302
ECR. See Exploration commitment review
EDA. See Event data analysis
Education of HSI specialists.
    See also Human-system integration,
      developing as a discipline
    opportunities for, 14
Electronic models, 25
Electronic Systems Center, 16
Emergency Care Research Institute, 110
Emergency medical missions, 15
Emergent behavior, 15, 53
Emergent requirements, 33
Emotional models, 251–252
Encyclopedias. See also Wikipedia
  online, user-constructed, 22
End-state operational system risks, 57
Energy systems, 255
Engineering development risk, management
    of, 59
Enterprise resource planning (ERP)
    package, 39
Environmental context, 5, 17, 139–150
  contributions to system design phases,
    149
  methods and respective sources of data,
    141
  overview, 139–141
  shared representations, 141–144
  strengths, limitations, and gaps, 149
  uses of methods, 144–149

"Envisioned world" problem, 163–164
EPIC model, 245, 321
"Epistemic status," 231
ERP. *See* Enterprise resource planning package
Errors
   operational stage risk of, 59
   taxonomies of, 328
ESDA. *See* Exploratory sequential data analysis
Ethical considerations, 6, 316–320
Ethnographic inquiry, 231
   contributions to the system design process, 154–156
   interviews, 153
   methods, 213
   observations, 153–154
   practices, 152–154
   principles, 150–152
   shared representations, 155
   strengths, limitations, and gaps, 155–157
European Union, 319
Evaluation, 56, 247–248, 281–282
   heuristic, 271–272
   of remaining plan activities, 90
   of success accomplishments, 90
   system-level, 14
Event data analysis (EDA), 5, 95, 177–188
   contributions to system design phases, 185–186
   ethical implications, 316–320
   examples of uses of, 180–181
   overview, 177–178
   shared representations, 178–179
   uses of methods, 180–185
Event trees, 260
Evolutionary system growth, 51
Evolvability, designing for, 26
Excel spreadsheets, 321
Expert COCOMO/COCOTS, 311
Exploration commitment review (ECR), 46–47
Exploration phase, 3, 246–247
Exploratory sequential data analysis (ESDA), 184

F

Failure modes, effects, and criticality analysis (FMECA), 259n.1

Failure modes and effects analyses (FMEA), 115, 124, 159, 253, 259n. 1, 260
   advantages and disadvantages of, 264
   of Symbiq™ IV Pump, 119–121
Failures. *See* Collaboration failures; Human-system failures; Product failures; System failures
Fallback plans, identification of, 89
Fault tree analysis (FTA), 253
   advantages and disadvantages of, 265
   and other technique variations, 260–262
   steps in performing, 264
FDA. *See* Food and Drug Administration
Feasibility
   evidence of, 45
   rationale for, 50
Feature needs
   large color touch screens, 111
   medication libraries with hard and soft dosage limits, 110–111
   semiautomatic cassette loading, 112–113
   special alarms with melodies, 111–112
   special pole mounting hardware, 113
   stacking requirements, 113–114
   and their rationales, 110–114
   tubing management, 114
"Feedreaders," 289
"Field modification," 28
Field observations, 5, 123, 150–157
   ethnographic practices, 152–154
   ethnographic principles, 150–152
Fitts's law, 321
Flash™ animations, 119, 119n.1
Flow models, 176
FMEA. *See* Failure modes and effects analyses
   steps in performing, 261
FMECA. *See* Failure modes, effects, and criticality analysis
Focus groups, 122
"Folksonomies," 22, 290
Food and Drug Administration (FDA), 110, 113
Formalization, 145
Formative evaluation, uses of methods in, 267–268
FTA. *See* Fault tree analysis
Full-scale warfare, 15
Function allocation, 131

Funders of research, lack of commitment to
    HSI by, 2, 5
The future, 7, 275–330
    conclusions and recommendations,
        296–330
    scenarios for, 277–295
Future-vision stories, 232
Future workshops, 171
Futures table, 144

G

Gantt charts, 209, 279–281
Global context, 16
Goal/task decompositions, 279–280
GOMS (goals, operators, methods, and
        selection rules) method, 167,
        242–243, 249–250, 281, 321
Google, 178
Government organizations, 4–5
Graphic user interface (GUI) simulations,
        119
    interactive builder, 32–33
Grounded theory, 152–153
Group narratives, 183
    "thinking with," 63
Groupware support systems, 38
Guidelines, 271

H

Habitability, in the military sector, 1
Hand-off functions, 94
*Handbook of Systems Engineering and
    Management*, 34
Hardware models, with integrated usability
        tests, 119–120
Harms, defining, 257
Health hazards. *See also* Safety and health
        considerations
    in the military sector, 18
Heuristic evaluation, 271–272
Hierarchical task analysis (HTA), 157–158
    formalism of, 166
    graphic representation of, 159
Hierarchies
    abstraction, 198
    decomposing, 283
    deep supplier, 50

High assurance, incremental development
        for accommodating, 49–51
High-level languages, 251
Holistic methods, 16
    in ethnography, 151
    of measuring risk, 83
Home media systems, 13
Hospira customer service organization, 110
Hospital systems, 12
HSI. *See* Human-system integration
HTA. *See* Hierarchical task analysis
Human capabilities and needs, considering
        early, 1
Human cognitive characteristics, 2
Human-computer interaction, 10
Human digital modeling, 221, 223
Human error analysis, 255–265
    contributions to system design phases,
        262
    general model of, for security screening,
        100
    identification of hazards, 257–259
    shared representations, 259–262
    strengths, limitations, and gaps,
        262–265
Human factors
    analysis of, 295
    events in the growth of, 10
    introducing early enough, 14
    professionals in, 59
Human Factors and Ergonomics Society,
        10, 125, 313
Human factors engineering, 1, 11
    in the military sector, 18
Human-in-the-loop evaluations/
        simulations, 87, 209, 232, 240–241,
        265
Human-intensive systems, future of, 3
Human-system domain experts, 2
Human-system engineering, 2
Human-system failures, 13
Human-system integration (HSI), 2, 4, 9,
        31
    accommodating the emergence of
        requirements, 303
    activities, participants, methods, and
        shared representation, 130
    beginning early and continuing
        throughout the development life
        cycle, 297

developing as a discipline, 7, 284–286, 312–313

modeling, 99

operational requirements in contracts and acquisition documents, 303–304

risks, 57

sizing the effort, 309–310

system development led by, 282–284

for UASS in the context of the risk-driven spiral, 96–97

Human-system integration (HSI) in the context of risk-driven incremental commitments, 98–103

accommodation to changing conditions and workplace requirements, 101–102

HSI methods tailored to time and budget constraints, 99–100

scalable methods, 102–103

shared representations used to communicate, 100–101

Human-system integration (HSI) in the incremental commitment model, 57–60, 94–96

Human-system integration (HSI) in the system development process, 55–74, 127–274

best practices for risk mitigation, 67–74

case studies, 91–125

conclusion, 66

defining opportunities and context of use, 55, 129, 135–188

defining requirements and design, 56, 129, 189–252

evaluating, 56

function allocation, 131

managing risks, 75–90

methods for evaluation, 129, 253–274

performance measurement, 131–133

shared representations, 61–66

the system development process, 31–54

Human-system integration methods tailored to time and budget constraints, 99–100

Human-system model development, 320–322

I

IBM/Rational Unified Process, 302

ICM. *See* Incremental commitment model

Identification

of fallback plans, 89

of hazards and when risk management is conducted, 257–259

of HSI contributors to system adaptability and resilience, 330

of risks, 78–84, 327–329

IEC. *See* International Electrotechnical Commission

IMPRINT (Improved Performance Research and Integration Tool), 19, 241, 249–250, 321

Incremental commitment model (ICM), 9, 23, 31, 36–51

for accommodating rapid change and high assurance, 49–51

activity categories and level of effort, 41

anchor point milestone feasibility rationale, 46

concurrent levels of activity view, 41–44

development commitment anchor point milestone review, 44–46

different risks creating different processes, 40

life-cycle process elaboration, 36, 45

milestone reviews, 37, 46–47

phases of, 44

principles, 33

process model generator view, 39–40

project experience with, 50–53

spiral view of, 47–49

top-5 projects explicitly using, 51, 51n. 1

Incremental growth, of system definition and stakeholder commitment, 32, 103–104

Individual stories, 231

Information, sharing across domains, 7

Input/output system diagrams, 142

Institute for Human and Machine Cognition, 315

Institute for Safe Medical Practices, 110

Institutionalization, of a system development process based on the success factors, 302

Insurgency suppression missions, 15

Integrated product team (IPT), 80–81, 283, 286–287, 298

structuring HSI-led system development, 284

Integrated usability tests, integrated
    hardware and software models with,
    119–120
Integration of human systems and systems
    engineering, 27, 145, 250–251,
    278–286, 298, 301–314
    accommodating the emergence of HSI
        requirements, 303
    defining opportunities and requirements
        and defining the context of use,
        279–280
    design solutions, 280–281
    developing HSI as a discipline,
        284–286, 312–313
    evaluation, 281–282
    fostering more synergy between
        research and practice, 314
    generating a baseline, 278–279
    HSI-led system development, 282–284
    humans in the design process, 1
    institutionalizing a system development
        process based on the success factors,
        302
    knowledge-based planning aids for HSI,
        310–312
    managing system development, 6, 305
    meaning of, 282
    operational requirements in contracts
        and acquisition documents, 303–304
    shared representations, 307–308
    sizing the HSI effort, 309–310
    systems of systems, 308–309
    traceability and requirements, 305–307
Interconnectedness and interdependency, 26
International Council on Systems
    Engineering, 313
International Electrotechnical Commission
    (IEC), 112
International Ergonomics Association,
    217n. 2, 313
International Journal of Human-Computer
    Studies, 131
International Journal of Human System
    Integration, 313
International Organization for
    Standardization. See ISO standards
Internet, the. See also Web 2.0
    influence on culture, 154
Interpretation, 175, 231
Interviews, 153
IPT. See Integrated product team
Iraq, current needs in, 93

ISO standards, 4, 115, 302
    ISO 9241-11, 192, 268, 271
    ISO/IEC 15288, 196, 310
    ISO/IEC 9126-1, 191
    ISO/PAS 18152, 44, 57, 311
    ISO/TR 18529, 310
Iteration, 48, 60
    system definition and development, 32
    system growth, 51
    usability tests, 122
IV pumps
    tube management features, 107
    two channel, 107

J

JSAF model, 244

K

Keystroke-level analysis, 13, 186, 249
Knowledge acquisition techniques, 161
Knowledge-based planning for HSI,
    286–287, 310–312
    tools for, 7

L

Labor savings, 14
Laboratory studies, 153
Lag sequential analysis, 184
Large-scale systems. See Systems of systems
LCA. See Life-cycle architecture package
Lead systems integrator (LSI), 15
Lean development process, 51
Lean methods, 37
Libraries. See Medication libraries
LibraryThing, 290
Life-cycle architecture (LCA)
    development phases, 3
    of the ICM and EDA, 185
    operational stage risk of high costs, 59
    package, 44, 50
    planning, 124
LIFT tool, 272
Likelihood levels, assessing, 82–83
Limitations, 249–252
    of cultural, team, and emotional
        models, 251–252
    ease of use, 249–250

of high-level languages, 251
of integration, 250–251
Limited warfare, 15
Link Trainer, 240
Linkage of system engineering principles to
    HSI activities that reduce risks, 58
LMM. *See* Lumbar motion monitor
Logistics planning tools, 311
Lose-lose situation, 38
Low-technology representations, 172–173,
    212, 212n. 1, 213
LSI. *See* Lead systems integrator
Lumbar motion monitor (LMM), 221

M

Macromedia Flash Player, 119n. 1
Manpower, personnel, and training (MPT)
    domains, 18
Manpower considerations, 1, 5, 11
    in the military sector, 18–19
MANPRINT (Manpower Personnel
    Integration) program, 10, 17, 24,
    296, 298, 307–308
Manufacturing sector, 17, 21
Maps, territory, 64
Market capture goals, 4
Marketing Requirement Document, 110
Markov modeling, 184
"Mash-up" technologies, 26, 289, 291
Matrix organization, 146
Maximizing the cost-effectiveness of
    usability evaluation, 326–327
Medical equipment
    possible harms and hazards from the
        use of, 258
    standards for, 114
    use of an automatic external
        defibrillator, 258
    use of an automatic needle injection
        device, 258
Medical Research Council Laboratory, 10
Medication libraries, with hard and soft
    dosage limits, 110–111
Mental workload, 207–208
Meta-design approaches, 293
Method acting, 234
Methods. *See also* Types of methods; Uses
    of methods
    application instrumentation, 270
    for assessing discomfort, 219

for assessing injury risk, 221
for assessing posture, 220
based on models and simulation, 270
collecting data from usage of an
    existing system, 270
issues and research needs, 116–117
satisfaction surveys, 270
tailoring to time and budget constraints,
    24, 299
types of, 6, 268–272
uses of, 266–272
web metrics, 270
Methods and shared representations,
    211–214
    ethnographic methods, 213
    low-technology representations,
        212–213
    scenarios, 211
    theatrical approaches, 213
    workshop methods, 213–214
Methods based on expert assessment of the
    characteristics of a system, 271–272
    cognitive walkthrough, 272
    guidelines and style guides, 271
    heuristic evaluation, 271–272
    usability walkthrough, 272
Methods based on observing users of a real
    or simulated system, 268–270
    formative methods, 268
    summative methods, 268–269
Methods for defining opportunities and
    context of use, 314–320
    tools to support capture and
        dissemination of results of context
        of use analyses, 315–316
    user participation in systems
        engineering and event data analysis
        and their ethical implications,
        316–320
Methods for defining requirements and
    design, 320–324
    human-system model development,
        320–322
    prototyping training and organizational
        design, 322–324
Methods for evaluation, 129, 253–274,
    324–330
    analysis of human error, 256–265
    identifying and assessing HSI
        contributors to system adaptability
        and resilience, 330

identifying and assessing HSI risks, 327–329
improving the communication of risk, 329–330
improving the use of usability objectives, 324–326
maximizing the cost-effectiveness of usability evaluation, 326–327
risk analysis, 253–256
usability methods, 265–274
Methods for mitigating fatigue, 226–229
assessment, 220–221
contributions to system design phases, 229
overview, 226–227
shared representations, 228
strengths, limitations, and gaps, 229
uses of, 227–228
Micro-Saint-based models, 321
Microergonomics interventions, 140
Microsoft Office, 270
Milestone B commitment, 39
Military sector context, 10, 12, 18–20. See also Command and control
habitability and survivability in, 1
manpower, 19
personnel, 19–20
training, 20
Mission-critical subsystems, 34
Mitigation efforts, "off the books," 89
MITRE Corp., 162, 311
Models, 3, 5, 7, 25, 240–252. See also Artifact models; Cultural models; Emotional models; Flow models; Hardware models; Human digital modeling; Human-system model development; Incremental commitment model; Network models; Physical models; Sequence models; Software models; Team models
contributions to system design phases, 246–248
derived from human cognitive operations, 242–243
overview, 240
strengths, limitations, and gaps, 248–252
that mimic human cognitive and perceptual-motor behavior, 244–246
types and uses of, 240–246
ModSAF model, 244

Motivation behind the design, 106
MPT. See Manpower, personnel, and training domains
Multidimensional scaling, 184
Multimedia documentaries, 173
Multiple systems. See Systems of systems
Multitasking, 207
Muscle Fatigue Assessment method, 220

N

Napping, strategic, 227
NASA. See National Aeronautics and Space Administration
National Academies
Committee on Human Factors, 2
study on organizational models, 252
National Aeronautics and Space Administration (NASA), 60n. 1
Near Earth Asteroid Rendezvous project, 144
TLX scales, 208
National Aerospace System, 241
National Institutes for Occupational Safety and Health (NIOSH), 219–220
National Science Foundation, 313
National Transportation Safety Administration, 10
Naval Postgraduate School, 285, 312
Navy Tactical Decision Support systems, 13
Near Earth Asteroid Rendezvous (NEAR) project, 144
Negative business outcomes. See also Customer observations
resulting from HSI faults, 259
Negotiation
facilitating, 64
terms oriented to, 34
Nested techniques, 144
Network management, 21
Network models, of human-system performance, 241–242
New technologies, 26
feasibility of inserting, 4
governmental and commercial uses of, 22
"Next-generation" intravenous infusion pump, 105–125
motivation behind the design, 106

summary of design issues and methods used, 124–125
user-centered design process in the ICM context, 106–124
NIOSH. *See* National Institutes for Occupational Safety and Health
Nonadvocate technical experts, 79
Nordic Musculoskeletal Questionnaire, 219
Norman, Don, 62–63
North Atlantic Treaty Organization, 313
Nuclear power plants, 21
work domain representation for a pressurized water reactor, 200
Nuclear Regulatory Commission, 262
NYNEX Science and Technology organization, 13

O

Observations, 153–154. *See also* Customer observations
Observer-participant approach, 153
Occupational Safety and Health Administration (OSHA), 10
Occupational repetitive action (OCRA) methods, 221
OCR. *See* Operations commitment review
OCRA. *See* Occupational repetitive action methods
Operation of the Defense Acquisition System, 2, 4–5, 14
Operational requirements, of HSI, 4
Operational return on investment, 31
Operational stage, 3, 248
Operational stage risks, 59
use-error-induced, 92
Operations commitment review (OCR), 47
Operator fatigue, 226
Opportunity-driven approach, to determining needs for HSI activity, adopting, 298
"Opt-in" and "opt-out" approaches, 320, 320n. 1
Optimization schemes, 140
Options assessment
assuming the risk, 87
avoiding the risk, 85–86
handling, 85
mitigating the risks, 87–88
transferring the risk, 86

Ordinal values, 82
Organization charts, 141–142
Organizational context, 5, 139–150
contributions to system design phases, 149
methods and respective sources of data, 141
overview, 139–141
shared representations, 141–144
strengths, limitations, and gaps, 149
uses of methods, 144–149
Organizational design
example of, 146
modeling approaches, 308
Organizational system scan, 144–147
Organizational variances, table of, 142
OSHA. See Occupational Safety and Health Administration
Ovako working posture analysis, 220
"Over-confidence" bias, 12

P

PageRank algorithms, 178n. 2
Paper prototypes, 119
Parameter estimation, 13
Part-task simulations, 249
Participatory analysis, 5, 95, 169–175, 210–216, 230
contributions to the system design process, 173, 214
fitting into the system development process, 174
methods, 211–214
overview, 169–173, 210–211
scenarios in, 172
shared representations, 173–174, 211–215
strengths, limitations, and gaps, 174–175, 215–216
workshops in, 170–172
Participatory workshops, 170–172
drawing and other visual workshops, 171–172
future workshops, 171
low-technology representations, 172–173
multimedia documentaries, 173
strategic design workshops, 171
Pass/fail reviews, 14

Pathfinder network scaling, 179, 179n. 3, 184
Pattern recognition, 318
PDR. *See* Product requirements document
Performance measurement, 131–133
Personas, 233–235, 279
  contributions to the system design process, 234
  shared representations, 233–234
  strengths, limitations, and gaps, 234–235
Personnel considerations, 1, 5, 11
  back-up, 12
  in the military sector, 18–20
"Personnel subsystems," 10
PERT charts, 209–210
Photo documentaries, 172
Physical ergonomics, 5, 217, 217n. 2, 218–223
  assessing, 207
  contributions to system design phases, 222
  overview, 217–218
  shared representations, 218–219
  strengths, limitations, and gaps, 222–223
  uses of methods, 219–221
Physical models, 25, 176
Physical performance characteristics, 2
Physical prototypes, foam model of a blood analyzer prototype, 237
Physical simulations, digital human, 243–244
PLIBEL, 219
Point-solution architecture, 33
Pole mounting hardware, 113
Policy recommendations, 4, 301–330
  methods for defining opportunities and context of use, 314–320
  methods for defining requirements and design, 320–324
  methods for evaluation, 324–330
  realizing the full integration of human systems and systems engineering, 301–314
Polyvinyl toluene sensors, 105
Port security, 97–105. *See also* Radiation portal monitoring (RPM) systems
  HSI in the context of risk-driven incremental commitments, 98–103

principles of system development in, 103–105
  use of work domain analysis in, 202
Power plants. *See also* Nuclear power plants
  accidents at, 198
  control rooms, 139, 204
"Practicum" environment, 286
Preventive action, 124
Price systems, 311
Principles-based comparison, of alternative process models, 34–36
Prioritized capabilities, specifying, 34
Prioritized risks, 84
Privacy
  of data, 319
  options in, 320
Private sector context, 4–5, 12, 20–22
Process control, 17, 21
Process model generator view, 39–40
Process tracing, 183
Product design methodologies, 2
Product failures, reducing risk of, 195
Product introduction, 124
Product requirements document (PDR), 119, 121
Product usability characteristics evaluation methods, 271–272
  automated methods based on rules and guidelines, 272
  methods based on expert assessment of the characteristics of a system, 271–272
Product variation, 145
Program award fee criteria, 4
Program impacts, assessing, 83–84
Program management risks, 57
Program managers, lack of commitment to HSI by, 2
Program schedules, 89–90
Progress monitoring, 14
Project Ernestine, 243
Protocols
  analysis of, 182
  RSS, 289
  think-aloud, 225
Prototypes, 3, 5–6, 25, 119, 235–239, 267, 324
  architectural, 236
  contributions to system design phases, 238

overview, 235–236
paper, 119
rapid, 22
shared representations, 236–237
strengths, limitations, and gaps,
    238–239
"throwaway," 212
training and organizational design,
    322–324
uses of methods, 236

Q

"Qualitative and quantitative personnel
    requirements inventory," 10
"Quality in use," evaluation of, 265
Quick Exposure Checklist, 220
Quick look reports, 60, 60n. 1

R

Radiation portal monitoring (RPM)
    systems, 98–99, 202
    large-scale, 97
Rapid change, 33
    incremental development for
        accommodating, 49–51
Ratio values, 82
Rational unified process (RUP), 37, 41, 51
R&D. *See* Research and development
Real options theory, 38
Reason's error classification, 257
Rebaselining, 32
Recommendations, 2, 4, 296–330
    adopting a risk- and opportunity-driven
        approach to determining needs for
        HSI activity, 298
    beginning HSI contributions to
        development early and continuing
        them throughout the development
        life cycle, 297
    designing to accommodate changing
        conditions and requirements in the
        workplace, 300–301
    ensuring communication among
        stakeholders of HSI outputs, 299
    integrating across human-system
        domains as well as across the system
        life cycle, 298
    tailoring methods to time and budget
        constraints, 299

Recording language, standard, 64
Recording technologies, 153
Reductions
    assessing achievement of, 90
    in the development effort, 195
Relationships, cause-effect, 50
Reliability, 12
Remotely piloted vehicles (RPVs), 92
Reports, 25
Representations. *See* Diagrams; Low-
        technology representations; Models;
        Prototypes; Reports; Shared
        representations; Simulations;
        Spreadsheets; Stories; Storyboards;
        Time lines
Representative methods, 162–165
    for defining opportunities and context
        of use, 137
    for defining requirements and design,
        190
    for evaluation, 254
Requirements
    analysis of, 4, 304
    classification of, 192
    "creep" of, 294
    specification of, 195
    specification of inappropriate, 3
Research agenda, 3, 5–7
    full integration of human systems and
        systems engineering, 6–7
    methods and tools, 5–6
    preliminary, 108–109
    shared representations, 5
Research and development (R&D), 86
    support for, 13
Research recommendations, 301–330
    methods for defining opportunities and
        context of use, 314–320
    methods for defining requirements and
        design, 320–324
    methods for evaluation, 324–330
    realizing the full integration of human
        systems and systems engineering,
        301–314
Residual risk, 259
Resilience, 6, 14, 309, 328, 330
Resources
    failure to assign, 14, 24
    suboptimal, 84, 145
Reusable components, 7, 33
Risk
    assuming, 87

avoiding, 85–86
identification of, 78–81
prioritizing, 84
residual, 259
transferring, 86
@Risk, 311
Risk analysis, 5, 78–84, 253–256
  assess likelihood and consequence
    levels, 82–83
  assessing program impacts, 83–84
  defining use error, 255–256
  determining level of, 83
  determining method of, 82
  overview, 253–256
  revised, 124
  steps in, 82
Risk-driven ICM approach, 51
  for accommodating rapid change and
    high assurance, 49
  adopting, 23–24
  to determine needs for HSI activity,
    adopting, 298
Risk-handling options, decision flow of, 85
Risk management, 48, 75–90, 104–105
  e-commerce web sites, 255
  early, 115–119
  energy systems, 255
  executing risk mitigation, 88–90
  handling options assessment, 85
  identification of hazards when
    conducting, 257–259
  risk-driven activity levels and anchor
    point milestones, 32–33
  techniques for, 255
  transportation systems, 255
  weapons systems, 255
Risk mitigation, 87–88
  best practices for, 67–74
  developing a plan, 88–89
  evaluating plan activities, 90
  evaluating success accomplishments, 90
  executing, 88–90
  identifying fallback plans, 89
  incorporating into program schedules,
    89–90
  progressive, 23
  steps in, 88
Risk of product failure, reducing, 195
Risk priority number (RPN) values, 115,
  119
Robust systems, 198

Role networks, 142–144
  for NASA's Near Earth Asteroid
    Rendezvous project, 144
Role variances, examples of, 150
Root concept, 231
RPM. See Radiation portal monitoring
  systems
RPN. See Risk priority number values
RPVs. See Remotely piloted vehicles
RSS protocol, 289
Rules and guidelines, automated methods
  based on, 272
RUP. See Rational unified process

S

Safety and health considerations, 1, 11
Safety-case submittals, 168
Safety-critical systems, 24, 34, 252
Sample size formula, 327
Satisfaction surveys, 270
Satisficing, 283. See also Stakeholders
  defining, 2n. 1
"Say-do-make" approach, 214
Scalable methods, 24, 102–103
  multidimensional, 184
Scenarios, 7, 211, 230–233, 280
  contributions to system design phases,
    232
  overview, 230
  in participatory analysis, 172
  shared representations, 231–232
  strengths, limitations, and gaps, 233
  uses of methods, 230–231
Scenarios for the future, 277–295
  integrated methodology, 278–286
  knowledge-based planning for HSI,
    286–287
  user participation, 288–295
Schematic representations, for a compact
  power plant control room, 204
Screening. See Security screening
Seaports. See Radiation portal monitoring
  (RPM) systems
SEAPRINT (Systems Engineering,
  Acquisition, and Personnel
  Integration), 18, 296
Search and rescue missions, 15
Second round prototypes, for interface to
  MRI device, 237

Security screening
    in complex labor situations, 104
    general model of human error analysis
        for, 100
    likely tightening of, 22
SEER/SEM, 311
Self-report instruments, 218–219
Sensors, polyvinyl toluene, 105
Sequence models, 157–159, 176
Service industries, 17
Service-oriented architectures (SOAs), 22,
    289–290
Shared language, 63
Shared representations, 141–144, 155,
    159–160, 166–167, 173–179,
    194–195, 201, 209, 215–219, 228,
    231–237, 259–262, 273, 307–308
    artifact model, 176
    attributes of good, 63–64
    composite stories, 231
    cultural model, 176
    cultural profile, 144
    for defining requirements and design,
        190
    in the design process, 64–66
    for evaluation, 254
    flow model, 176
    and FMEA, 259–260
    and FTA, 260–262
    future-vision stories, 232
    futures table, 144
    individual stories, 231
    input/output system diagram, 142
    organization charts, 141–142
    physical model, 176
    providing a basis for controlling costs,
        195
    reducing risk of product failure, 195
    reducing the development effort, 195
    and role networks, 142–144
    sequence model, 176
    for specification of requirements, 195
    table of organizational variances, 142
    tracking evolving requirements by
        providing a format to document
        usability requirements, 195
    usefulness of, 62–63
Shared representations for communication,
    5, 100–101
    among members of the development
        team, 195

of concepts to engineering staff, 100
    creating, 25
    between customers and suppliers, 195
    of HSI issues and opportunities, 61–66
Signal detection theory, 242, 321
Simulations, 3, 5, 7, 25, 240–252
    contributions to system design phases,
        246–248
    overview, 240
    part-task, 249
    strengths, limitations, and gaps,
        248–252
    types and uses of, 240–246
Single-user systems, 21
Situation awareness, 11, 139, 223–226
    contributions to system design phases,
        225
    measuring, 224–225
    overview, 223–224
    strengths, limitations, and gaps, 225–226
Situation Awareness Global Assessment
    Technique, 224
Situation Awareness Rating Technique, 225
SOAs. *See* Service-oriented architectures
Social network analysis, 185
"Social software" services, 22, 289
"Social tagging," 22
Socially constructed processes, design as,
    61, 63
Sociotechnical systems approach, 141,
    148–149
Software models, with integrated usability
    tests, 119–120
Software Technology Risk Advisor, 311
"Sourcing," of information, 22
Space program, 248. *See also* National
    Aeronautics and Space
    Administration
Special causes, 141
Spimes, 294
Spiral models, 34, 37, 39, 47–49
    development of, 35
    simplified view of the ICM, 48
    win-win, 51
Spreadsheets, 5, 25
Stacking requirements, 113–114
"Staged world" techniques, 163–164
Stakeholders, 2, 5, 11
    analyzing, 148–149
    concurrence of, 40
    conflicting requirements of, 15

of HSI outputs, ensuring
    communication among, 299
satisficing, 31–32, 48, 283
success-critical, 38, 103
user-centered activities for, 196
Standard recording language, 64
Standardized interface, 22
Standish Group, 191
Stories, 5, 25, 183
Storyboards, 7, 280
Straddle carriers, 102
Strategic design workshops, 171
Style guides, 271
Subjectivity issues, 219
Suboptimal resources. *See* Resources
Success-critical stakeholder satisficing, 103
Successful system development
    concurrent system definition and
        development, 32
    incremental growth of system definition
        and stakeholder commitment, 32
    iterative system definition and
        development, 32
    principles for, 2–3, 32–33
    risk-driven activity levels and anchor
        point milestones, 32–33
    stakeholder satisficing, 32
Summative methods, 267–270
Supplier hierarchies, deep, 50
Survivability, 11
    in the military sector, 1, 18
"Sweeps," 162
Symbiq™ IV Pump, 105–107, 114–115,
    125, 159
    excerpts from failure modes and effects
        analyses (FMEA), 120–121
Synergy between research and practice
    fostering more, 7, 314
    lack of, 14
System design phases, 11
    architecting and design, 247
    contributions to, 149, 160, 167,
        185–186, 196, 205–206, 209, 222,
        225, 229, 232, 238, 246–248, 262,
        273
    evaluation, 247–248
    exploration and valuation, 246–247
    operation, 248
System design process, contributions to,
    154–155, 173, 177, 214, 217, 234
System developers, 14

System development principles, 103–105
    concurrent system definition and
        development, 105
    incremental growth of system definition
        and stakeholder commitment,
        103–104
    risk management, 104–105
    success-critical stakeholder satisficing,
        103
System development process, 31–54
    conclusion, 53–54
    evolving nature of system requirements,
        33–34
    incremental commitment model, 36–39
    institutionalizing based on success
        factors, 302
    participatory methods fitting into, 174
    principles-based comparison of
        alternative process models, 34–36
    principles for successful system
        development, 32–33
    project experience with ICM principles,
        51–53
    views of the incremental commitment
        model, 39–51
System diagrams, inputs and outputs, 142
System engineers, 2
System failures, catastrophic, 9
System-level evaluation, 14
System life-cycle processes, 196
    activity level of HSI methods across
        phases of, 56
    issues involved in, 2
System performance, compromises in, 24
System requirements
    emergent, 33
    evolving nature of, 33–34
    rapid change, 33
    reusable components, 33
System resilience. *See* Resilience
System safety, in the military sector, 18
System scoping, 3
System simulations. *See* Simulations
Systems engineering for user participation,
    291–295
Systems of systems, 6, 14, 36, 300, 308–309
    complexity of, 1, 4, 308
    defining, 15
    very large, 50

T

TADMUS (Tactical Decision Making Under Stress) program, 13
Task analysis, 5, 157–161
  contributions to system design phases, 160
  overview, 157–159
  relationship to, 165
  shared representations, 159–160
  strengths, limitations, and gaps, 160–161
  traditional, 201
  uses of methods, 160
Task flow diagrams, 115, 118
Taxonomies, of error, 328
Team models, 12, 251–252
Technique for human error rate prediction (THERP), 256
Technologies. *See also* New technologies
  "mash-up," 26, 289, 291
  potential insertion opportunities for, 105
  recording, 153
  wearable, 292
Territory maps, 64
Testing
  of alarm criticality and alerting, 120–122
  of display readability, 122
  rapid, 22
  of usability requirements, 194
Theater Response Package, 16
Theatrical approaches, 213, 215
Themes, 23–27
  adopting a risk-driven approach, 23–24
  creating shared representations for communication, 25
  designing to accommodate changing conditions and requirements in the workplace, 26
  integrating HSI contributions across life-cycle phases and human-system domains, 27
  tailoring methods to time and budget constraints, 24
Theory-based analysis, 99
Theory W approach, 38
THERP. *See* Technique for human error rate prediction
Think-aloud protocols, 225

Threat-based RPM display, graphical representation of work flow with, 101
Threat detection, 99
Three Mile Island accident, 1, 256, 328
"Throwaway" prototypes, 212
Time constraints, 23
  tailoring methods to, 24
Time of day, and alertness level, 228
Time lines, 7, 279
TIPS cards, 123
TLX scales, 208
Tools. *See also* individual tools
  for product design, 2
  to support capture and dissemination of results of context of use analyses, 315–316
Top-5 projects, explicitly using ICM principles, 51, 51n. 1
Touch screens, large color, 111
Traceability, 6
  and requirements, 305–307
Tracking evolving requirements, by providing a format to document usability requirements, 195
Trade-offs, 3, 19, 34, 140
Training considerations, 1, 5, 11
  deficiencies in, 20
  in the military sector, 18, 20
Transportation systems, 255
Trustworthiness, 12
Tubing management, 114
Types of methods, 268–272. *See also* Methods; Uses of methods
  expert-based evaluation, 272
  product usability characteristics evaluation, 271–272
  user behavior evaluation, 268–270
Types of models and simulations, 240–246
  digital human physical simulations, 243–244
  human-in-the-loop simulation, 240–241
  models derived from human cognitive operations, 242–243
  models that mimic human cognitive and perceptual-motor behavior, 244–246
  network models of human-system performance, 241–242
  signal detection theory, 242

U

UASs. *See* Unmanned aerial systems
Unintended relations and features,
    detection of, 62
Unmanned aerial systems (UASs), 92–97
    conclusion and lessons learned, 96–97
    hypothetical case, 93–94
    in the ICM context, 94–96
U.S. Army, 10, 18–19, 241
U.S. Department of Defense (DoD), 2,
        4–5, 10, 14, 18–19, 241, 250, 297,
        301–304, 313
    development milestone reviews, 23, 37
    DoD Instruction 5000.2, 2, 4–5, 14,
        302
    Milestone B commitment, 39
U.S. Department of Health and Human
        Services, 271
U.S. Department of Homeland Security
        (DHS), 97
U.S. Navy, 18–19, 250
U.S. Rehabilitation Act, 245
US WEST, 13
Usability
    approaches to ensuring, 266
    contributions to system design phases,
        196, 273
    evaluation methods, 5, 232, 265–274
    of an existing system, measuring, 193
    improving the use of objectives,
        324–326
    overview, 191–192, 265–266
    practitioners of, 274
    quantifying, 325
    setting objectives, 115
    shared representations, 194–195, 273
    strengths, limitations, and gaps, 197,
        273–274
    tools to support capture and
        dissemination of results, 315–316
    uses and types of methods, 193–194,
        266–272
    walkthrough, 272
Usability requirements, 191–197
    specifying for new systems, 193–194
USC COCOMO/COSYSMO, 311
Use-error faults, 254
    defining, 255–256
    risk analysis, 159, 255

Use-error-induced operational risks, 92
Use of methods, 193–194, 208. *See also*
        Methods; Types of methods
    instructions for development and
        testing, 123
    measuring usability of an existing
        system, 193
    shared representations, 62–63
    specifying usability requirements for the
        new system, 193–194
    testing whether usability requirements
        have been achieved, 194
User-based evaluation methods, types of,
        269
User behavior evaluation methods,
        268–270
    methods based on models and
        simulations, 270
    methods based on observing users of a
        real or simulated system, 268–270
    methods that collect data from usage of
        an existing system, 270
User-centered design process in the ICM
        context, 106–124
    activities for stakeholder requirements,
        196
    contextual inquiry, 114–115
    design decisions, 109
    early risk management, 115–119
    feature needs and their rationales,
        110–114
    field studies, 123
    focus groups, 122
    instructions for use development and
        testing, 123
    integrated hardware and software
        models, 119–120
    iterative usability tests, 122
    life-cycle planning, 124
    preliminary research, 108–109
    product introduction, 124
    prototypes, 119
    revised risk analysis, 124
    setting usability objectives, 115
    tests of alarm criticality and alerting,
        120–122
    tests of display readability, 122
    validation usability tests, 123–124
User-created dynamic pages, 22

User participation in systems engineering,
        288–295
    approaches to capturing user input,
        288–291
    ethical implications, 316–320
Uses of methods, 144–149, 160, 167,
        180–185, 201–205, 219–221,
        227–231, 236
    assignment and diagnosis, 185
    cultural analysis, 147–148
    data analysis, 183–184
    data collection, 183
    data representation, 184
    ethnographic inquiry, 231
    in formative and summative evaluation,
        267
    human digital modeling, 221
    interpretation, 231
    methods for assessing discomfort, 219
    methods for assessing fatigue, 220–221
    methods for assessing injury risk, 221
    methods for assessing posture, 220
    organizational system scan, 144–147
    other example applications, 203–205
    problem scenarios and claims, 231
    root concept, 231
    stakeholder analysis, 148–149
    strengths, limitations, and gaps,
        187–188
    use of work domain analysis in the port
        security case study, 202
Uses of models and simulations, 240–246
    digital human physical simulations,
        243–244
    human-in-the-loop simulation, 240–241
    models derived from human cognitive
        operations, 242–243
    models that mimic human cognitive and
        perceptual-motor behavior, 244–246
    network models of human-system
        performance, 241–242
    signal detection theory, 242
USS *Vincennes*, Iranian Air Bus downed by,
        13, 328
UTOPIA project, 65, 239

V

V-model, 37, 39
    updates, 34

Validation usability tests, 123–124
Valuation commitment review (VCR),
        46–47
Valuation phase, 3, 246–247
Value-based systems and software
        engineering, 38
Variability, maximization of, 153
VCR. *See* Valuation commitment review
Vincennes. See USS *Vincennes*
Visual workshops, 171–172
Visualizations, novel, 203
Voice recognition applications, 13

W

Walkthroughs. *See* Cognitive walkthroughs
Warfare, limited or full-scale, 15
Waterfall models, 34
    sequential, 34, 39
"Weak links," 330
Weapons systems, 255
Wearable technologies, 292
Web 2.0, 22, 26, 288, 290–291, 294, 305,
        316, 318
Web metrics, 270
Web sites, designing, 157
"Weblogs," 22, 289. *See also* "Blogs"
WebSAT, 272
Whole-systems approach, 139
Wikipedia, 290
Win-lose situations, 38
Win-win spiral process, 51
Wireframes, 119
Work-arounds, 26
Work-centered design approaches, 139
Work domain analysis, 197–207
    contributions to system design phases,
        205–206
    overview, 197–200
    representation for a pressurized water
        reactor nuclear power plant, 200
    shared representations, 201
    strengths, limitations, and gaps,
        206–207
    use in the port security case study, 202
    uses of methods, 201–205
Work flow
    graphical representation of, 101
    problems with, 187
Workload, managing, 19

Workload assessment, 207–210
contributions to system design phases, 209
overview, 207–208
shared representations, 209
strengths, limitations, and gaps, 209–210
use of method, 208
Workplace investigations, 175
Workplace requirements, accommodation to, 101–102

Workshop methods, 213–214, 280. *See also* Drawing workshops; Future workshops; Participatory workshops; Strategic design workshops; Visual workshops
Workstations, 12
World War II, 10

X

XML interface, 22, 289

Y

Yahoo!, 291